A Book Of

PHARMACEUTICAL ORGANIC CHEMISTRY

SIMPLIFIED

For
S. Y. B. Pharm [Semester III and IV]
As Per New Revised Syllabus of Pune University

Dr. K. S. Jain

M. Pharm., Ph.D., FIC
Principal and Professor
Shri Jain Vidyaprasarak Mandal's
S.F. Jain College of Pharmacy, 60/61, D2 Telco Road,
Acharya Anand Rushiji Marg,
Chinchwad, Pune - 411 019

Dr. P. B. Miniyar

M. Pharm., Ph.D., FAGE
Professor and Head
(Department of Pharmaceutical Chemistry)
Sinhgad Technical Education Society's
Sinhgad Institute of Pharmacy, Narhe, Pune - 411 041

N1657

PHARMACEUTICAL ORGANIC CHEMISTRY - SIMPLIFIED (Sem. I & II) ISBN : 978-93-5164-341-8

Second Edition : July, 2015
© : Authors

The text of this publication, or any part thereof, should not be reproduced or transmitted in any form or stored in any computer storage system or device for distribution including photocopy, recording, taping or information retrieval system or reproduced on any disc, tape, perforated media or other information storage device etc., without the written permission of Authors with whom the rights are reserved. Breach of this condition is liable for legal action.

Every effort has been made to avoid errors or omissions in this publication. In spite of this, errors may have crept in. Any mistake, error or discrepancy so noted and shall be brought to our notice shall be taken care of in the next edition. It is notified that neither the publisher nor the authors or seller shall be responsible for any damage or loss of action to any one, of any kind, in any manner, therefrom.

Published By :
NIRALI PRAKASHAN
Abhyudaya Pragati, 1312, Shivaji Nagar,
Off J.M. Road, Pune – 411005
Tel - (020) 25512336/37/39, Fax - (020) 25511379
Email : niralipune@pragationline.com

Printed By :
Repro Knowledgecast Limited
Thane

◆ DISTRIBUTION CENTRES

PUNE
Nirali Prakashan : 19, Budhwar Peth, Jogeshwari Mandir Lane, Pune 411002, Maharashtra
Tel : (020) 2445 2044, 66022708, Fax : (020) 2445 1538
Email : bookorder@pragationline.com, niralilocal@pragationline.com

Nirali Prakashan : S. No. 28/27, Dhyari, Near Pari Company, Pune 411041
Tel : (020) 24690204 Fax : (020) 24690316
Email : dhyari@pragationline.com, bookorder@pragationline.com

MUMBAI
Nirali Prakashan : 385, S.V.P. Road, Rasdhara Co-op. Hsg. Society Ltd.,
Girgaum, Mumbai 400004, Maharashtra
Tel : (022) 2385 6339 / 2386 9976, Fax : (022) 2386 9976
Email : niralimumbai@pragationline.com

◆ DISTRIBUTION BRANCHES

JALGAON
Nirali Prakashan
Maharashtra, Tel : (0257) 222 0395, Mob : 94234 91860

KOLHAPUR
Nirali Prakashan : New Mahadvar Road, Kedar Plaza, 1st Floor Opp. IDBI Bank
Kolhapur 416 012, Maharashtra. Mob : 9850046155

NAGPUR
Pratibha Book Distributors : Above Maratha Mandir, Shop No. 3, First Floor,
Rani Jhanshi Square, Sitabuldi, Nagpur 440012, Maharashtra
Tel : (0712) 254 7129

DELHI
Nirali Prakashan : 4593/21, Basement, Aggarwal Lane 15, Ansari Road, Daryaganj
Near Times of India Building, New Delhi 110002
Mob : 08505972553

BENGALURU
Pragati Book House : House No. 1, Sanjeevappa Lane, Avenue Road Cross,
Opp. Rice Church, Bengaluru – 560002.
Tel : (080) 64513344, 64513355,Mob : 9880582331, 9845021552
Email:bharatsavla@yahoo.com

CHENNAI
Pragati Books : 9/1, Montieth Road, Behind Taas Mahal, Egmore,
Chennai 600008 Tamil Nadu, Tel : (044) 6518 3535,
Mob : 94440 01782 / 98450 21552 / 98805 82331,
Email : bharatsavla@yahoo.com

niralipune@pragationline.com | www.pragationline.com
Also find us on   www.facebook.com/niralibooks

Foreword ...

I have read the book **"Pharmaceutical Organic Chemistry-Simplified" for S. Y. B. Pharm. Sem. III and IV** written by **Dr. K. S. Jain** and **Dr. P. B. Miniyar**, for M/s Nirali Publications, Pune. The authors have rich experience in teaching the subject with a few books and several publications to their credit. This book has been written for the students of Second year B.Pharm. and consists of 09 chapters following the revised syllabus of the second year B.Pharmacy course implemented by Savitribai Phule Pune University, with effect from the academic year 2014-15.

The style of presentation of this book is rather unique, giving a deeper understanding of the subject. Many modern concepts are explained with simplicity and ease. Keeping in mind the importance of the subject-organic chemistry from Pharmacy point of view, the authors have strived to make the contents of the chapters very simple, lucid and easy to understand with numerous structures, reaction schemes, figures, examples and illustrations.

I feel the book shall be really welcomed by both the students, as well as, the subject teachers as a complete package covering the subject syllabus. There are question banks provided at the end of each of the chapters, solving which shall help the students to face the exams with much confidence.

I congratulate the authors for bringing out this book and wish them the very best success in this noble effort.

Dr.L.V.G Nargund M.Pharm., Ph.D., F.I.C
Director & Professor,
Nargund College of Pharmacy
Dr. K.S. Nargund Pharmaceutical & Chemical Research Foundation
Dattatreyanagar, Banashankari III Stage, Bangalore – 560 085

Preface ...

The successful release and warm welcome received from students and teachers for our book **Pharmaceutical Organic Chemistry - Simplified F.Y.B. Pharm.: Semester I and II**, has proved like an inductive effect for us to resonate and perform one more addition reaction in this series Happily, the reaction has been successful, yields quantitative, purity excellent and cost much affordable for the end users. This new product, **Pharmaceutical Organic Chemistry - Simplified S.Y. B. Pharm.: Semester III and IV**, by M/s. Nirali Prakashan, Pune, can be considered as the successive analogue of our earlier product.

The book comprises of total 09 chapters, exactly in the same order and of same contents as prescribed in the syllabus of the University. The Chapters like 1. Stereochemistry, 2. Molecular Rearrangement Reactions and 5. Heterocyclic Chemistry have been much simplified to the need and grasp of the students with sufficient illustrations and examples.

Chapters; 6. Introduction to Combinatorial Chemistry, 7. Reterosynthesis (Disconnection Approach) and 9. Nanochemistry and Microwave Assisted Synthesis; cover the modern concepts and aspects of pharmaceutical organic chemistry and are explained with sufficient cases-in-points and illustrations so that students find them interesting.

The remaining three chapters; 3. Chemistry of Amino Acids, 4. Polycyclic Compounds and 8. Chemistry of Carbohydrates are presented in very simple, easy to understand manner with numerous figures, structures, reaction schemes, tables, examples and illustrations. All the nine chapters have rich Question Banks at the end. Thus, keeping in with our tradition this book too is unique in its style, presentation and simplicity.

Once again we expect good and positive response for this book by both the students, as well as, the subject teachers for its quality and style of presentation, contents and lucid explanatory language. The coverage of syllabus is complete and sincere reading and solving of questions provided in the question banks, can assure the students of a good grasp of the basics, as well as, gaining confidence to appear for any viva voce or exam.

Special mention is made of the efforts, co-operation and encouragement provided for this task by Mr. Jigneshbhai Furia, Ms. Chaitali, Mr Akbar, Mr. Ravi and all Staff of Nirali Prakashan, Pune.

We wish an enjoyable learning for the students and satisfactory teaching for the teachers of the subject - **Pharmaceutical Organic chemistry**.

Authors

Date : 24th October, 2014 (Balipratipada)

Contents ...

1. Stereochemistry	1.1 – 1.48
2. Molecular Rearrangement Reactions	2.1 – 2.22
3. Chemistry of Amino Acids	3.1 – 3.18
4. Polycylic Compounds	4.1 – 4.22
5. Heterocylic Chemistry	5.1 – 5.84
6. Introduction to Combinational Chemistry	6.1 – 6.8
7. Retro-synthesis (Disconnection Approach)	7.1 – 7.26
8. Chemistry of Carbohydrates	8.1 – 8.22
9. Nanochemistry and Microwave Assisted Synthesis	9.1 – 9.8
Index	I.1 – I.1

Chapter 1 …

STEREOCHEMISTRY

CONTENTS

- Stereoisomerism, Geometrical isomerism
- E & Z nomenclature, Optical isomerism
- Chirality, Fischer representation
- R & S nomenclature
- Diastereomerism
- Resolution of Racemic modification
- Newmann and Sawhorse representation
- Conformational isomerism
- Conformational isomerism in ethane and n-butane
- Conformations of cyclohexane
- Monoalkyl and dialkyl cyclohexanes
- Conformation in decalin

INTRODUCTION

Stereochemistry is a branch of organic chemistry which deals with structure of compounds in three dimensions and hence can be termed as chemistry or study of compounds with respect to the arrangements and movements of different atoms or group of atoms in space. The word is derived from Greek word (Stereos = "three"-dimensionality).

Stereochemistry also deals with stereo-isomerism and stereo-chemical reactions of organic compounds.

FOUNDERS OF STEREOCHEMISTRY

Biot realised in 1815 that the solutions of many naturally occurring compounds rotate the *plane of polarization* of plane polarized light.	**Pasteur** recognized in 1850 that the *optical activity* was caused by an asymmetric arrangement of atoms in a molecule.	**van't Hoff** with **Le Bel** described in 1874 how the atoms of a molecule are actually arranged in *space*.

Significance of stereochemistry in biological activity:

Stereochemistry plays a major role in the pharmacological properties of a drug because:
1. Any change in stereo chemistry of the drug affects its pharmacological activity
2. The isomeric pairs have different physical properties (partition coefficient, pKa, etc.) and thus, differ in pharmacological activity or drug action.

Sometimes, even toxic and non-toxic nature of two isomers depends on their 3D arrangements in space, which results in binding or not binding at specific sites of receptors.

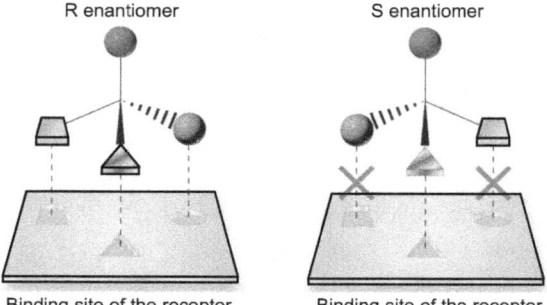

Fig. 1: Drug Receptor interactions

Pharmacodynamics:

Differences in configuration (*e.g.* stereochemistry) of compounds, can lead to startling differences in the biological effect. The wrong configuration will lack required interactions or add undesired ones. Receptors are often chiral and racemic mixture of a drug forms two diastereomeric complexes, as follows:

$$[Drug]_R + [Drug]_S + [Receptor]_S$$
$$\Updownarrow$$
$$[[Drug]_R [Receptor]_S] + [[Drug]_S [Receptor]_S]$$

Two different diastereomeric complexes having different energies and stabilities.

There are numerous examples of stereoisomeric drugs differing vastly in their biological actions. Enantiomers can have different activities.

Dextropropoxyphene : analgesic   Levopropoxyphene : antitussive

Dextro isomer of propoxyphene is analgesic, while levo isomer of propoxyphene is anti-tussive.

S, S-Ethambutol is tuberculostatic while, the R, R-isomer is toxic and can cause blindness.

(S,S)-Ethambutol (Anti-TB)   (R,R)-Ethambutol (Blindness)

S-Limonene has lemon odor while, its R-isomer has orange odor.

S-Limonene (Lemon)   R-Limonene (Orange)

Pharmacokinetics:

The significance of stereochemistry lies in the very specific interactions between enzymes and substrates, which affect the ADME (Absorption, Distribution, Metabolism and Excretion) of drugs. Fate of a drug in the body, right from the time it enters in the body, until its bi-products are eliminated from the body, depends on its ADME.

Absorption: It is the process of movement of unchanged drug from the site of administration to systemic circulation.

Stereoisomers with structural similarities to endogenous entities and nutrients display difference in their permeability rates across the G.I. membrane and hence in their bioavailability.

For example:

1. The (−) enantiomer of bupivacaine is slowly absorbed and has longer duration of action than the (+) enantiomers of bupivacaine.
2. The drug (−) S-propranolol has three-times greater ability to penetrate the membrane barriers as compared to R-enantiomer.
3. The (−) enantiomer of methotrexate is actively absorbed but, the (+) enantiomer of methotrexate is passively absorbed.

Distribution: It is the process of transportation of a drug in the body compartments, often through biding with carrier proteins. The interaction of enantiomers with a plasma protein yields a diastereomeric association.

For example:
1. The (−) Enantiomer of indacrinone shows 0.9% binding to plasma protein, while the (+) enantiomer of indacrinone shows only 0.3% binding.
2. Human albumin binds R-propranolol more strongly than the S-form.

Metabolism is the conversion of drug molecule, from one chemical form to another form. Stereochemical factors play an important role in the metabolism of drugs.

Most enzymes show stereoselectivity but, not stereospecificity. One of the various stereoisomers enters into biotransformation pathway, preferentially over others.

For example: Decarboxylation of S-α-methyldopa leads to S-α-methyldopamine, but no reaction occurs for R-α-methyldopa.

Excretion: The process of removal of drugs or their metabolites from the body. Kidney is the main organ of excretion. Excretion also takes place through intestine, skin, breast and hair.

For example:
1. Enantiomers of terbutaline, disopyramide and pindolol exhibit stereoselective renal clearance.
2. Levofloxacin is excreted as unchanged drug in urine, but its racemate, ofloxacin is eliminated as desmethyl or N-oxide metabolites with less than 5% unchanged drug from the kidney.

ISOMERISM

There are many compounds which have equal number of like atoms. These compounds have the same molecular formulae but, differ from each other in physical and chemical properties, and are called *Isomers*. This phenomenon exhibited by such compounds is called as *Isomerism*. (in *Greek ; isos* means *equal* and *meros* means *parts*)

There are mainly two types of Isomerism:
1. Structural Isomerism
2. Stereoisomerism

1.1 STRUCTURAL ISOMERISM (CONSTITUTIONAL ISOMERISM)

Compounds that have same molecular formulae but, differ in connectivity of atoms, resulting in different structural formulae are termed **Structural Isomers**. When the isomerism is due to difference in the arrangement of atoms within the molecule without any reference to space, it is called **Structural Isomerism** (same molecular formula but, different structural formulae).

Structural Isomerism is of five types:
(i) Chain Isomerism
(ii) Positional Isomerism
(iii) Functional Isomerism
(iv) Metamerism
(v) Tautomerism

1.1.1 Chain or Skeletal Isomerism

Compounds having same molecular formulae but, differ in order (connectivity) in which the carbon atoms are bonded to each other are called as chain or skeletal isomers.

For example: Isomers differ in the way of carbon bonding or connectivity.

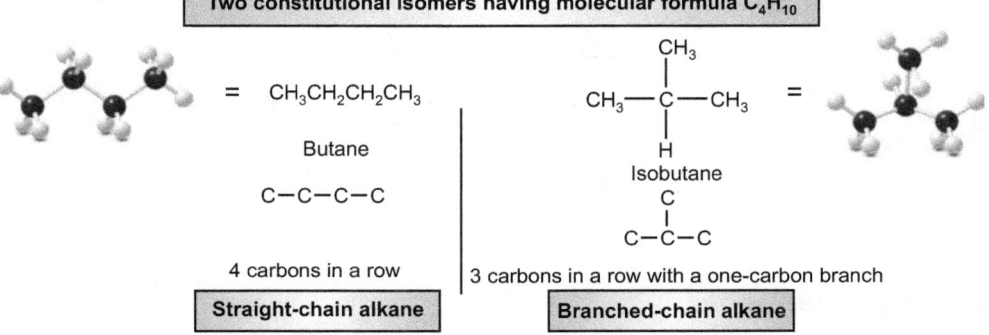

Two constitutional isomers having molecular formula C_4H_{10}

$CH_3CH_2CH_2CH_3$
Butane
C—C—C—C
4 carbons in a row
Straight-chain alkane

CH_3—$\overset{\displaystyle CH_3}{\underset{\displaystyle H}{C}}$—$CH_3$
Isobutane
C—C—C with C branch
3 carbons in a row with a one-carbon branch
Branched-chain alkane

1.1.2 Positional Isomerism

Compounds having same molecular formulae, but differ in the position of a functional group on the carbon chain.

For example,

CH_3—CH_2—CH_2—CH_2—Br
1-Bromobutane

CH_3—$CH(Br)$—CH_2—CH_3
2-Bromobutane

CH_3—CH_2—CH_2—OH
n-Propyl alcohol

CH_3—$CH(OH)$—CH_3
iso-Propyl alcohol

CH_3—CH_2—CO—CH_2—CH_3
3-Pentanone

CH_3—CO—CH_2—CH_2—CH_3
2-Pentanone

o-Nitrophenol

p-Nitrophenol

1.1.3 Functional Isomerism

Compounds having same molecular formulae but, different functional groups.

For example:

CH_3-CH_2-OH — Ethyl alcohol

CH_3-O-CH_3 — Dimethyl ether

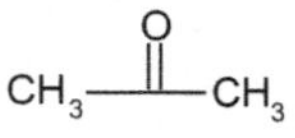

$CH_3-\underset{\underset{O}{\|}}{C}-CH_3$ — Acetone

$CH_3-CH_2-\underset{\underset{O}{\|}}{C}-H$ — Propionaldehyde

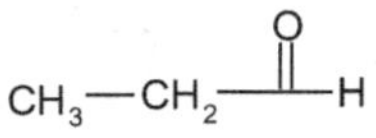

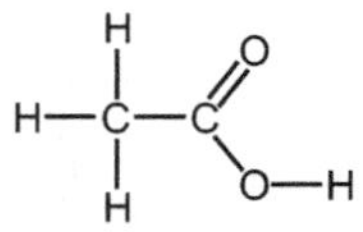

Acetic acid

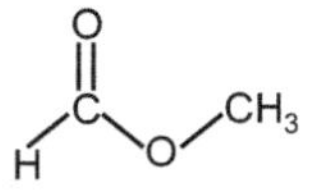

Methyl formate

1.1.4 Metamerism

This type of isomerism is due to unequal distribution of carbon atoms on either side of the same functional group.

For example:

$CH_3-CH_2-O-CH_2-CH_3$ — Diethyl ether

$CH_3-O-CH_2-CH_2-CH_3$ — Methylpropyl ether

$CH_3-CH_2-NH-CH_2-CH_3$ — Diethylamine

$CH_3-CH_2-CH_2-NH-CH_3$ — Methylpropylamine

1.1.5 Tautomerism

Tautomers are compounds whose structures differ in arrangement of atoms and exist in dynamic equilibrium as an inter-converting mixture.

For example:

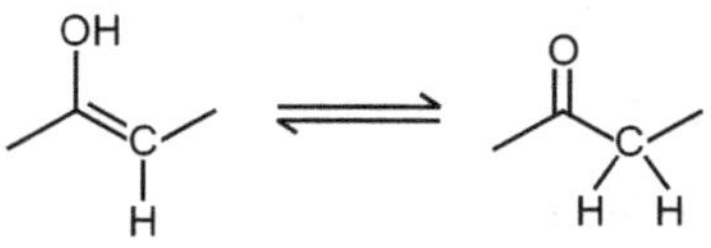

Enol form ⇌ Keto form

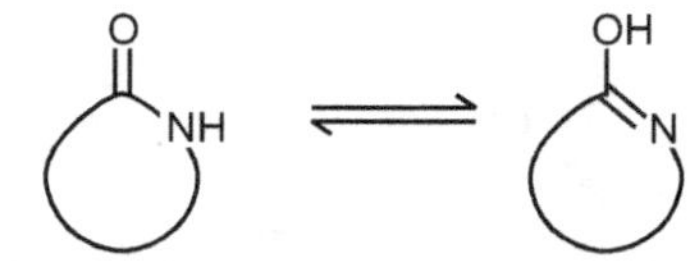

Lactam form ⇌ Lactim form

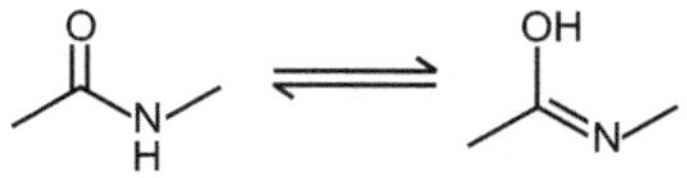

Amide form ⇌ Imidic acid form

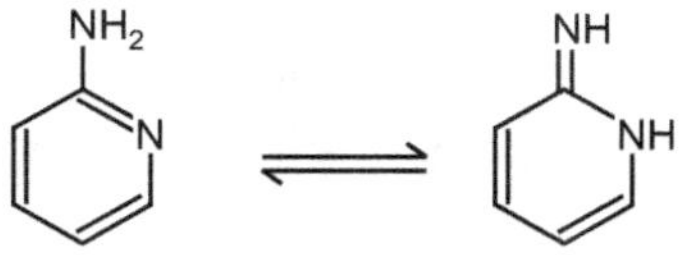

Amine form ⇌ Imine form

s-Triazine-2,4,6-triol ⇌ s-Triazine-2,4,6-trione

1.2 STEREOISOMERISM

"Stereoisomers have the same atomic connectivity but, they differ in the spatial arrangements or orientation of the constituent atoms".

Stereoisomers are further classified as *configurational isomers* and *conformational isomers*. Configurational isomers are further classified as *optical isomers* and *geometrical isomers*. The concept of **Dynamic stereochemistry** explains the difference between them.

Configurational isomers	Conformational isomers
• Refers to the arrangement of bonds and can be changed only by breaking bonds.	• Refers to the arrangement of atoms in molecules that can arrive by the free rotation of atoms about a single chemical bond and can be changed without breaking a bond.
• e.g.: D- and L- configurations of organic molecule can only be changed by breaking one or more bonds.	

1.2.1 Configurational Isomerism

The particular arrangement of atoms in space (spatial arrangement) that is characteristic of a given molecule is named as its **configuration**. The different types of configurations encountered are dealt with separately in details, under different subtypes.

Optical Isomers (R vs S, D vs L) — **Geometric Isomers** (Cis (Z) vs Trans (E))

- (R)/(S): CHO, OH, CH₂OH arrangements
- L-Alanine / D-Alanine
- cis-2-Butene (Z)-2-Butene / trans-2-Butene (E)-2-Butene

1.2.2 Conformational Isomerism

Describes the different spatial arrangements of atoms or groups in a molecule that can arise due to rotations around single bonds.

| Newman Projection | Sawhorse Projection | Fischer Projection |

GEOMETRICAL ISOMERISM

The geometrical isomers have different arrangement of groups across the plane of double bond in acyclics or across the plane of single bond in cyclics. Geometrical isomerism is a property exhibited by particular kind of diastereomers with restricted rotation either due to double bonds or cyclic rings (Diastereomers are stereoisomers that are not mirror images of each other).

1. **In Alkenes:**
   - Have sp^2 Hybridized C-C double bond.
   - This C-C double bond consists of a σ bond and π bond.
   - Restriction of C-C double bond rotation.
   - *Trans* form more stable than *cis*-form.

   For example:

   trans-2-Butene   cis-2-Butene
   (Opposite sides)   (Same sides)

2. **In Cyclic Rings:**
   Must have two different groups on different carbon atoms on the ring.

cis-1,2-Dimethylcyclopropane   trans-1,2-Dimethylcyclopropane

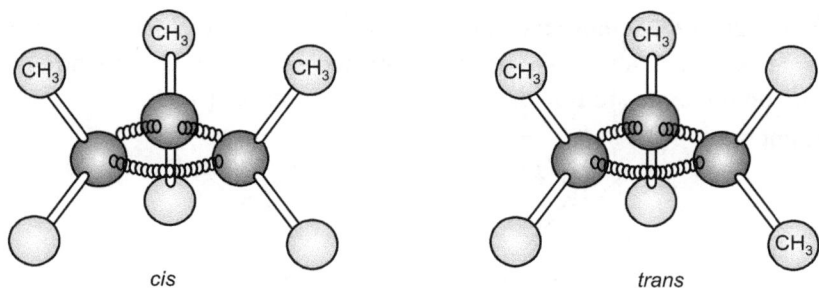

cis   trans

3. **No *cis / trans* isomers:**

   A few cases do exist, where there is no *cis / trans* isomerism, despite presence of a double bond/ring in the structure and hence, there is no optical activity. (This is because, one group is not common to either of the connecting atoms of the double bond/ring).

   Lets see some more details on Geometrical Isomerism with few more examples;

   cis-Crotonic acid   trans-Crotonic acid

   2-Methylcyclopropane carboxylic acids

Properties:

1. Different physical properties
2. Non-identical chemical properties
3. Different rates of reactions in both chemical and biological media.

Geometrical isomers can be interconverted by the rotation about the double bond or the rigid part (ring) theoretically. But, in practice this needs very high energy. Methods of interconversion are known but usually they result in mixture of cis and trans isomers.

Nomenclature of Geometrical Isomers: The compound with similar atoms/groups on the same side of double bond as in I is termed as *cis* and compound with similar atom/group on the opposite side of bond as in II is termed as *trans*.

For example:

trans-2-Butene (Opposite sides)   cis-2-Butene (Same sides)

II   I

However, if three or four different atoms/group of atoms are attached to the double bonded carbon atoms then it is not possible to use *cis/trans* terminology. Hence, in 1960s Cahn, Ingold and Prelog (CIP) proposed a nomenclature based on a set of priorities and sequence rules named as the *E-Z system of nomenclature.*

The E-Z system of Nomenclature: *(Useful particularly when four different groups attached to ethenylic carbon atoms)*

This system is based on the priorities of groups given by the convention.

Step 1: Write the structural formula of the compound clearly showing double bond/ring along with all the substituents.

Step 2: Using priority rules (sequence rules) to assign priority to each atom bonded to one of the carbon atom and similarly repeat it for the other atom, depending on the atomic number of the atom.

Step 3: If substituents of identical priority are on the same side of the double bond/ring then the configuration is termed as *Z* isomer standing for *Zussman* (meaning together in *German*) and if they are on the opposite sides of the double bond then the compound is designated as *E* isomer (from the *German* word *Entegegen* meaning opposite).

(Z)-1-Bromo-1-chloropropane $CH_3 > H$
     $Br > Cl$

(Z)-3-Chloro-2-hexene $CH_3 > H$
     $Cl > CH_2CH_2CH_3$

cis and trans can be corrected with Z and E, as follows:

cis-2-Butene (Z)-2-Butene

trans-2-Butene (E)-2-Butene

OPTICAL ISOMERISM

Optical isomerism is the property exhibited by the compounds having the same structures, but different configurations and bearing an ability to rotate the plane polarized light. A pair of optical isomers has similar physical and chemical properties and their distinguishing character being only their ability to rotate the plane of plane polarized light in opposite directions (but, in equal magnitude). Such a pair of optical isomers is termed as *enantiomers*. (*Enantio* meaning opposite in Greek) This property of rotating the plane of plane polarized light is referred to as **optical activity**.

Light propagates in all directions and when propagating in any direction light vibrates in all the planes. When ordinary light is passed through a Nicole prism (consisting of Canada Balsum; pieces of calcite, $CaCO_3$ arranged in a definite manner) or polarizer, light is found to vibrate in only one single plane, and is said to be plane polarized or simply polarized light.

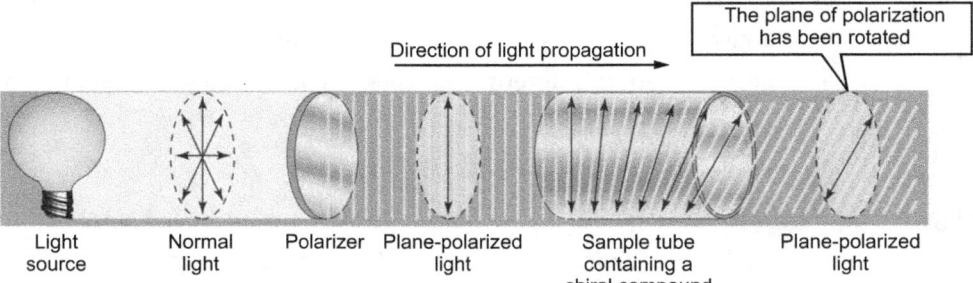

Fig. 2: Optical Activity: Ability to rotate the plane of plane-polarized light

Optical activity in a compound is detected and measured by means of *Polarimeter*. When a solution of known concentration of an optically active material is placed in a polarimeter, the beam of polarized light is rotated through a certain number of degrees, either to right (clockwise) or to the left (anticlockwise). The compound which rotates the plane of polarized light to the right (clockwise) is said to be **dextrorotatory** and is indicated by the sign **(+)**. The compound which rotates the plane of polarized light to the left (anticlockwise) is said to be *levorotatory* and is indicated by the sign (−). The magnitude of rotation, in degrees, is referred to as observed rotation [α]. *e.g,.* Lactic acid rotates the plane to the right and is termed as (+) Lactic acid.

Specific Rotation:

It is defined as the angle of rotation exhibited by 1 gm / ml solution of substance in tube of 1 decimeter (10 cm) length. Consider a system in which the plane of polarized light is rotated through α degree at a temperature of t°C and using the sodium D – line as the source. The specific rotation $[\alpha]_D^t$ is given by formula;

$$[\alpha]_D^t = 100\,\alpha\,/\,ld \quad \text{in case of pure liquid sample}$$

$$[\alpha]_D^t = 100\,\alpha\,/\,lc \quad \text{in case of solution of a compound}$$

where,

α = Observed angle of rotation
l = Length of the tube in decimeters
d = Density of pure liquid
c = The number of grams of solute per 100 ml solvent

Specific rotation varies with both wavelength of light and the temperature chosen but, is constant at a given temperature as any other physical property like, refractive index etc. Usually specific rotation is determined using D-line of Sodium (589.3 nm) at 20°C.

ASYMMETRY/CHIRALITY

Any geometric figure which cannot be superimposed on its mirror image is termed as "*Chiral*" based on Greek word "*Chiros*" meaning hand and chirality means handedness, meaning, not superimposable with their mirror images.

Achiral means that the object has a plane of symmetry.

- Hands, gloves are prime examples of chiral objects.
  They have a "left" and a "right" version.
- Butter fly, is an example of achiral objects as its mirror image is super impossible on its original image.
- Organic molecules can be Chiral or Achiral

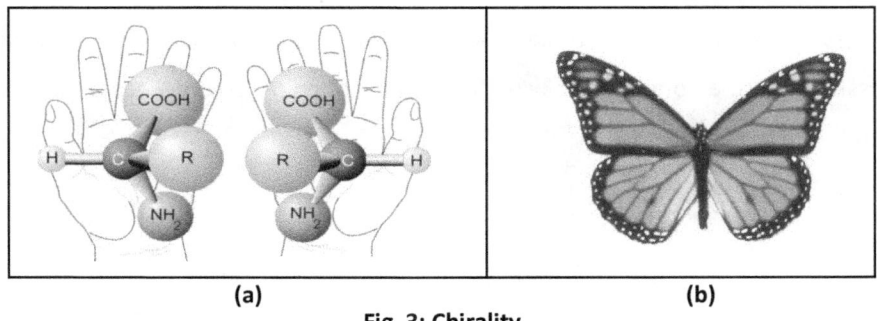

(a) (b)
Fig. 3: Chirality

Earlier term asymmetric carbon was being used to refer a carbon atom bonded to four different atoms or groups of atoms.

For example, there is one chiral centre (sterocentre) in 2-butanol, two chiral centres in tartaric acid and four chiral centres in glucose.

$$\underset{L\,(+)\,2\text{-Butanol}}{H-\overset{C_2H_5}{\underset{CH_3}{\overset{|}{C}}}-OH} \qquad \underset{D\,(+)\,2\text{-Butanol}}{HO-\overset{C_2H_5}{\underset{CH_3}{\overset{|}{C}}}-H}$$

Both second and third carbon atoms are chiral in tartaric acid and any compound with 2 chiral centers can exist as four isomeric forms ($2^2 = 4$).

(2R,3S Tartaric acid)   (2R,3R Tartaric acid)

(2S,3S Tartaric acid)   meso Tartaric acid

Observing the structure of glucose with 4 chiral carbons, a maximum of 16 isomers are possible. Thus, a compound having 'n' number of chiral carbons has a maximum of 'n^2' number of isomers.

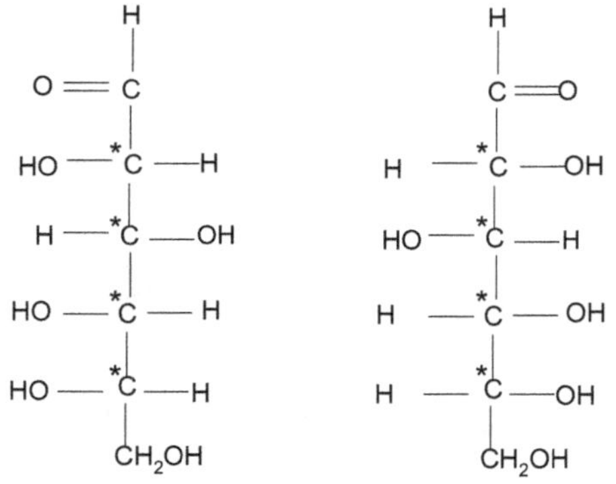

L-Glucose   D - Glucose

Molecular Symmetry and Chirality:

A molecule can have only one mirror image. If the image is superimposable on the original, the molecule is called **Achiral.**

On the other hand, if it is not superimposable on the original then, the molecule and its mirror image form two distinct species called, enantiomers giving rise to a type of stereoisomerism i.e., enantiomerism.

In lactic acid, the two forms of lactic acid are mirror images of each other but not superimpossible. The former is dextrorotatory i.e., it turns the plane of the polarized light to the right and the levorotatory i.e., it turns the plane of polarized light to left.

For example:

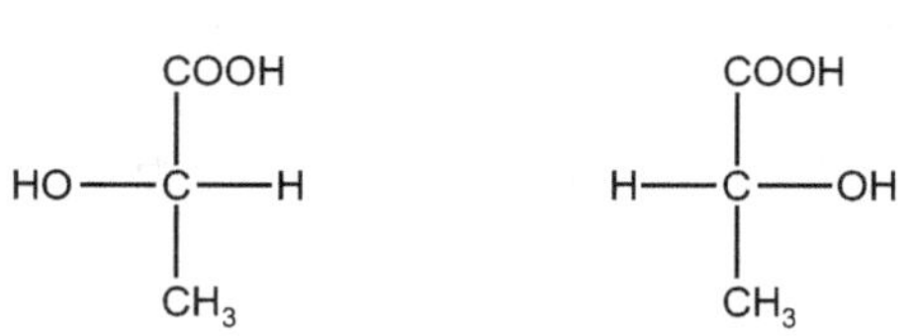

D (+) Lactic acid   L (−) Lactic acid

There are usually two ways of deciding whether a given molecule is optically active or not. One is to construct the model of a molecule and then to build the mirror image of this model. If the model and its mirror image are superimposable, the molecule is not optically active. The second way is to look for symmetry elements in the molecule. If it has none of these elements, it is active. (even though it may have a simple axis of symmetry).

There are 3 main elements of symmetry *viz.*,

1. Plane of symmetry
2. Centre of symmetry and
3. Alternating axis of symmetry.

Presence of any of thease makes a molecule optically inactive.

1. Plane of symmetry: It is a plane which divides the molecule into two identical halves which are mirror images of each other.

Plane of symmetry (σ)

Chloroform has three planes of symmetry, each containing an H-C-Cl grouping.

2. Center of symmetry: A point through which a lines passes to opposite sides and meets the same atoms. It is present in cyclic compounds having even number of carbon atoms.

Consider a molecule given below.

The above molecule has center or point of symmetry at the center of the ring.

3. Alternating axis of symmetry: A molecule possess n-fold of alternating axis, which on rotating through an angle of $360°/n$ about the axis, followed by reflection, in a plane perpendicular to the axis, shows identical mirror image.

Consider the molecule given below;

An alternating or rotating-reflection axis of symmetry of order n (S_n) is an (n-fold) axis such that a rotation of 360°/n around it followed by reflection in a plane perpendicular to the axis generates a structure indistinguishable from the original.

The molecule in above examples, has a fourfold alternating axis of symmetry passing through the center of the ring and at right angles to it.

Its mirror image is superimposable with the original molecule by turning the ring upside down and rotating it 90° around the axis.

Symmetry designations:

Term	Alternating Axis	Simple Axis	Optical Activity
Symmetric	Present	May/ may not be present	Inactive
Dissymmetric	Absent	May/ may not be present	Usually active
Asymmetric	Absent	Absent	Usually active

1.2.2.3 Optical Isomers

1. **Enantiomers and Enantiomerism:**

   Enantiomers can be defined as non-superimposable mirror images

   In short;
   - Molecules that have one carbon with four different substituents have a non-superimposable mirror image.
   - Have tetrahedral structure.
   - **Enantiomers** = non-superimposable mirror image stereoisomers. (derived from Greek word, 'Enantio" = Opposite, 'morphs' = form)
   - Enantiomers have identical physical properties.

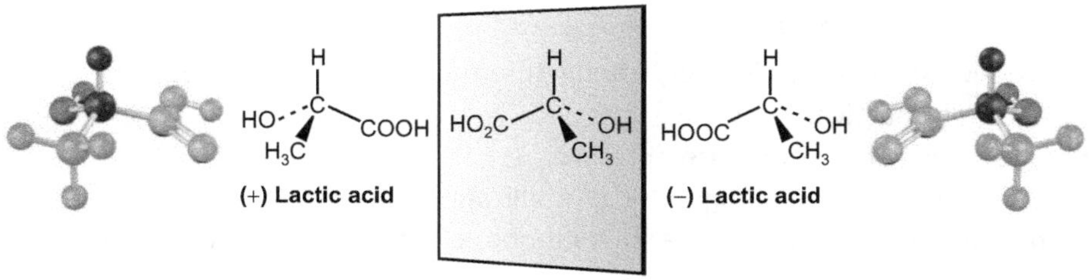

PHARMACEUTICAL ORGANIC CHEMISTRY - II   STEREOCHEMISTRY

(+) Lactic acid   (−) Lactic acid

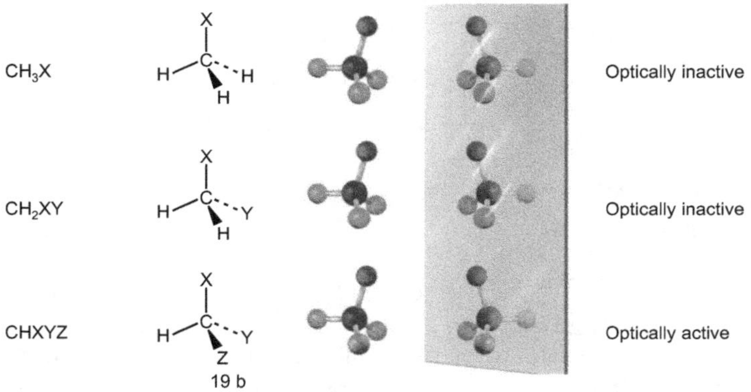

CH₃X   Optically inactive

CH₂XY   Optically inactive

CHXYZ   Optically active

Fig. 4

Examples of enantiomers include glyceraldehydes, tartaric acid, lactic acid, secondary butyl chloride, chloroiodomethane sulphonic acid etc.

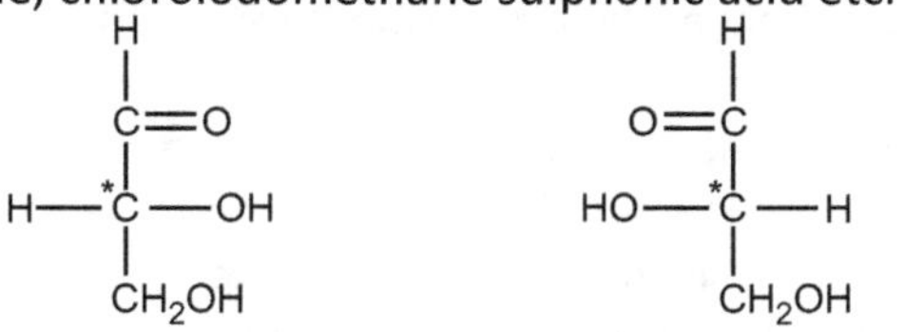

D-Glyceraldehyde   L-Glyceraldehyde

All these compounds contain at least one *chiral* or *asymmetric* centre. *Stereocenters* (sometimes called chiral centers, or stereogenic centers) are carbons that have four non-identical substituents on them.

Enantiomerism is also exhibited by compounds in which chiral carbon is generated by connecting to different isotopes of the same element. E.g., α-Deuteroethylbenzene.

It should be noted that all the compounds have mirror images and in most of the compounds they are superimposable on each other as in methane. An important property of enantiomers is that interchange of any two groups at the stereocenter converts one enantiomer into other.

2. **Diastereomers:**

Diastereomers are non-enantiomeric stereoisomers that are not mirror images of each other *i.e.*, diastereomers are stereoisomers that are not enantiomers. They have two or more stereocenters and differ in the orientation of at least one of them.

In brief *diastereomers* are:
- Non-identical mirror images, having different physical properties.
- Optically inactive.
- Their rates of reactions are different.
- Separation by chromatography, crystallization is easier.
- n = number of chiral centres, 2n = number of enantiomers and diastereomers.

[Diagram showing four Fischer projections I, II, III, IV of 2,3-dichloropentane. I and II are Enantiomers; III and IV are Enantiomers; II and III are Diasteriomers.]

Considering the above structures of 2,3-dichloropentane, it can be concluded that the pairs, I and II & III and IV, are enantiomers as they are non-superimposable mirror images of each other. Now lets us consider other pairs, *i.e.*, between the pair I and III/ IV or the pair II and III/ IV, it can be seen that eventhough, they are **stereoisomers**, they are **non-mirror images** and hence are termed *diastereomers*.

Now lets consider the stereoisomers of tartaric acid; here the meso-tatraic acid is a diastereomer of each of the enantiomers. The pairs of enantiomers have the opposite configuration at every stereocenter i.e., enantiomeric tartaric acids are (2R, 3R) and (2S, 3S). While, a diastereoisomer i.e., meso-tartaric acid has one stereocenter of common configuration, the other is of opposite configuration (2R, 3S). *(We may see the R, S nomenclature in next section)*

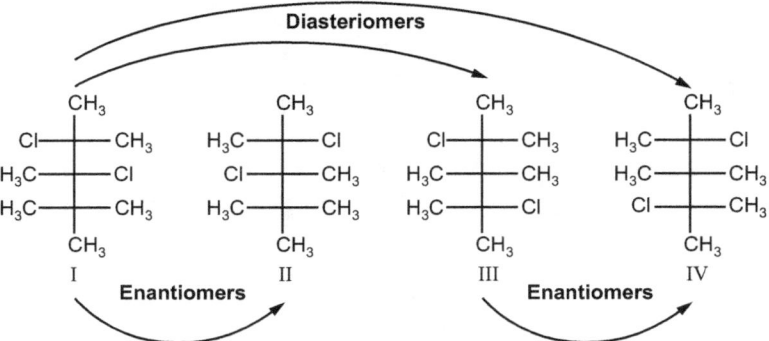

(2R,3S Tartaric acid) Meso   (2R,3R Tartaric acid)   (2S,3S Tartaric acid)

(2R,3R) and (2S,3S) are Enantiomers; Meso and the enantiomers are Diasteriomers.

To summarize in form of a table:

Stereisomer	Enantiomer	Diastereomer
2R, 3R	2S, 3S	2R, 3S and 2S, 3R
2S, 3S	2R, 3R	2R, 3S and 2S, 3R
2R, 3S	2S, 3R	2R, 3R and 2S, 3S
2S, 3R	2R, 3S	2R, 3R and 2S, 3S

2. (a) **Epimers:** When two diastereomers differ in the stereochemistry at only one stereocenter then these are called *epimers*.

For example: Glucose and galactose are epimers at C_4. Similarly, glucose and mannose are epimers at C_2.

D-Galactose   D-Glucose   D-Mannose

2. (b) **Anomers:** In the pyranose structure of glucose the –OH group at C_5 attacks the aldehyde (C_1) to form a hemiacetal. A new stereocenter at C_1 is generated and a pair of diastereomers is formed. These are called anomers.

α-Glucose   β-Glucose

In other words, two isomers differ with respect to the configuration (α or β) of OH group at the anomeric carbon.

Properties:

Diastereomers have different physical properties like, M.P., B.P., solubility, retention times and R_f values and have different rates of reactions (chemical properties) even in achiral environments.

Meso Compounds:

An achiral compound with chiral centers is called a *meso* compound and it has a plane of symmetry.

The two structures on the right in the figure are identical so the compound (*2R, 3S)* is achiral. Or in other words the half part of the molecule is exactly the mirror image of other half part.

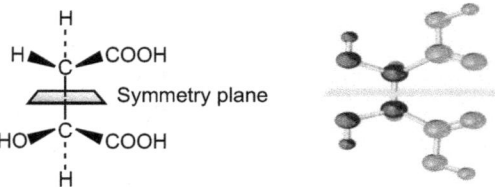

Thus, it is a case of identical substitution on both chiral centers

Fig. 5

RESOLUTION OF RACEMIC MODFICATIONS

A substance composed of equimolar amounts of a pair of enantiomers is called as "racemic modification".

The process of separation of pure enantiomer from their racemic modification is called "resolution".

It has a great practical importance in the study of naturally occurring optically active compounds.

Following are the different five methods of separation of a racemic mixture.
1. Mechanical separation
2. Preferential crystallization by innoculation
3. Chromatographic separation
4. Biochemical separation
5. Separation by conversion into diastereomers.

1. Mechanical separation

Pasteur used this process to separate (+) tartaric acid and (−) tartaric acid from the (±) conglomerate of tartaric acid. The (+) and (−) forms have opposite crystalline shapes. The crystals of opposite facets are to be seen distinctly under a microscope. Then with the help of tweezer the two types of crystals are to be picked up one by one and to be collected in separate containers.

This process has some demerits:

(a) No value in practice.

(b) It is not applicable to the racemic and solid solutions.

(c) Distinctive crystals facets are seldom found in a racemic mixture and this makes the separation trouble some and incomplete.

(d) The process is tedious.

(e) The process has historical interest only.

2. Preferential crystallization by Inoculation

- Mainly applied to a racemic mixture.
- Here, the greater affinity of each enantiomer for the molecules of its own kind than the other enantiomer is exploited.
- Here, the pure crystal of one enantiomer is inoculated in a saturated solution of the racemic mixture.
- The molecules of this enantiomer from the solution start depositing on the crystal and it grows in size.
- A crystal of an isomorphous substituent may be used for inoculation.
- Racemic compounds of greater solubility in a solvent can also be separated.
- It has a great practical importance in purification of enantiomers.

Example: Phenylmethylcarbonyl hydrogen phthalate is purified 95% by this method using a small crystal of its pure enantiomer in CS_2 medium.

3. **Chromatographic - Separation**
   - Enantiomers react with an optically active reagent at different rates and produce distereomers of different stabilities.
   - A solution of racemic form in a choosen solvent is allowed to pass slowly down an optically active adsorbent like starch.
   - The enantiomers are adsorbed by the active adsorbent at different rates to form distereomers of different stabilities.
   - The column is washed (eluted) with a suitable solvent.
   - The enantiomer forming less stable distereomer comes down the column faster than the other and the eluents are collected in separate vessels.

     Example: (±) - Mandelic acid is resolved almost completely using starch as an adsorbent.
   - Paper chromatography can also be used. Here cellulose acts as an optically active substance.
   - The process is very useful in deciding whether, the given substituent is dl pair or a compound containing symmetric molecule.
   - If elution is found to be optically active, the subsistent under investigation is definitely a dl-pair.
   - If not, it consists of a symmetric moleculae.

4. **Biochemical separation**
   - It was discovered by Pasteur.
   - The chemical reaction occurs with the help of bio-catalysts (enzymes) and is called as biochemical separation.
   - Living organisms contain optically active bio-catalysts called enzymes.
   - When living organisms are added or developed in a racemic modification, they eat up an enantiomer preferentially leaving the other behind and separation occurs.

     Example: *Penicllium glaucum*, a mould, eats up preferentially (±) – ammonium tartrate when, added to (±) ammonium tartarate.

   Since, biological processes are highly specific, the method leads to a high extent of resolution provided proper organism is employed for the same.

The following are the limitations of a biochemical separation:

(a) It is difficult to find out proper organism, which is specifically effective.

(b) One gets only one of the enantiomers, at the expense of the other.

(c) Dilute solution must be used; otherwise organism may die and hence, small amount of resolved product is obtained.

5. **Separation by conversion into distereomers:**

   - Enantiomers have identical physical properties while, distereomers have different physical properties.
   - This fact is utilised here to resolve a racemic mixture.
   - The racemic form is allowed to react with an optically active substance, two distereomeric derivatives are then formed.
   - These have different solubilities and boiling points. So by fractional crystallization, the solid distereomers can be separated.
   - Now-a-days gas chromatography is also used to separate the distereomers and fractional distillation has minimum scope.

Schematic representation

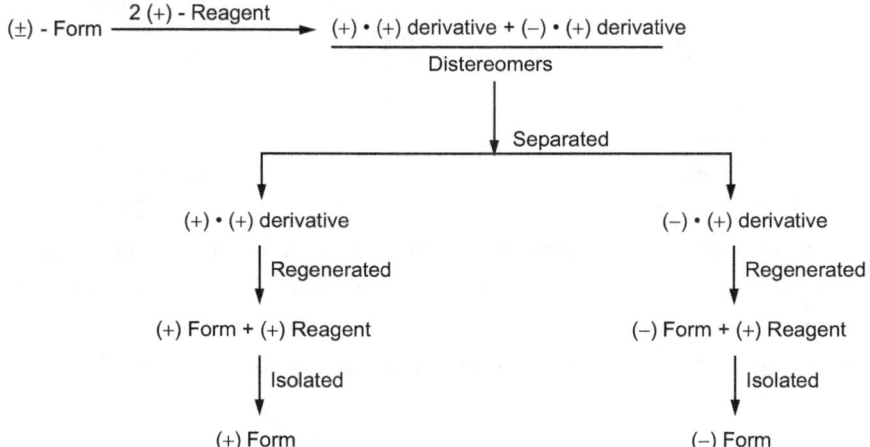

   - The process is mainly applied to acids and bases, as well as, alcohols, aldehydes, ketones, hydrocarbons, amino acids etc.

Example: Acids are converted into two distereomeric salts by the reaction of optically active bases. The bases used are alkaloids e.g., strychnine, ephedrine, quinine, morphine, brucine etc. Mehtylamines and phenethylamines are also used.

- The diastereomers are then separated by fractional distillation.
- Each of the diastereomers is then hydrolysed with dil. HCl to generate the enantiomers.

(−) Ephedrine

Menthylamine derivative

FISCHER PROJECTIONS

A Fischer projection provides an easy way to draw 3-dimensional molecules on paper. All atoms are projected onto one plane. These are flat drawings that represent a 3D molecule. A chiral carbon is at the intersection of the horizontal and vertical lines. Horizontal lines are forward, out-of-plane; while, vertical lines are behind the plane. E.g., Lactic Acid.

(S)-Lactic acid perspective drawing

(S)-Lactic acid Fischer projection

Fischer's rules showing the arrangement around an asymmetric carbon are as follows:

1. The carbon chain of the compound is arranged vertically with most oxidized carbon at the top.
2. Represent the asymmetric carbons at the intersection of crossed lines.

Groups attached to the vertical lines are understood to be going back behind the plane of the paper. (away from the viewer)

3. Groups attached to the horizontal lines are understood to be coming forward out of the plane of the paper. (towards the viewer)

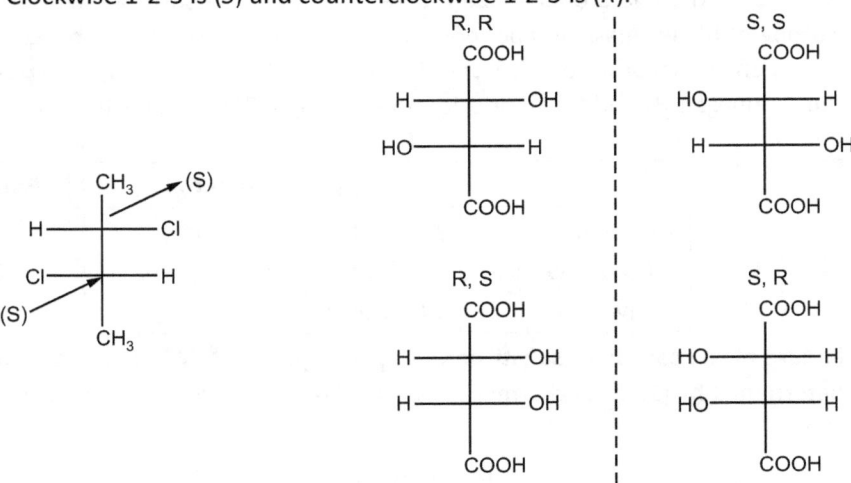

4. Rotation of 180° in plane doesn't change the molecule.
5. Do not rotate 90°. It changes the conformation from R to S or *vice versa*, as seen below.

6. Lowest priority (usually H) comes forward, so assignment starts from backwards.
7. Clockwise 1-2-3 is (*S*) and counterclockwise 1-2-3 is (*R*).

Erythro and Threo system of nomenclature:
- Nomenclature is used only in those compounds, which have only two chiral carbons.
- If two identical groups in Fischer projection formula are on the same side = ***erythro form***; and if they are on the opposite sides = ***threo form***.

CH₃	CH₃	CH₂CH₃	CH₂CH₃
H——Cl	H——Cl	H——Br	H——Br
H——Cl	Cl——H	Cl——H	H——Cl
C₂H₅	C₂H₅	CH₃	CH₃
Erythro form	Threo form	Threo form 3-Bromo-4-chloropentane	Erythro form 3-Bromo-2-chloropentane

R AND S NOMENCLATURE (THE CAHN-INGOLD–PRELOG NOMENCLATURE - C.I.P.RULES)

In 1960s Cahn, Ingold and Prelog proposed a methodology for the nomenclature of compounds containing chiral centres so as to assign absolute configuration based on a set of sequence and priority rules.

RULE 1: Assigning Priorities: Sequence Rules

Look at the four atoms directly attached to the stereogenic center (*). Assign priorities based on atomic number to all four atoms. Priority 1 is assigned to the atom or group of highest atomic number, priority 4 to the lowest.

(I) **Isotopes:** If the two atoms happen to be isotopes of the same element, then the isotope of higher mass number gets higher priority. Simplest possible example is hydrogen and its other two isotopes in methanol. Ofcourse, **OH gets top priority**. But amongst T, D and H the priority order shall be **T > D > H**, which is explained below.

		Mass number	Priority
	T (Tritium)	3 (1 proton + 2 neutrons)	1
	D (Deuterium)	2 (1 proton + 1 neutron)	2
	H (Hydrogen)	1 (1 proton)	3

(II) **Nature of the carbon of substituent alkyl groups (1°/2°/3°):** If priority cannot be determined by (1), it is determined by a similar comparison of atoms working out from

$$H-\underset{H}{\overset{H}{C}}-\underset{H}{\overset{H}{\underset{2}{C}}}-\underset{Cl}{\overset{H}{\underset{3}{C}}}-H \quad \overset{4}{}$$

In the methyl group, the second atoms are H, H, H whereas in the ethyl group, they are C, H, H. The priority sequence is therefore Cl, C₂H₅, CH₃, H.

(III) A double or triple bond to an atom, **A**, is considered as equivalent to two or three single bonds to **A**:

(IV) Type of substitutent group/atom: If the four atoms attached to the chiral centre, all are different, the priority depends on the atomic number, with the atom of higher atomic number getting higher priority.

Examples:

Bromochloroiodo methane	Chloroiodomethanesulphonic acid
(structure with I, Br, Cl, H; priorities 1,2,3,4)	(structure with I, HO$_3$S, Cl, H; priorities 1,3,2,4)
I > Br > Cl > H	I > Cl > S > H
Atomic No. 53 35 17 1	Atomic No. 53 17 16 1

The general sequence for substituent groups/atoms as per priority is as follows:

–I > –Br > –Cl > –SH > –F > –OOCR > –OR > –OH > –NO$_2$ > –NHCOR > –NR$_2$ > –NHR > –NH$_2$ > –CCl$_3$ > –COCl > –COOR > –COOH > –CONH$_2$ > –COR > –CHO > –CN > –CH$_2$OH > –C$_6$H$_5$ > –CR$_3$ > –CH$_3$ > –H

RULE 2: Visualization of proper orientation:

- Visualise the compound/molecule oriented in such a way that the ligand (bond) of lowest priority is directed away from the viewer. (working in 3D, rotate molecule so that lowest priority group is in back.)
- Then observe the arrangement of remaining ligands (bonds)
  - if in proceeding from ligand of highest priority to the ligand of second priority and then to the ligand of third priority, the viewers eye travels in clockwise direction, then the configuration is specified as *R* (Latin *rectus* means right) and
  - if counter clockwise, then it is specified as *S* (Latin *sinister* means left).
- Alternatively, draw an arrow in a circular fashion from highest priority to lowest. If the arrow orientation is clockwise the designation is *R*. Conversely, if the arrow orientation is counterclockwise then the designation is *S*.

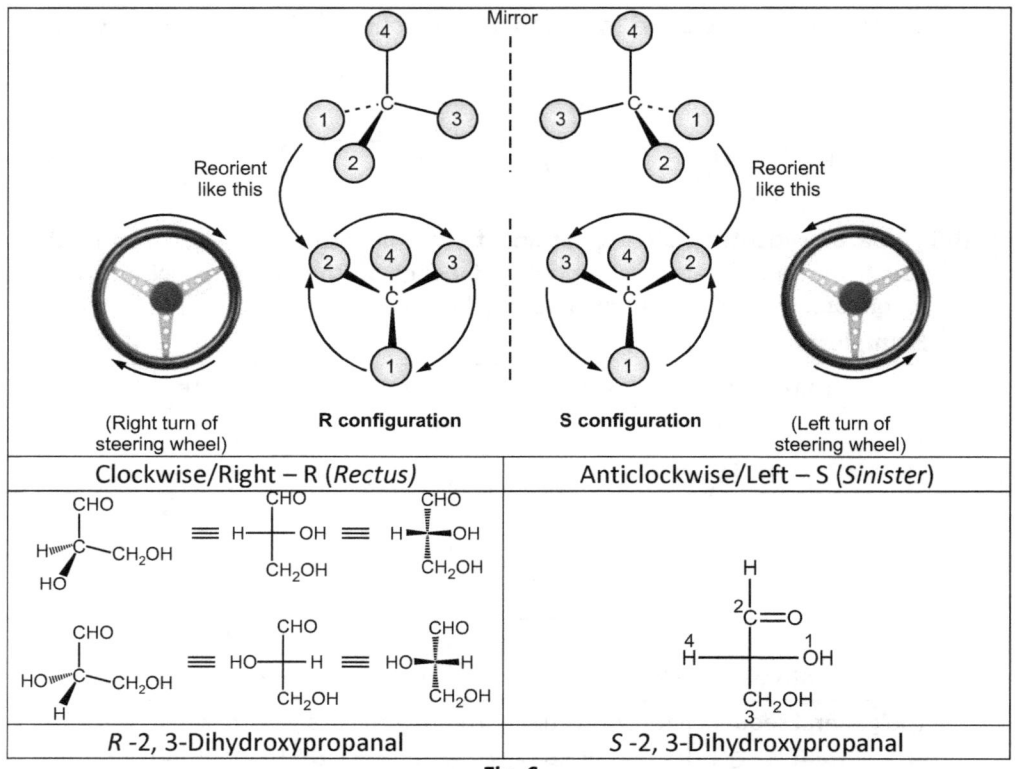

Fig. 6

RULE 3:

In case, there are more than one chiral carbon in the molecule, then configuration is assigned for each chiral centre by applying the above procedure to each of them.

Select one of the chiral carbons and then apply the above method and specify the configuration for the selected carbon and then repeat the procedure for the second chiral carbon. Then designate configuration for the molecule using symbols *R* and *S*, along with locant of carbon in parentheses.

e.g., 2, 3-dichloropentane
Carbon at 2 position (2nd carbon) Chloro > Chloropropyl > Methyl > Hydrogen
Carbon at 3 position (3rd carbon) Chloro > Chloroethyl > Ethyl > Hydrogen

2-R,3-R

1.3 CONFORMATIONAL ISOMERISM

Isomers which can be converted into each others by rotation about a single bond are called as *conformational isomers or conformers or rotational isomers.*

This isomerism arises due to the ability of a single bonded carbon to rotate about the bond axis freely, *i.e.,* rotation about single bonds is not restricted. Therefore, molecule exists in number of forms and there exist energy barriers between these forms.

There are different ways to represent these conformational isomers, which are discussed here.

1.3.1 Newmann Projections

Newman projections are the way of drawing conformation.

The molecule in a Newman projection is viewed along the C-C bond axis in such a way that the second carbon lies directly behind the first carbon as depicted.

For example:

The front carbon and the atoms bonded to it are represented by the centre of circle and the lines originating from it. While, the rear carbon with its bonded atoms are represented by periphery of circle and lines originating from the circumference.

- **Eclipsed:** Groups of front and rear carbon overlap (dihedral angle: 0° or 120°).
- **Staggered:** Rear groups rotate upside down, staggered symmetrical. (dihedral angle: 60°)
- **Skew:** They lie in between or intermediate of the above two forms.

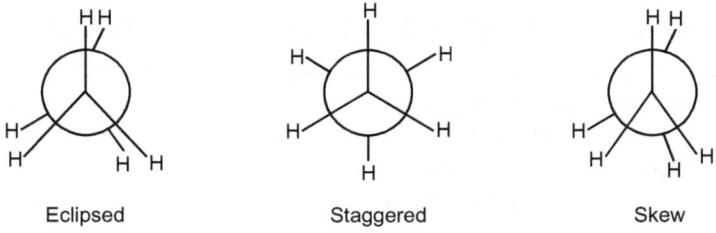

Eclipsed   Staggered   Skew

If we visualize three dimensionally, the eclipsed and staggered conformations they appear as follows:

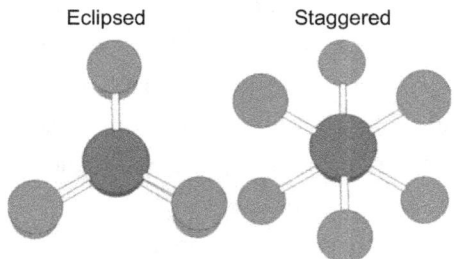

Relative Stability: Staggered > Skew > Eclipsed

1.3.2 Sawhorse Projections

In a Sawhorse formula, C-C bond is viewed sideways (diagonally from one side), while, in case of Newmann projection C-C bond lies along the vision.

Newmann projection   **Sawhorse projection**

A Sawhorse projection really represents the different spatial arrangements of atoms or groups in a molecule that arise due to a rotation (torsion) around single bond axis, as viewed along its axis.

1.3.3 Conformational Isomerism and Conformational Analysis

The various shapes that a molecule can adopt by rotation about single bonds are called *conformations*. This phenomena of ready interconversion amongst isomers is exhibited as the compound exists in a dynamic equilibrium mixture of a number of continuously changing, energy dependent conformations which, differ from one another in the degree of rotations about one or more single bonds. (dihedral/torsion angle).

Conformational isomers are a class of stereo isomers as they differ only in the spatial arrangements of atoms or groups.

For example, ethane interconverts millions of times per second at 25°C. However, the configurations of ethylene (ethene) derivatives do not interconvert spontaneously even at 200°C. In principle one could stop interconversions of conformational isomers by sufficient cooling. Hence, distinction between configuration and conformation is based on the ability of the compound to interconvert at room temperature, 25°C. The interconversion of conformers is energy dependant. The study of relative stability of different conformers along with potential energy of the compound and correlation to its chemical and physical properties is termed as *Conformational analysis*.

1.3.4 Conformations of Ethane

Potential energy curve obtained for ethane, with one carbon being stationary and the other rotating freely about C-C bond axis would be as follows;

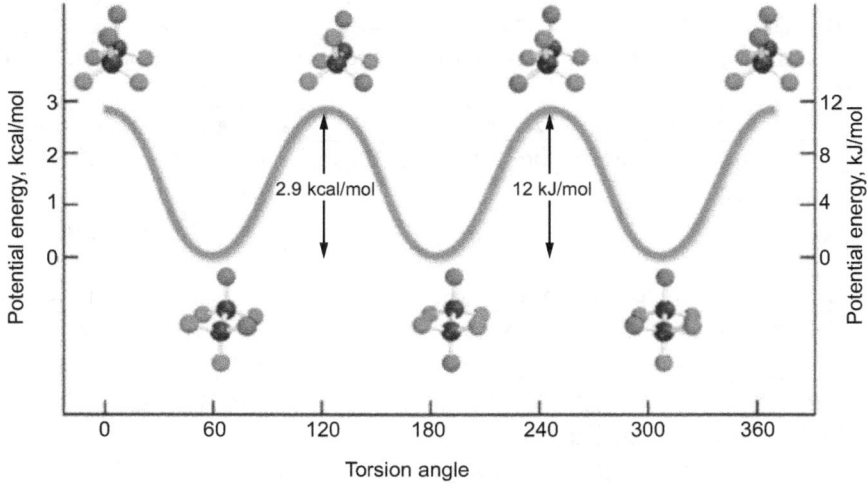

Fig. 7: Energy *versus* dihedral (torsion) angle for ethane

See the H-H eclipsing interaction = 4 kJ/mol. The barrier to C-C rotation for ethane is 12 kJ/mol; between Staggered and Eclipsed = 2.8-2.9 kcal/mol.

The potential energy diagram shows three energy minima corresponding to *staggered conformations* of 60°, 180° and 300° dihedral angles.(Hydrogen atoms are as far apart as possible). Similarly, there are three energy maxima of *eclipsed conformation* with dihedral angle of 0°, 120° and 240°. (Hydrogen atoms are near each other). As staggered conformation corresponds to energy minima, it happens to be most stable conformation while eclipsed conformation is at energy maxima and represents transition state. The energy difference between the two conformers is close to about 3 kcal/mol (12 kJ/mol). The destabilization associated with the eclipsing of bonds on adjacent atoms is called torsional strain in eclipsed ethane and is due to the slight repulsion of electron pairs of adjacent C-H bonds as they rotate past one another in converting from one staggered conformation to another. Three pairs of eclipsed bonds produce about 3 kcal/mol (12 kJ/mol) of torsional strain in ethane. The activation energy for rotation about the C-C bond in ethane is small, the thermal energy from the surroundings is sufficient to cause staggered conformations of ethane to interconvert millions of times each second at RT.

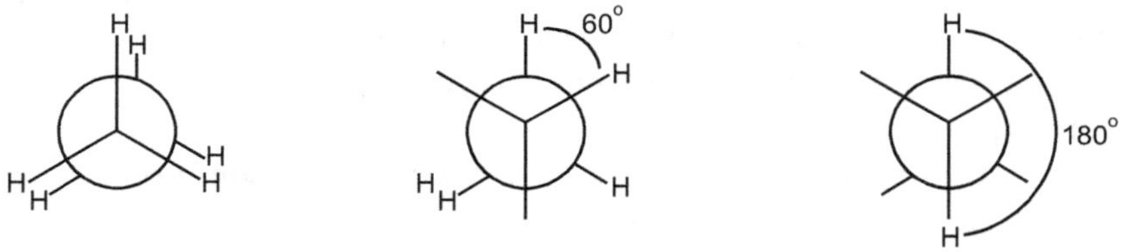

| | Eclipsed conformer (Torsional angle = 0°) | Gauche conformer (Torsional angle = 60°) | Anti conformer (Torsional angle = 180°) |

The following table lists differences between conformational and configurational isomers.

	Conformational isomers	**Configurational isomers**
1.	Arise due to rotation about flexible single bond.	Rigid, due to difference in arrangement of groups on a chiral carbon or about a rigid part of a molecule.
2.	Non-isolable at room temperature	Isolable and easy to separate.
3.	Interconvertible by rotation about a single bond.	Not easily convertible as bond breaking and making is involved.
4.	Low energy barrier (upto 50 kJ/mol).	Higher energy (more than 50 kJ/mol).

1.3.5 Conformations of Butane

In ethane all the staggered conformations are equivalent, on the other hand in butane, there are two different staggered conformations. In one of these (synclinal), there is a gauche relationship between methyl groups. While, in the other conformation the relationship is anti-periplanar. These staggered conformations are free of torsional strain. However, the anti-periplanar conformer is the most stable, because the methyl groups are far apart. The methyl groups in the gauche conformations are close enough to each other, so that the Van der Waals forces between them are repulsive; the electron clouds of the two groups are so close that they repel each other. The repulsion causes the gauche conformation to have approximately 0.9 kcal/mol(3.8 kJ/mol) more energy than the anti-conformation. The eclipsed conformations represent energy maxima in potential energy diagram.

The potential energy diagram depicts four distinct changes in energy profile (*i.e.,* crest or troughs) corresponding to four conformers. A fully eclipsed conformation (syn-periplanar), two partially eclipsed conformations (anticlinal) and a fully staggered conformation (gauche or synclinal).

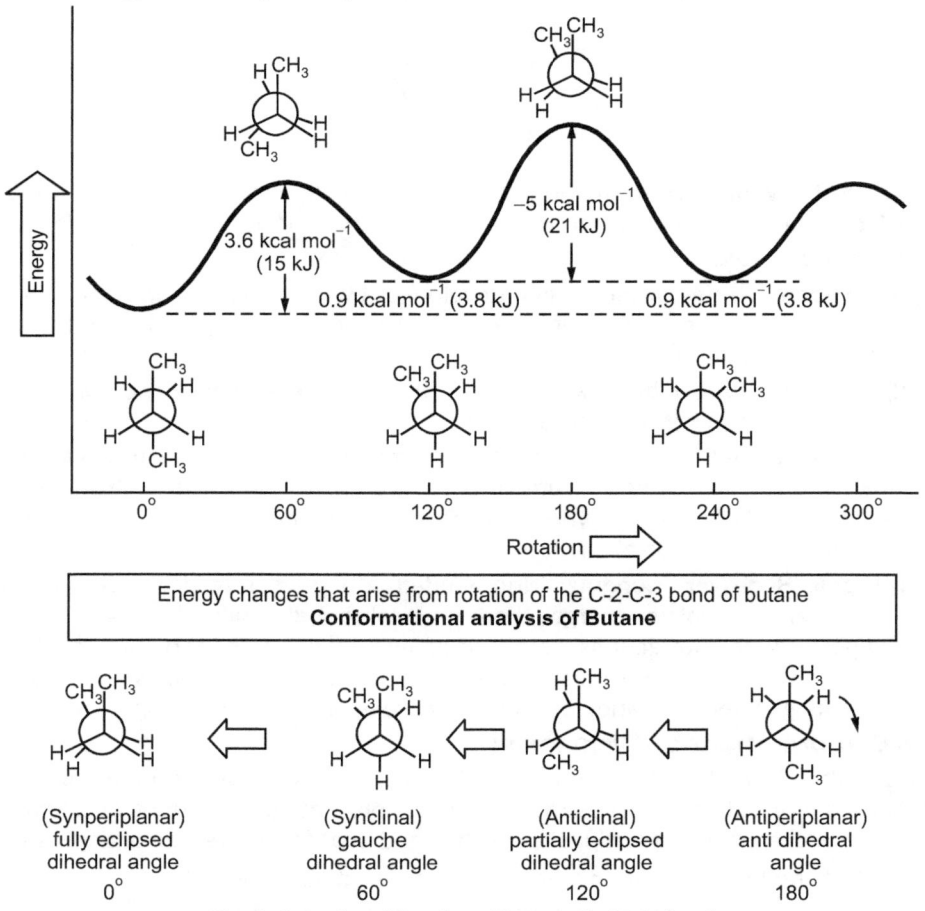

Fig. 8: Rotational barrier of butane is 25 kJ/mol

Stability: Anti-periplanar > Anti-clinal > Syn-clinal > Syn-periplanar.

Synperiplanar	Synclinal	Anticlinal	Antiperiplanar
0°	60°	120°	180°

```
        0°
   -30°   30°
        Peri
   Syn
Clinal     Clinal
   Anti
  -150°  150°
        Peri
        180°
```

The most favoured conformation of a compound depends on four main factors. These factors are *torsional strain, angle strain, van der Waal's strain* and *intra/inter molecular interactions.*

(a) **Torsional strain** is the strain developed by *bond pair-bond pair repulsion* between atoms or groups of atoms on each carbon atom (non-bonded atoms of each carbon atom).

(b) **Angle strain:** Any bond angle other than the ideal bond angle, *i.e.*, 109° 28 results in strain known as angle strain.

(c) **van der Waal's strain:** Strain due to proximity of atoms *i.e.*, when two atoms not bonded to each other are forced to be at a distance less than the sum of their van der Wall's radii. (Hydrogen-120 pm, Nitrogen-150 pm, Oxygen-140 pm where *pm* stands for *pico meter*)

(d) **Dipole/Hydrogen bonding:** Non-bonded atoms if forced to be proximate and carry opposite charge then physical bonding like hydrogen bonding, dipole-dipole interactions takes place and stabilizes a particular conformer. Similarly, if atoms of similar charges are proximate then repulsion takes place resulting in destabilization or requires more energy to be held together.

1.3.6 Conformations of Cyclohexane

Molecular formula of cyclohexane is C_6H_{12}. Based on tetrahedral theory, cyclohexane molecule can exist as *chair* and *boat* conformations, both of which are non-planar and puckered conformations. Both chair and boat forms are free of angle strain.

- Most stable and common acyclic ring; internal angles are 120°.
- Favoured four conformations, chair, half-chair, boat, and twist-boat.

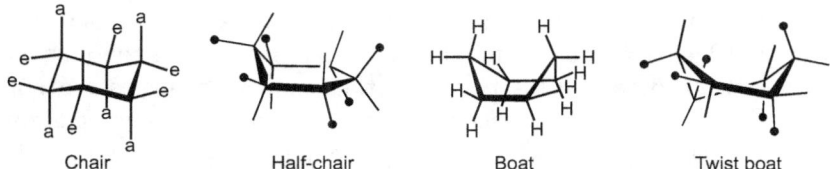

Chair   Half-chair   Boat   Twist boat

1.3.7 Equatorial and Axial bonds in Chair form of Cyclohexane

- **Axial:** "perpendicular" to the "plane of the ring".
- **Equatorial:** "parallel" to the "plane of the ring".

There are all twelve carbon-hydrogen bonds in cyclohexane molecule consisting of two sets of six bonds each. A set of six bonds are parallel to the axis of symmetry or perpendicular to plane of the molecule (above and below) termed as **axial bonds**. Out of the six axial bonds three are above and three are below the plane of molecule. Other set of six bonds are inclined at an angle of 109° 28' to the axis of symmetry (in the plane of molecule) known as **equatorial bonds**.

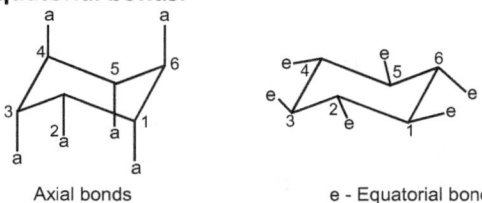

Axial bonds   e - Equatorial bonds
                           a - Axial bonds

(a) Chair conformation of Cyclohexane: In chair conformation, all carbon-carbon bonds are staggered and exist predominantly in a non-planar, puckered conformation.

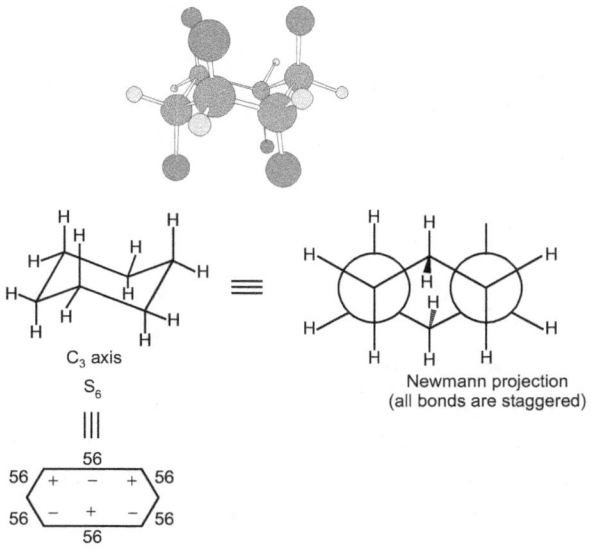

In chair conformation all bonds are staggered (Newmann projection) and hence torsional strain (Pitzer strain) is minimized. Interactions between neighboring methylene groups as in gauche butane leads to steric strain and bond angles are not exactly 109°30' but 111°. In *Newmann* projection the angle formed between adjacent carbon atoms is not exactly 60° but is 56° resulting in puckering of the ring. The chair conformation is symmetrical as vertical axis C_3 passing through center of chair, as well as, S_6 axis and it also has center of symmetry. This results in a puckered non-planar structure.

(b) Boat conformation of Cyclohexane:

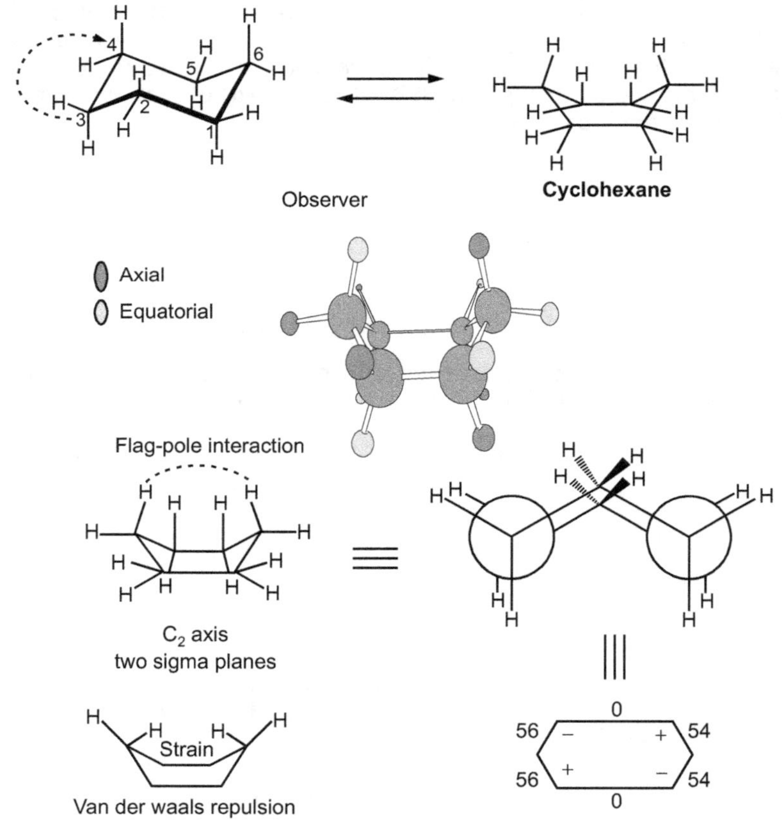

In boat conformation, there are four staggered (gauche) and two eclipsed butane like units. Hydrogen atoms at C_1 and C_4 are termed as flagpole hydrogen atoms and are at a distance of 183 pm which is less than the sum of their van der Waal's radii. (250 pm). Staggered (gauche) pairs of carbons are C_1 / C_2, C_3 / C_4, C_4 / C_5 & C_6 / C_1 and eclipsed pairs are C_2 / C_3 and C_5 / C_6. There is complete eclipsing of hydrogen atoms attached to carbon atom forming side CH_2-CH_2 bonds. Hydrogen atoms on C_1 and C_4 (*Flagpole* hydrogens) interfere with each other sterically in transannular interaction. Therefore, Boat form is less stable than chair form. The boat conformation has one C_2 axis and two sigma planes.

Twist Boat Conformation of Cyclohexane: The *twist boat* conformation of cyclohexane experiences three forms of strain. They are bond angle strain, eclipsing strain (torsional strain) and transannular strain (across the ring strain).

- Less the torsional strain, flagpole hydrogen moves away.
- They show skew conformation.
- More stable than boat conformation (has 1.5 kcal/mole energy less than boat form).

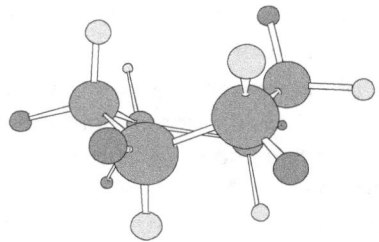

Chair conformation has minimum energy since it is free from bond angle and eclipsing strain. Chair form experiences only steric strain which is due to the gauche - butane like interaction between neighbouring methylene groups. Boat conformation has higher energy due to eclipsing side carbons and transannular interaction between flagpole hydrogen atoms.

Therefore, boat conformation can be stabilized by moving apart the flagpole hydrogen atoms. The conformation with flagpole hydrogen atoms moved apart is known as *"Twist boa*t" which has minimum transannular interaction between flagpole hydrogen atoms and also in it the torsional strain relieved. In this process the symmetry of twist boat is lost and molecule becomes chiral.

Boat   Twist boat (Chiral)

Half-chair Conformation of Cyclohexane

- It is a transition state with **C₂ symmetry** generally considered to be on the pathway between chair and twist-boat.
- It involves rotating one of the **dihedrals** to zero in such a way that the four adjacent atoms are coplanar and the other two atoms are out of plane.

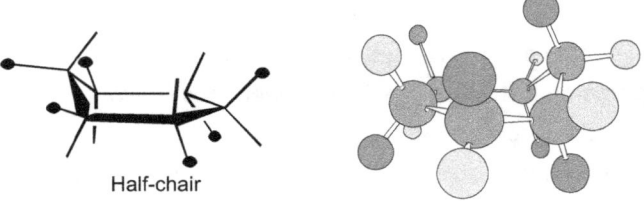

Half-chair

Potential Energy Profile Diagram of Cyclohexane-Conformational analysis of cyclohexane – stereochemistry of cyclohexane system

One chair conformation of cyclohexane can be easily converted into an alternate chair conformation. Two *chair* and two *twist boat* conformations are intermediates and are at energy minima while two *half chair* conformations and *full boat* conformations are at energy maxima. Chair conformation of cyclohexane is perfectly staggered and hence is free from torsional strain and angle strain. Boat conformation of cyclohexane experiences steric strain due to flagpole interaction (H-H) and torsional strain. Hence, the boat conformation of cyclohexane is less stable than the chair conformer by about 6 kcal/mol (25 kJ/mole).

Some of steric and torsional strains in the boat conformer can be relieved by twisting. Twist boat conformer is less stable than the chair conformer by about 5 kcal/mol (21 kJ/mol) but, is more stable than the boat conformer.

The highest energy barrier is transition state conformation called the half chair. It can be attained by moving C_1, C_2, C_3 and C_4 of chair into one plane and C_6 above and C_5 below the plane and contains many eclipsed C-H bonds. As four carbon atoms are forced to occupy the same plane the conformer is at energy maxima. The chair conformer can attain least stable half chair conformation by gaining 10.8 kcal/mol (45 kJ/mol) of energy. The half chair on loss of energy is converted to either chair or twist boat conformer and the twist boat conformer in turn can attain boat conformation by gaining energy. As the maximum energy gradient for interconversion of conformers of cyclohexane is 10.8 kcal/mol (45 kJ/mol) which can be easily obtained at room temperature by cyclohexane molecule from surroundings, interconversion of one chair conformer to other through a half chair, twist boat, boat, twist boat and half chair conformers occurs very rapidly. This process of interconversion, also known as ring flipping is fast and occurs at a rate of 1,00,000 times/sec. at RT which is depicted in the potential energy diagram below.

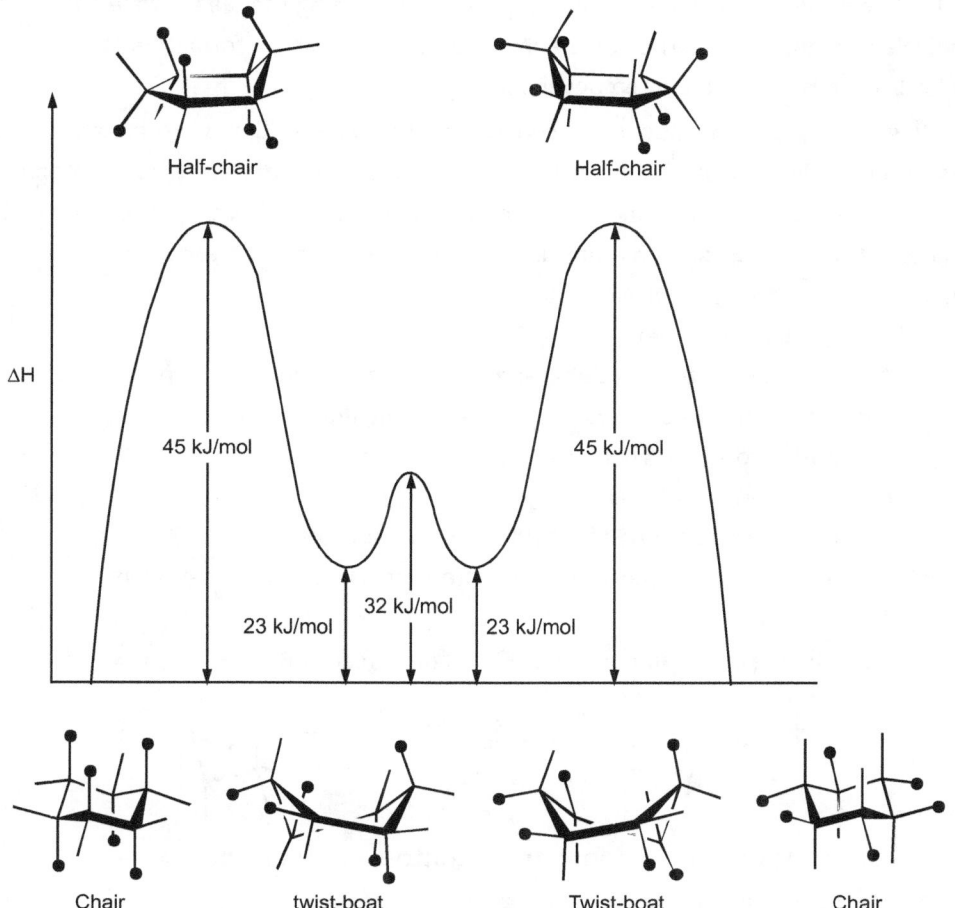

Fig. 9: Energy Profile diagram for conformation of Cyclohexane

Stability order: Chair > Twist boat > Boat > Half chair

Readily interconvertible forms.

At room temperature in the cyclohexane molecule a chair conformer interconverts rapidly to a mirror image chair conformation. This conversion is called as ring flip. During one cycle of interconversion, all *axial* bonds are converted to *equatorial* bonds and all *equatorial* bonds become *axial* bonds. The *equatorial – axial* interconversion is so rapid that all hydrogen atoms on cyclohexane can be considered as equivalent. The proton NMR shows only one signal at room temperature indicating that all hydrogen atoms are equivalent. The energy barrier between the alternate chair conformation is only about 11 kcal/mol and hence the interconversion.

Ring flipping is slowed down on cooling to less than –80°C and proton NMR shows two different signals clearly indicating that the *axial* and *equatorial* Hydrogen atoms are not identical at –80°C. Flipping of the molecule is slowed down sufficiently, so that *equatorial* and *axial* Hydrogen atoms are differentiated as two different sets of protons, each set giving different ^{1}H NMR signals.

Ring-Flipping in Cyclohexane:
- At room temperature, cyclohexane interconverts, rapidly to a mirror image chair conformation. This conversion is called as Ring flip.
    - All equatorial → Axial
    - All axial → Equatorial
- Cis- and Trans- relations of substituents do not change.
- The energy barrier between the alternate chair conformation is only about 11 kcal/mol.
- Ring flipping is fast and occurs 1,00,000 times/sec at RT.

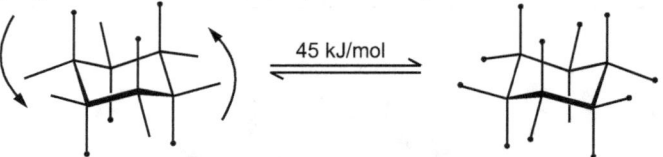

1.3.8 Conformation of Cyclohexane - Conformational Analysis
- Most stable and common cycloalkane.
- If it was totally planar, bond angle would have been 120° (deviating from normal sp^3 angle of 109.5°, leading to instability).

Two major and two minor conformations exist:
1. If 4 carbons of the ring i.e., in one plane and other 2 carbons are above the plane it is **boat conformation**.
2. If 4 carbons of the ring lie in one plane and one is above and one is below the plane it is **chair conformation**.

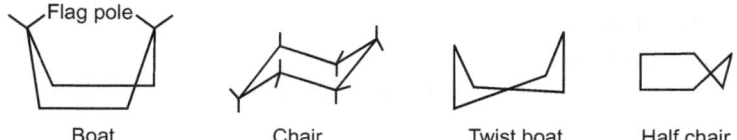

The other two conformations of cyclohexane are **twist boat** and **half chair**.

Chair form is most favourable as bonds remain tetrahedral and so no angle strain. Also groups remain staggered with less torsion strain.

Boat form slightly less favourable as groups are eclipsed causing torsional strain (flag pole interactions). Thus, boat form has 6.9 kcal/mole energy more than chair form.

Twist boat is stable than boat by 1.5 kcal/mole, because groups are rather skew and no eclipsed. Therefore, lesser torsional strain. Half chair form has the highest energy i.e., around 11 kcal/mole higher than chair form.

Thus, order of stability is **chair > twist boat > Boat > half chair.**

Ring Flipping

Cyclohexane has two identical and readily interconvertible chair forms and are mirror images of each other. This interconversion process is called **"ring flipping"**, whereby an axial group of one form gets converted to equatorial of other form.

α and β-bonds: Each carbon atom of chair form has one axial and one equatorial bond. Thus total 6 + 6 = 12 bonds. The six bonds which are upwards (above plane of ring) are called β-bonds, while the remaining which are downwards (below plane of ring) are called as α-bonds. In general axial bonds produce more steric strain as they hold their groups parallel to groups of other axial bonds.

Monosubstituted cyclohexanes

Two conformations axial or equatorial (of the substituents). Axial is less stable than equatorial, because of 1, 3 and 1, 5 interactions with the 2-H atoms. Equitorial is less crowded and so more stable and has 95% abudance.

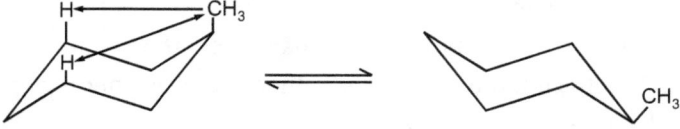

Disubstituted cyclohexanes:
1, 1-Disubstituted cyclohexane

If both substituents are identical and on same carbon, both structures are equivalent.

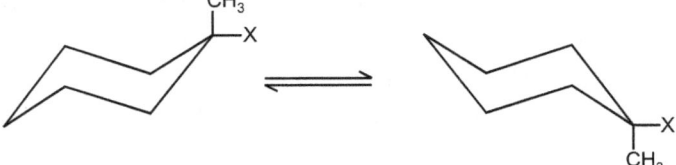

But if both substitutents are different, then bulky group occupy equatorial positions.

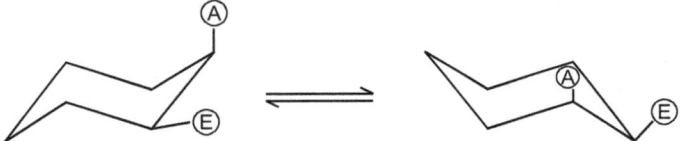

1, 2-Disubstituted cyclohexane
Two types *cis* and *trans*

In *cis* 1, 2-disubstituted cyclohexane, one substituent is axial and other is equatorial.

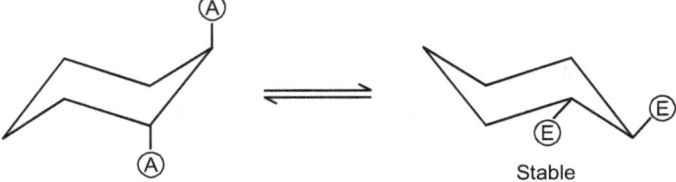

These structures are in dynamic equilibrium and readily interconvertible. They are non-super impossible mirror images - enantiomers.

In *trans* 1, 2-disubsituted cyclohexanes, either both substituents are axial or both are equatorial. The two forms are not mirror images of each other. The structure in which both substituents are equatorial is more stable.

Stable

1, 3-Disubstituted cyclohexane

cis 1, 3-disubstituted form is more stable than *trans*. The diequatorial form is stable than the diaxial. If both subtitutents are same then the *cis* isomer may possess plane of synmmetry and become optically inactive.

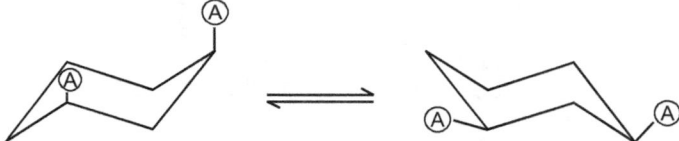

In the *trans* 1, 3-disubstituted form, one substitutent is always axial and other is equatorial. No plane of symmetry.

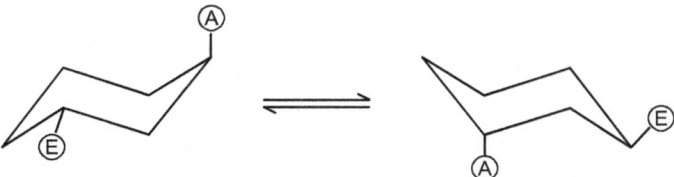

1, 4-Disubstituted cycloalkanes

cis: If one substituent is axial, other is equatorial. If both substituents are identical then both conformers are equally stable.

trans: In case of *trans* conformers both substituents should be either axial or both should be equatorial. The diequatorial conformer is always more stable. If posses both 1 and 4-substituents identical then, a plane of symmetry passes through the C_1 and C_4 atoms making them optically inactive.

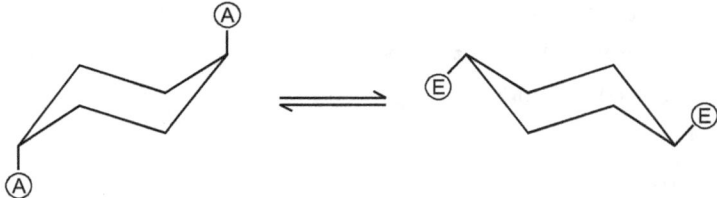

1.3.9 Conformational Analysis of Decalin

Declain (Decahydronaphthalene) is a bicyclic compound in which two cyclohexane rings are fused with each other across a common single bond. The fusion bond hydrogens if both are axial it is *trans* decalin, but if they are both equatorial it is *cis*-decalin.

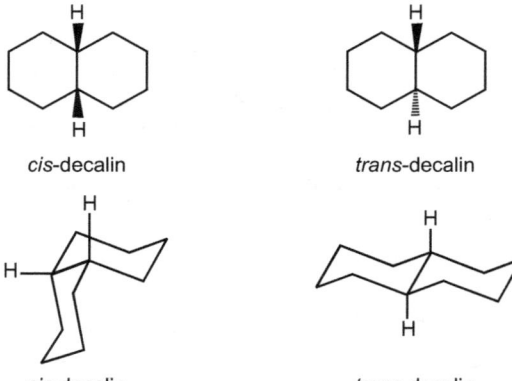

cis-decalin is a chiral molecule in which, two hydrogens attached at the point of fusion between two rings lie on the same side of ring. Any substituents attached in cis-decalin adopt equatorial orientation due to conformational flipping. cis-decalin is less stable than trans-decalin which is having more energy of about 2.7 kcal/mole.

trans-decalin is achiral, rigid and may possess centre of symmetry. The two hydrogens are attached at the point of fusion between two rings lie on the opposite side of the ring in trans-decalin. Hence trans-decalin is more stable than cis-decalin by about 2.7 kcal/mole as compared to the cis-form.

QUESTION BANK

1. Define the following with example:
   (i) Enantiomers
   (ii) Diastereomers
   (iii) Geometrical Isomerism
   (iv) Meso compounds
   (v) Chirality
   (vi) Optical activity
   (vii) Conformational isomer
   (viii) Configurational isomer
   (ix) Racemic modification
   (x) Specific rotation
   (xi) Atropisomers

2. What are distereomers? Explain with suitable examples.
3. Draw Fischer projections for the following:
   (i)   Meso 2,3–Dichlorobutane
   (ii)   (2S, 3S)-Tartaric acid
   (iii) 2-Chlorobutane
   (iv)   (2R, 3S)-2-chlorobutanol
   (v)   2-Iodobutane
   (vi)   (R) 3-Methylpentanol
   (vii) Meso-Tartaric acid
   (viii) (R)-2-Butanol
4. Draw stereoisomers of the following compounds:
   (i)   2-Chlorobutane
   (ii) 4, 4-Diethyl 2-hexane
   (iii) 2-Butene
   (iv) 1, 3-Pentadine
   (v)   3-Iodopentane
5. Assign E and Z configurations to the following:
6. Draw structures of
   (i) 3-bromo-(3Z, 5E)-octadiene
   (ii) 3S-Bromo-2S-hydroxybutane
7. Assign R or S configurations to the following:
   (i)   (ii)
   (iii)   (iv)
   (v)   (vi)

(vii) [structure: H, COOH, H₃C, OH on chiral carbon]

(viii) [structure: OH, H, CH₃, OH, H, CH₃]

(ix) [Fischer projection: COOH, H—Br, H—Cl, CH₃]

(x) [Newman projection: CH₃, Cl, H, H, Cl, CH₃]

(xi) [Newman projection: CH₃, H, Br, Br, H, CH₃]

(xii) Me₂N—C(OH)(OMe)—NH₂

8. Describe chirality with suitable examples.
9. What are the configurational and conformational isomers? Give the methods of determination of configuration of geometrical isomers based on physical properties.
10. What is the atropisomerism? Explain it with suitable examples.
11. Discuss the stereospecific and strereoselective reactions with suitable examples.
12. Why chair conformation is more stable than boat conformation? Explain.
13. Draw Newmann projection formulae for all the conformations of 1,2 and 1, 4-dimethylcyclohexane. Comment on their stability.
14. Draw the Newmann projection formulae for n-butane and discuss the energy profile diagram of the same.
15. What do you mean by Racemic Modification? Explain with suitable examples the various methods used for resolution of racemic modification?
16. Explain, why *trans* decalin is more stable than cis decalin?

17. What do you mean by flagpole interactions in cyclohexane?
18. What is ring flipping? Explain with structure.
19. Give the conformational analysis of cyclohexane.
20. What is stereoisomerism? Enumerate differences between conformational and configurational stereoisomers.
21. Comment on the following, in brief:
    (i) Axial methylcyclohexane is less stable than equatorial methylcyclohexane.
    (ii) Stereochemistry of decalin
    (iii) 1, 3-Diaxial interaction
    (iv) *trans* 1, 2-dimethylcyclohexane is more stable than its cis isomer.
    (v) Cyclohexane is more stable in chair form than boat form.
    (vi) Advantages of Z/E nomenclature over *cis* and *trans* nomenclature with examples.
    (vii) Catalytic hydrogenations are found to be always in *syn* conformers.
22. Discuss all possible isomers of 1, 2-dimethylcyclohexane and explain which is the more stable conformation.
23. Discuss all possible conformations of cyclohexane and explain the most stable conformation with diagram.
24. Discuss about the different elements of symmetry of a molecule and explain the criteria for the optical rotation.
25. Write the priority rules for assigning E/Z and R/S configuration.
26. Explain the terms with example:
    (i) Angle strain
    (ii) Torsional strain
    (iii) Steric strain
    (iv) Dipole-dipole interactions.
27. Write a note on equatorial and axial bonds in cyclohexane.
28. Between menthol and neomenthol the most preferred conformation is menthol. Explain with structures.
29. Write short notes on the following:
    (a) Conformational analysis of n-butane
    (b) Racemic Modification
    (c) Geometrical isomerism and structural isomerism
    (d) Conformations of decalin.
    (e) Stereospecific and stereoselective reactions.
    (f) Atropisomerism
    (g) Limitations of D and L method of nomenclature.

30. Give reasons:
    (i) *cis* and *trans* does not mean Z and E
    (i) *meso* compounds do not exhibit optical rotation
    (iii) cis-2-butene is less stable than *trans*-2-butene.
31. Explain the possible conformations of cyclobutane with help of figures.
32. What is dihedral angle in a stereoisomer?
34. Discuss chair, boat and twist boat conformation of cyclohexane molecule.
35. Configuration is most common terminology used in stereochemistry. Discuss it.
36. Give an account on *syn* and *anti* addition reactions with special emphasis on stereochemistry.

■■■

Chapter 2 ...

MOLECULAR REARRANGEMENT REACTIONS

CONTENTS

- Rearrangement of electron deficient systems, Migration to Oxygen, Nitrogen and Carbon, Mechanism and Stereochemistry of Bayer-Villiger oxidation and Dakin oxidations, Wagner- Merewein rearrangements, Pinacol-Pinacolone rearrangement, Beckmann, Curtius, Lossen, Hoffman and Schmidts rearrangements.
- Rearrangements of electron rich system inclusive of Stevens', Sommlet, Favoroski, Neber and Benzilic acid rearrangement.
- Rearrangement to aromatic nucleus including mechanism of Fries and Claisen rearrangement.
- Pericyclic Reactions: Electrocyclic, Cycloaddition and Sigma tropic reactions (Cope rearrangement).

INTRODUCTION

Molecular rearrangements are organic reactions which involve migration of an atom or group from its original position to an adjacent atom or near adjacent atom. Most rearrangements are intramolecular processes.

CLASSIFICATION

There are four major types:

1. **Rearrangements of electron deficient systems (Nucleophilic rearrangement reactions):**

   Migrating group is a nucleophile ($Nu^\ominus$) and migrated on electrophile ($E^\oplus$).

   (a) Electron deficient oxygen:
   (i) Bayer-Villiger oxidation
   (ii) Dakin oxidation.

   (b) Electron deficient nitrogen:
   (i) Hoffman rearrangement
   (ii) Curtius rearrangement
   (iii) Lossen rearrangement
   (iv) Schmidt rearrangement
   (v) Beckmann rearrangement

(c) **Electron deficient carbon:**
  (i) Wagner Meerwein rearrangement
  (ii) Pinacol - Pinacolone rearrangement
  (iii) Benzilic acid rearrangement

2. **Rearrangement of electron rich system (Electrophilic rearrangement reactions)**
   Migrating group is electrophile ($E^\oplus$) and migrated on electron rich centre.
   (i) Steven's rearrangement
   (ii) Sommlet rearrangement
   (iii) Favoroskii rearrangement
   (iv) Neber rearrangement

3. **Rearrangement to aromatic nucleus (Aromatic rearrangements):**
   (i) Fries rearrangement
   (ii) Claisen rearrangement

4. **Pericyclic rearrangements:**
   (Migration to double/triple bonds sigmapior)
   (i) Cope rearrangement

REARRANGEMENTS OF ELECTRONIC DEFICIENT OXYGEN

1. BAYER-VILLIGER OXIDATION

Definition: The oxidation of ketones to esters or their hydrolysed products (carboxylic acid) with hydrogen peroxide or organic peroxy acids (peracetic acid, perbenzoic acid, pertrifluoroacetic acid) is known as *"Bayer-Villiger rearrangement"*.

Reaction:

$$R-\underset{\underset{O}{\|}}{C}-R' + R''-COOOH \longrightarrow R-\underset{\underset{O}{\|}}{C}-OR' + R''-COOH$$

Mechanism:

Step 1: Hydrolysis of peroxyacids to form a nucleophile and an electrophile.

$$RCOOOH \rightleftharpoons R''COOO^\ominus + H^\oplus$$
            Peroxy carboxylate   Electrophile
            ion (Nu)

Step 2: Protonation of ketone to form resonance stabilized carbocation.

$$R-\underset{\underset{O}{\|}}{C}-R' \xrightarrow{H^\oplus} R-\underset{\underset{\overset{\oplus}{O}H}{\|}}{C}-R' \longleftrightarrow R-\underset{\underset{\oplus}{|}}{\overset{OH}{C}}-R'$$
                                    (Ia)   (Ib)

Structure (Ib) is more stable than (Ia).

Step 3: Attack of nucleophile, loss of R"COO$^\ominus$ and migration of alkyl group R' to electron deficient oxygen atom.

$$R-\underset{\underset{O-O-\underset{\parallel}{C}-R''}{|}}{\overset{\overset{OH}{|}}{C}}-R' \xrightarrow{-R''COO^\ominus} R-\underset{\underset{:\overset{\oplus}{O}}{|}}{\overset{\overset{OH}{|}}{C}}\!\!\dashv R' \longrightarrow R-\underset{\underset{OR}{|}}{\overset{\overset{OH}{|}}{C}}\oplus$$

Step 4: Loss of proton and formation of an ester.

$$R-\underset{\underset{OR'}{|}}{\overset{\overset{O-H}{|}}{C}}\oplus \xrightarrow{-H^\oplus} R-\overset{\overset{O}{\parallel}}{C}-OR'$$

Applications:

1. **For the preparation of esters and acids:**

$$R-\overset{\overset{O}{\parallel}}{C}-R' \xrightarrow{RCO_3H} RCOOR' \xrightarrow{HOH} R-COOH + R'-OH$$

Example:

$$C_6H_5-\overset{\overset{O}{\parallel}}{C}-CH_3 \xrightarrow{CF_3\,CO_3H} CH_3-\overset{\overset{O}{\parallel}}{C}-OC_6H_5$$

2. **For the preparation of anhydrides:**

$$CH_3-\overset{\overset{O}{\parallel}}{C}-\overset{\overset{O}{\parallel}}{C}-CH_3 \xrightarrow{RCO_3H} CH_3-\overset{\overset{O}{\parallel}}{C}-O-\overset{\overset{O}{\parallel}}{C}-CH_3$$

Diacetyl   Acetic anhydride

3. **For the preparation of Lactones:**

Cyclohexanone $\xrightarrow{RCO_3H}$ (ϵ-Caprolactone)

2. DAKIN OXIDATION

Definition: The replacement of an aldehyde (or ketonic) group of the *o*-hydroxy, *p*-hydroxy or *o*-aminobenzaldehyde by a hydroxyl group by the action of alkaline hydrogen peroxide (H_2O_2) is known as **"Dakin-Oxidation"**.

Reaction:

o-Hydroxy benzaldehyde $\xrightarrow{\text{Alkaline } H_2O_2}$ Catechol

Mechanism: It is quite similar to Bayer-Villiger oxidation.
Step 1: Addition of nucleophile (hydroperoxide anion to the carbonyl carbon).

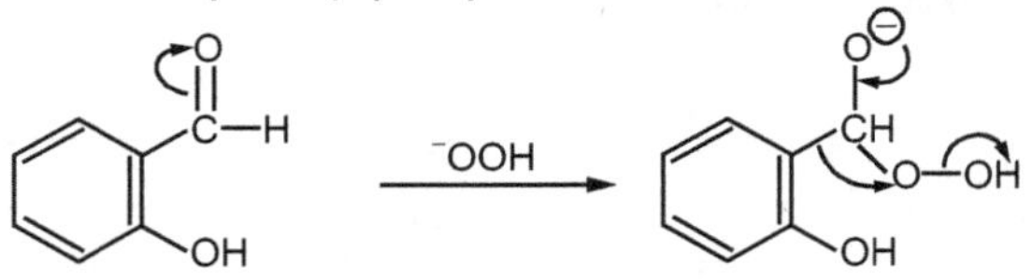

Step 2: 1, 2, Acyl migration, hydroxide elimination and formation of ester.

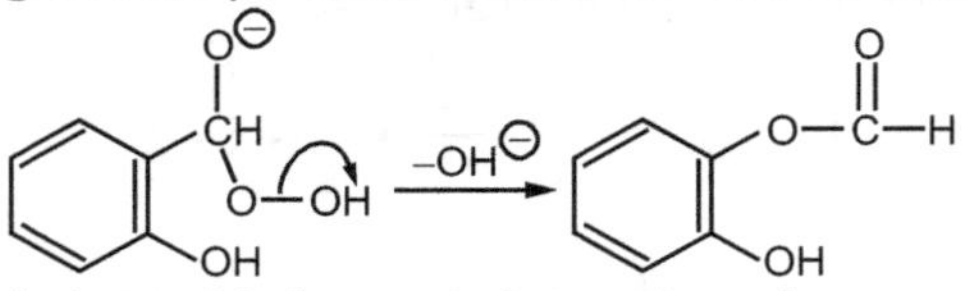

Step 3: Formation of phenoxide ion and abstraction of proton to form catechol.

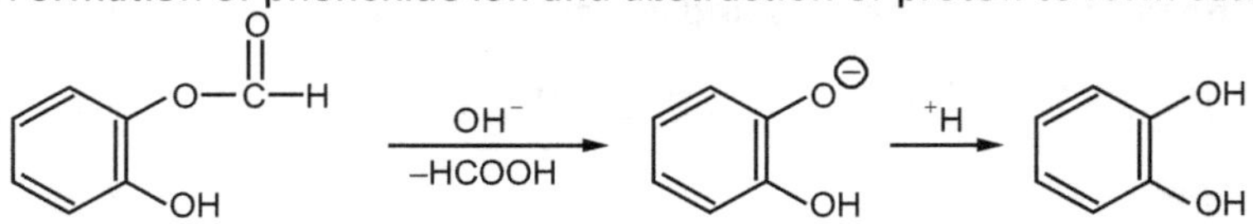

Application:
1. It is used for synthesizing polyhydric phenols from naturally occurring hydroxyl aldehydes.

o-Vanillin → Pyrogallol 1-monomethyl ether

REARRANGEMENTS OF ELECTRON DEFICIENT NITROGEN ATOM

The migration of an alkyl or aryl group with its bonding pair of electrons from carbon to the adjacent nitrogen atom.

General Reaction:

$R-C=N-X \longrightarrow R-N=C=O$

X =	Br	→ Hoffmann
X =	$-\overset{+}{N}\equiv N$	→ Curtius
X =	$-\overset{+}{N}\equiv N$	→ Schimdt
X =	$-OCOR$	→ Lossen
X =	$-OH$	→ Beckmann

Hoffmann Rearrangement:

$R-CONH_2 \xrightarrow{NaOBr} R-N=C=O \xrightarrow{H_2O} R-NH_2$

Curtius Rearrangement:

$$R-CON_3 \xrightarrow{\Delta} R-N=C=O \xrightarrow{H_2O} R-NH_2 \xrightarrow{RNCO} R\,NH\,CO\,NHR$$

$$\downarrow C_2H_5OH \qquad\qquad \text{Hydrolysis}\uparrow$$

$$R-NHCOOC_2H_5$$

Schmidt Rearrangement:

$$R-COOH \xrightarrow{HN_3} R-N=C=O \xrightarrow{H_2O} R-NH_2$$

Lossen Rearrangement:

$$R-CONH-OH \xrightarrow{H^{\oplus}} R-N=C=O \xrightarrow{H_2O} R-NH_2$$

Beckmann Rearrangement:

$$\underset{R'}{\overset{R}{>}}C=N-OH \longrightarrow R-CONHR'$$

3. HOFFMANN REARRANGEMENT

Definition: This rearrangement is the conversion of an amide to primary amine with one carbon atom less by the action of alkaline hypohalite (NaOBr) or bromine in alkali.

This reaction (shall not be confused with Hoffmann elimination) is also known as Hoffmann degradation of amides.

Reaction:

$$\underset{\text{Amide}}{R-\overset{O}{\overset{\|}{C}}-NH_2} + NaOBr \longrightarrow \underset{\text{Isocyamate}}{R-N=C=O}$$

$$\downarrow \text{Hydrolysis}$$

$$\underset{\text{Amine}}{R-NH_2}$$

Mechanism:

Step 1: Addition of Br⁻ by means of NaOBr.

$$\underset{\text{Amide}}{R-\underset{O}{\overset{\|}{C}}-NH_2} + OBr^{\ominus} \longrightarrow \underset{\text{N-Bromo amide}}{R-\underset{O}{\overset{\|}{C}}-\underset{H}{N}-Br}$$

Step 2: Abstraction of Proton by a base.

$$R-\underset{O}{\overset{\|}{C}}-\underset{H}{N}-Br + OH^{\ominus} \xrightarrow{H_2O} \underset{\text{A bromo amide anion}}{R-\underset{O}{\overset{\|}{C}}-\overset{\ominus}{N}-Br}$$

Step 3: Concerted step (main step)

$$[R-\underset{\underset{O}{\|}}{C}-\underset{\ominus}{\ddot{N}}-Br] \xrightarrow{-Br^{\cdot\cdot}} [R-\underset{\underset{O}{\|}}{C}-\ddot{N}\oplus]$$
Nitrene

$$R-\underset{\underset{O}{\|}}{C}-\underset{\ominus}{\ddot{N}}-Br \longrightarrow O=C=N-R$$
Isocyanate

↓ Hydrolysis

$$R-NH_2$$

Applications:
1. **For the preparation of primary aliphatic and aromatic amines.**

Benzoic acid (COOH) $\xrightarrow[FeBr_2]{Br_2}$ m-Br-COOH $\xrightarrow[(ii)\ NH_3]{(i)\ SOCl_2}$ m-Br-CONH$_2$ $\xrightarrow[KOH]{Br_2}$ m-Bromo aniline (NH$_2$, Br)

2. **For the synthesis of anthranilic acid (most important industrial application)**

Phthalimide $\xrightarrow{NaOH}$ (COOH, CONH$_2$) $\xrightarrow[2.\ H_3O^{\oplus}]{1.\ Br_2 + NaOH}$ Anthranilic acid (COOH, NH$_2$)

4. CURTIUS REARRANGEMENT

Definition: Pyrolysis of an acyl azide, which loses nitrogen and then rearranges to an isocynate is called as *"Curtius rearrangement"*.

Reaction:

$$R-\underset{\underset{Acyl\ azide}{}}{\overset{O}{\overset{\|}{C}}}-N_3 \xrightarrow[-N_2]{\Delta} \underset{Isocyanate}{R-\ddot{N}=C=O}$$

Mechanism:

$$R-\overset{O}{\overset{\|}{C}}-\ddot{N}=\overset{\oplus}{N}=\overset{\ominus}{\ddot{N}} \xrightarrow{-N_2} R-\overset{O}{\overset{\|}{C}}-\ddot{N} \longrightarrow O=C=N-R$$

Urea and urethane are side products in Curtius rearrangement.

$$R-N=C=O \xrightarrow{H_2O} [R-NH-COOH] \xrightarrow{-CO_2} R-NH_2$$

Carbamic acid

$$\downarrow C_2H_5OH \qquad \qquad \uparrow Hydrolysis \qquad \qquad \downarrow R'-N=C=O$$

$$R-NH-COOC_2H_5 \qquad \qquad \qquad R-NH-\underset{\underset{O}{\|}}{C}-NH-R'$$

Urethane (Carbamates)   Substituted urea

Applications:
1. **For the preparation of primary amines.**

$$C_6H_5CH_2COOC_2H_5 \longrightarrow C_6H_5CH_2CON_3 \xrightarrow[H_2O]{\Delta} C_6H_5CH_2NH_2$$

Ethylphenyl acetate   **Azide**   **Benzylamine**

2. **For the preparation of amino acids.**

$$\underset{\text{Cyano acetic ester}}{\overset{CN}{\underset{COOR}{\overset{|}{CH_2}}}} \xrightarrow[\substack{(1)\ R-X \\ (2)\ NH_2NH_2 \\ (3)\ HNO_2}]{} \underset{\text{Acyl oxide}}{R-CH\overset{COOH}{\underset{CON_3}{}}} \xrightarrow[\substack{(1)\ C_2H_5OH \\ (2)\ HCl}]{HCl} \underset{\alpha\text{ - Amino acid}}{R-CH\overset{COOH}{\underset{NH_2}{}}}$$

5. LOSSEN REARRANGEMENT

Definition: *o*-Acyl derivative of hydroxamic acids gives isocyanates when treated with base. This is known as *"Lossen rearrangement"*.

Reaction:

$$R-\underset{\underset{O}{\|}}{C}-NHOCOR' \xrightarrow{OH^\ominus} R-N=C=O$$

(R' = Ac)

$$\downarrow$$

$$R-NH_2$$

Mechanism:

Step 1: Abstraction of proton from N atom.

$$R-\underset{\underset{O}{\|}}{C}-\underset{H}{\overset{\cdot\cdot}{N}}-OCOR' \xrightarrow[-H^\oplus]{OH^\ominus} R-\underset{\underset{O}{\|}}{C}-\underset{\ominus}{\overset{\cdot\cdot}{N}}-O-\underset{\underset{O}{\|}}{C}-R$$

Step 2: Elimination of – OCOR' group and migration of R group with its bonded electron on nitrene.

$$R-\underset{\underset{O}{\|}}{C}-\underset{\ominus}{N}-O-\underset{\underset{O}{\|}}{C}-R' \longrightarrow O=C=N-R$$

$$\downarrow H_2O$$

$$R-NH_2$$

Applications:

1. For the preparation of primary amines.

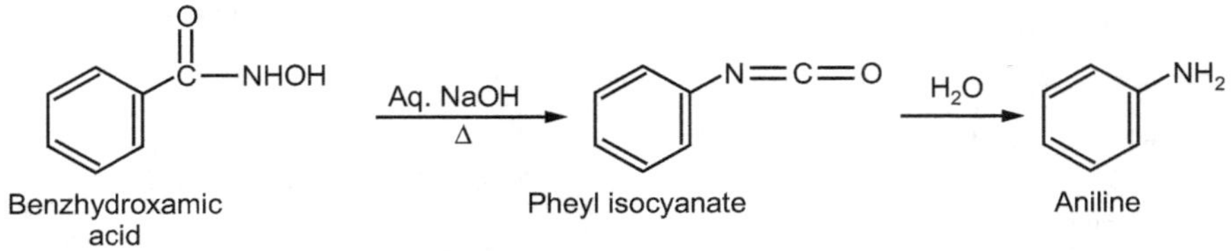

Benzhydroxamic acid (PhC(=O)-NHOH) $\xrightarrow{\text{Aq. NaOH}, \Delta}$ Phenyl isocyanate (Ph-N=C=O) $\xrightarrow{H_2O}$ Aniline (Ph-NH$_2$)

2. For the conversion of carboxylic acid into primary amines.

$$CH_3CH_2COOH \xrightarrow{SOCl_2} CH_3CH_2COCl \xrightarrow{NH_2OH} CH_3CH_2CONHOH$$
Propionic acid → Propionyl chloride → Ethyl hydroxamic

$\xrightarrow{OH^-}$ $CH_3-CH_2-N=C=O$ (Ethyl isocynate) → $CH_3-CH_2-NH_2$ (Ethylamine)

6. SCHMIDT REARRANGEMENT

Definition: This arrangement is actually called by the name Schmidt reaction, involving the addition of hydrazoic acid to carboxylic acid in presence of H_2SO_4 or Lewis acid.

Reaction:

$$R-COOH + HN_3 \text{ (Hydrazoic acid)} \xrightarrow{H^+ (H_2SO_4)} R-N=C=O \longrightarrow R-NH_2$$

Mechanism:

$$R-\underset{O}{\underset{\|}{C}}-OH \xrightarrow{H^+} R-\underset{O}{\underset{\|}{C}}-\overset{+}{O}H_2 \longrightarrow R-\underset{O}{\underset{\|}{\overset{+}{C}}}$$

$$R-\underset{O}{\underset{\|}{\overset{+}{C}}} + HN_3 \longrightarrow [R-C(=O)-\overset{+}{N}H-N=N] \longrightarrow O=C=\overset{+}{N}-R \xrightarrow{-H^+} O=C=N-R \xrightarrow{\text{Hydrolysis}} R-NH_2$$

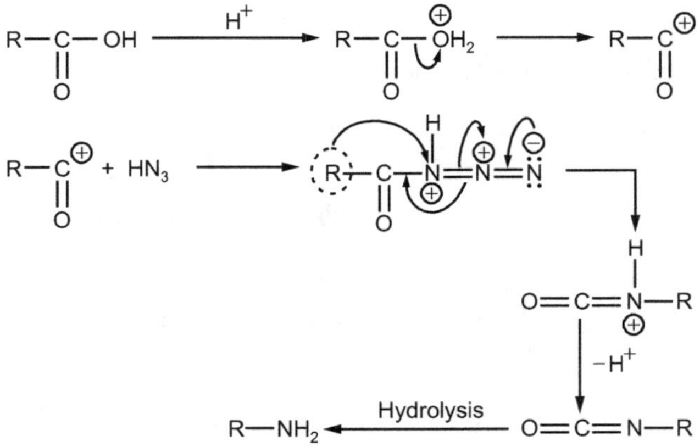

Applications:

1. **In the preparation of primary amines:** More widely used than Hoffmann and Curtius rearrangements for this purpose. This reaction must be carried out with caution due to explosive and poisonous nature of the hydrazoic acid.

$$C_6H_5CH_2COOH + N_3H \xrightarrow[CHCl_3]{H_2SO_4} C_6H_5CH_2NH_2 + N_2\uparrow + CO_2\uparrow$$

Phenylacetic acid → Benzylamine

2. **For the preparation of lactams.**

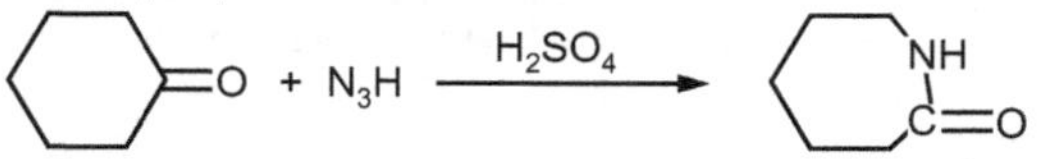

Cyclohexanone + N_3H $\xrightarrow{H_2SO_4}$ Caprolactum

7. BECKMANN REARRANGEMENT

Definition: The conversion of ketoximes to N-substituted amides by heating with some acidic reagents *viz.* concentrated H_2SO_4, PCl_5, P_2O_5, $SOCl_2$ etc. is known as **"Beckmann rearrangement"**.

Reaction:

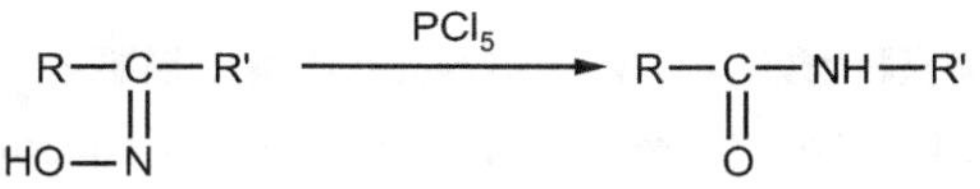

$$\underset{\underset{HO-N}{\|}}{R-C-R'} \xrightarrow{PCl_5} \underset{\underset{O}{\|}}{R-C-NH-R'}$$

Ketoxime → N-Substituted amide

Mechanism:

Step 1: Protonation of ketoxime and loss of water to yield carbonium ion.

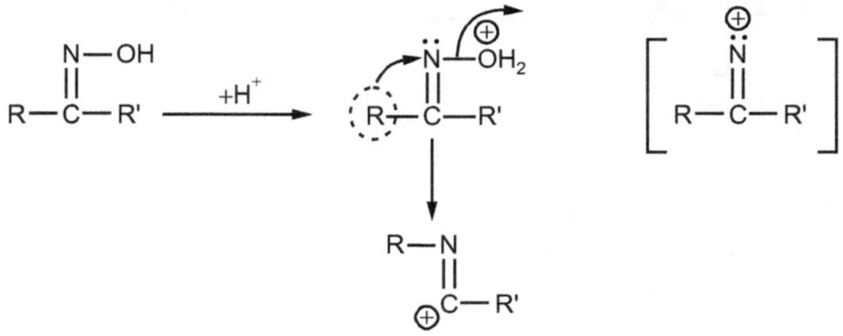

Step 2: Addition of water on carbonium ion followed by loss of proton yields N-substituted amide.

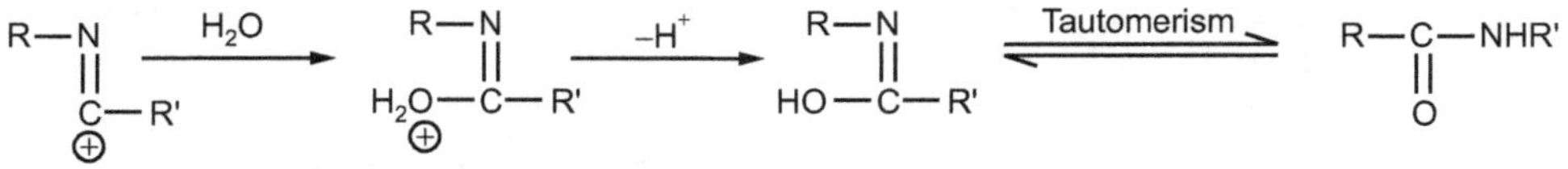

In this rearrangement, the shift or migration of group is always trans (anti) to the leaving group.

Applications:

1. For ring expansion.

Example: oximes of *cyclic* ketone gives ring enlargement.

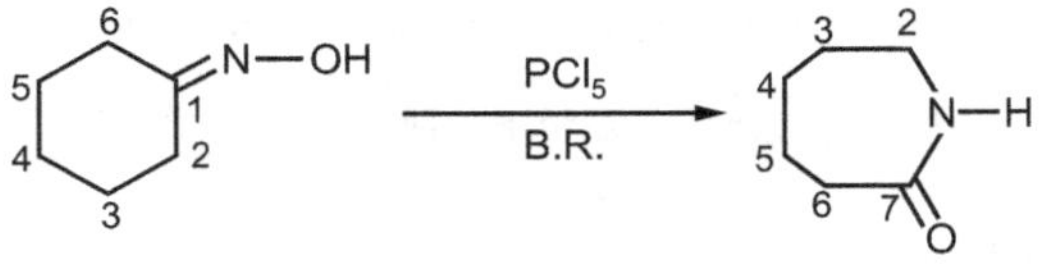

Cyclohexanone oxime → (PCl₅, B.R.) → Caprolactum (Raw material for nylon type of polymer)

2. Synthesis of isoquinoline.

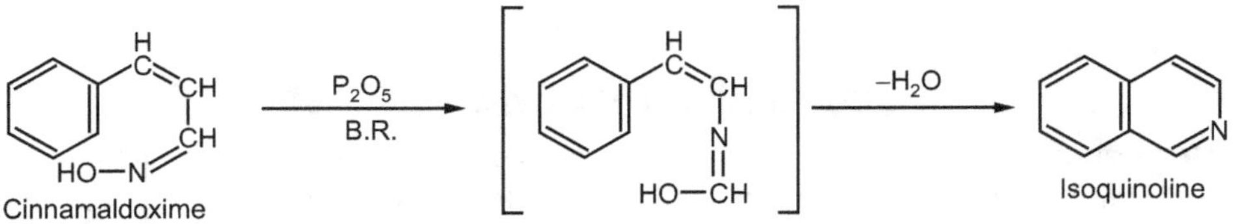

Cinnamaldoxime → (P₂O₅, B.R.) → [intermediate] → (−H₂O) → Isoquinoline

REARRANGEMENTS OF ELECTRON DEFICIENT CARBON

8. WAGNER-MEERWEIN REARRANGEMENT

Definition: The rearrangement involves formation of more stable carbocation from less stable carbocation.

Reaction:

$$CH_3-\underset{CH_3}{\underset{|}{\overset{CH_3}{\overset{|}{C}}}}-\overset{\oplus}{C}H_2 \longrightarrow CH_3-\underset{CH_3}{\overset{\oplus}{C}}-CH_2-CH_3$$

neo-pentyl → iso-pentyl

Mechanism:

Step 1: Formation of carbocation.

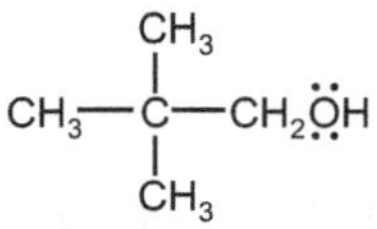

$$CH_3-\underset{CH_3}{\underset{|}{\overset{CH_3}{\overset{|}{C}}}}-CH_2\ddot{O}H \xrightarrow{H^+} CH_3-\underset{CH_3}{\underset{|}{\overset{CH_3}{\overset{|}{C}}}}-CH_2-\overset{\oplus}{O}H_2$$

neo pentyl alcohol

$$\downarrow -H_2O$$

$$CH_3-\underset{CH_3}{\underset{|}{\overset{CH_3}{\overset{|}{C}}}}-\overset{\oplus}{C}H_2 + H_2O$$

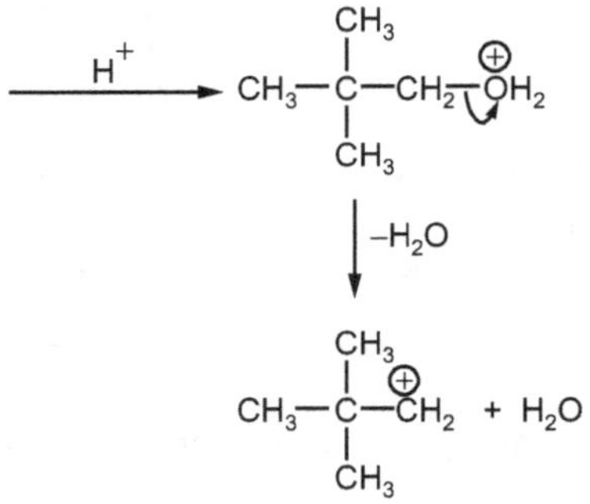

Step 2: Rearrangement of carbocation (1, 2-shift).

$$CH_3-\underset{\underset{CH_3}{|}}{\overset{\overset{CH_3}{|}}{C}}-\overset{+}{C}H_2 \xrightarrow{\text{1,2-shift}} CH_3-\underset{\underset{+}{|}}{\overset{\overset{CH_3}{|}}{C}}-CH_2-CH_3$$

$$\downarrow -H^+$$

$$CH_3-\underset{\underset{CH_3}{|}}{C}=CH-CH_3$$

2-Methyl-2-butene

Applications:

1. For ring contractions.

2-Amino cyclohexanol $\xrightarrow{HNO_2}$ [diazonium intermediate] $\xrightarrow[-H_2O]{-N_2}$ Cyclopentanlal (CHO)

2. Used in commercial synthesis of camphor from α-pinene.

α-Pinene $\xrightarrow[-20°C]{HCl}$ Camphor

9. PINACOL - PINACOLONE REARRANGEMENT

Definition: The conversion of pinacols (1,2-glycols) to ketones or aldehyde by means of mineral acids, acid chloride or other electrophilic reagents is known as *Pinacol-Pinacolone rearrangement*.

Reaction: Examples:

1.
$$CH_3-\underset{\underset{OH}{|}}{\overset{\overset{CH_3}{|}}{C}}-\underset{\underset{OH}{|}}{\overset{\overset{}{}}{C}}-CH_3 \xrightarrow[30\% H_2SO_4]{\Delta} CH_3-\overset{\overset{O}{||}}{C}-\underset{\underset{CH_3}{|}}{\overset{\overset{CH_3}{|}}{C}}-CH_3$$

Pinacol
(2,3-Dimethyl-2,3-butanediol)

Pinacolone
(Methyl-t-butyl ketone)

2.
$$CH_3-\underset{\underset{OH}{|}}{\overset{\overset{CH_3}{|}}{C}}-\underset{\underset{OH}{|}}{CH_2} \longrightarrow CH_3-\underset{\underset{H}{|}}{\overset{\overset{CH_3}{|}}{C}}-\overset{\overset{}{}}{\underset{\underset{O}{||}}{CH}}$$

2-Methylpropane 1,2-diol

Isobutyraldehyde

Mechanism:

Step 1: Formation of carbocation.

$$CH_3-\underset{\underset{OH}{|}}{\underset{|}{C}}(CH_3)-\underset{\underset{OH}{|}}{\underset{|}{C}}(CH_3)-CH_3 \underset{-H^+}{\overset{+H^+}{\rightleftharpoons}} CH_3-\underset{\underset{OH}{|}}{\underset{|}{C}}(CH_3)-\underset{\underset{\overset{+}{O}H_2}{|}}{\underset{|}{C}}(CH_3)-CH_3 \xrightarrow{-H_2O} CH_3-\underset{\underset{OH}{|}}{\underset{|}{C}}(CH_3)-\overset{+}{\underset{|}{C}}(CH_3)-CH_3$$

Step 2: 1, 2, shift, migration of – CH_3 group.

$$CH_3-\underset{OH}{\underset{|}{C}}(CH_3)-\overset{+}{C}(CH_3)-CH_3 \xrightarrow{1,2\ shift} \left[CH_3-\overset{+}{\underset{OH}{\underset{|}{C}}}-\underset{CH_3}{\underset{|}{C}}(CH_3)-CH_3 \longleftrightarrow CH_3-\underset{\overset{+}{O}H}{\underset{|}{C}}(CH_3)=\underset{CH_3}{\underset{|}{C}}(CH_3)-CH_3 \right] \xrightarrow{-H^+} CH_3-\underset{O}{\underset{||}{C}}-\underset{CH_3}{\underset{|}{C}}(CH_3)-CH_3$$

  Rearranged carbonium ion | Stabilised carbonium | Pinacolone

Applications:

1. **For the preparation of carbonyl compounds.**

$$CH_3-\underset{\underset{CH_3}{|}}{C}=CH_2 \xrightarrow{Cl_2} CH_3-\underset{\underset{Cl}{|}}{\overset{CH_3}{\underset{|}{C}}}-CH_2Cl \xrightarrow[(2)\ H^+]{(1)\ Ag_2O} CH_3-\underset{\underset{H}{|}}{\overset{CH_3}{\underset{|}{C}}}-\overset{H}{\underset{}{C}}=O$$

Isobutylene → Isobutyraldehyde

2. **Ring expansion of cyclic ketones**

   Example: Synthesis of cycloheptanone from cyclohexanone.

   Cyclohexanone $\xrightarrow{CH_3NO_2}$ 1-Nitromethyl-cyclohexanol $\xrightarrow{Reduction}$ (1-aminomethylcyclohexanol) $\xrightarrow[-H^+]{NaNO_2/HCl,\ 0-5°C}$ Cycloheptanone

10. BENZILIC ACID REARRANGEMENT

Definition: α-Diketones are converted into α-hydroxy acids by base catalysed rearrangement is known as **"Benzilic acid rearrangement"**.

Reaction: Examples:

(1) $C_6H_5-\underset{O}{\underset{||}{C}}-\underset{O}{\underset{||}{C}}-C_6H_5 \xrightarrow[Ethanol]{KOH} C_6H_5-\underset{\underset{C_6H_5}{|}}{\overset{OH}{\underset{|}{C}}}-COO^-K^+ \xrightarrow{H^+} C_6H_5-\underset{\underset{C_6H_5}{|}}{\overset{OH}{\underset{|}{C}}}-COOH$

Benzil → Benzilic acid

(2) Furil $\xrightarrow[EtOH]{KOH}$ Furilic acid

Mechanism:

Step 1: Attack of – OH (nucleophile) on carbonyl group.

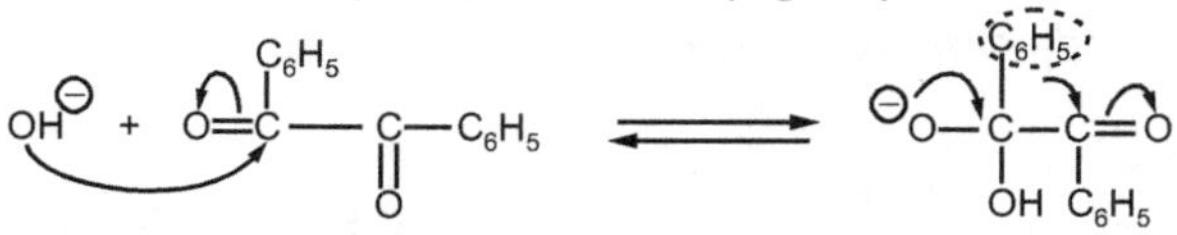

[Mechanism diagram: OH⁻ attacks the carbonyl carbon of benzil (C₆H₅–CO–CO–C₆H₅) giving tetrahedral intermediate with O⁻, OH and C₆H₅ groups]

Step 2: 1, 2 Shift (Migration of – C₆H₅ group)

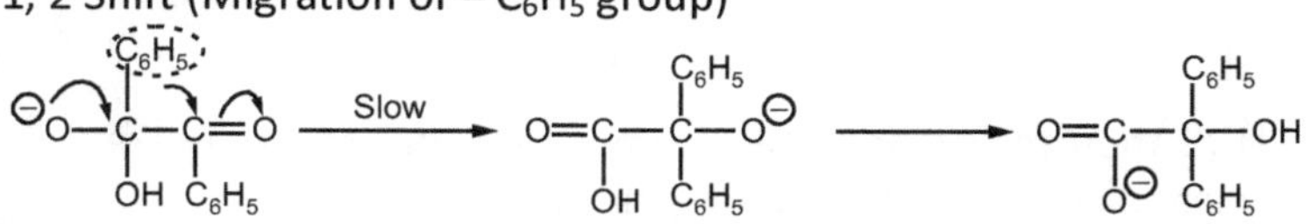

[Mechanism diagram showing slow 1,2-phenyl shift yielding the benzilate anion, then protonation to give benzilic acid: O=C(C₆H₅)–C(OH)(C₆H₅)–COO⁻ → final acid]

Applications:

1. Synthesis of furilic acid from furil.

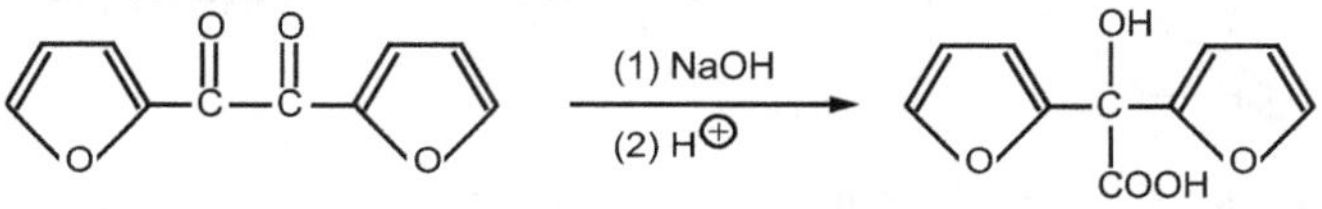

[Reaction: Furil (bis-furan-2-yl diketone) + (1) NaOH (2) H⁺ → Furilic acid (bis-furan-2-yl hydroxy acid with –C(OH)(COOH)–)]

Furil → Furilic acid

2. Synthesis of citric acid from ketopinic acid.

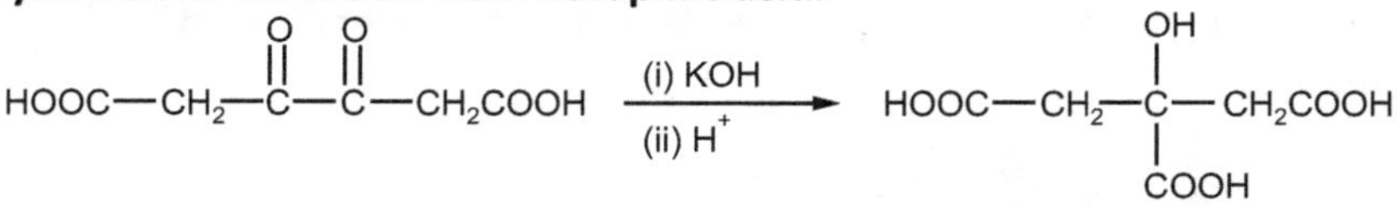

$$HOOC-CH_2-\underset{O}{\overset{\|}{C}}-\underset{O}{\overset{\|}{C}}-CH_2COOH \xrightarrow[\text{(ii) H}^+]{\text{(i) KOH}} HOOC-CH_2-\underset{\underset{COOH}{|}}{\overset{\overset{OH}{|}}{C}}-CH_2COOH$$

Ketopinic acid → Citric acid

REARRAGEMENT OF ELECTRON RICH SYSTEMS

11. STEVEN'S REARRANGEMENT

Definition: The rearrangement of keto-quaternary ammonium or sulphonium salts to amino ketones under the influence of a strong base such as NaOR or NaNH₂ is known as *Steven's rerrangement*.

Examples:

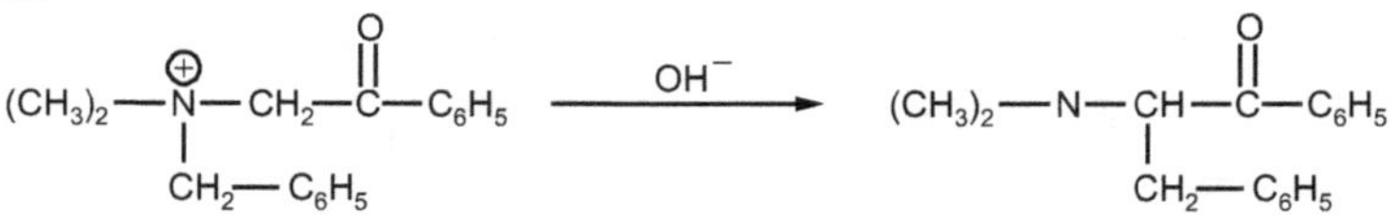

$$(CH_3)_2-\overset{+}{\underset{\underset{CH_2-C_6H_5}{|}}{N}}-CH_2-\overset{O}{\overset{\|}{C}}-C_6H_5 \xrightarrow{OH^-} (CH_3)_2-N-\underset{\underset{CH_2-C_6H_5}{|}}{CH}-\overset{O}{\overset{\|}{C}}-C_6H_5$$

Benzyldimethyl-phenacyl ammonium ion → α-Dimethylamino-α-benzyl acetophenone

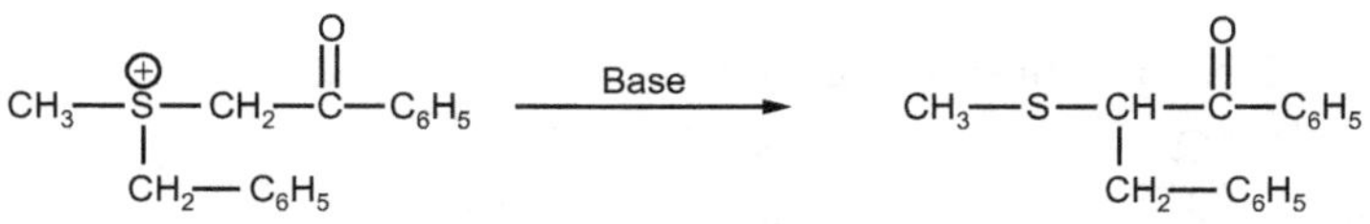

$$CH_3-\overset{+}{\underset{\underset{CH_2-C_6H_5}{|}}{S}}-CH_2-\overset{O}{\overset{\|}{C}}-C_6H_5 \xrightarrow{\text{Base}} CH_3-S-\underset{\underset{CH_2-C_6H_5}{|}}{CH}-\overset{O}{\overset{\|}{C}}-C_6H_5$$

Benzylmethyl-phenacyl sulphonium ion → α-Methylmercapto-α-benzyl acetophenone

Mechanism:

Step 1: Abstraction of proton from α-carbon by a base to yield "**YLIDE**" is a species in which adjacent atom bears formal opposite charge.

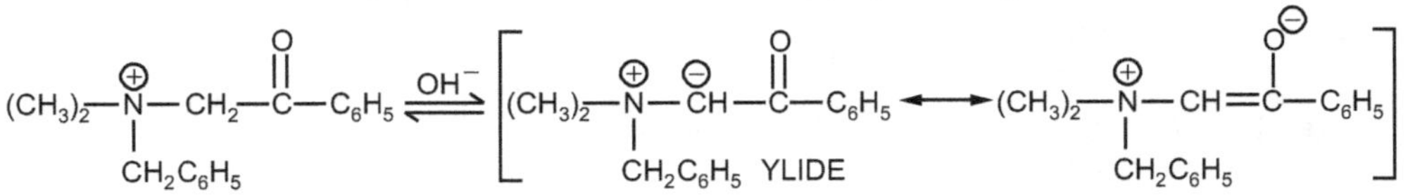

$$(CH_3)_2-\overset{\oplus}{\underset{\underset{CH_2C_6H_5}{|}}{N}}-CH_2-\overset{O}{\overset{\|}{C}}-C_6H_5 \overset{OH^-}{\rightleftharpoons} \left[(CH_3)_2-\overset{\oplus}{\underset{\underset{CH_2C_6H_5}{|}}{N}}-\overset{\ominus}{CH}-\overset{O}{\overset{\|}{C}}-C_6H_5 \longleftrightarrow (CH_3)_2-\overset{\oplus}{\underset{\underset{CH_2C_6H_5}{|}}{N}}-CH=\overset{O^{\ominus}}{\overset{|}{C}}-C_6H_5 \right]$$

$$\text{YLIDE}$$

Step 2: YLIDE then may rearrange to amino ketone *via* or concerted 1, 2 shift or radical-pair mechanism or ion-pair mechanism.

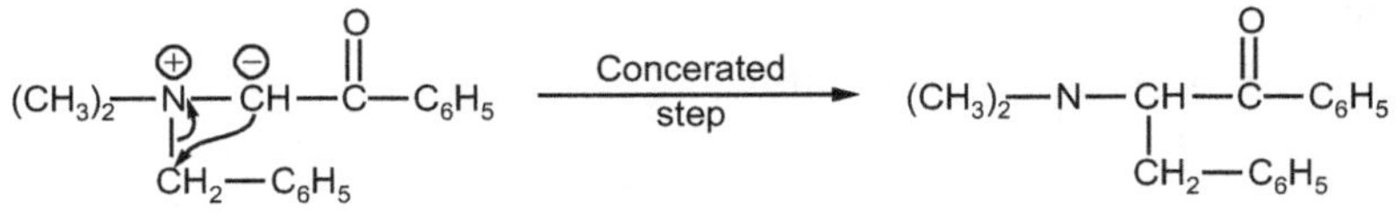

$$(CH_3)_2-\overset{\oplus}{\underset{\underset{CH_2-C_6H_5}{|}}{N}}-\overset{\ominus}{CH}-\overset{O}{\overset{\|}{C}}-C_6H_5 \xrightarrow{\text{Concerated step}} (CH_3)_2-N-\underset{\underset{CH_2-C_6H_5}{|}}{CH}-\overset{O}{\overset{\|}{C}}-C_6H_5$$

12. SOMMELET REARRANGEMENT (Sommelet - Hauser)

Definition: Benzyl quaternary ammonium salts on reaction with alkali metal amides give benzyl tertiary amines. This is called as *"Sommelet rearrangement"*.

Reaction:

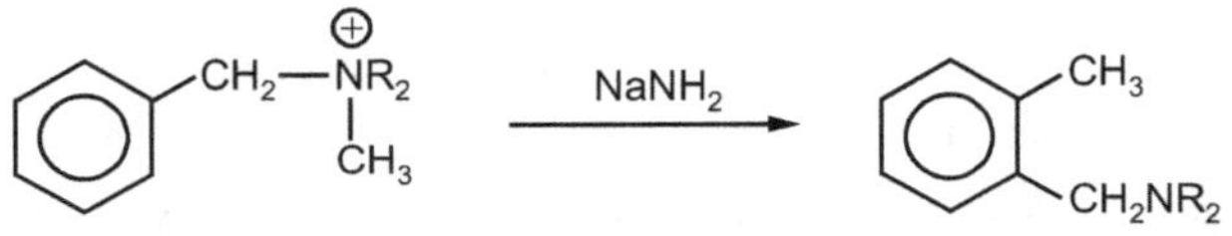

Ph-CH$_2$-$\overset{\oplus}{N}$R$_2$(CH$_3$) $\xrightarrow{NaNH_2}$ o-CH$_3$-C$_6$H$_4$-CH$_2$NR$_2$

Mechanism:

Step 1: Abstraction of proton from benzylic hydrogen (more acidic) by a base to yield a **YLIDE**.

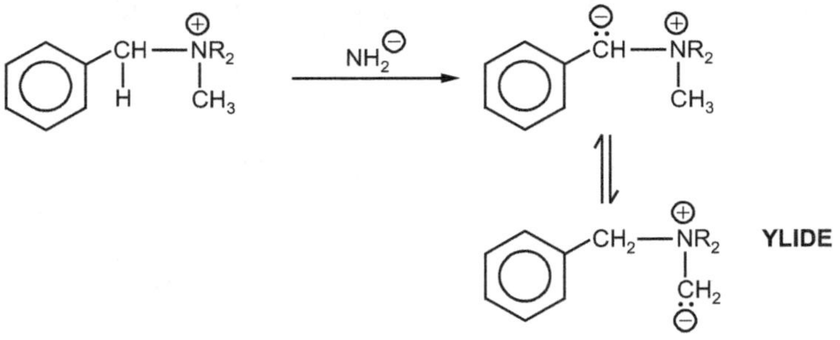

Ph-CH(H)-$\overset{\oplus}{N}$R$_2$(CH$_3$) $\xrightarrow{NH_2^{\ominus}}$ Ph-$\overset{\ominus}{CH}$-$\overset{\oplus}{N}$R$_2$(CH$_3$)

$\updownarrow$

Ph-CH$_2$-$\overset{\oplus}{N}$R$_2$($\overset{\ominus}{\underset{..}{C}H_2}$)   **YLIDE**

Step 2: [2, 3]-Sigmatropic rearrangement.

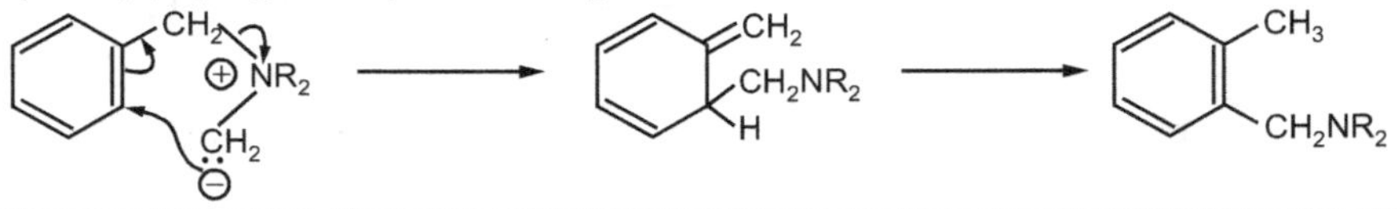

Applications:

1. This rearrangement is useful for the preparation of aromatic aldehydes.

   Examples:

   (a) p-Bromobenzyl bromide + (CH$_2$)$_6$N$_4$ (Hexamethylene tetramine) $\xrightarrow{CH_3COOH, \Delta}$ p-Bromobenzaldehyde

   (b) 2-Chloromethylthiophene + (CH$_2$)$_6$N$_4$ $\xrightarrow{CH_3COOH, \Delta}$ Thiophene 2-aldehyde

2. **For the preparation of amines.**

   Example:

   Benzyl chloride + (CH$_2$)$_6$N$_4$ (Hexamethylene tetramine) $\xrightarrow{\text{Excess } NH_3, \Delta}$ Benzylamine

3. **For the preparation of an aminoketone.**

   p-Nitrobromoacetophenone $\xrightarrow[2.\ NH_3/\Delta]{1.\ (CH_2)_6\ N_4 \cdot HCl}$ p-Nitrobenzoylmethylamine
   (Intermediate for **Chloromycetin** synthesis)

13. FAVORSKII REARRANGEMENT

Definition: Transformation of α-haloketones to esters *via* base-catalysed rearrangement is called *"Favorskii rearrangement"*.

Reaction:

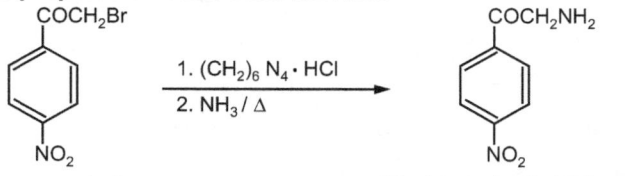

α-Haloketone → Ester

Mechanism:

Step 1: Abstraction of α-hydrogen

Step 2: Formation of cyclopropanone ring

Step 3: Abstraction of proton from solvent.

Application:

1. For ring contraction in cyclic system

   2-Chlorocyclohexanone → Methyl cyclopentane carboxylate (with MeO$^\ominus$)

14. NEBER REARRANGEMENT

Definition: α-Aminoketones can be prepared by treatment of ketoxime tosylates with a base (ethoxide ion) or pyridine. This is known as *"Neber rearrangement"*.

Reaction:

$$R-CH_2-\underset{\underset{N-OTs}{\|}}{C}-R' \xrightarrow{\ ^\ominus OEt\ } R-CH_2-\underset{\underset{NH_2}{|}}{\overset{\overset{O}{\|}}{C}}-R'$$

Ketoxime tosylate → α-Aminoketone

R = aryl, alkyl or hydrogen
R' = aryl, alkyl but not hydrogen

Mechanism:

Step 1: Abstraction of the acidic proton by a base to form carbocation.

Step 2: Rearrangement of the carbocation to form "**Azirine**" intermediate.

Step 3: Hydrolytic ring opening of azirine to form the α-amino ketone.

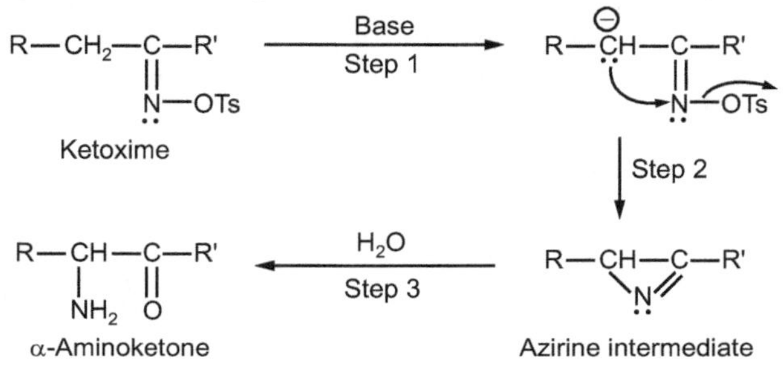

REARRANGEMENT OF AROMATIC NUCLEUS

15. FRIES REARRAGEMENT

Definition: Phenolic esters rearrange to *o*- and *p*-acyl phenols in presence of Lewis acids (AlCl$_3$). This is known as *"Fries rearrangement"*.

Reaction:

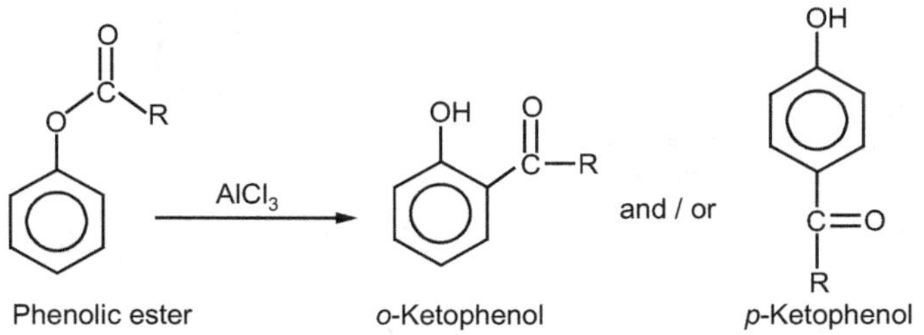

Mechanism:

Step 1 : Complex formation

Step 2 : Intramolecular mechanism

Step 3 : Hydrolysis of stable product gives acylphenol

[Reaction scheme showing Fries rearrangement mechanism with Steps I, II, III producing o-Hydroxy acetophenone and p-Hydroxy acetophenone]

Photo-Fries rearrangement: This rearrangement is same as Fries-rearrangement. Here UV light is used as catalyst instead of $AlCl_3$.

Both *o*- and *p*-migrations are observed.

Applications:

1. **For the synthesis of adrenaline (Cardiac stimulant).**

Catechol + $ClCH_2COCl$ (Chloroacetyl chloride) $\xrightarrow[\text{Esterification}]{\text{Pyridine}}$ [ortho-hydroxyphenyl chloroacetate]

$\xrightarrow[\text{AlCl}_3/\text{CS}_2]{\text{CH}_3\text{NH}_2 / \text{H}_2}$

(±) Adrenaline [3,4-dihydroxyphenyl-CH(OH)·CH$_2$·NHCH$_3$]

2. Fries rearrangement is useful for the preparation of aromatic hydroxyketones, since direct acylation of phenols gives very poor yields.

16. CLAISEN REARRANGEMENT

Definition: Arylalkyl ethers when heated without solvent rearranges to *o*-allyl phenol. This is known as *"Claisen rearrangement"*. But, if both ortho positions are blocked then the allylic group will migrate to the para position.

Reaction:

Phenylallyl ether → o-Allylphenol (Δ, 200°C)

Mechanism: Reaction proceeds *via* cyclic transition state. Dienone is formed as an intermediate which tautomerises to alkyl phenol.

Applications:

1. **Allyl ethers of enols undergo Claisen rearrangement to form ketone.**

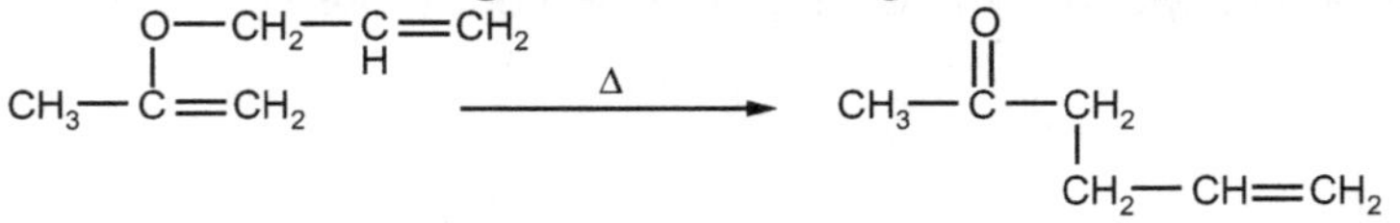

$$CH_3-\overset{O-CH_2-\underset{H}{C}=CH_2}{\underset{}{C}}=CH_2 \xrightarrow{\Delta} CH_3-\overset{O}{\underset{}{C}}-\underset{CH_2-CH=CH_2}{CH_2}$$

2. **Allylarylamines gives allylaniline.**

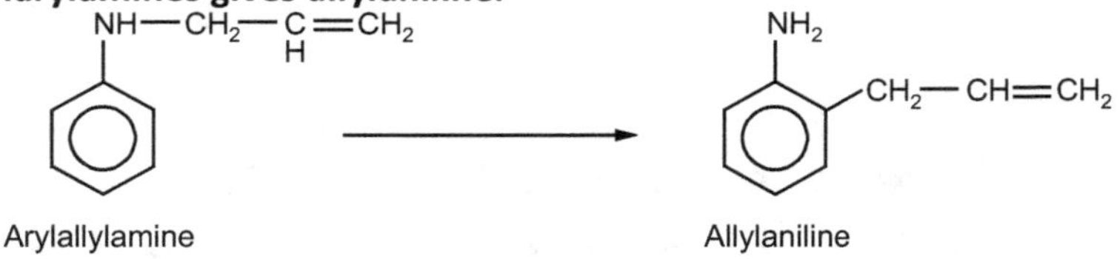

Arylallylamine → Allylaniline

3. **For the synthesis of eugenol.**

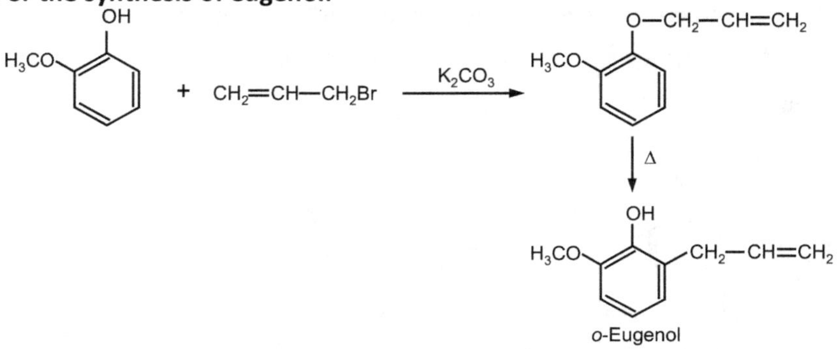

o-Eugenol

PERICYCLIC REARRANGEMENT

17. COPE REARRANGEMENT

Definition: The *Cope rearrangement* is simply a [3,3]-sigmatropic 1,5-diene isomerisation.

Reaction:

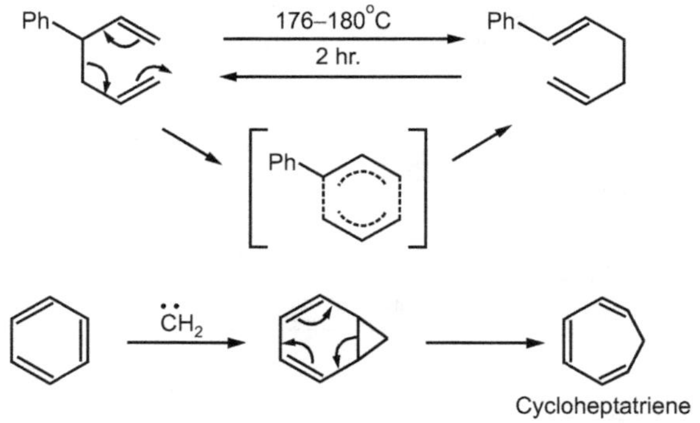

176–180°C, 2 hr.

Cycloheptatriene

Oxy-cope rearrangement:

3-Hydroxy 1,5-hexadiene →[3,3] Sigmatropic rearrangement

Stereochemistry: The stereochemical outcome of this rearrangement is a chain shaped transition state.

Example, Meso 3, 4-dimethyl-1, 5-hexadiene gives cis-trans-2, 6-octadiene.

Meso-3, 4-dimethyl-hexa-1,5-diene → Chair form → Z,E-2,6-octadiene (cis-trans isomer)

Application:

1. For expansion of cyclobutane ring to a 1, 5-cyclooctadiene ring.

QUESTION BANK

1. Classify various rearrangement reactions with suitable example of each type.
2. What do you mean by a 1, 2-shift? Explain it with suitable examples.
3. What is YLIDE ion? Explain it with suitable examples.
4. Write down definition, reaction, mechanism and applications of any two rearrangements belonging to the type "Rearrangements for electron deficient carbon atom".
5. Explain any two nucleophilic rearrangements of electron deficient nitrogen atom.

6. Explain the rearrangements of your choice w.r.t. definition, reaction, mechanism and application from the rearrangements belonging to the following classes:
   (i) Electron deficient carbon atom
   (ii) Electron deficient nitrogen atom
   (iii) Electron deficient oxygen atom
   (iv) Sigmatropic rearrangement or Migration to electron rich centre.
7. Explain the rearrangements w.r.t. definition, reaction, mechanism and application from the following:
   (i) Pinacol-pinacolon rearrangment
   (ii) Curtius rearrangement
   (iii) Stevens rearrangement
   (iv) Sommlet rearrangement
   (v) Claisen rearrangement
   (vi) Fries rearrangement
8. Discuss how Claisen rearrangement is intramolecular with suitable examples.
9. What do you mean by sigmatropic rearrangement reaction? Explain it with suitable examples.
10. Give reasons
    (a) In Oxy – Cope rearrangement, isomeric diene is not obtained.
    (b) Curtius rearrangement gives urea derivatives as side products.
11. Write short notes on
    (a) Bayer – Villiger oxidation
    (b) Beckmann rearrangement
    (c) Cope rearrangement
    (d) Wagner – Meerwin rearrangement
    (e) Hofmann rearrangement
    (f) Wolf rearrangement
    (g) Willgerodt rearrangement
    (h) Lossen rearrangement
    (i) Witting rearrangement
    (j) Dakin oxidation
    (k) Sigmatropic rearrangement
    (l) Cycloaddition reaction
    (m) Free radical rearrangement
    (n) Benzilic acid rearrangement
    (o) Curtius rearrangement
    (p) Schimdt rearrangement

■■■

Chapter 3 ...

CHEMISTRY OF AMINO ACIDS

CONTENTS

- Classification and structures of natural amino acids
- Iso electric point
- General methods of preparation of amino acids
- Peptide bonds

1. INTRODUCTION

Proteins, from the Greek word *proteios*, meaning first, are a class of organic compounds mainly containing carbon, nitrogen and oxygen. They are present in every living cell and are vital to each of them. In the form of skin, hair, callus, cartilage, muscles, tendons and ligaments, proteins hold together, protect and provide structure to the body of a multicelled organism. In the form of enzymes, hormones, antibodies and globulins, they catalyze, regulate, and protect the body chemistry. In the form of hemoglobin, myoglobin and various lipoproteins, they effect the transport of oxygen and other substances within an organism.

Amino acids are the basic building blocks of proteins.

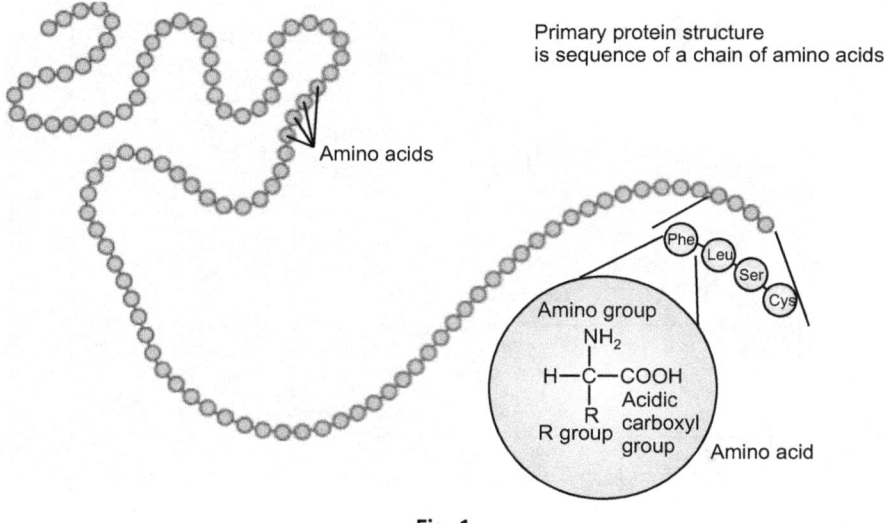

Fig. 1

2. STRUCTURE AND CLASSIFICATION OF NATURAL AMINOACIDS

Amino acids are bifunctional molecules: The common feature of all amino acids is the presence of at least one amino group and one carboxylic acid group in thier chemical structure. Both inter and intra molecular reactions between basic and acidic functions play an important role in the physical and chemical properties of these small, difunctional compounds.

Structure:

Aminoacids: General structure

Hydrolysis of proteins by boiling aqueous acid or base yields an assortment of small molecules identified as *α-aminocarboxylic acids* or simply called as *natural α-amino acids.* More than twenty such components have been isolated, and the most common, twently of these are listed.

Table 1: Natural α-Amino Acids.

Name	Structure	Structure	Name
Alanine Ala A MW = 89	$^-OOC-CH(H_3N^+)-CH_3$	$H-CH(NH_3^+)-COO^-$	Glycine Gly G MW = 75
Valine Val V MW = 117	$^-OOC-CH(H_3N^+)-CH(CH_3)_2$	$HO-CH_2-CH(NH_3^+)-COO^-$	Serine Ser S MW = 105
Leucine Leu L MW = 131	$^-OOC-CH(H_3N^+)-CH_2-CH(CH_3)_2$	$OH-CH(CH_3)-CH(NH_3^+)-COO^-$	Threonine Thr T MW = 119
Isoleucine ISO I MW = 131	$^-OOC-CH(H_3N^+)-CH(CH_3)-CH_2-CH_3$	$HS-CH_2-CH(NH_3^+)-COO^-$	Cysteine Cys C MW = 121
Phenylalanine Phe F MW = 131	$^-OOC-CH(H_3N^+)-CH_2-C_6H_5$	$HO-C_6H_4-CH_2-CH(NH_3^+)-COO^-$	Tyrosine Tyr Y MW = 181
Tryptophan Trp W MW = 204	$^-OOC-CH(H_3N^+)-CH_2$-indole	$NH_2-C(=O)-CH_2-CH(NH_3^+)-COO^-$	Asparagine Asn N MW = 132

Methionine Met M MW = 149	⁻OOC–CH(H₃N⁺)–CH₂–CH₂–S–CH₃		H₂N–C(=O)–CH₂–CH₂–CH(NH₃⁺)–COO⁻	Glutamine Gln Q MW = 146
Proline Pro P MW = 115	⁻OOC–CH–CH₂–CH₂–CH₂–NH (ring)		H₃N⁺–CH₂–(CH₂)₃–CH(NH₃⁺)–COO⁻	Lysine Lys L MW = 146
Aspartic acid Asp D MW = 133	⁻OOC–CH(H₃N⁺)–CH₂–COO⁻		H₂N–C(=NH₂⁺)–NH–(CH₂)₃–CH(NH₃⁺)–COO⁻	Arginine Arg R MW = 174
Glutamic acid Glu E MW = 147	⁻OOC–CH(H₃N⁺)–CH₂–CH₂–COO⁻		(imidazole)–CH₂–CH(NH₃⁺)–COO⁻	Histidine His H MW = 155

Some common features of these amino acids can be noted. With the exception of proline, they are all 1° amines; and with the exception of glycine, they are all chiral. The configuration of the chiral amino acids are the same when written as a Fischer projection formulae and is defined as the **L-configuration** by Fischer.

Applying the Cahn-Ingold-Prelog notation, all these natural chiral amino acids, with the exception of cysteine, have an S-configuration.

Classification:

(a) Based on polarity of the molecule:

Table 2

Non-Polar aliphatic	Non-polar aromatic	Polar uncharged	Polar positive charge	Polar negative charge
Glycine	Phenylalanine	Serine	Histidine	Aspartic acid
Alanine	Tyrosine	Tyrosine	Arginine	Glutamic acid
Valine	Tryptophan	Asparagine	Lysine	
Leucine	Histidine	Glutamine		
Isoleucine				
Proline				

(b) Based on acidic/ basic nature of the molecule:

Table 3

Acidic	Basic	Neutral
Aspartic acid Glutamic acid	Lysine Arginine Histidine	Glycine, Alanine etc.

(c) Based on the R group

Table 4

Branched alkyl group	Aliphatic chain	Aromatic ring	Heterocyclic ring
Valine Leucine Isoleucine	Leucine Glycine Alanine	Tyrosine Phenylalanine	Histidine *(Imidazole ring)* Trptophan *(Indole ring)*

(d) Based on additional functional groups

Table 5

Extra Amino group	Extra Carbonyl group	Extra Amide group	Extra Thiol/Thio group
Lysine Arginine	Aspartic acid Glutamic acid	Asparagine Glutamine	Cysteine Methionine

(e) Essential and non essential amino acids

Based on the nutritional requirements; all amino acids which cannot be prepared by the human body (or animals body) are called *essential amino acids*, (since, they are essential in the diet). Plants prepare these amino acids and can act as a source for these amino acids.

Methionine, arginine, tryptophan, valine, leucine, isoleucine, phenylalanine, histidine, lysine are essential amino acids.

Out of these, histidine and arginine are not biosynthesized in children, but can be in sometimes biosynthesised adults. Hence, they are called *semi-essential amino acids.*

Amino acids which can be prepared by the body are called *non essential amino acids*. They are glycine, alanine, serine, aspartic acid, asparagine, glutamine, tyrosine, glutamic acid and proline.

Table 6

Essential amino acids	Non-Essential amino acids
Methionine, Arginine, Tryptophan, Valine, Leucine, Isoleucine, Phenylalanine, Histidine, Lysine	Glycine, Alanine, Serine, Aspartic acid, Asparagine, Glutamine, Tyrosine, Glutamic acid, Proline.

3. THE ISOELECTRIC POINT

A prominent characteristic of amino acids is their amphoteric character. They can function as acids or bases. Amino acids actually exist as inner salts, zwitterions.

$$\overset{+}{N}H_3$$
$$|$$
$$CH_3CHCOO^-$$

Alanine inner salt

Physical properties of amino acids are consistent with the highly polar inner salt structure. The precise structure of an amino acid is determined by the pH of the medium in which the acid is dissolved.

At low pH (less than 2) an amino acid such as glycine exists as the protonated cation (A). At high pH (greater than 10) amino-carboxylate anion (C) is the principal form. Between these extremes in pH, the inner salt B will be present along with varying amounts of A or C.

$$\overset{+}{N}H_3CH_2COOH \underset{+H^\oplus}{\overset{-H^+}{\rightleftharpoons}} \overset{+}{N}H_3CH_2COO^- \underset{+H^\oplus}{\overset{-H^+}{\rightleftharpoons}} NH_2CH_2COO^-$$

A (cation)　　　　　B (zwitterian)　　　　　C (anion)

The pH at which the amino acid is in an electrically neutral form [(B) for glycine] which is also known as the isoelectric point; pI. The pI lies halfway between the pKa^1 and pKa^2 values for most amino acids.

$$pI = 1/2(pKa^1 + pKa^2)$$

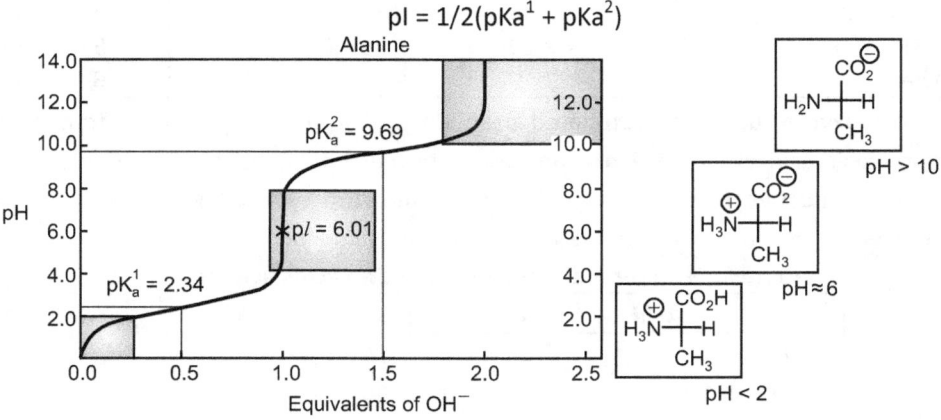

Fig. 2

At low pH values the amino acid resembles a typical diprotic acid. Data from titration with aqueous base gives a titration curve which indicates that the carboxylic acid has a pKa value of about 2.3 and the ammonium ion has a pKa value near 9.5.

The pI for an amino acid which possesses two amino or two carboxylic acid groups lies halfway between the pKa values of the two singly charged forms.

Table 7 Values for pKa's and pI's for amino acids

Amino Acids	pKa^1	pKa^2	pKa^3	pI
Alanine	2.34	9.69		6.01
Arginine	2.01	9.04		10.76
Asparagine	2.02	8.80	12.48	5.41
Aspartic Acid	2.10	3.86		2.98
Cysteine	1.86	8.35	9.82	5.11
Glutamic acid	2.10	4.07	10.34	3.08
Glutamine	2.17	9.13	9.47	5.70
Glycine	2.35	9.78		6.07
Histidine	1.77	6.10		7.64
Isoleucine	2.32	9.76	9.18	6.04
Leucine	2.33	9.74		6.04
Lysine	2.18	8.95		9.74
Methionine	2.28	9.21	10.53	5.74
Phenylalanine	2.58	9.24		5.91
Proline	2.00	10.60		6.30
Serine	2.21	9.15		5.68
Threonine	2.09	9.10		5.60
Tryptophan	2.38	9.39		5.88
Tyrosine	2.20	9.11		5.66
Valine	2.29	9.72	10.07	6.00

The carboxyl group of a protonated α-amino acid is more acidic than that of a monocarboxylic acid by about 2 pKa units. This property is attributed to the electron withdrawing inductive effect of the adjacent ammonium cation. As the ammonium group moves farther from the carboxy group, the pKa^1 value increases.

Table 8: Structural effects on the amino acids acidity

Acid	pKa^1	pKa^2
CH_3COOH	4.76	–
$^+NH_3CH_2COOH$	2.35	9.8
$^+NH_3CH_2CH_2COOH$	3.60	10.19
$^+NH_3CH_2CH_2CH_2COOH$	4.03	10.40
$^+NH_3CH_2CH_2CH_2CH_2COOH$	4.21	10.69
$^+NH_3CH_2CH_3$	–	10.81

Interestingly, the acidity of the ammonium cation in the presence of a carboxylate anion is greater than anticipated. Acidity changes with the distance between the two functional groups as is expected, but the intrinsic acidity is greater than that of a model ammonium cation.

4. PREPARATION/SYNTHESIS OF α-AMINO ACIDS

(i) Amination of α-bromocarboxylic acids: The following equation, provides a straightforward method for preparing alpha-aminocarboxylic acids. The bromoacids, in turn, are conveniently prepared from carboxylic acids by reaction with $Br_2 + PCl_3$.

(ii) Gabriel synthesis: Reaction of potassium phthalimide and bromo malonic ester give the phthalimide substituted malonic ester which has an acidic hydrogen, activated by the two ester groups. It is alkylated, followed by the base catalyzed hydrolysis of the phthalimide moiety and the esters. Further, acidification and thermal decarboxylation, produces an amino acid and phthalic acid.

(iii) Strecker synthesis: Its an elegant procedure, which assembles an α-amino acid from ammonia (the amine precursor), cyanide (the carboxyl precursor) and an aldehyde. This reaction is essentially an imino analogy of cyanohydrin formation. The α-aminonitrile formed in this way can then be hydrolyzed to an amino acid under either acid or base catalysis.

(iv) By resolution of racemic mixtures:

The three synthetic procedures described above and many others that can be conceived usually give racemic amino acid products. If pure **L** or **D** enantiomers are desired, it is necessary to resolve these racemic mixtures. A common method of resolving racemates is by diastereomeric salt formation with a pure chiral acid or base. This is illustrated for a generic amino acid in the following scheme.

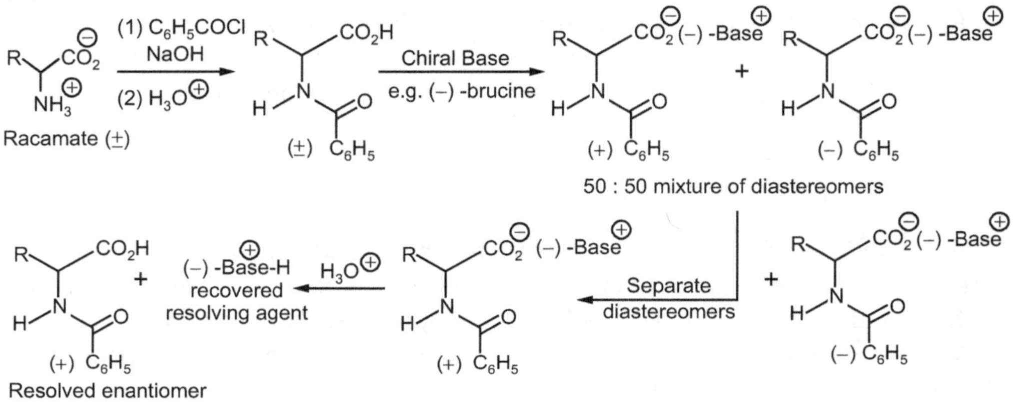

Using the acidic COOH group

In the initial display, the carboxylic acid function contributes to diastereomeric salt formation. The racemic amino acid is first converted to a benzamide derivative to remove the basic character of the amino group. Next, an ammonium salt is formed by combining the carboxylic acid with an optically pure amine, such as brucine (an analog of strychnine). Since, the amino acid moiety is racemic and the base is a single enantiomer **(L)**, an equimolar mixture of diastereomeric salts is formed. Diastereomers may be separated by crystallization, chromatography or other physical manipulation. In this way one of the isomers may be isolated for further treatment.

In this illustration it is the (+) : (−) diastereomer. Finally the salt is broken by acid treatment, giving the resolved (+)-amino acid derivative together with the recovered resolving agent (the optically active amine). The same procedure could be used to obtain the (−)-enantiomer of the amino acid.

Using the Basic NH$_2$ Group

Since, amino acids are amphoteric, resolution could also be achieved by using the basic character of the amine function. For this approach an enantiomerically pure chiral acid such as tartaric acid is needed as the resolving agent. The carboxylic acid function is first esterified, so that it will not compete with the resolving acid.

Resolution by enzymatic discrimination

Resolution of aminoacid derivatives may also be achieved by enzymatic discrimination in the hydrolysis of amides. For example, an aminoacylase enzyme from pig kidneys cleaves an amide derivative of a natural L-amino acid much faster than it does the D-enantiomer. If the racemic mixture of amides is treated with this enzyme, the L-enantiomer (whatever its rotation) will be rapidly converted to its free zwitter ionic form, whereas the D-enantiomer will remain largely unchanged. Here, the diastereomeric species are transition states rather than isolable intermediates. This separation of enantiomers, based on very different rates of reaction, is called **kinetic resolution**.

(v) Erlenmeyer-Plöchl azlactone and amino acid synthesis: This method first involves the formation of an azalactone by the intramolecular cyclization of an acylglycine in the presence of acetic anhydride.

The next step is reaction of the azalactone with a carbonyl compound followed by mild hydrolysis (*drastic hydrolysis gives the α-oxo acid directly*) leading to the unsaturated α-acylamino acid which, on reduction yields the substituted amino acid.

Substituted amino acid.

If, $R_1 = R_2 = H$, then the amino acid formed is alanine;
If, $R_1, R_2 = PhCH_2$, then the amino acid formed is phenylalanine.

(v) Knoop synthesis: An α-keto acid on treatment with NH_3 forms an imine which on catalytic reduction gives an amino acid.

$CH_3COCOOH$ (Pyruvic acid) $\xrightarrow{NH_3}$ imine $\xrightarrow{H_2/Pd \text{ or } Na/C_2H_5OH}$ amino acid

5. CHEMICAL TESTS FOR AMINO ACIDS

(a) **Biuret test:** This test is positive for compounds containing more than one peptide linkage, e.g., proteins and their hydrolytic products. It is also positive for compounds which contain two carbonyl groups, joined together or through a single atom of nitrogen or carbon and similar substances which contain $CSNH_2$, $-C(NH)NH_2$ or CH_2NH_2 groups, which also respond to the test.
Test: 2 ml of protein solution + 1 ml of 40% NaOH + 1-2 drops of 1% copper sulfate violet colour indicates the presence of peptide linkage.

(b) **Ninhydrin colour test (Nin-Reaction of aminoacids):** This reaction was discovered by Ruhemann who found that α-amino-acids when warmed with triketo + hydrindene hydrate (Ninhydrin) gave a fine blue colour. β and γ-amino-acids hardly reacted and α-aminoacids when substituted on the amino or carboxyl group (e.g., proline), gave a negative reaction.

Test 2 ml of protein solution + 0.5 ml ninhydrine solution gives blue colour.

(c) **Millon Test (Tyrosine):** Neutral protein solution reacts with acidified mercuric chloride to form a yellow precipitate of mercury protein-complex. This complex forms a nitrate complex with sodium nitrate solution on warming, developing a red colour.
Test: Add 1 ml of acidified solution of protein (with suphuric acid) to 1 ml of acid mercuric sulfate, (10% mercuric sulfate in 10% sulphuric acid) and boil (1 min). Yellow ppt. Cool under tap water + 1% $NaNO_2$ (aq. solution). On gentle warming it turns red.

(d) **Xanthoprotein Test:** Proteoses and peptones do not form precipitates with nitric acid, but their solutions when made alkane, first become yellow and then orange. In this test a white precipitate of protein formed after the addition of nitric acid is due to the formation of meta proteins, that are insoluble in nitric acid. The nitro compounds from the protein molecule containing benzene ring, e.g., tyrosine, tryptophan, phenylalanine develop a yellow colour. These nitro compounds in alkaline medium ionize freely and produce a deep yellow orange colour.
Test : To 2 ml of protein solution, add 1 ml of conc. nitric acid white precipitate forms. Boil it, so the colour changes to yellow. Cool the test tube and add 2 ml of 20% of aq. sodium hydroxide (or ammonia) solution to make alkaline. Deep orange colour develops.

(e) Sakaguchi test (Arginine): Arginine in presence of alcoholic α-naphthol forms a complex with sodium hypochlorite developing a bright red colour.

Test: 3 ml protein solution + 1 ml 5% sodium hydroxide + 2 drops of pure alcoholic α-naphthol + 1 drop 10% sodium hypochlorite; mix well, brown red colour develops.

6. REACTIONS OF AMINO ACIDS

Amino acids undergo most of the chemical reactions characteristic of each function, assuming the pH is adjusted to an appropriate value.

(a) Esterification of carboxylic acid: Usually conducted under acidic conditions, as shown in the two equations written below. Under such conditions, amine functions are converted to their ammonium salts and carboxylic acids are not dissociated. The first equation is a typical Fischer esterification involving methanol. The initial product is a stable ammonium salt. The amino ester formed by neutralization of this salt is unstable, due to acylation of the amine by the ester function.

The second reaction illustrates benzylation of the two carboxylic acid functions of aspartic acid using *p*-toluenesulfonic acid as catalyst. Once the carboxyl function is esterified, zwitterionic species are no longer possible and the product behaves like any 1°-amine.

(b) Acylation (Protection) of amino function: In order to convert the amine function of an amino acid into an amide, the pH of the solution must be raised to 10 or higher, so that free amine nucleophiles are present in the reaction system. Carboxylic acids are converted to carboxylate anions at such a high pH, and do not interfere with amine acylation reactions. The following two reactions are illustrative.

In the first, an acid chloride serves as the acylating reagent. This is a good example of the superior nucleophilicity of nitrogen in acylation reactions, as compared to water and hydroxide anion present as competing nucleophiles. A similar selectivity favoring amines is observed in the Hinsberg test.

The second reaction employs an anhydride-like reagent for the acylation. This is a particularly useful procedure in peptide synthesis, due to the ease with which the t-butylcarbonyl (t-BOC) group can be removed at a later stage. Since, amides are only weakly basic (pKa ~ – 1), the resulting amino acid derivatives do not display zwitterionic character, and may be converted to a variety of carboxylic acid derivatives.

(c) Specific oxidation: The mild oxidant, iodine reacts selectively with certain amino acid side groups. These include, the phenolic ring in tyrosine and the heterocyclic rings in tryptophan and histidine, to yield products of electrophilic iodination. In addition, the sulfur group in cysteine and methionine are also oxidized by iodine. Quantitative measurment of iodine consumption has been used to determine the number of such residues in peptides.

The basic functions in lysine and arginine are the onium cations at pH less than 8, and are unreactive in that state. **Cysteine** is a thiol and like most thiols it is oxidatively dimerized to a disulfide, which is sometimes listed as a distinct amino acid under the name **cystine**. Disulfide bonds of this kind are found in many peptides and proteins. For example, the two peptide chains that constitute insulin are held together by two disulfide links. Our hair consists of a fibrous protein called keratin, which contains unusually large proportion of cysteine. In the manipulation called "permanent waving", disulfide bonds are first broken and then created after the hair has been reshaped. Treatment with dilute aqueous iodine oxidizes the methionine sulfur atom to a sulfoxide.

Cysteine-Cystine Interconversion

(d) **Decarboxylation of amino acids:** Amino acids can be successfully decarboxylated under mild coniditons like heating with barium hydroxide.

(e) **N-Alkylation/Acylation:** Under normal conditions, N-alkylation/acylation is preferred to C-alkyation acylation.

(f) **Reduction:** The carboxylic acid function is reduced to 1° alcohol by LiAlH$_4$ more effectively than NaBH$_4$.

Summary of the reactions given by amino acids is as follows:

The above discussed and other reactions of amino acids are summarised next page.

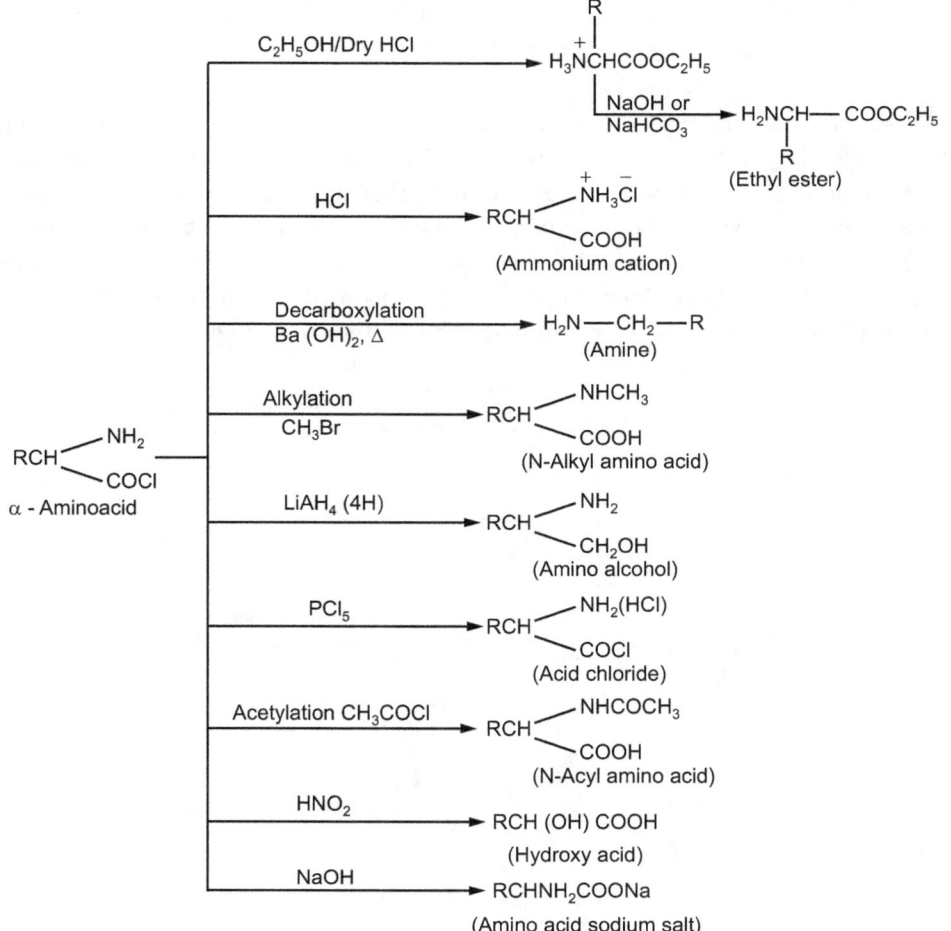

7. THE PEPTIDE BOND

If the amine and carboxylic acid functional groups in amino acids are joined together to form amide bonds, a chain of amino acid units, called a **peptide**, is formed. A simple tetrapeptide structure is shown in the following diagram. By convention, the amino acid component retaining a free amine group is drawn at the left end (the N-terminus) of the peptide chain, and the amino acid retaining a free carboxylic acid is drawn on the right (the C-terminus).

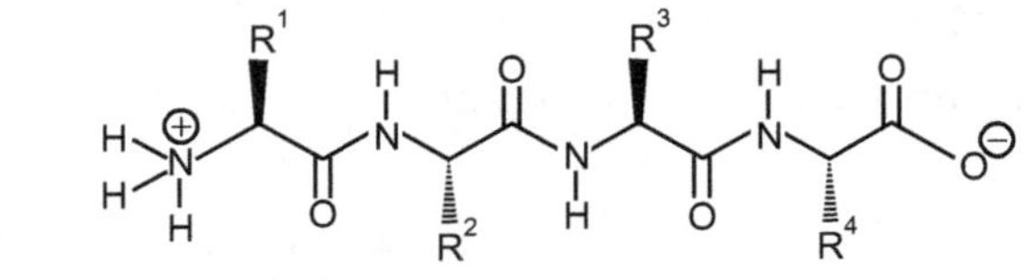

N-terminus   C-terminus

The conformational flexibility of peptide chains is limited chiefly to rotations about the bonds leading to the alpha-carbon atoms. This restriction is due to the rigid nature of the amide (peptide) bond. As shown in the following figure, nitrogen electron pair delocalization into the carbonyl group results in significant double bond character between the carbonyl carbon and the nitrogen. This keeps the peptide links relatively planar and resistant to conformational change. This aspect of peptide structure is an important factor influencing the conformations adopted by proteins and large peptides.

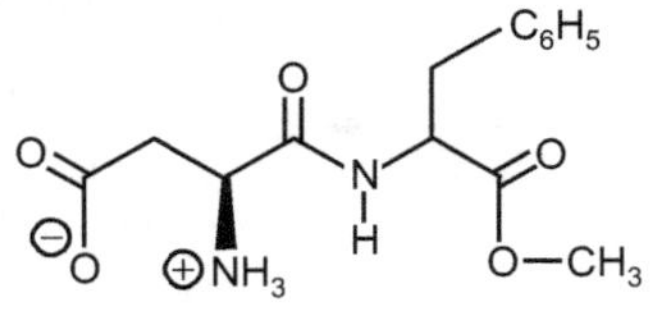

Asp-Phe-OCH$_3$
Aspartame

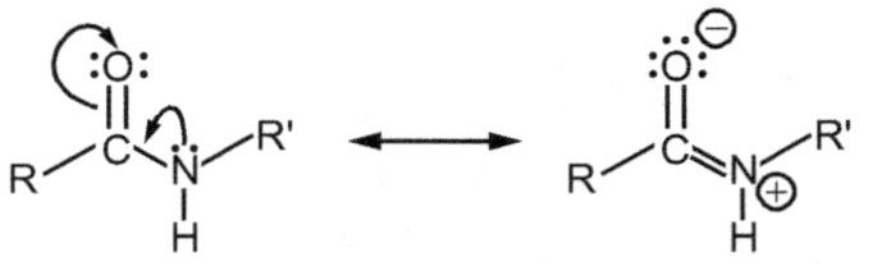

C—N double character in amide (peptide) bonds

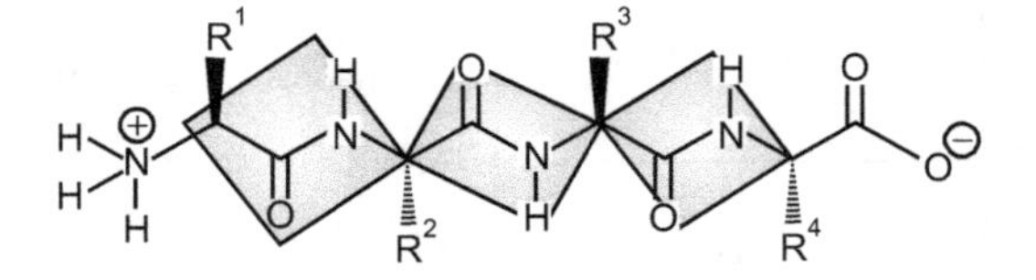

Planar peptide bond segments

Fig. 3

TERMINAL RESIDUE ANALYSIS

Discovering the structures and functions of proteins in living organism is an important tool for understanding cellular processes. This allows drugs that target specific metabolic pathways to be invented more easily.

The structures of peptides are confirmed by terminal residue analysis, particularly at C and N terminal. The identification of N-terminal amino acid residue of the peptide chain is known as **N-terminal analysis**.

N-terminal amino-acid analysis helps in identifying the sequence of amino acid present in the peptides. The two commonly used methods for N-terminal analysis are:

1. Sanger's method (2,4-DNFB)
2. Edman's method (Phenyl isothiacyanate)

The C-terminal analysis would greatly help in verifying the primary structure of proteins predicted from DNA sequences. The number of methods for C-terminal analysis are as follows:

1. Enzymatic method (carboxypeptidase)
2. Hydrazinolysis

N-terminal Analysis

1. **Sanger's method (2,4-DNFB)**

In this technique, a peptide is treated with 2, 4-dinitrofluorobenzene (DNFB). As a result, fluorine of DNFB undergoes nucleophilic substitution by the free amino group of the peptide and yields N-dinitro phenyl derivative of peptide. The subsequent peptide derivative is hydrolysed to the component of amino acids. The process is repeated for several times until all the amino acids present in peptide chain are identified.

2. Edman's method:

In this method, the reaction takes place between the free amino group of N-terminal amino acid and phenyl isothiocyanate (Edman's reagent) in presence of dilute alkali. The phenyl isothiocyanate derivative of peptide undergoes hydrolysis to give phenylthiohydantoin residue, which is then identified. This procedure can be repeated again to identify the next amino acid.

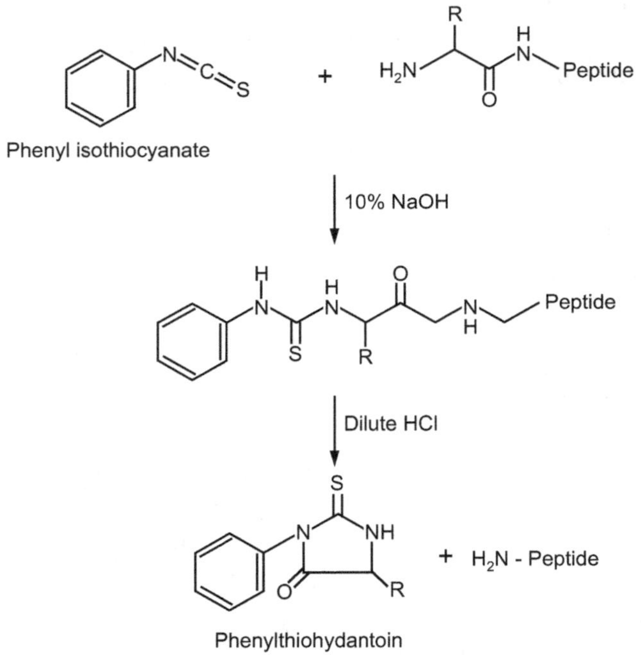

C-Terminal Analysis

1. Enzymatic method:

This method is useful for the identification, quantitative estimation and determination of the sequence of amino acid present in a protein. In this method the enzyme carboxypeptidase attacks proteins or peptides only at the end, which contains the free carboxyl group.

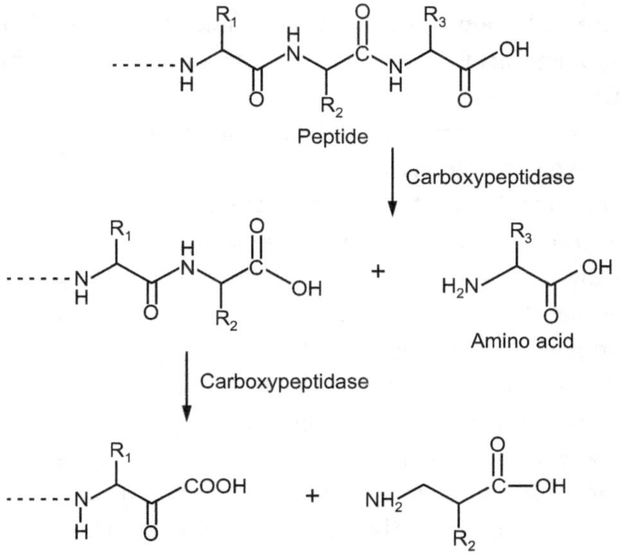

2. Hydrazinolysis:

In this method, the peptides are heated with anhydrous hydrazine at 100°C, which converts all of the amino acids, except C-terminal amino acids into acid hydrazides. The products are then separated by cation-exchange resin chromatography.

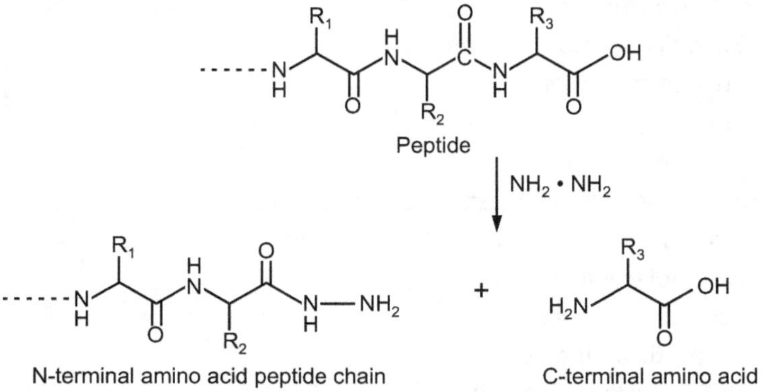

QUESTION BANK

1. What are amino acids? Discuss any three methods of syntheses of amino acids.
2. How will you synthesize the following amino acids?
   (i) Isoleucine
   (ii) Arginine
   (iii) Threonine

3. Discuss Strecker, Koop and Gabriel Phthalimide syntheses of amino acids.
4. What are amino acids? Give the synthesis of glycine by different methods of amino acids syntheses.
5. What are proteins? Discuss in brief about structure of proteins.
6. Define and explain *iso*-electric point of amino acids
7. Write a note on primary structure of proteins.
8. Draw the structures of the following peptides.
   (i) Gly- Gly
   (ii) Gly – Ala – Phe
9. Write a brief account on peptide linkage and its geometry.
10. Classify the amino acids according to 'R' group attached.
11. What are proteins? Discuss their importance.
12. Explain the synthesis alanine using Erlenmeyer azalactone method.
13. Why amino acids are called as amphoteric compounds?
14. What is the effect of pH on the structure of amino acids?
15. Enlist the natural amino acids.
16. Enlist some biologically important proteins and write their medicinal importance.
17. How will you prepare amino acids from halogen acids?
18. Write short notes on:
    (i) Biologically important peptides
    (ii) Protein structure
    (iii) Erlenmeyer Azalactone synthesis
    (iv) Peptide-linkage
19. Discuss simple chemical tests to detect amino acids.
20. Give structures (two from each):
    (i) Non-polar amino acids
    (ii) Polar amino acids
    (iii) Aromatic amino acids
    (iv) Heterocycle amino acids
21. Elaborate on the terminal residue analysis for the characterization of peptides.

■■■

Chapter 4 ...

POLYCYLIC COMPOUNDS

CONTENTS

Synthesis and reactions of:
- Naphthalene
- Phenanthrene
- Anthracene

NAPHTHALENE

Naphthalene is a bicyclic aromatic hydrocarbon in which two benzene rings are fused together at *o*-positions.

Source and Extraction:

(i) Naphthalene is obtained from coal tar and petroleum oil.

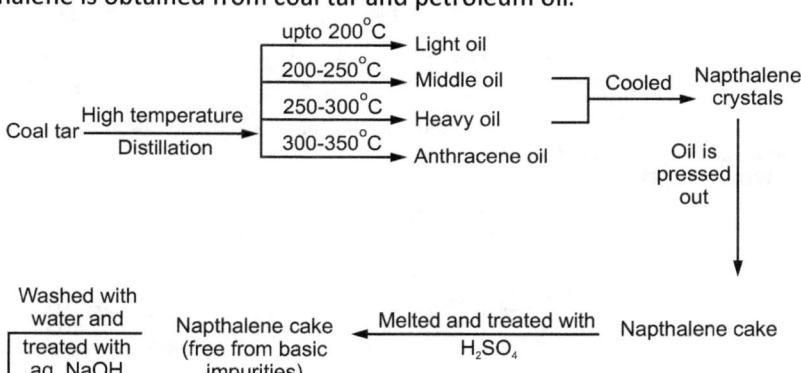

Structure:

Numbering and Resonating forms

Isomerism and nomenclature of naphthalene derivatives:

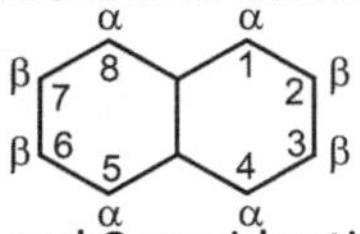

Positions 1, 4, 5 and 8 are identical (α-positions)
Positions 2, 3, 6 and 7 are identical (β-positions)

1. Naphthalene consists of two benzene ring fused at *o*-positions. It is proved by following observations:

On oxidation naphthalene gives phthalic acid. Thus, naphthalene contains benzene ring with two side chains in *o*-position.

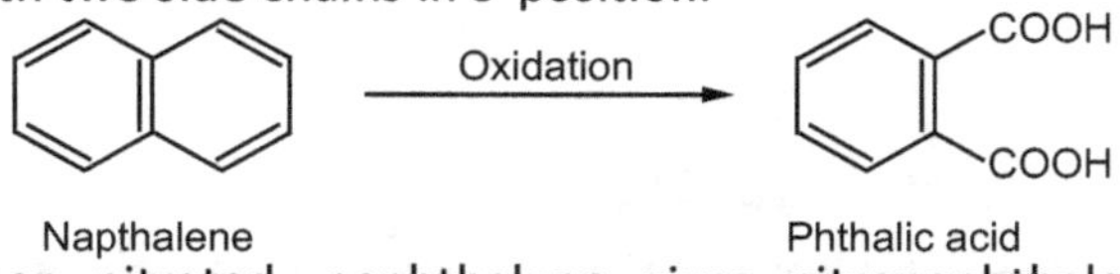

Napthalene → (Oxidation) → Phthalic acid

When nitrated, naphthalene gives nitronaphthalene which on oxidation yields *o*-nitrophthalic acid.

This indicates that the nitro group is in the benzene ring and that it is the side chain which is oxidised, through the oxidative cleavage of the adjacent ring.

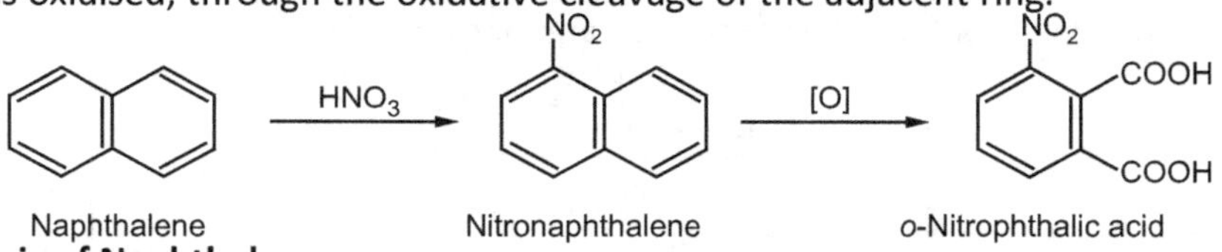

Naphthalene → (HNO₃) → Nitronaphthalene → [O] → *o*-Nitrophthalic acid

Synthesis of Naphthalene :

1. Haworth synthesis:

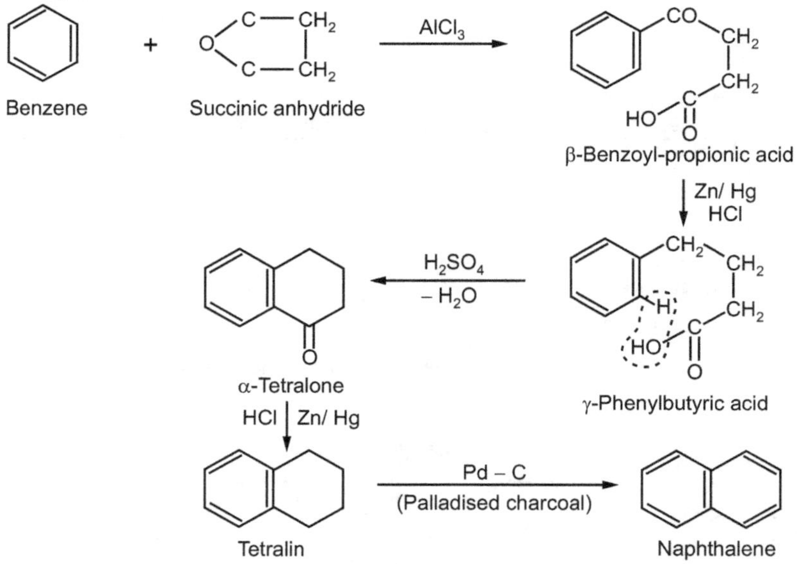

Benzene + Succinic anhydride → (AlCl₃) → β-Benzoyl-propionic acid → (Zn/Hg, HCl) → γ-Phenylbutyric acid → (H₂SO₄, –H₂O) → α-Tetralone → (HCl, Zn/Hg) → Tetralin → (Pd–C, Palladised charcoal) → Naphthalene

In the first step β-benzoylpropionic aicd is formed *via* Friedel-Crafts acylation by the reaction between benzene and succinic anhydride in presence of aluminium chloride. This upon Clemmensen reduction gives γ-phenylbutyric acid, which on heating with conc. H_2SO_4 gives α-tetralone by ring closure. α-Tetralone on Clemmensen reduction forms tetralin which on heating with selenium gives naphthalene.

2. From 4-Phenyl-2-butenoic acid:

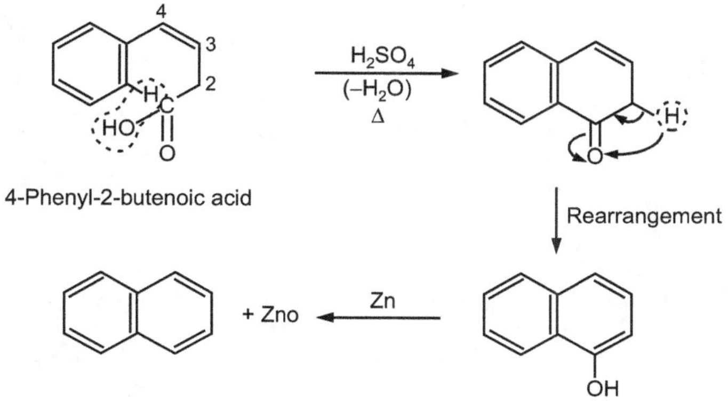

Naphthalene α-Naphthol

When 4-phenyl-2-butenoic acid is heated in presence of conc. H_2SO_4, α-naphthol is formed. This on distillation with zinc dust gives naphthalene.

3. From 4-Phenyl-1-butene:

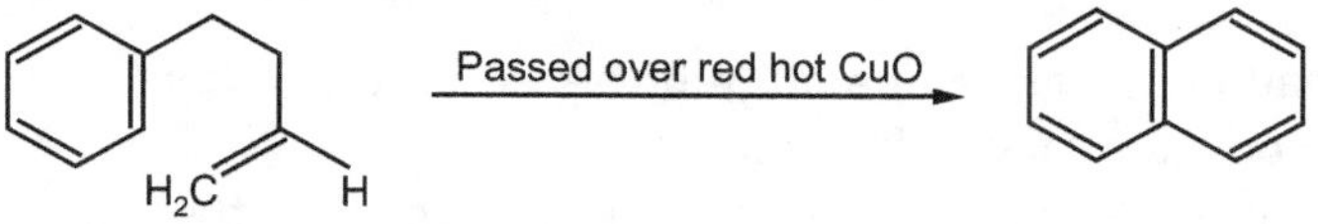

4-Phenyl-1-butene Naphthalene

When 4-phenyl-1-butene is passed over red hot cuprous oxide it cyclises to naphthalene.

Properties:

Naphthalene is less aromatic than benzene and therefore, it is more reactive than the latter. Thus, electrophilic substitution rections of naphthalene occur faster than that of benzene.

All the H atoms in benzene are equivalent and hence benzene forms only one monosubstituted derivative.

In naphthalene, however, α-H and β-H are not equivalent. The resonance hybrid of the σ-complex for the α-attack is found to be more stable than the resonance hybrid of the σ-complex for the β-attack.

Thus, we see that the resonance hybrid of the α-complex formed through the α-attack contains 7 resonating structures. While, that formed through the β-attack affords 6 such resonating structures.

Therefore, electrophilic substitution on naphthalene occurs mostly at α-position.

The reversible sulphonation at high temperature however, occurs at the β-position since, this gives a thermodynamically stable product.

(i) An activating group at 1-position directs an electrophile to the 4-position preferentially and to a lesser extent to the 2-position. If such a group is present at the position-2, it directs the electorphile to take up the position-1.

(ii) A deactivating group directs the attacking electrophile to take a position in the second ring (adjacent ring).

Chemical Reactions:
1. Oxidation:

Naphthalene undergoes oxidation:
- With CrO_3/CH_3COOH at 250°C → 1,4-Napthaquinone
- With $KMNO_4/H_2SO_4$ → Phthalic acid
- With V_2O_5/O_2 at 480°C → Phthalic anhydride

Naphthalene + $2 O_3$ → Napthalene diozonide $\xrightarrow{H_2O / Zn}$ Phthaladehyde

Similarly, naphthalene can also be oxidised to varying degress, by subtle use of reaction conditions and reagents, leading to 1, 4-naphthaquinone, phthalic acid and phthalic anhydride.

Ozonolysis of the naphthalene ring at two double bonds proceeds through the diozonide ultimately, leading to the dialdehyde, phthaldehyde.

2. Reduction:

Naphthalene undergoes reduction:
- With Na/EtOH at 78°C → 1,4-Dialine
- With Na/Isoamyl alcohol at 132°C → Tetraline
- With H_2/Pt or Ni → Decalin

Naphthalene can be reduced partially to completely to the corresponding dehydro, tetrahydro and decahydro derivatives under a variety of reaction conditions using appropriate reagents as depicted above.

3. Halogenation:

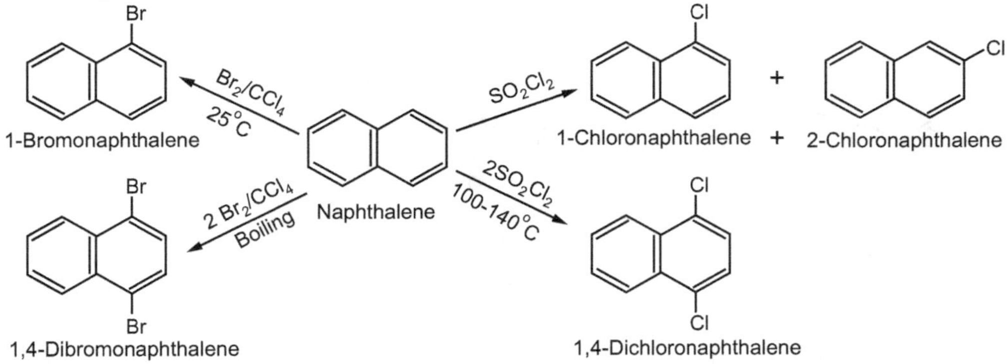

Chlorination of naphthalene using sulfuryl chloride leads to a product mixture of the 1-chloro and 2-chloronaphthalene, when the reagent is used in equimolar quantities. However, doubling the molar ratio of the chlorinating agent leads to 1,4-dichloro naphthalene. Similar, observations are observed in case of bromination. However, it is more specific and leads to only 1-bromo derivative under equimolar quantities.

4. Nitration:

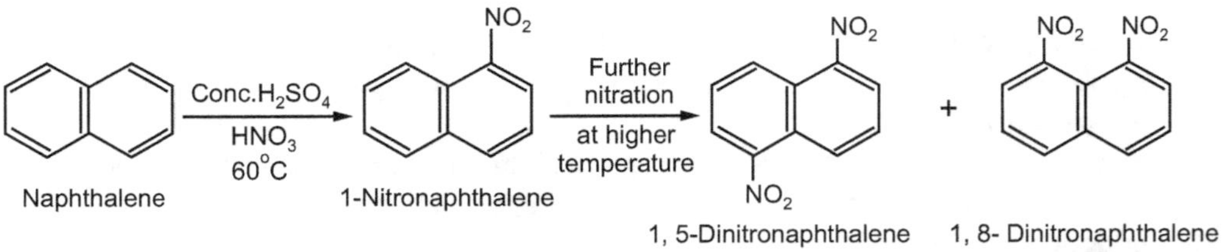

Naphthalene undergoes initial nitration at position 1. Further nitration of 1-nitronaphthalene leads to 1,5- and 1,8-dinitronaphthalene.

5. Sulphonation:

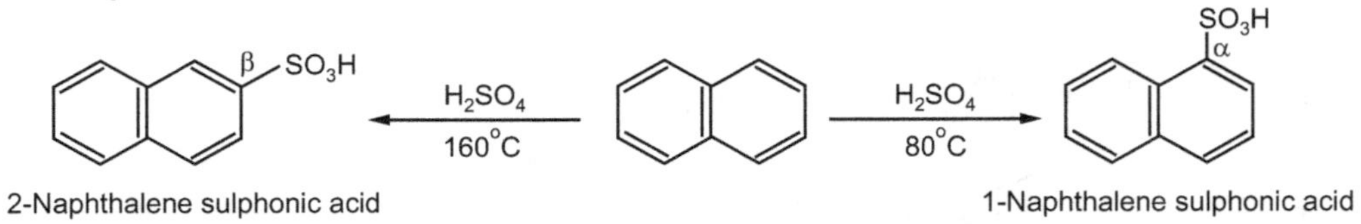

Naphthalene with sulfuric acid at lower temperature undergoes sulfonation at the postion-α. However, at higher temperature sulfonation occurs at β-positions.

6. Chloromethylation:

Naphthalene →(HCHO/HCl, CH₃COOH)→ 1-Chloromethyl naphthalene

Under classical formylating condition (HCHO-HCl in acetic acid), 1-chloromethyl naphthalene is obtained from naphthalene.

7. Friedel-Crafts acylation:

1-Acetylnaphthane ←(AlCl₃/CH₃COCl, C₆H₅NO₂)← Naphthalene →(AlCl₃/CH₃COCl, CS₂ or C₂H₂Cl₂)→ 1-Acetyl naphthalene

Proper selection use of solvent decides the product fate (nature) for the F.C. acetylation of naphthalene. Milder condition employed using low boiling solvents like CS$_2$ or DCM afford the expected α-acetyl derivative. Use of higher boiling solvents like nitrobenzene affords the β-acetylnaphthalene.

8. Friedel-Crafts (F.C.) Alkylation:

Naphthalene →(MeI, AlCl₃)→ 1-Methylnaphthalene + 2-Methylnaphthalene

Naphthalene →(Et-Br, AlCl₃)→ 2-Ethylnaphthalene

While, F.C. methylation of naphthalene leads to the product mixture of the α- and β-methyl derivatives; the F.C. ethylation though slightly less yielding, offers only the β-ethylnaphthalene.

Preparation of Naphthalene derivatives:

1. α-Naphthylamine:

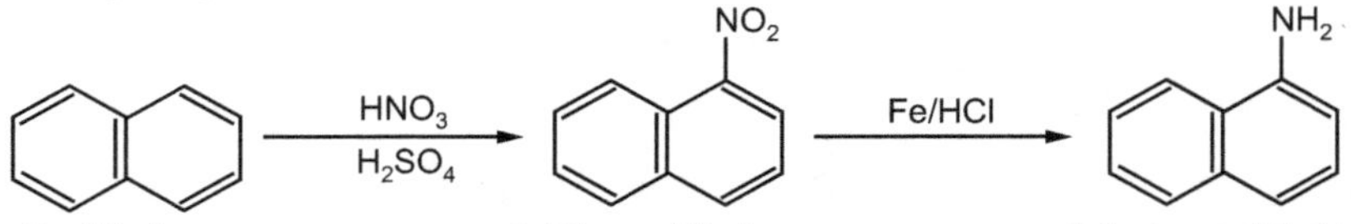

Naphthalene → (HNO$_3$/H$_2$SO$_4$) → 1-Nitronaphthalene → (Fe/HCl) → 1-Aminonaphthalene

1-Aminoinaphthalene can be obtained from naphthalene through the conventional two step nitration followed by reduction process.

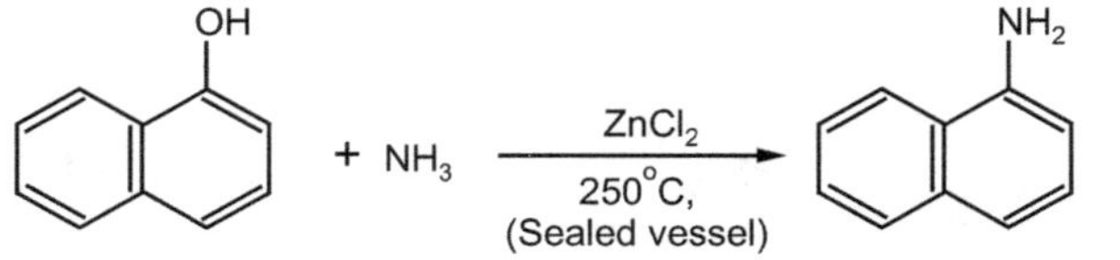

1-Naphthol + NH$_3$ → (ZnCl$_2$, 250°C, Sealed vessel) → 1-Aminonaphthalene

Alternatively, a single step process using α-naphthol and ammonia is sealed vessel using high temperature and ZnCl$_2$ catalyst, is more productive.

2. β-Naphthylamine

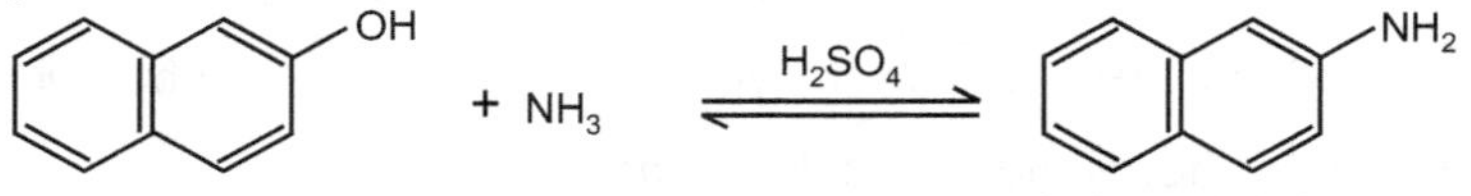

2-Naphthol + NH$_3$ ⇌ (H$_2$SO$_4$) → 2-Aminonaphthalene

β-Naphthol with ammonia under acidic catalysis affords the β-aminonaphthalene.

3. α-Naphthol:

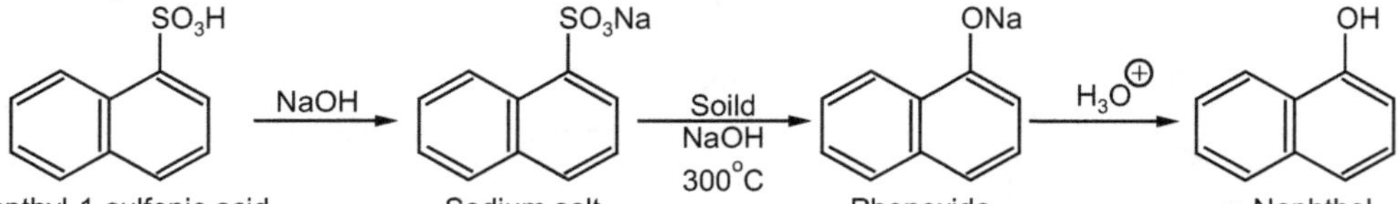

Napthyl-1-sulfonic acid → (NaOH) → Sodium salt → (Solid NaOH, 300°C) → Phenoxide → (H$_3$O$^+$) → α-Naphthol

The conventional use of naphthyl-1-sulfonic acid, its fusion with NaOH, followed by hydrolysis to α-napthol, follows the same route like benzene sulfonic acid to phenol.

4. β-Naphthol:

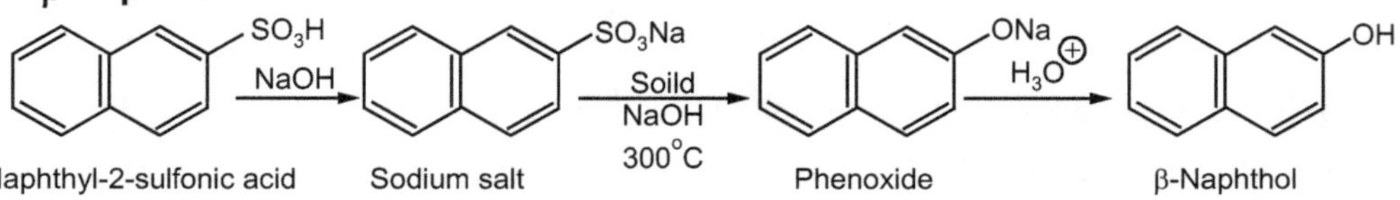

Naphthyl-2-sulfonic acid → (NaOH) → Sodium salt → (Solid NaOH, 300°C) → Phenoxide → (H$_3$O$^+$) → β-Naphthol

β-naphthol is also prepared similarly from naphthyl-2-sulfonic acid.

5. Naphthoic acids:

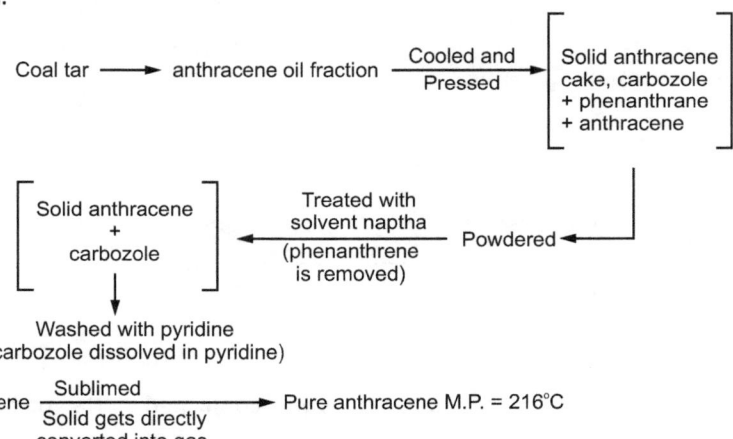

1-Acetylnapthalene → Naphthoic acid
(1. NaOH/I_2, 2. H_3O^+)

1- and 2-napthoic acids are obtained from the corresponding 1-acetyl and 2-acetyl-naphthalenes, through the oxidative action of sodium hypoiodide, followed by hydrolysis.

ANTHRACENE

Anthracene is obtained from the anthracene oil fraction of coal-tar and is purified by sublimation.

Coal tar → anthracene oil fraction —Cooled and Pressed→ [Solid anthracene cake, carbozole + phenanthrane + anthracene]

[Solid anthracene + carbozole] ←Treated with solvent naptha (phenanthrene is removed)— Powdered ←

↓

Washed with pyridine
(carbozole dissolved in pyridine)

Anthracene —Sublimed / Solid gets directly converted into gas without liquid stack→ Pure anthracene M.P. = 216°C

Anthracene is a tricyclic aromatic hydrocarbon in which three benzene rings are fused together in a linear manner. It undergoes substitution reactions *viz.,* halogenation, nitration and sulphonation.

Positions of double bonds in anthracene:

Resonance structures of Anthracene

Numbering of Positions:

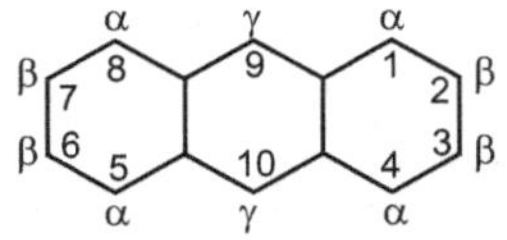

[Anthracene numbering diagram: positions 1,2,3,4,5,6,7,8,9,10 with α at 1,4,5,8; β at 2,3,6,7; γ at 9,10]

Synthesis:

1. Haworth Synthesis :

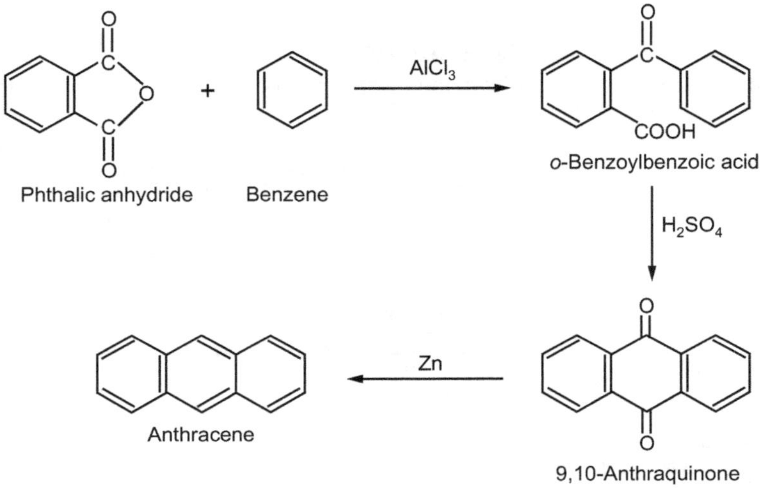

Phthalic anhydride + Benzene →(AlCl₃) o-Benzoylbenzoic acid →(H₂SO₄) 9,10-Anthraquinone →(Zn) Anthracene

Anthracene contains three benzene rings was confirmed by Haworth. In this method of synthesis, phthalic anhydride and benzene are reacted in presence of AlCl₃ to form o-benzoylbenzoic acid. This on heating with conc. H_2SO_4 dehydrates to 9, 10-anthraquinone, which on distillation with zinc dust gives anthracene.

2. Elbs reaction

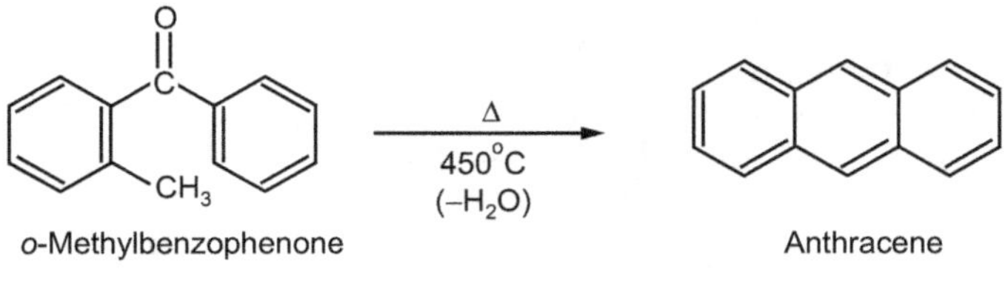

o-Methylbenzophenone →(Δ, 450°C, −H₂O) Anthracene

A polynuclear hydrocarbon is prepared by pyrolysis of diaryl ketone. This is called as **"Elbs reaction"**. o-Methylbenzophenone upon heating at 450°C loses a water molecule and forms anthracene.

3. Friedel-Craft's Reaction

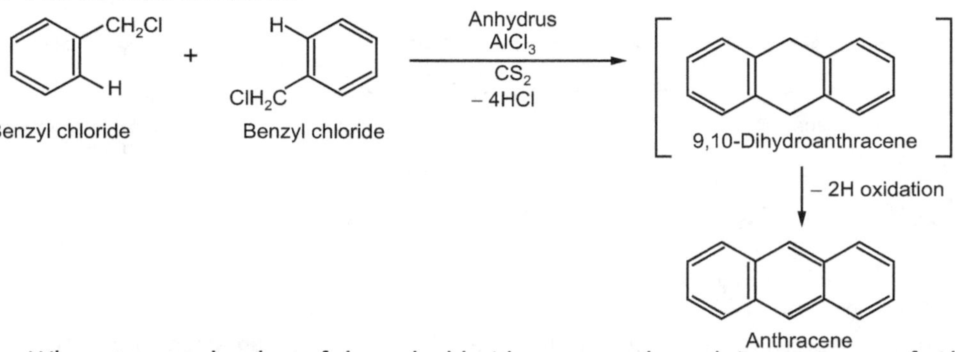

Benzyl chloride + Benzyl chloride → (Anhydrous AlCl₃, CS₂, –4HCl) → [9,10-Dihydroanthracene] → (–2H oxidation) → Anthracene

When two molecules of benzyl chloride are condensed in presence of $AlCl_3$, 9,10-dihydro-anthracene is formed, which on mild oxidation loses two hydrogen atoms to give anthracene.

4. From benzene and methylene dibromide

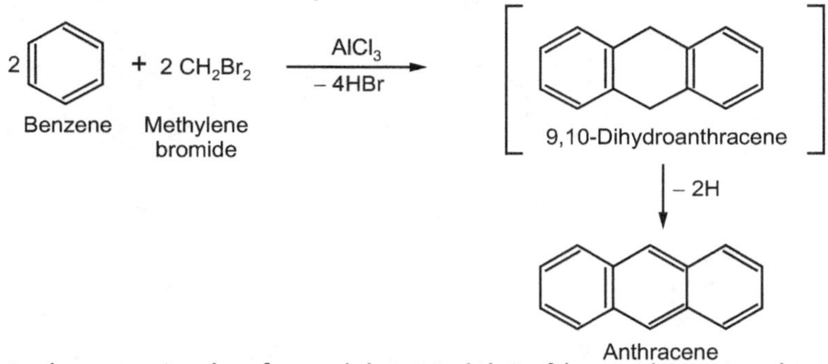

2 Benzene + 2 CH_2Br_2 (Methylene bromide) → ($AlCl_3$, –4HBr) → [9,10-Dihydroanthracene] → (–2H) → Anthracene

Anthracene is also formed by Friedel-Craft's condensation between 2 moles of benzene and 2 moles of methylene dibromide.

Chemical Reactions:

Antracene gives both electrophilic substitution and addition reactions equally well. These reactions occur at its 9 and 10 positions. Anthracene has resonance energy (28 kcal/mole per ring) which is lower than that of benzene ring (30 kcal/mole). Hence, it is less aromatic than benzene.

1. Oxidation:

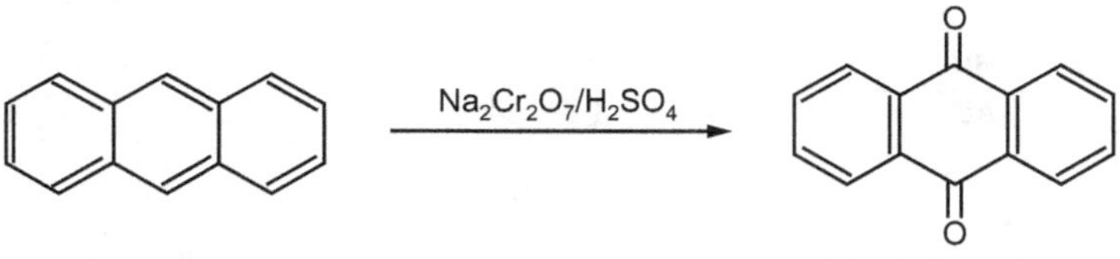

Anthracene → ($Na_2Cr_2O_7/H_2SO_4$) → 9,10-Anthraquinone

Anthracene yields 9,10-anthraquinone upon oxidation in presence of sodium dichromate and sulphuric acid.

2. Reduction:

Anthracene → (Ni/H₂, 225°C) → 1,2,3,4,5,6,7,8-octahydroanthracene → (Ni/H₂) → Completely reduced product

Anthracene → (Alcohol, Na-Hg) → 9,10-Dihydroanthracene

Anthracene can be reduced in presence of zinc amalgam to form 9,10-dihyroanthracene. Whereas if reduced in presence of Raney Ni at 225°C, it gives octahydroanthracene which can be further reduced to its fully saturated form.

3. Halogenation:

Anthracene → (Cl_2/CS_2 or SO_2Cl_2) → 9,10-dichloroanthracene → (NaOH, Δ, −HCl) → 9-chloroanthracene

Anthracene → (X_2/CCl_4 Reflux, X = Cl, Br) → Mono-haloanthracene + Dihaloanthracene

Anthracene monohalide and dihalide is formed by the reaction between anthracene with chlorine or bromine without any catalyst.

4. Nitration:

Anthracene → (HNO_3, Ac_2O, 15-20°C) → 9-Nitroanthracene + 9,10-Dinitroanthracene

Anthracene forms a mixture of 9-nitro and 9,10-dinitroanthracenes when treated with conc. HNO_3 and acetic anhydride.

5. Sulphonation:

Anthracene + H₂SO₄ in glacial acetic acid → Anthracene 1-sulphonic acid + Anthracene 2-sulphonic acid

Anthracene + Glacial acetic acid, Excess of conc. H₂SO₄ →
- (At low temperature) 1,8-Anthracene disulphonic acid
- (At high temperature) 2,7-Anthracene disulphonic acid

Anthracene undergoes sulphonation at high temperatures to form anthracene 2-sulphonic acid. Where as, at low temperatures it yields anthracene 1-sulphonic acid.

6. Formylation (Vilsmeier-Haack method):

Anthracene + PhN(Me)CHO (Methyl phenyl formamide) —POCl₃→ Anthracene 9-aldehyde + N-Methylaniline

7. Diels-Alder Reaction:

Anthracene + Maleic anhydride —Δ→ 9,10-Anthracene maleic anhydride

Anthracene + benzene —Δ→ (C₆H₄ bridged adduct)

Anthracene undergoes the Diels-Alder reaction in the 9, 10-positions to form endo-anthracene maleic anhydride.

Synthesis of Anthracene Derivatives:

1. Alizarin (1, 2-dihydroxyanthraquinone)

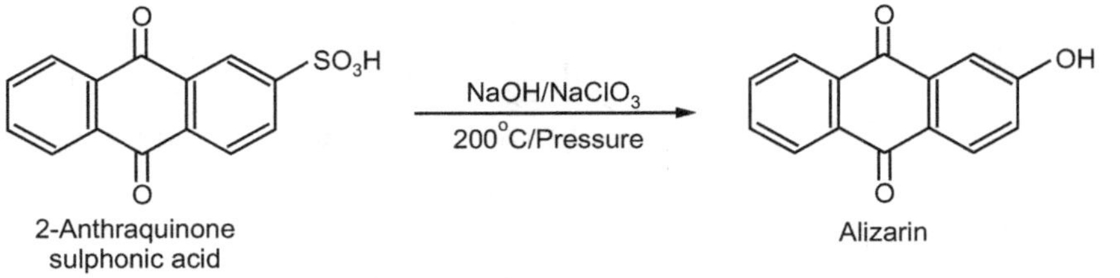

2-Anthraquinone sulphonic acid → (NaOH/NaClO₃, 200°C/Pressure) → Alizarin

When 2-anthraquinone sulphonic acid is fused with sodium hydroxide and sodium chlorate (NaClO₃) at 200°C under pressure, forms alizarin. Alizarin was once used as dye of splendid red colour.

2. 2-Aminoanthraquinone:

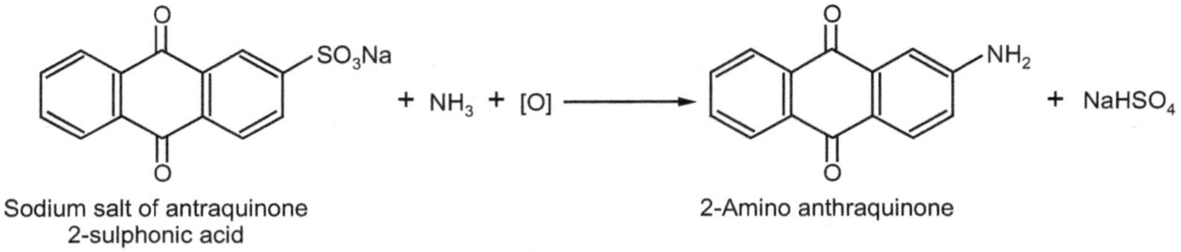

Sodium salt of antraquinone 2-sulphonic acid + NH₃ + [O] → 2-Amino anthraquinone + NaHSO₄

It is an intermediate in the preparation of indathrene dyes.

3. 1 and 2-Hydroxyanthracenes (Anthrols):

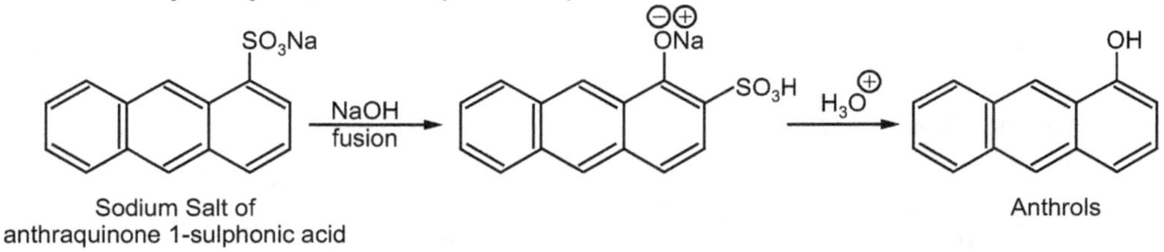

Sodium Salt of anthraquinone 1-sulphonic acid → (NaOH fusion) → intermediate → (H₃O⁺) → Anthrols

1- and 2-Hydroxyanthracenes are known as anthrols. 1- Anthrol is yellow solid where as, 2-anthrol is brownish solid.

4. 9-Hyroxyanthracene (Anthranol)

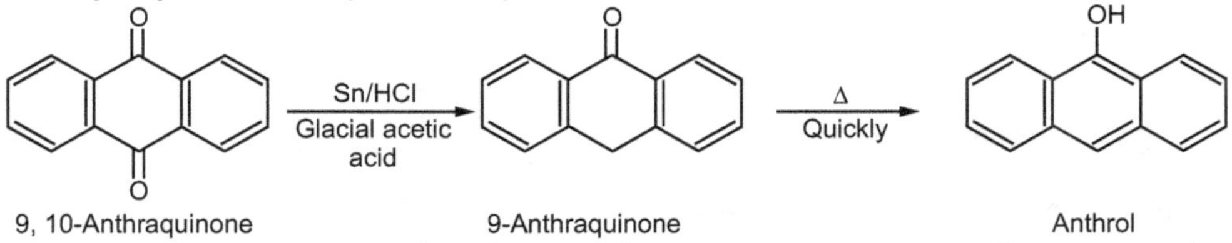

9, 10-Anthraquinone → (Sn/HCl, Glacial acetic acid) → 9-Anthraquinone → (Δ, Quickly) → Anthrol

9, 10-Anthraquinone is reduced to 9-anthraquinone in presence of tin as a catalyst, which quickly converts into anthrol upon heating.

5. 9, 10-Dihydroxyanthracene (Anthraquinol)

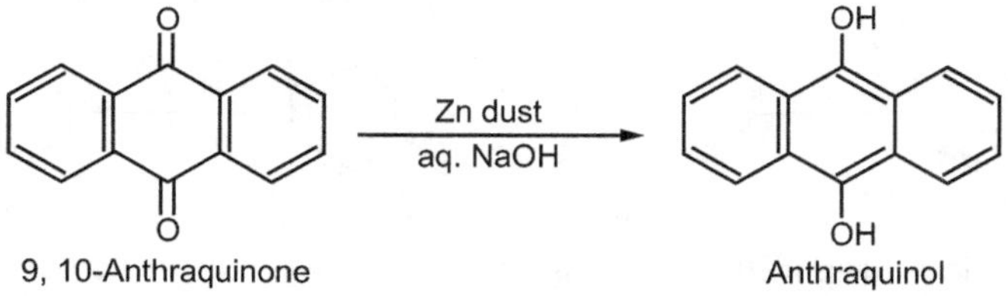

9, 10-Anthraquinone →(Zn dust, aq. NaOH)→ Anthraquinol

Reduction of anthraquinone with zinc dust and aqueous NaOH gives anthracene 9, 10-diol or anthraquinol.

6. 1 and 2-Anthroic acids

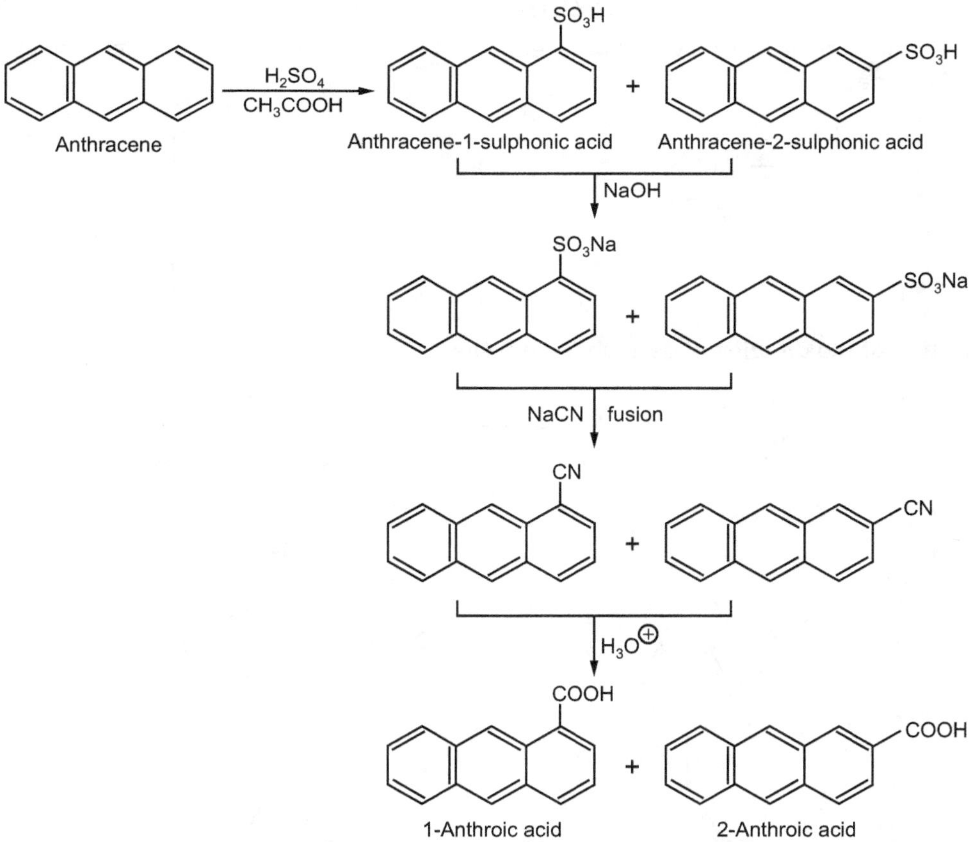

Anthracene →(H_2SO_4, CH_3COOH)→ Anthracene-1-sulphonic acid + Anthracene-2-sulphonic acid

↓ NaOH

Sodium anthracene-1-sulphonate + Sodium anthracene-2-sulphonate

↓ NaCN fusion

1-Cyanoanthracene + 2-Cyanoanthracene

↓ H_3O^+

1-Anthroic acid + 2-Anthroic acid

1 and 2-Anthroic acids are prepared by the hydrolysis of corresponding cyanides (prepared by the fusion of sodium sulphonates with sodium cyanide).

7. 9-Anthroic acid *via* 9-carbonyl chloride

Anthracene → (COCl, 160°C, Δ) → Anthracene-9-acid chloride → (H_3O^+) → 9-Anthroic acid

9-Anthroic acid is prepared by heating anthracene with oxyalyl chloride at 160°C.

It is structurally related to certain alkaloids *e.g.*, morphine, steroids, *e.g.*, cholesterol.

It occurs in the anthracene oil fraction of coal-tar. It is separated from anthracene by means of solution in solvent naptha.

PHENANTHRENE

Phenanthrene is a tricyclic non-linear fused ring system and an angular isomer of anthracene.

Position of the double bonds in phenanthrene:

Synthesis:

1. Haworth Synthesis:

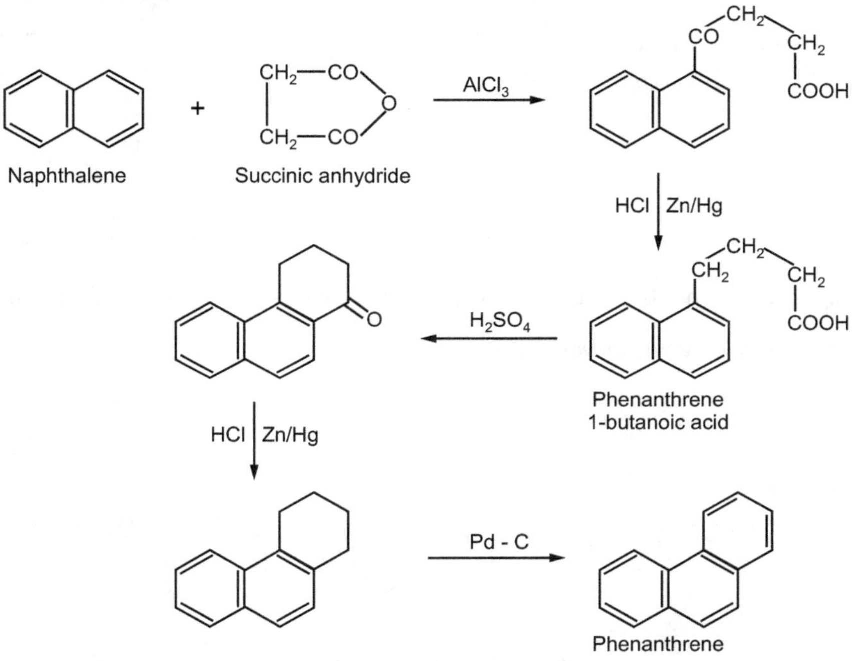

Naphthalene + Succinic anhydride →(AlCl₃) [aroyl-propionic acid] →(HCl, Zn/Hg) Phenanthrene 1-butanoic acid →(H₂SO₄) [tricyclic ketone] →(HCl, Zn/Hg) [tetrahydrophenanthrene] →(Pd-C) Phenanthrene

Naphthalene when condensed with succinic anhydride in presence of AlCl₃ yields, the ketonic acid. This acid is reduced under Clemmensen conditions. The ring closure takes place in presence of conc. H_2SO_4. Finally, reduction followed by aromatisation gives phenanthrene.

2. Bardhan-Sengupta Synthesis:

Step 1: Synthesis of 1-bromo-2-phenylethane

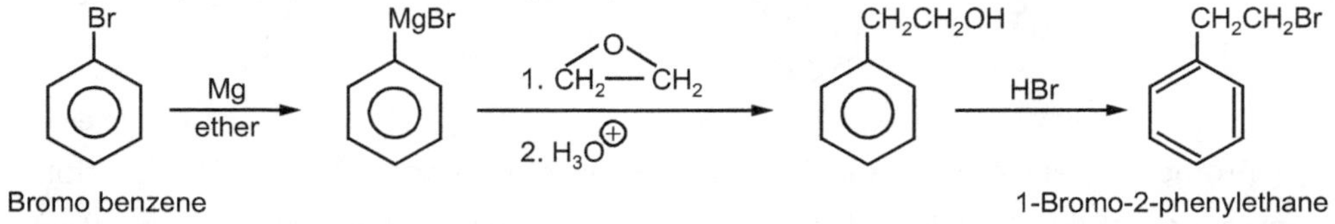

Bromo benzene →(Mg, ether) PhMgBr →(1. ethylene oxide; 2. H_3O^+) PhCH₂CH₂OH →(HBr) 1-Bromo-2-phenylethane

1-Bromo-2-phenylethane is prepared from bromobenzene by reaching it with magnesium in ether, ethylene oxide and hydrogen bromide.

Step 2: Synthesis of 2-carbethoxycyclohexanone.

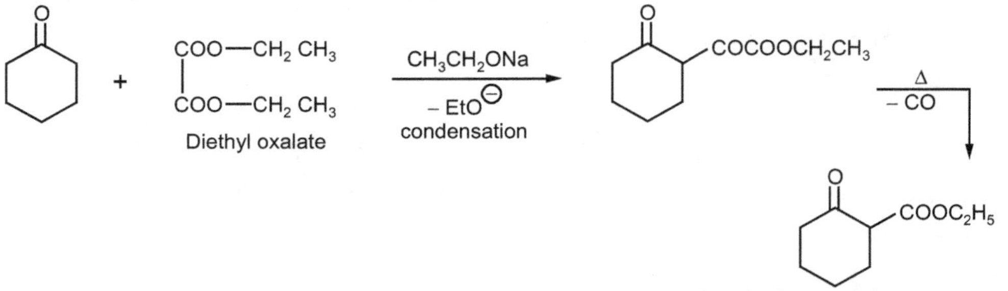

2-carbethoxycyclohexanone

When cyclohexanone is condensed with diethyl oxalate in presence of sodium ethoxide it gives 2-carbethoxycyclohexanone.

Step 3:

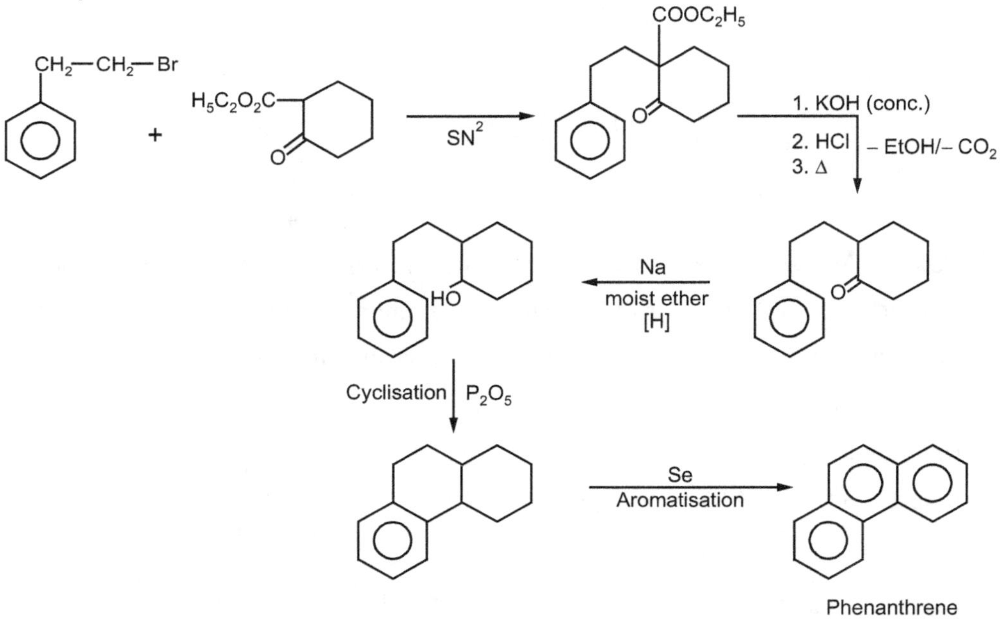

Phenanthrene

1-Bromo-2-phenylethane and 2-carbethoxycyclohexanone undergo SN^2 reaction in presence of KOH, followed by reduction and further dehydrative cyclisation in presence of P_2O_5. The cyclised intermediate on heating with selenium aramatizes to phenanthrene.

3. Bogert - Cook Synthesis:

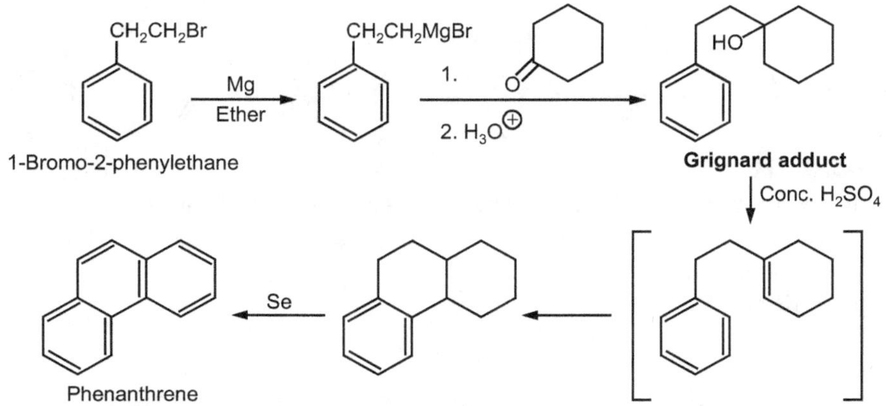

1-Bromo-2-phenylethane is reacted with magnesium in ether followed by cyclohexanone and hydrolysis undergoes ring closure. The intermediate formed undergoes aromatisation, yields phenanthrene.

Chemical Reactions:

1. Oxidation:

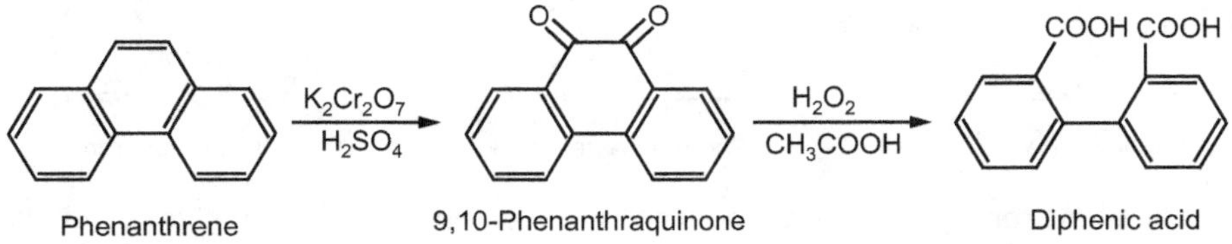

Phenanthrene undergoes oxidation with potassium dichromate and H_2SO_4, to form 9, 10-phenanthraquinone. Further oxidation of it with H_2O_2 under acidic conditions yields the diphenic acid.

2. Reduction:

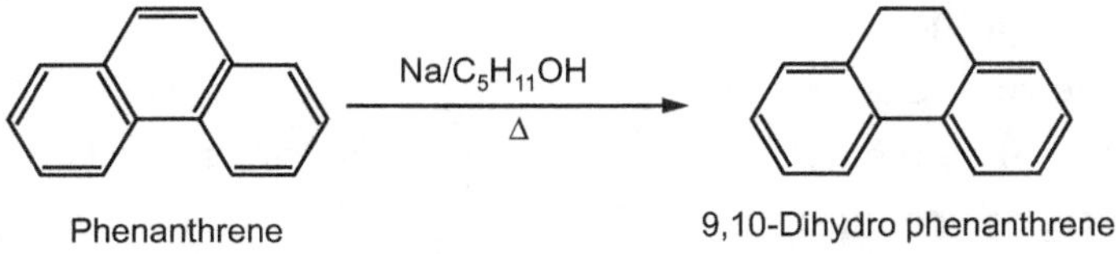

Phenanthrene undergoes reduction in presence of sodium in *iso*-pentanol to form 9, 10-dihydro phenanthrene.

3. Halogenation:

Phenanthrene →(Cl₂ / CCl₄)→ 9,10-Dichloro phenanthrene →(Δ, –HCl)→ 9-Chloro phenanthrene

Reaction with Cl_2 in CCl_4 and phenanthrene yields 9,10-dichloro-phenanthrene at room temperature. This upon heating loses of molecule of HCl to give 9-chlorophenanthrene.

4. Nitration:

Phenanthrene →(Conc. HNO_3 / Conc. H_2SO_4)→ 9-Nitrophenanthrene

Phenanthrene when reacted with conc. nitric acid and sulphuric acid gives 9-nitrophenathrene.

5. Sulphonation:

Phenanthrene →(Conc. H_2SO_4)→ 2-Phenanthrene phonic acid + 3-Phenanthrene sulphonic acid

Phenanthrene reacts with concentrated sulphuric acid to give a mixture of 2-phenanthrene sulphuric acid and 3-phenanthrenesulphonic acid.

QUESTION BANK

1. Write the structural formulae and numbering for the following:
   (a) Naphthalene
   (b) Anthracene
   (c) Phenanthrene

2. Give any three methods of syntheses and chemical reactions for the following polycyclic compounds:
   (i) Napthalene
   (ii) Phenanthrene
   (iii) Anthracene

3. How is naphthalene commercially obtained?
4. What happens when,
   (a) Naphthalene is treated with concentrated sulphuric acid at 165°C.
   (b) Naphthalene is warmed with concentrated nitric acid in the presence of sulphuric acid.
   (c) Naphthalene is heated with oxygen in the presence of vanadium pentoxide.
5. How will you syntheses the following compounds from naphthalene?
   (a) α-Naphthalenesulphonic acid
   (b) β-Naphthalenesulphonic acid
   (c) β-Acetyl naphthalene
   (d) Phthalic anhydride
   (e) α-Naphthol
   (f) β-Naphthol
   (g) α-Naphthoic acid
6. Write the resonance structures for anthracene.
7. How is anthracene isolated from coal-tar?
8. How is anthracene synthesized?
9. What happens when anthracene is treated with,
   (a) Bromine in CCl_4
   (b) Nitric acid and acetic acid
   (c) Sodium and ethyl alcohol
   (d) Sodium dichromate and sulphuric acid
   (e) Oxidation in the presence of V_2O_5 at 500°C
10. How will you syntheses anthracene from benzene?
11. How will you syntheses anthraquinone from naphthalene?
12. How will you syntheses alizarin from benzene?
13. What will happen when,
    (a) Phenanthrene is treated with $K_2Cr_2O_7$.
    (b) Anthracene is treated with nitric acid in acetic anhydride at 15 to 20°C.

14. Write a note on:
    (a) Nitration of napthalene
    (b) Bardhan Sengupta synthesis
    (c) Haworth synthesis of napthalene
    (d) Reactions of naphthalene
15. Discuss structure of phenanthrene.
16. Describe Haworth's method of synthesis of phenanthrene.
17. How will you prepare the following:
    (a) Diphenic acid
    (b) 9, 10-Dihydrophenanthrene
    (c) 9-Chlorophenanthrene
    (d) 9-Nitrophenanthrene
    (e) 2 and 3-Phenanthrene sulphonic acids.

■■■

Chapter 5 ...

HETEROCYCLIC CHEMISTRY

CONTENTS
- Structures, Numbering and Corresponding Drugs of the following Heterocyclic Compounds: Furan, Thiophene, Pyrrole, Pyrazole, Thiazole, Imidazole, Oxazole, Isoxazole, Hydantoin, Pyridine, Pyridazine, Pyrimidine, Indole, Benzfuran, Benzthiazole, Benzimidazole, Benzoxazole, Quinoline, Isoquinoline, Quinazoline, Cinnoline, Purine, Xanthine, Pteridine and Coumarin.
- Synthesis and Reaction of the following compounds: Furan, Pyrrole, Indole, Imidazole, Pyridine and Quinoline.

Introduction:
Heterocyclic compounds are cyclic compounds which contain atoms other than carbon and hydrogen in the ring. The common heteroatoms are oxygen, nitrogen and sulphur. The chemistry which deals with the preparation, reactions and structures of such compounds is called as *"heterocyclic chemistry"* and constitutes about 60% of organic chemistry literature.

Heterocyclic chemistry is important from the points of view of pharmaceuticals, agrochemicals, insecticides, polymers, dyes etc. Many of the drugs, as well as, biologically important molecules like, hemoglobin, vitamins, alkaloids, nucleic acids (DNA, RNA), chlorophyll, as well as, caffeine in tea-coffee, are heterocyclic compounds.

NOMENCLATURE OF HETEROCYCLIC COMPOUNDS

There are two main systems of nomenclature for heterocyclic compounds:
1. Systematic nomenclature system – (The Hansch - Wildman system)
2. Trivial nomenclature system.

1. The Systematic Nomenclature System (Hansch-Wildman nomenclature system)

It is the most common systematic method of nomenclature which specifies;
- Ring size
- Nature/Type
- Positions of hetero atoms.

Rules

(a) Combination of prefix with stem
  (i) **Prefix** indicates the heteroatom. It is derived from the heteroatom(s) present in the heterocyclic compound under consideration.
   - Oxygen (O) - *Oxa*
   - Nitrogen (N) - *Aza*
   - Sulfur (S) - *Thia*
   - Phosphorous (P) - *Phospha*
   - Boron (B) - *Bora*

   e.g., Oxazole and Thiazole.

(ii) If heteroatom present twice, thrice or four times etc.., then prefix becomes **di-, tri, tetra-, penta-** etc. **e.g.,** Diazole, Diazine, Triazole, Tetrazole and Pentazole.

(iii) Preference for prefix is to be given in order O > S > N > P > Si
e.g., Oxazole, Thiazole, Oxathiole.

(b) Stem indicates ring size and whether it is saturated or unsaturated.

(i) **Suffix used for nitrogen containing heterocyclic compounds**

Ring size	Unsaturated	Saturated
3 member	-irine	-iridine
4 member	-ete	-etidine
5 member	-ole	-olidine
6 member	-ine	-inane
7 member	-epine	-epane
8 member	-ocine	-ocane
9 member	-onine	-onane
10 member	-ecine	-ecane

(ii) **Suffix used for non-nitrogen containing heterocyclic compounds**

Ring size	Unsaturated	Saturated
3 member	-irene	-irane
4 member	-ete	-etane
5 member	-ole	-olane
6 member	-ine	-ane
7 member	-epine	-epane
8 member	-ocine	-ocane
9 member	-onine	-onane
10 member	-ecine	-ecane

(c) State of Hydrogenation also to be indicated by prefix, dihydro, tetrahydro etc. and also number of atoms which are reduced or position that is reduced should be indicated. e.g., 2H, 3H, 4H etc.

(d) Numbering:

(i) The numbering is always started from the heteroatom and again in same preference:

O > S > N > P > Si

(ii) If more than one heteroatom is present, then both heteroatoms should get minimum numbers in same preference order.

2. Trivial Nomenclature System.
(a) Monocyclic heterocyclic compounds:
(i) 3-Member with 1-heteroatom

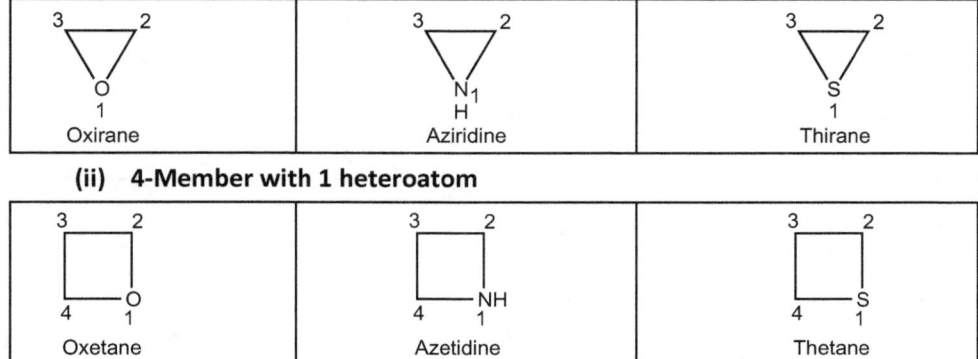

(ii) 4-Member with 1 heteroatom

(iii) 5-Member 1 heteroatom

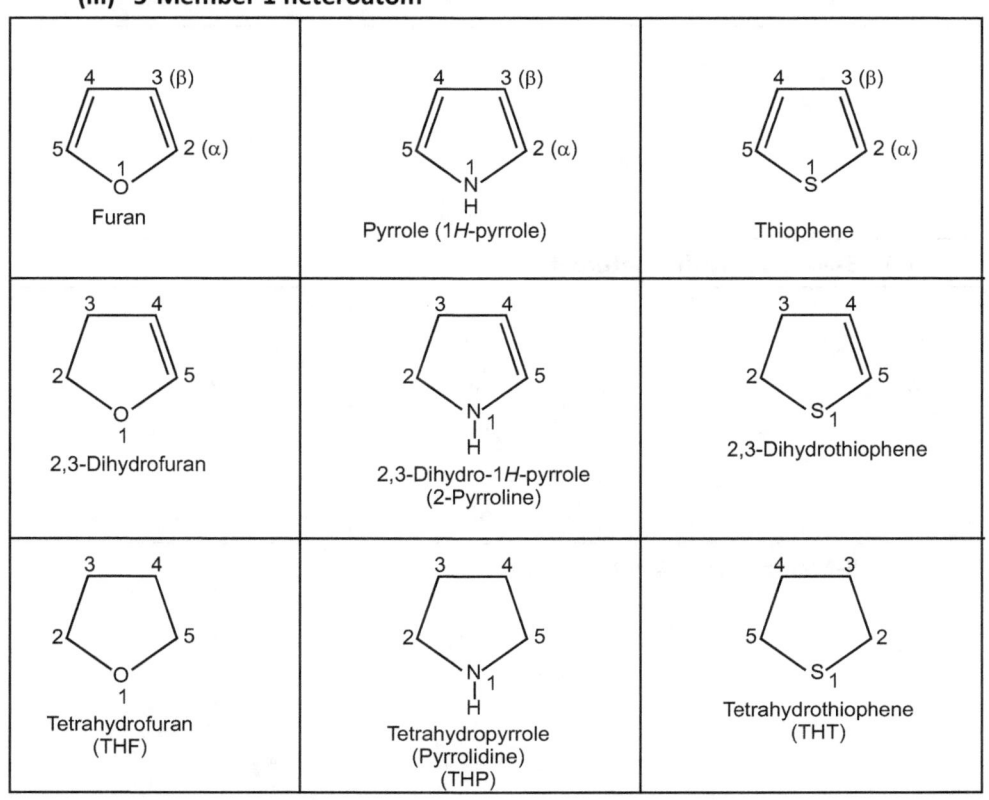

(iv) 5-Member with 2 heteroatoms

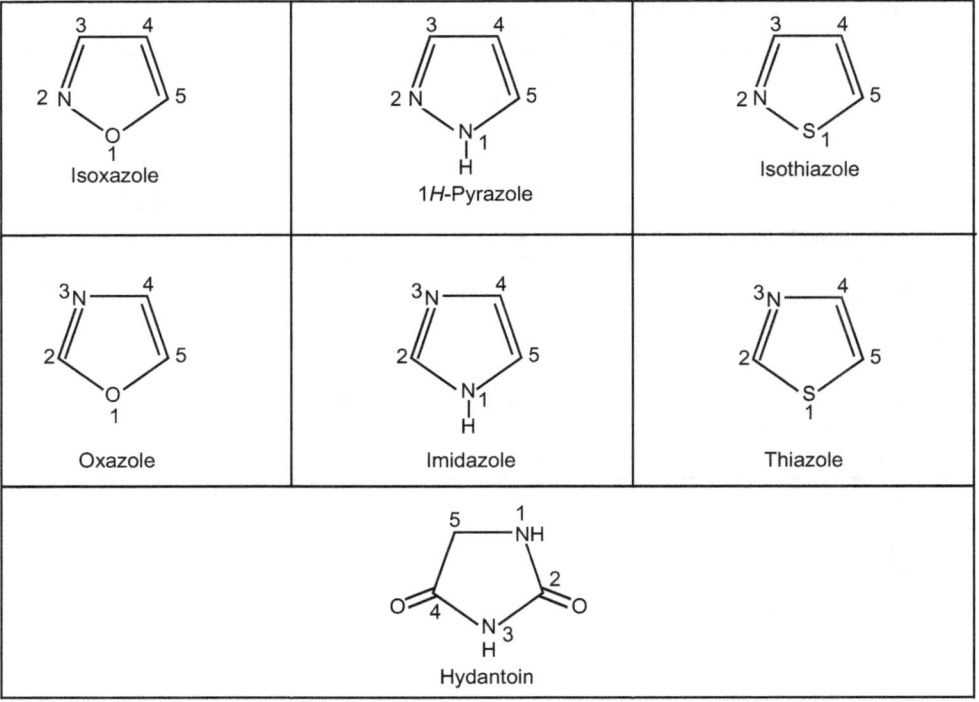

(v) 5-Member with 3 heteroatoms

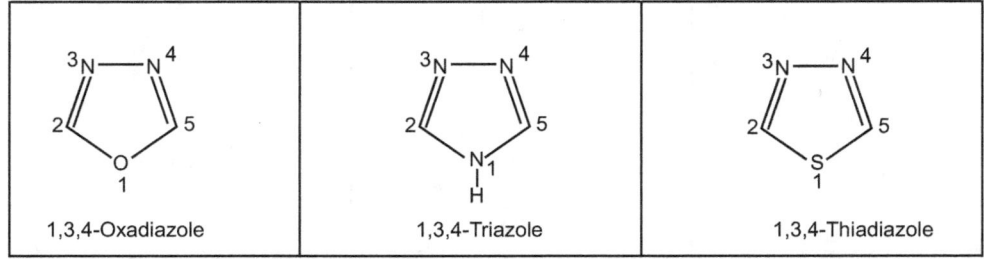

(vi) 5-Member with 4 heteroatoms

1H-Tetrazole

(vii) 6-Member with 1 heteroatom

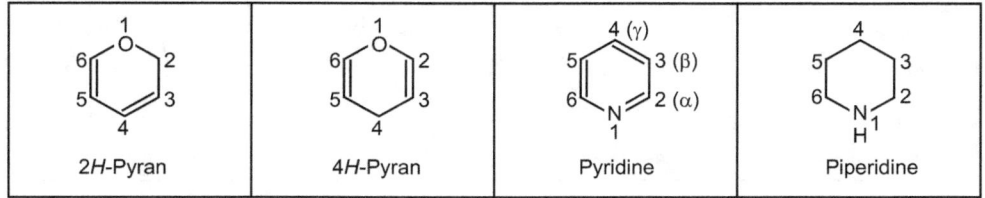

| 2H-Pyran | 4H-Pyran | Pyridine | Piperidine |

(viii) 6-Member with 2 heteroatoms

| Pyridazine | Pyrimidine | Pyrazine | Piperazine |
| 1H-Thiazine | Morpholine | 1,4-Oxazine | 1,4-Dioxane |

(ix) 6-Member with 3 heteroatoms

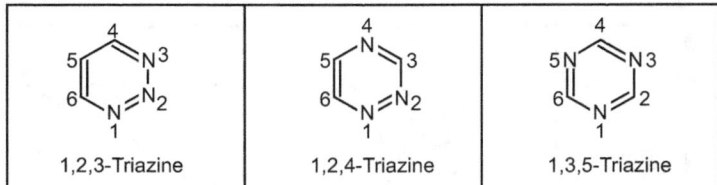

| 1,2,3-Triazine | 1,2,4-Triazine | 1,3,5-Triazine |

(x) 6-Member with 4 heteroatoms

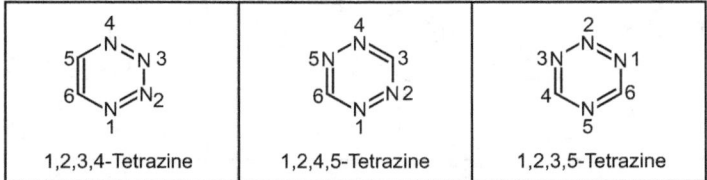

| 1,2,3,4-Tetrazine | 1,2,4,5-Tetrazine | 1,2,3,5-Tetrazine |

(xi) 7-Member with 1 or 2 heteroatoms

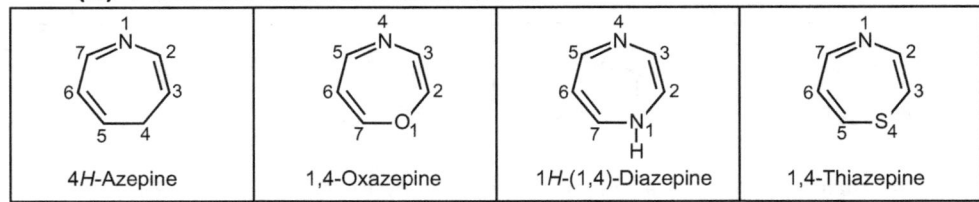

| 4H-Azepine | 1,4-Oxazepine | 1H-(1,4)-Diazepine | 1,4-Thiazepine |

(b) Fused heterocyclic compounds

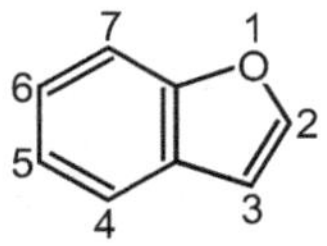 Benzfuran	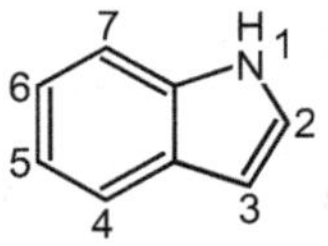 Indole	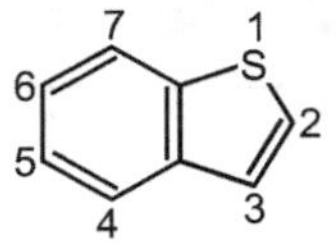 Benzothiophene
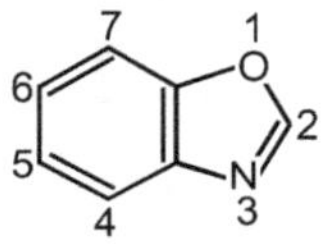 Benzoxazole	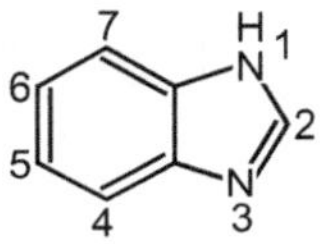 Benzimidazole	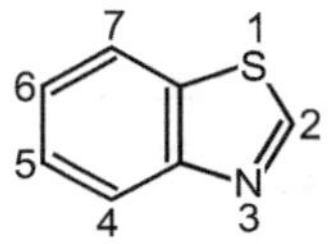 Benzthiazole
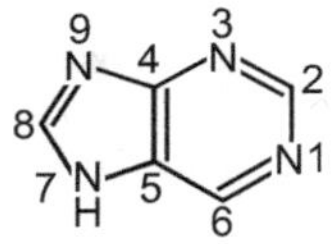 Purine	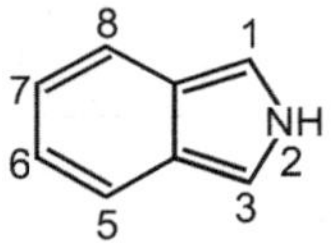 Isoindole	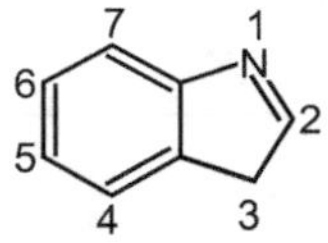 3H-Indole
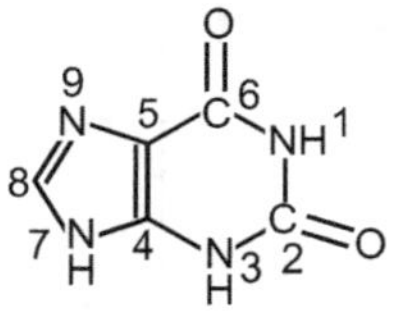 Xanthine	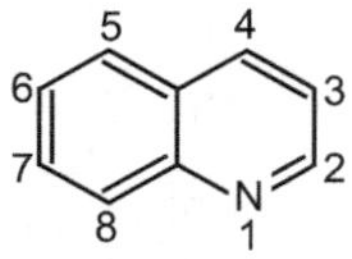 Quinoline	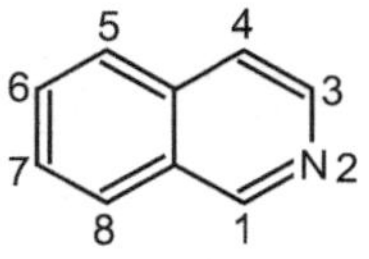 Isoquinoline
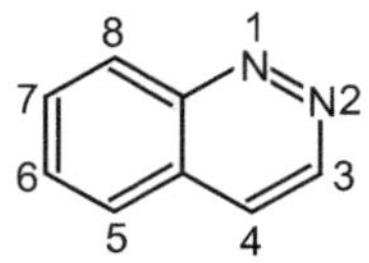 Cinnoline	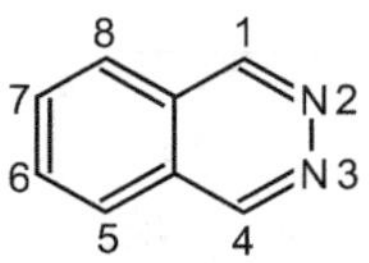 Phthalazine	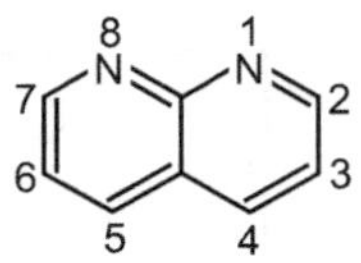 1,8-Naphthyridine

4H-Quinolizine	Pteridine (Pyrimidine + Pyrazine)	2H-Chromene
Coumarine	β-Carboline	4H-Carbazole
9H-Carbazole	Naphtho (2,3-b) thiophene	Xanthene
Phenoxazine	Phenothiazine	Phenazine

CORRESPONDING DRUGS OF HETEROCYCLIC COMPOUNDS

1. **Furan:**

   It is a potentially bioactive heterocycle and there are numerous examples of drugs having furan nucleus in their structure exhibiting a wide range of biological activities, like diuretic, vitamins, anti-protozoal, anti-bacterial, anti-amoebic, anti-ulcer, NSAID etc.

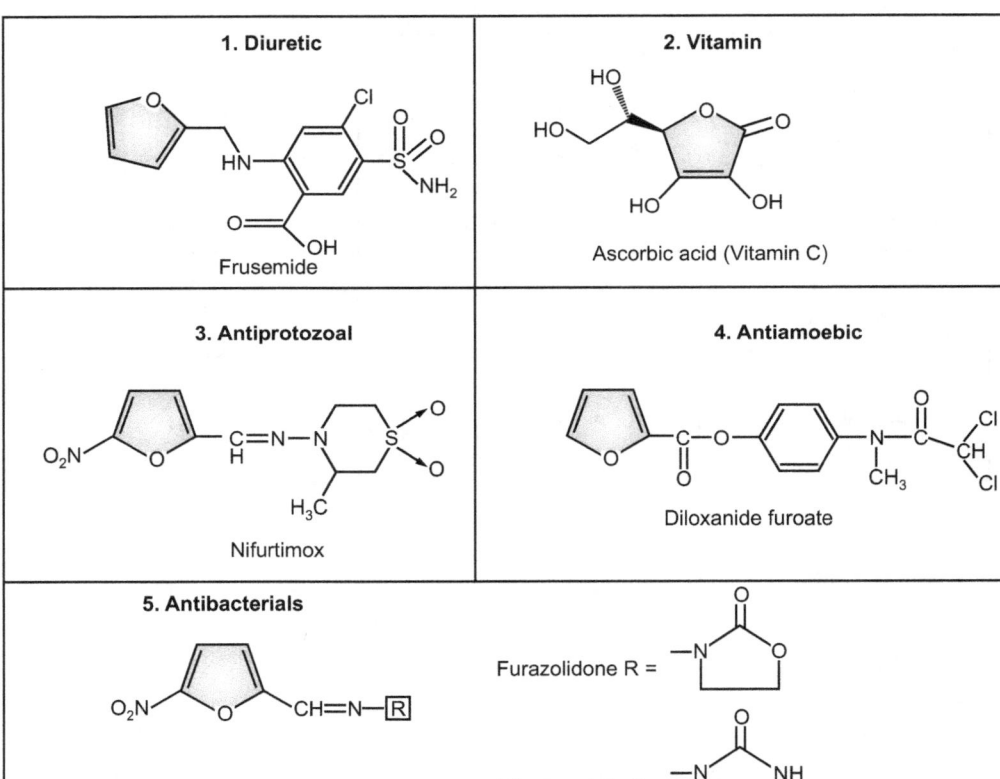

2. Thiophene:

Pharmaceutical chemist is interested in thiophene derivatives because of the concept of bioisosterism. Aromaticity of thiophene with its six π-electrons is electronically and sterically similar to benzene (as well as furan and pyrrole). As a result of this, of this thiophene analogues of biologically active benzene derivatives may well exhibit similar activities.

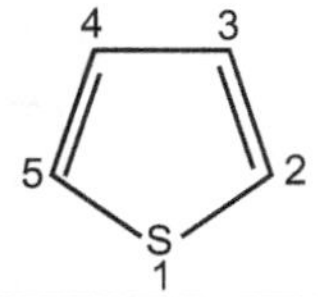

1. Antihistaminic
Methapyrilene

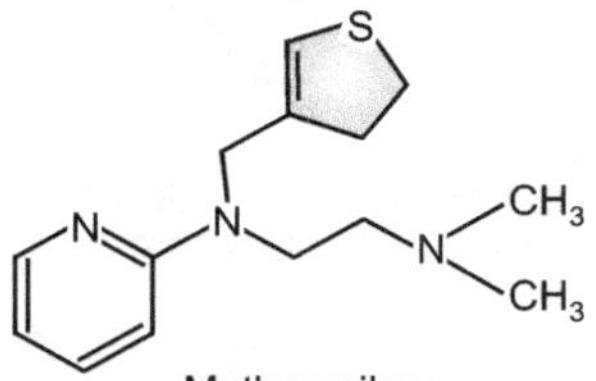

2. NSAID
Surofen

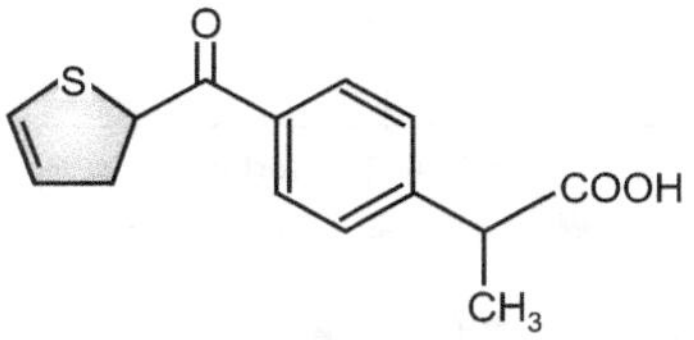

3. Antibiotics
Ticarcilline

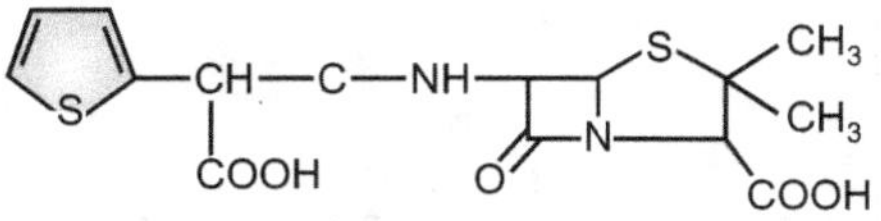

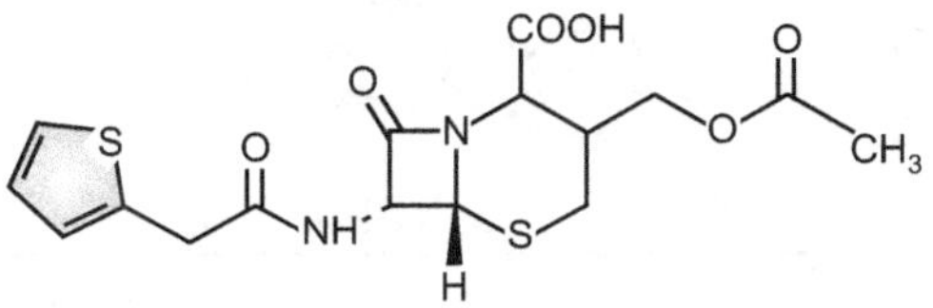

Cefalothin

4. Antineoplasic
Ralfitrexed

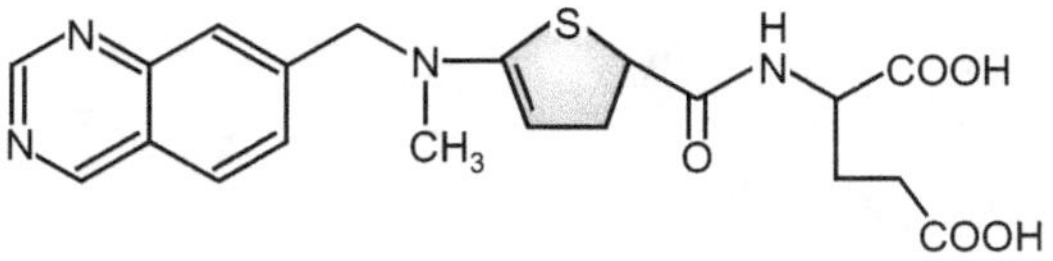

5. Antidepressant
Duloxetine

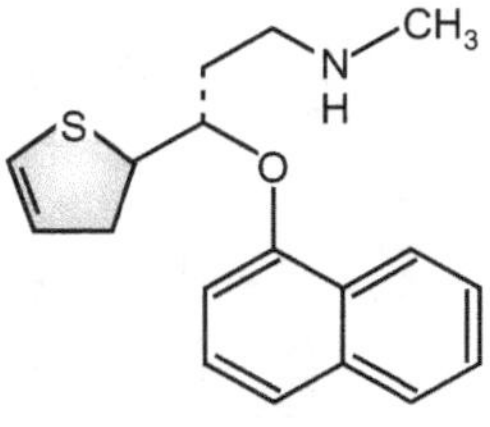

3. Pyrrole:

Pyrroles are found in a variety of biological contexts, as parts of vitamin cofactors and natural products. Common naturally produced molecules containing pyrrole include vitamin B_{12}, bile pigments like **bilirubin** and **biliverdin**, **porphyrins** of heme, **chlorophyll** and porphyrinogens. Pyrroles are also found in several drugs, including **atorvastatin, ketorolac** and **sunitinib**.

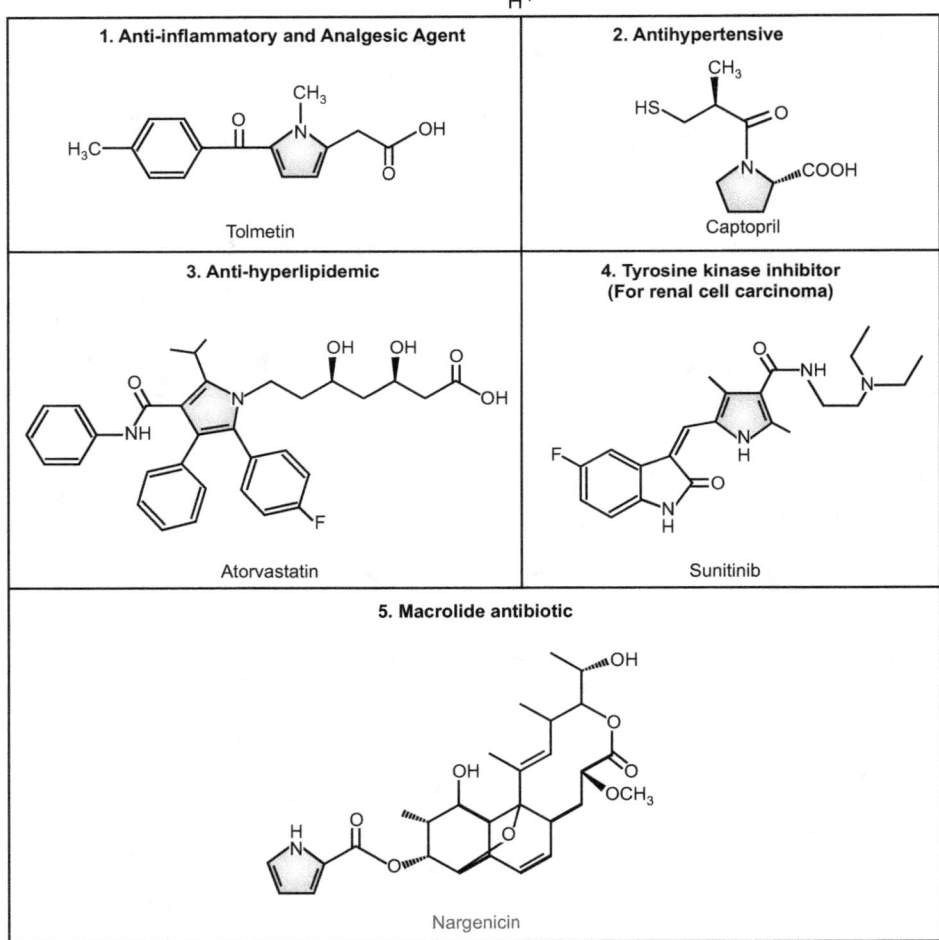

4. Pyrazole:

The pyrazole ring is present as the core or scaffold in a variety of leading drugs such as **celecoxib** (NSAID, COX-2 inhibitor), **sildenafil** (Viagra: a drug used to correct erectile dysfunction), **difenamizole** (fungicidal) and **rimonabant** (anti-obesity) etc. Pyrazole analogues have found building blocks in organic synthesis for designing pharmaceutical and agrochemicals.

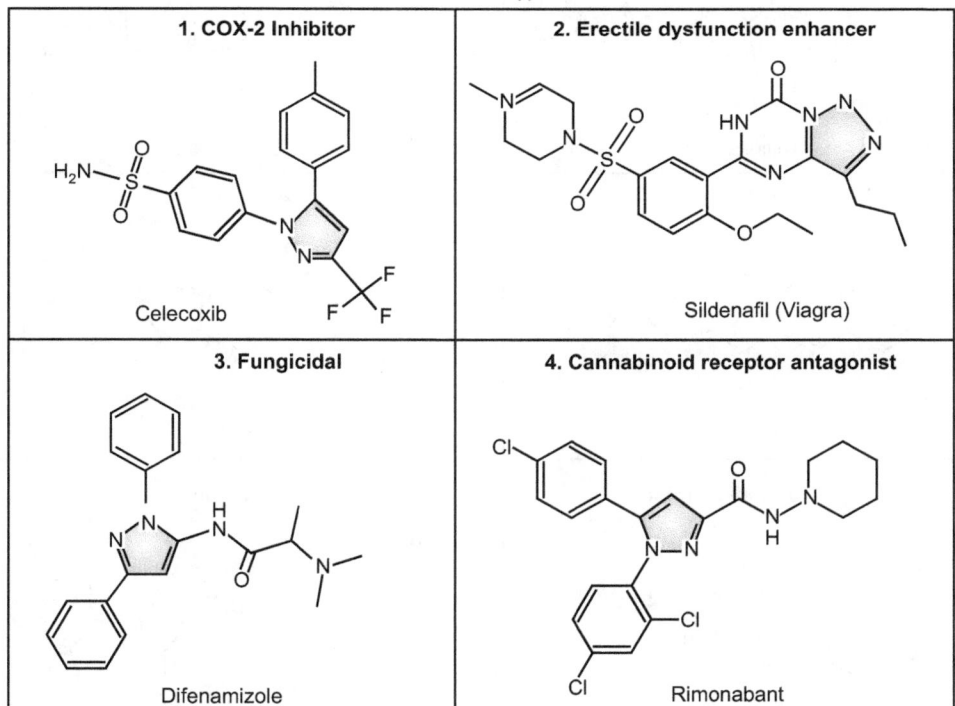

5. Thiazole:

Drugs containing thiazole core or scaffold include, **thifluzamide**, **tricyclazole**, and **thiabendazole** are used for controlling various agricultural pests. Another widely used thiazole derivative is the non-steroidal anti-inflammatory drug **meloxicam**.

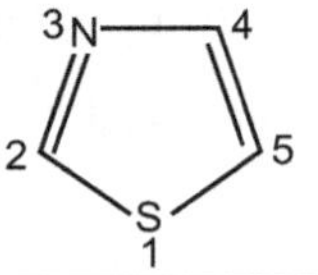

1. Antifungal	2. Anthehelmintic
Thifluzamide	Thiabendazole
3. NSAID	4. Vitamin
Meloxicam	Thiamine
5. Anti-microbial	6. Antibiotic
Sulphathiazole	Cefixime

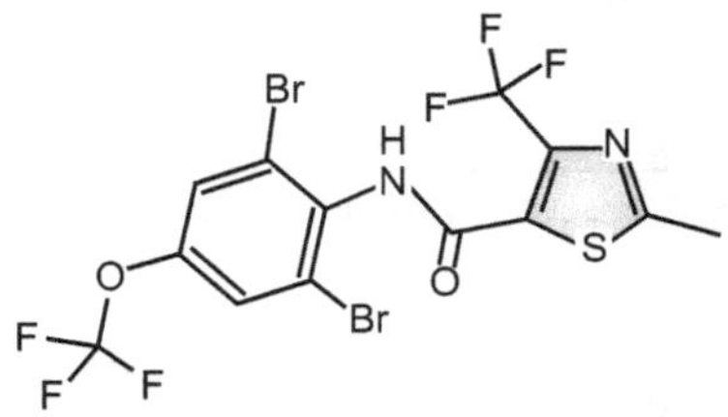

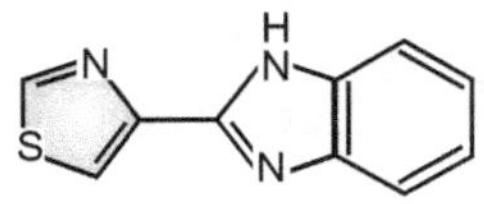

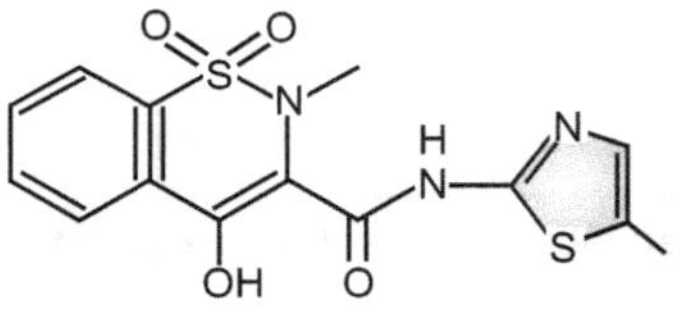

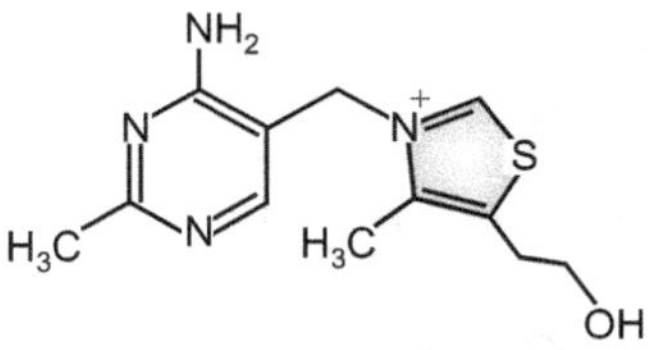

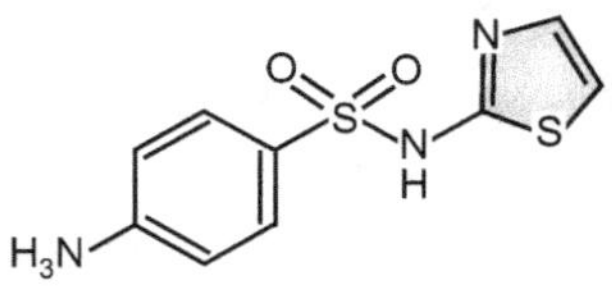

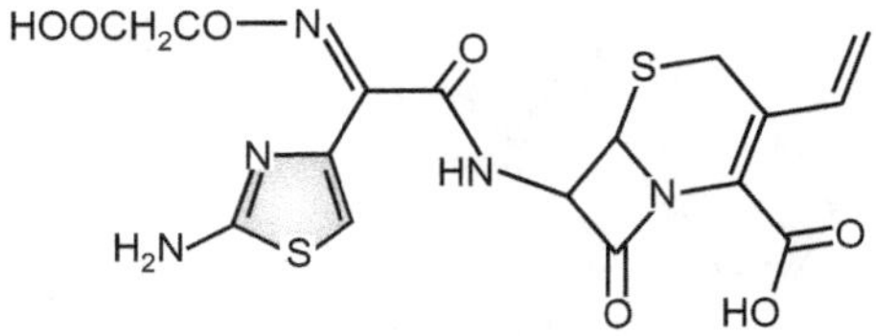

6. Imidazole:

Imidazole is found in many important biological molecules. The most obvious is the amino acid, histidine, which has an imidazole side chain. Histidine is present in many proteins and enzymes and plays a vital part in the structure and binding functions of hemoglobin. Many drugs contain an imidazole ring and are used as antifungal, antiprotozoal and antihypertensive medications. Some drugs containing an imidazole ring include **nitroimidazoles** like **ketoconazole**, **miconazole**, and **clotrimazole** as well as the sedative **midazolam**. Imidazole is also present in the anticancer medication mercaptopurine, which combats leukemia.

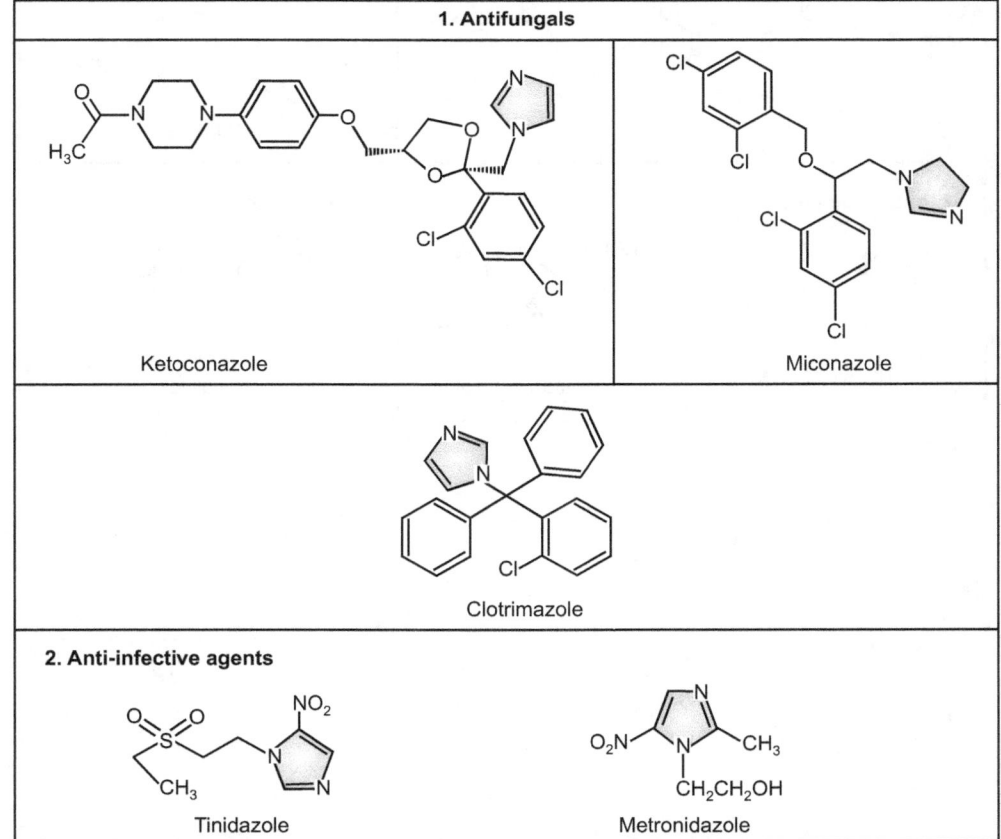

7. Oxazole:

Darglitazone is a member of the thiazolidinedione class of drugs and an agonist of peroxisome proliferator-activated receptor-γ (PPAR-γ), used in the treatment of metabolic disorders such as type II diabetes. **Ditazole** is a platelet aggregation inhibitor.

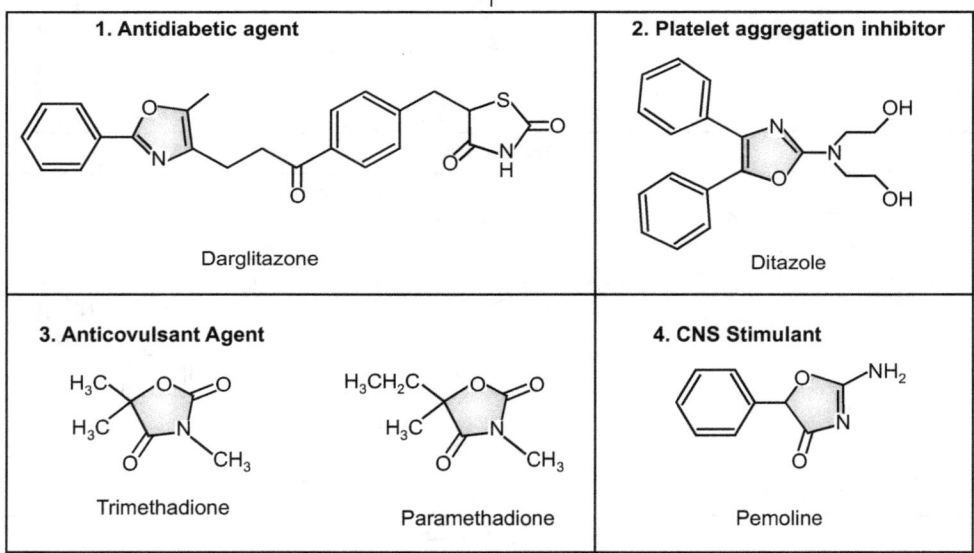

8. Isoxazole:

Isoxazole derivatives such as **sulfamethoxazole, sulfisoxazole, oxacillin** and **cycloserine** have been in commercial use for many years. **Cycloserine** is the best known antibiotic drug that possess anti-tubercular and anti-bacterial activities in treatment of leprosy.

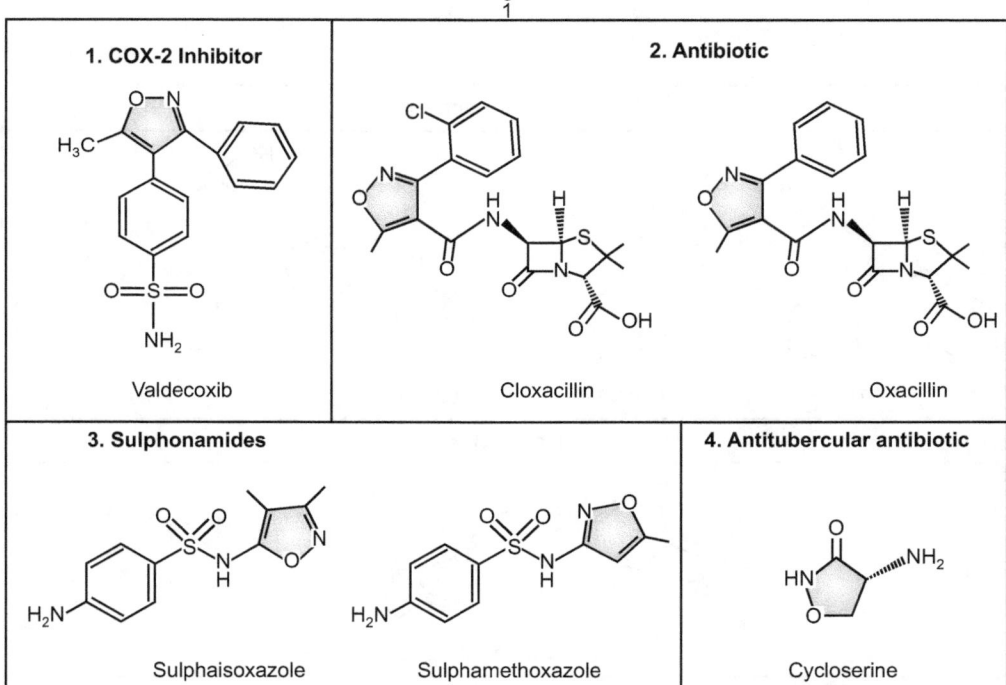

9. Hydantoin:

Hydantion group can be found in several medicinally important compounds. In pharmaceuticals, 'hydantoins' most often refer to anticonvulsants; **phenytoin**, **mephenytoin**, **ethotoin** and **fosphenytoin** (prodrug of phenytoin) are used as anticonvulsants in the treatment of seizure disorders. The hydantoin derivative **dantrolene** is used as a muscle relaxant in malignant hyperthermia and is also used in neuroleptic malignant-syndrome, spasticity, and ecstasy intoxication.

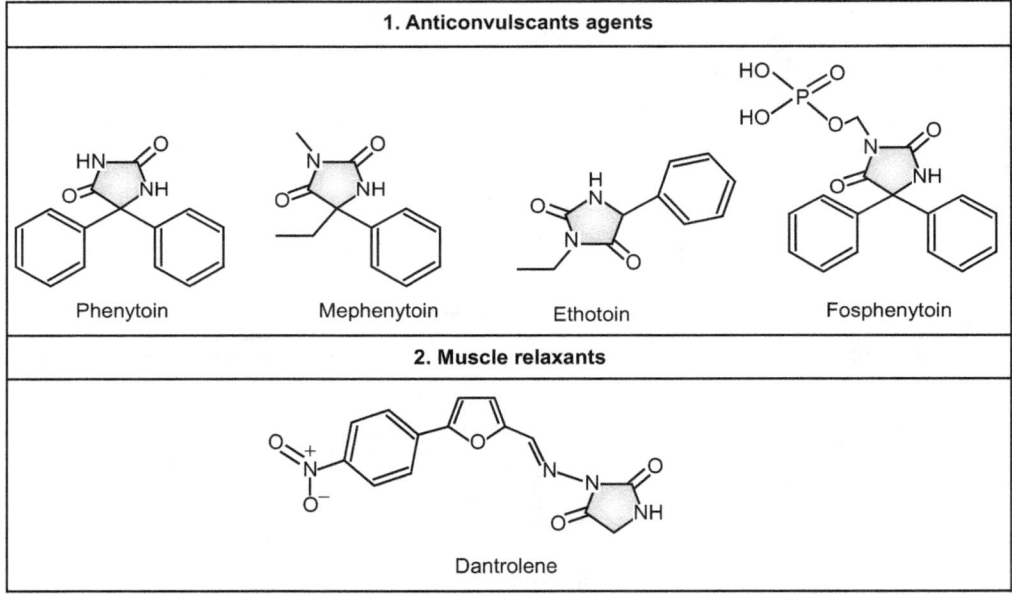

10. Pyridine: It is used in the synthesis of **sulfapyridine** (anti-bacterial), tripelennamine and **mepyramine** (anti-histaminic) and *in-vitro* synthesis of DNA drugs. The drug molecule containing pyridines in ring structure are **niacin** and **pyridoxal** (B-complex vitamin), **isoniazid** (anti-tubercular), **bisacodyl** (laxative) and many other drugs.

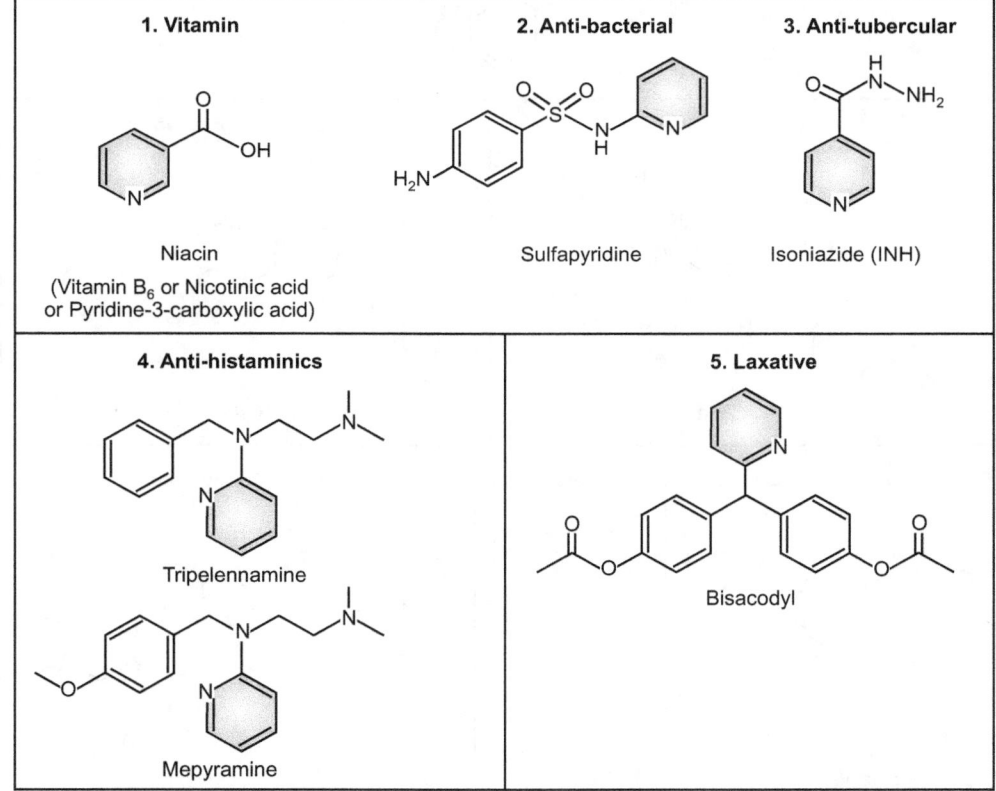

11. Pyridazine:

It is a popular pharmacophore. It is found in the structures of several drugs such as **cadralazine** (antihypertensive), **minaprine** (antidepressant), **pipofezine** (tricyclic antidepressant), **hydralazine** (vasodilator, smooth muscle relaxant) and **cefozopran** (fourth-generation cephalosporin).

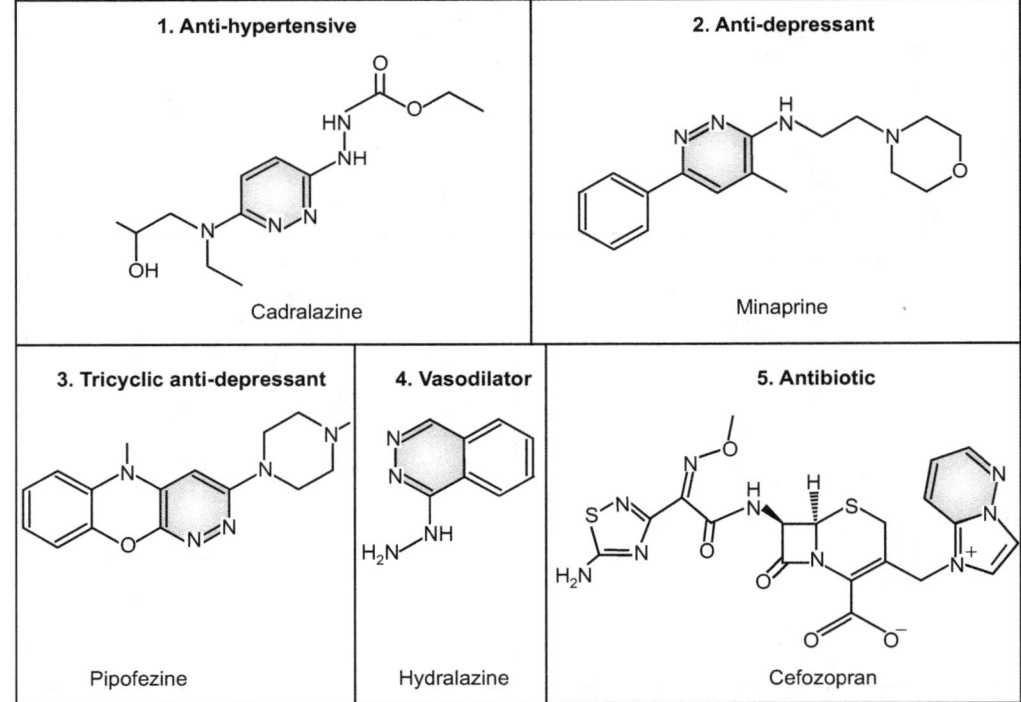

12. Pyrimidine:

The pyrimidine ring system has wide occurrence in nature as substituted and ring fused compounds, including the nucleotides, **thiamine (vitamin B$_1$)** and **alloxan**. It is also found in many synthetic compounds such as **barbiturates** and the HIV drug, **zidovudine**. **Trimethoprim** is a bacteriostatic antibiotic used mainly in the prevention and treatment of urinary tract infections.

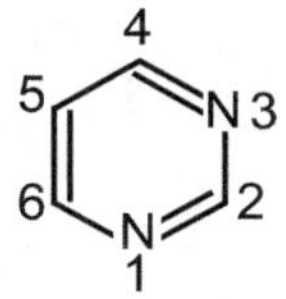

Anti-neoplastic agent	Sedative and hypnotic agent	Bacteriostatic agent
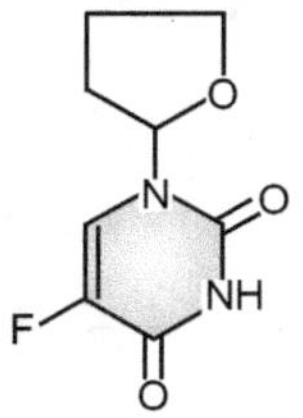 Tegafur	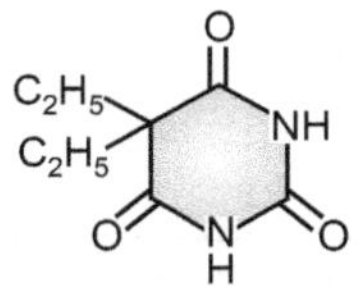 Barbitone	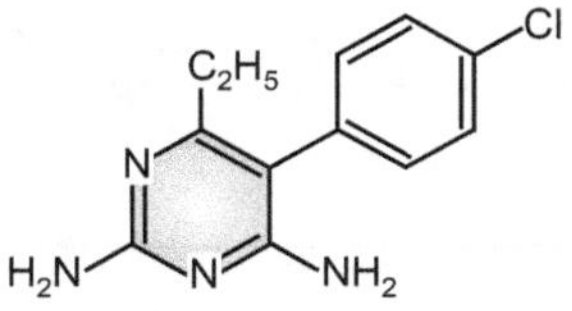 Pyrimethamine

Anti-fungal agent	Sulfonamide antibacterial agent
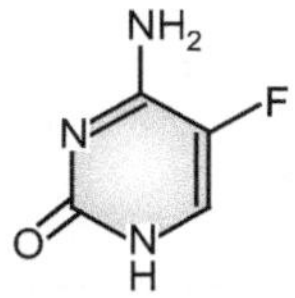 Zidovudine	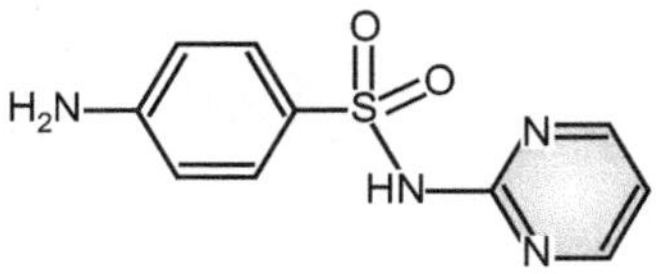 Sulfadiazine

13. Indole:

It is a common component of fragrances and the precursor to many pharmaceuticals. The amino acid **tryptophan** is an indole derivative and the precursor of the neurotransmitter **serotonin**. There are many alkaloids which contain the indole core. The ergot alkaloids , **lysergic acid, physostigmine** etc. Some of the drugs like **reserpine** (antipshychotic, antihypertensive) come under this category. Other indolic compounds include the plant hormone **auxin** (indolyl-3-aceticacid, IAA), the anti-inflammatory drug, **indomethacin**, the non-selective betablocker drug, **pindolol,** and the naturally occurring psychedelic hallucinogen **dimethyltryptamine**.

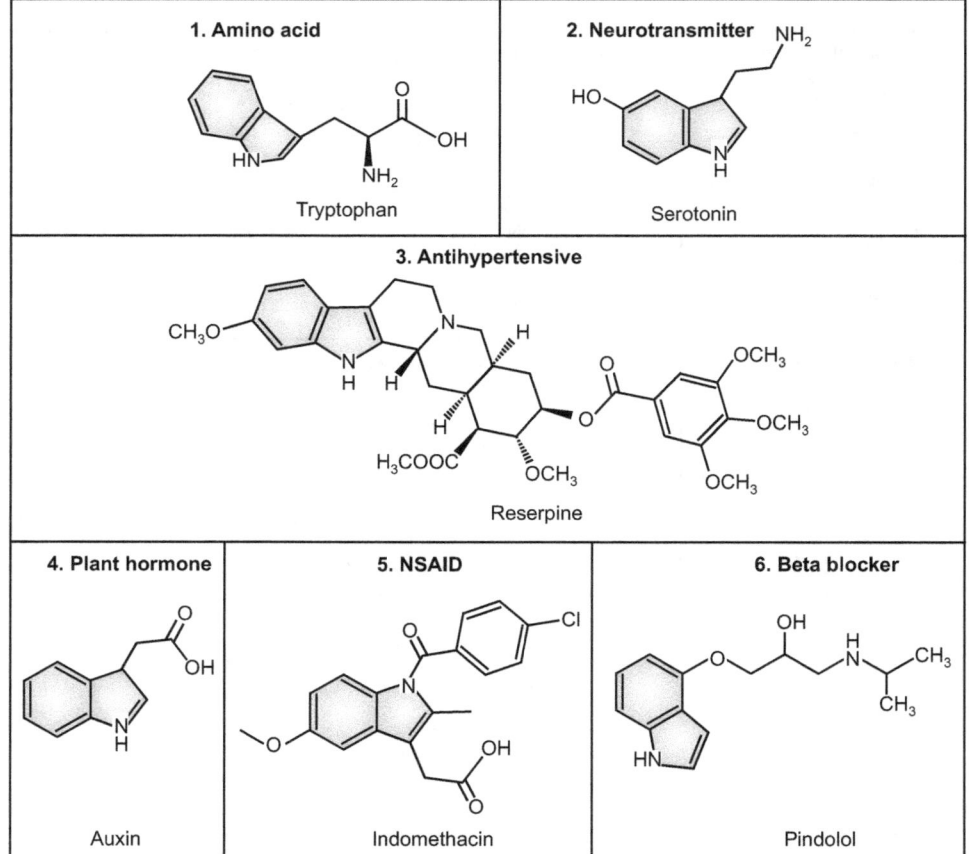

14. Benzofuran:

It is the "parent" of many related compounds with more complex structures. For example, **psoralen** is a benzofuran derivative that occurs in several plants and is used in treatment of skin problems like psoriasis, eczema, vitilgo. Another example includes, the selective phosphoinositide-3-kinase α inhibitor **liphagal**. Of the naturally occurring phenolic benzofuran derivatives thunberginols A-F, thunberginol F is a benzfuran derivative and is used as antiallergic and antimicrobial. **Amiodarone** is an antiarrhythmic agent used for various types of cardiac dysrhythmias, both ventricular and atrial. **5-(2-aminopropyl) benzofuran (5-APB)** is a triple monoamine reuptake inhibitor as well as being a potent agonist for the 5-HT$_{2A}$ and 5-HT$_{2B}$ receptors.

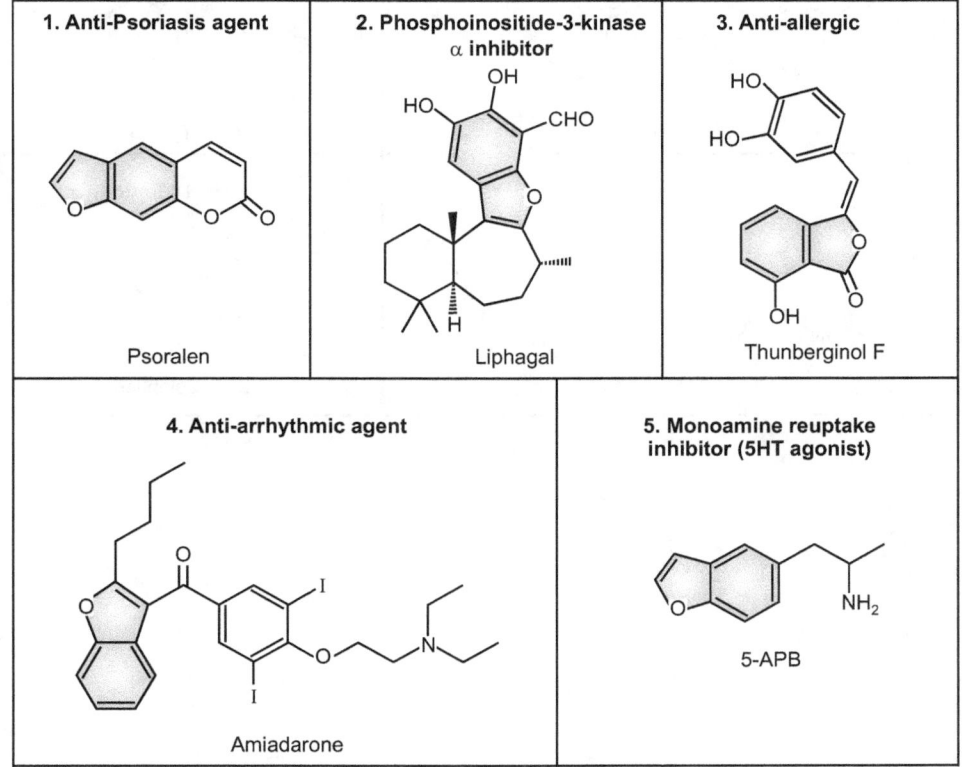

15. Benzothiazole:

Although the parent compound, benzothiazole is not widely used, many of its derivatives are found in commercial products or in nature. A derivative of benzothiazole is the light-emitting component of **luciferin**, found in fireflies. Some drugs contain this group, an example being **riluzole**. Used to treat amyotrophic lateral sclerosis **phortress** is an anticancer compound in advanced stages of clinical trials.

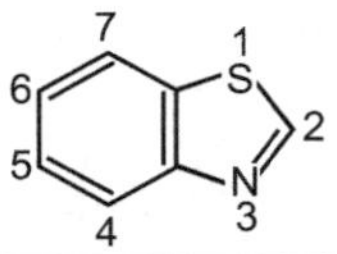

1. Light emmiting component	2. Amyotrophic lateral sclerosis
Luciferin	Riluzole
3. Anti-cancer	4. Diuretics
Phortress	Ethoxzolamide

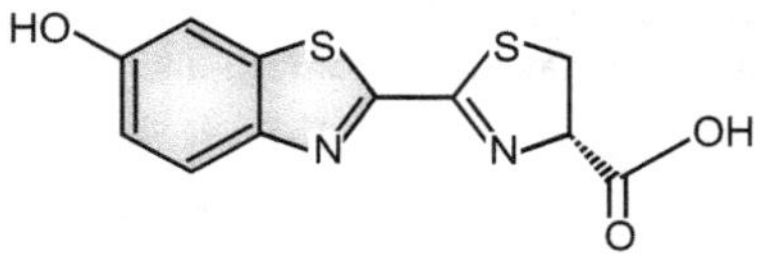

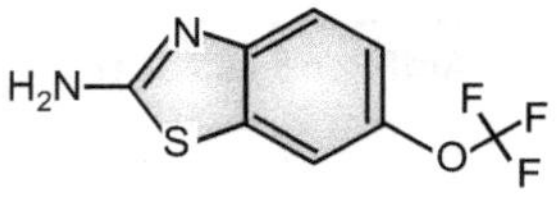

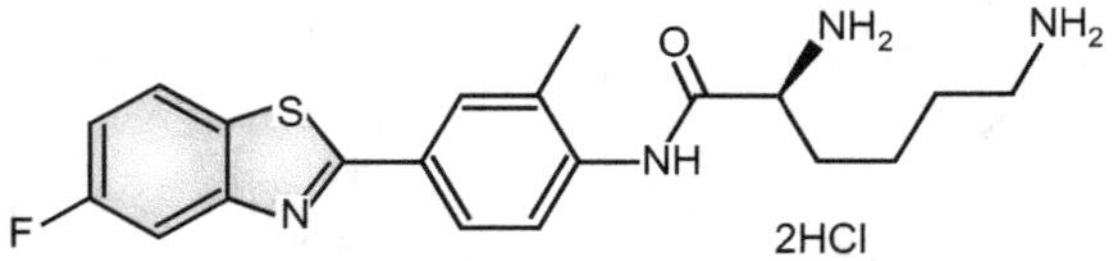

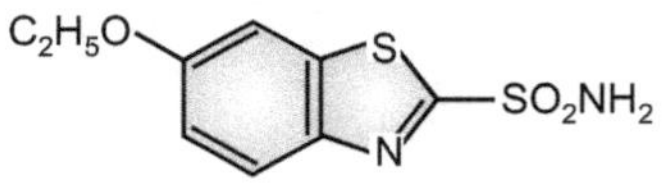

16. Benzimidazole:

The most prominent benzimidazole compound in nature is N-ribosyl-dimethylbenzimidazole, which serves as an axial ligand for cobalt in vitamin B_{12}. **Mebendazole** (or MBZ) is a benzimidazole drug used to treat infestations by worms including pinworms, roundworms, tapeworms, hookworms and whipworms. **Thiabendazole** or **TBZ** is a fungicide and parasiticide. Another drug, **albendazole**, or, **eskazole**, is a benzimidazole drug used for the treatment of a variety of parasitic worm infestations. **Dovitinib,** is the latest benzimidazole anticancer drug acting through multikinase inhibition. **Bendamustine** is a nitrogen mustard, used in the treatment of chronic lymphocytic leukemia and lymphomas.

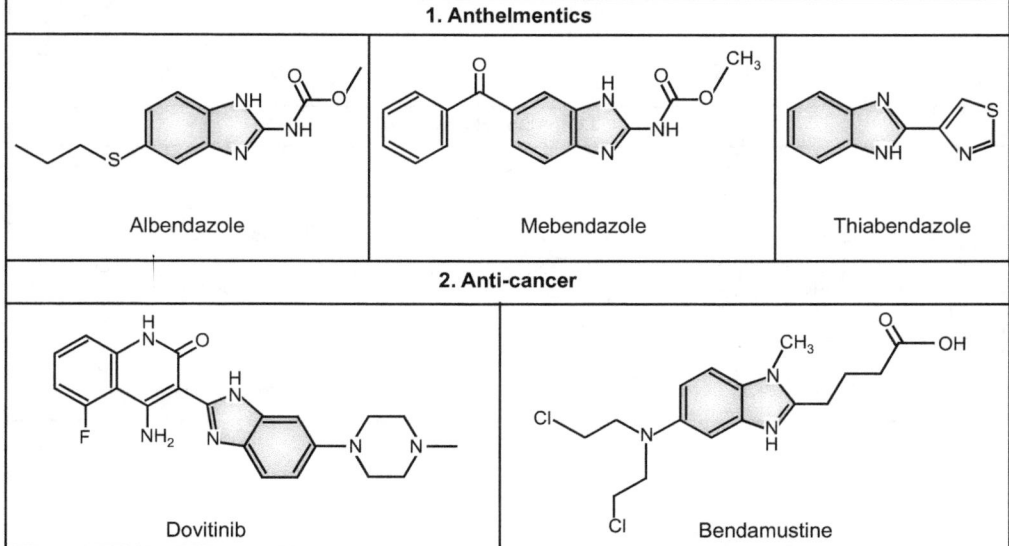

17. Benzoxazole:

Being a heterocyclic compound, benzoxazole finds use in research as a starting material for the synthesis of larger, usually bioactive structures. It is found within the chemical structures of pharmaceutical drugs such as the anti-inflammatory agent **flunoxaprofen**, novel antibacterial, **boxazomycin B**, the antibiotic active against gram positive bacteria and fungi, **calcymycin** and well known muscle relaxant **chloroxazone** to treat muscle spasms, etc. **Flunoxaprofen**, also known as **priaxim**, is a chiral non-steroidal anti-inflammatory drug.

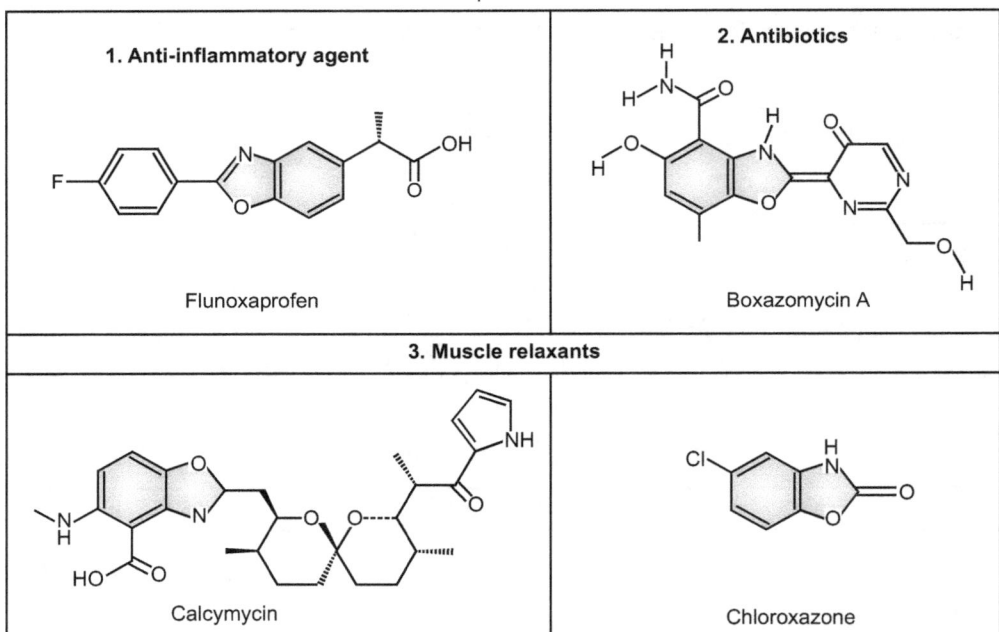

18. Quinoline:

Quinoline itself has few applications, but many of its derivatives are useful drugs as the antimalarials, **quinine, chloroquin, primaquin, mefloquin, quinocide** etc. The widely used antibacterials, **ciprofloxacin** and analogs are quinolin-3-carboxylic acids. The 8-hydroxyquinolines, represented by **clioquinol** are antiameobics and antiparasitic drugs. **Praziquantel** is another antiparasitic drug.

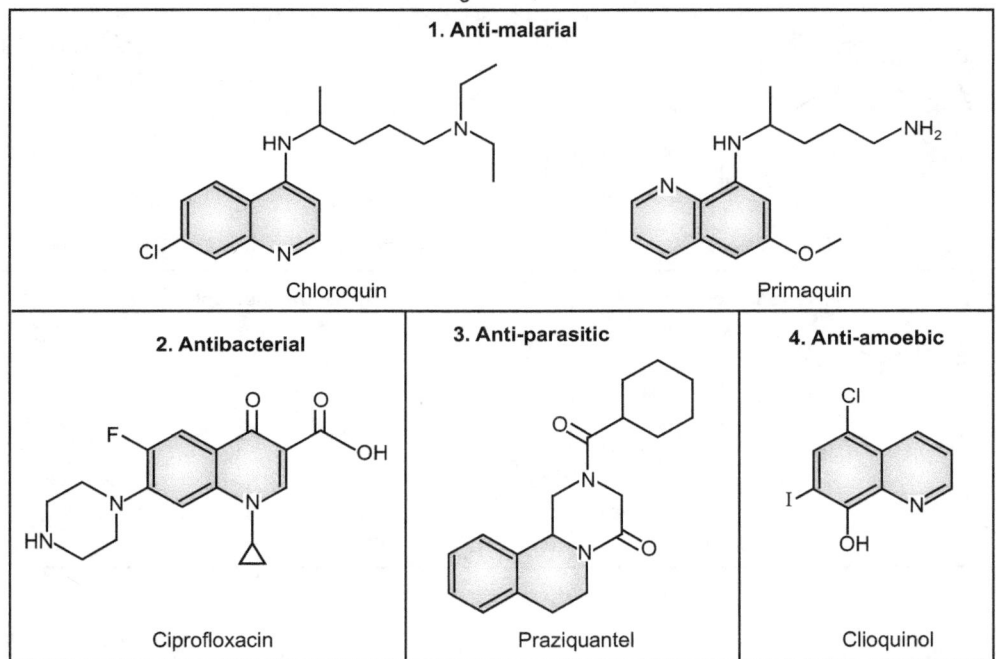

19. Isoquinoline:

Isoquinoline is the structural backbone in many naturally occurring alkaloids including **papaverine** and **berberine.** Anesthetic drug **dimethisoquin** is another example. Similarly, antihypertensive drugs, such as **debrisoquin**.

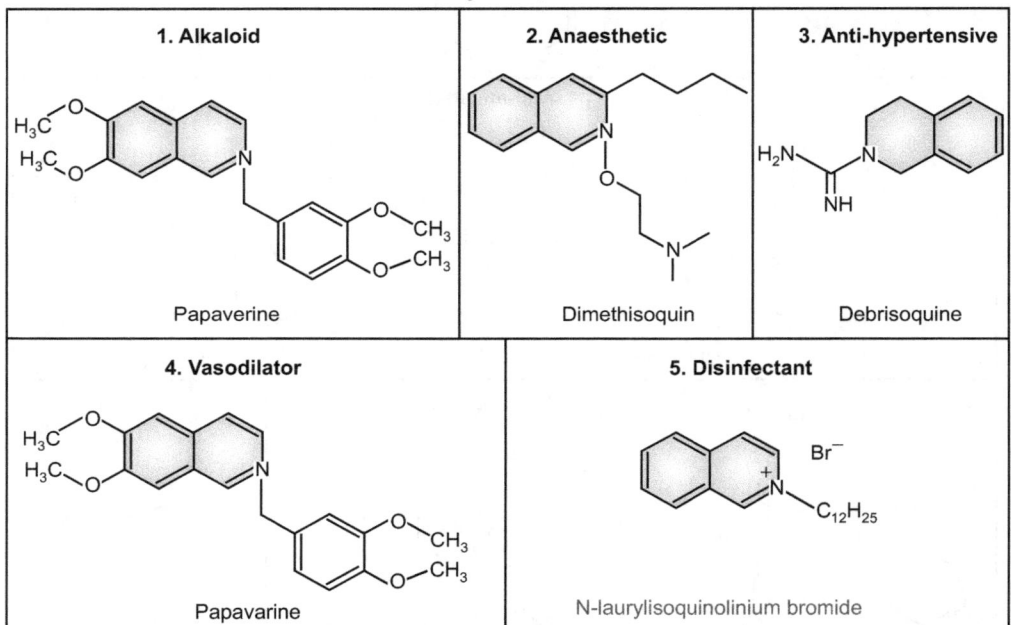

20. Quinazoline:

Medicinally, it appears in many drugs useful in various areas especially, as antimalarial agents, as antihypertensive agents (prazosin and doxazosin analogs), as, well as anticancer agents (gefitinib analogs). Another example of a compound containing the quinazoline structure is hypnotic sedative drug, methaqualone.

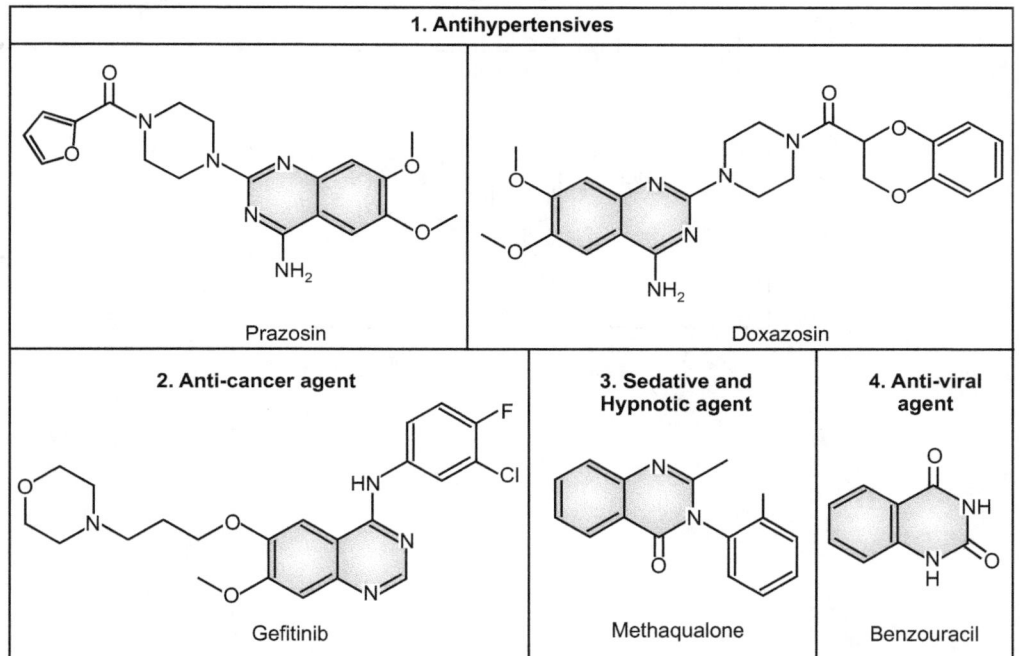

21. Cinnoline:

There are not many examples of drugs bearing cinnoline nucleus. One of the examples is **cinoxacin**, an antibiotic used against UTI.

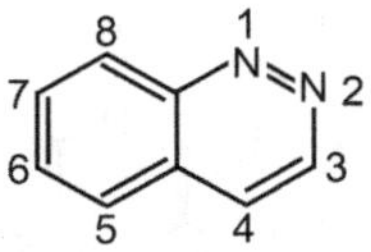

Cinnoline

Antibiotic

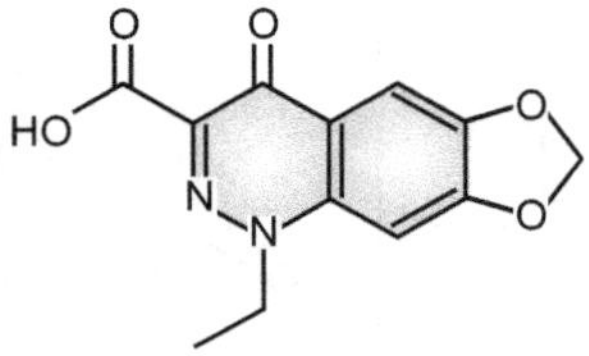

Cinnoxacin

22. Purine:

Many naturally occurring bioactive molecules are purines. Two of the five bases in nucleic acids, **adenine** and **guanine** are **purines**. Other notable purines are **hypoxanthine, xanthine, theobromine, caffeine, uric acid** and **isoguanine**. Many of the anti-viral agents are in clinical practice are purine derivatives.

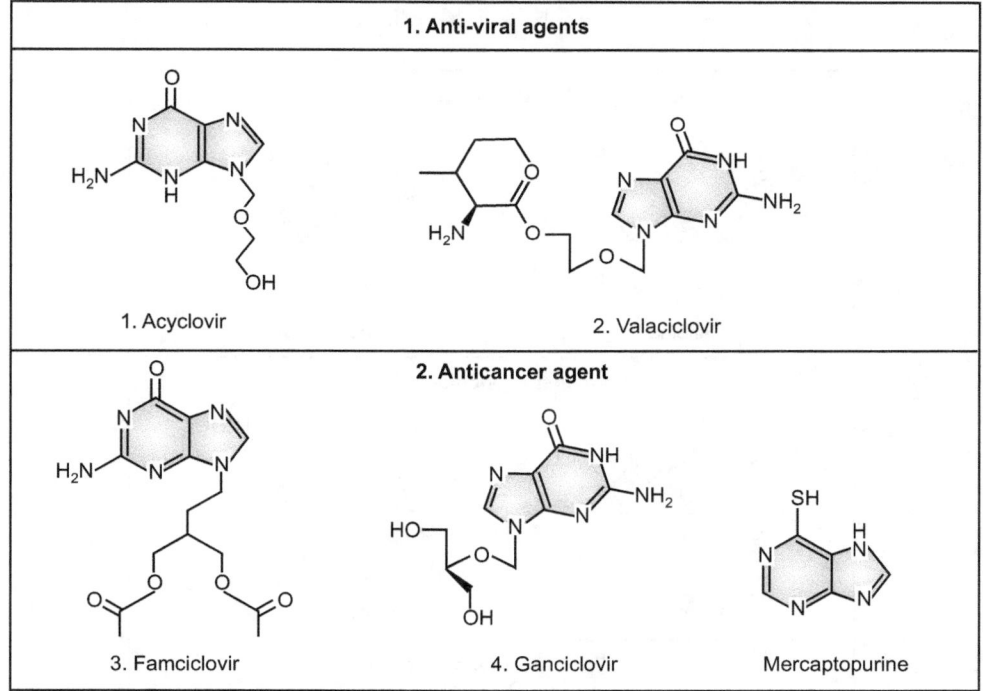

23. Xanthine:

It is a purine base found in the body tissues and fluids of human and in other organisms. A number of stimulants are derived from xanthine, including **caffeine** and **theobromine**. **Theophylline**, used in therapy for COPD and asthma under a variety of brand names. **Hypoxanthine** is a naturally occurring purine derivative. **Allopurinol** is used primarily to treat hyperuricemia and its complications, including chronic gout.

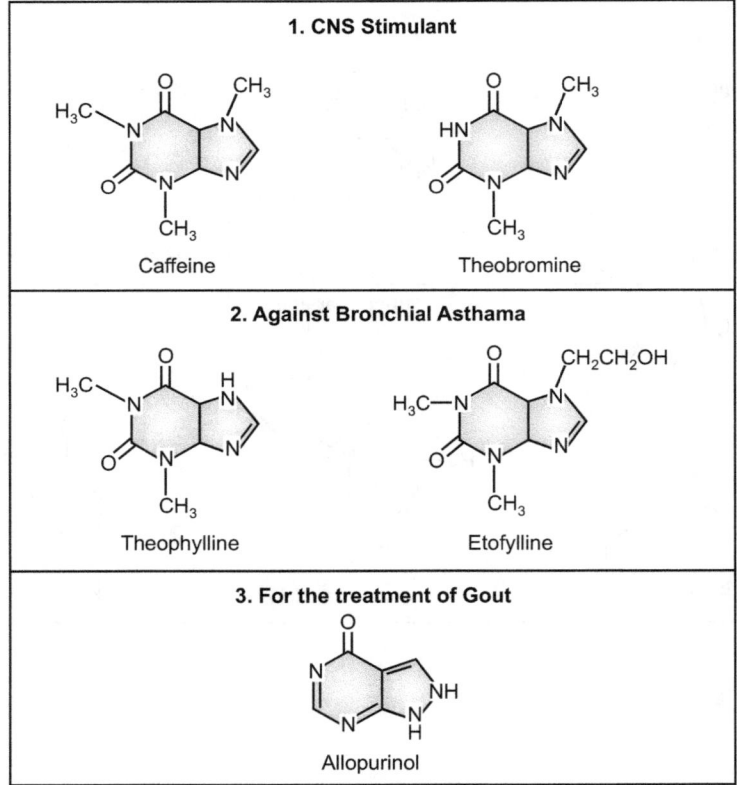

24. Pteridine:

Pteridine is an aromatic chemical compound composed of fused pyrimidine and pyrazine rings. Pteridine, is a precursor in the synthesis of dihydrofolic acid in many microorganisms. The enzyme dihydropteroate synthetase is inhibited by Sulfonamide antibiotics. Many pteridine derivatives are used as anti-cancer agents.

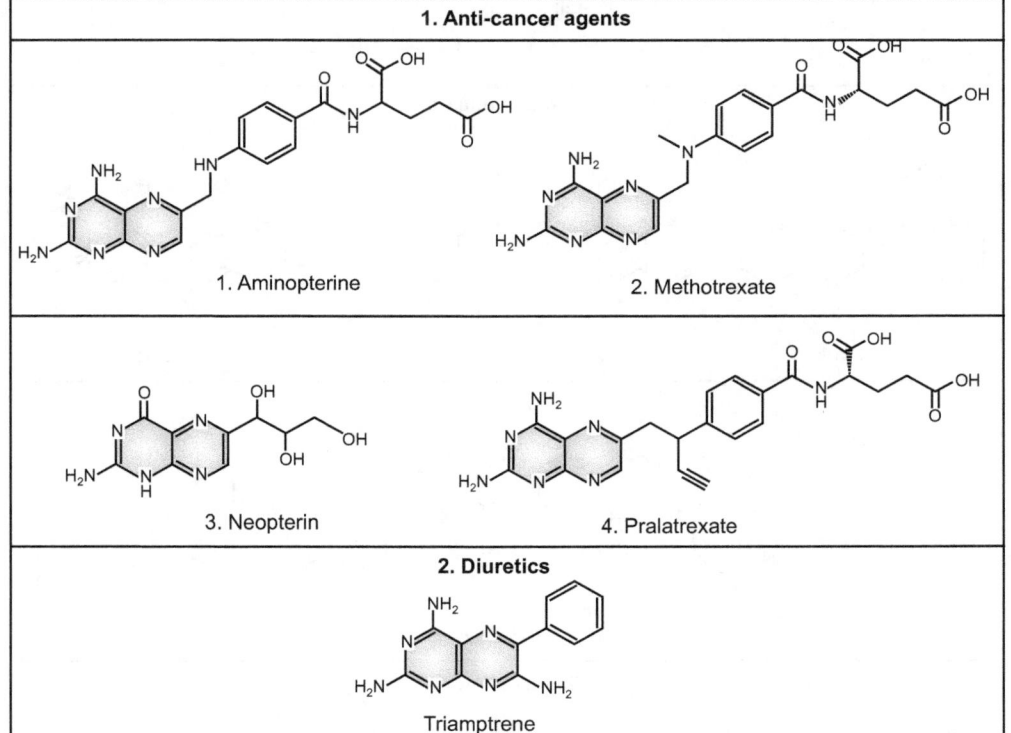

Pteridine

1. Anti-cancer agents

1. Aminopterine
2. Methotrexate
3. Neopterin
4. Pralatrexate

2. Diuretics

Triamptrene

25. Coumarin:

It is a fragrant organic chemical compound in the benzopyrone chemical class found in many plants. Some naturally occurring coumarin derivatives include **umbelliferone** (7-hydroxycoumarin), **aesculetin** (6,7-dihydroxycoumarin), **herniarin** (7-methoxy-coumarin), **psoralen** and **imperatorin**. Reported biological activities in coumarins include, anti-HIV, anti-tumor, anti-hypertension, anti-arrhythmia, anti-inflammatory, anti-osteo-porosis, antiseptic and analgesic. **Carbocromen** is a vasodilator.

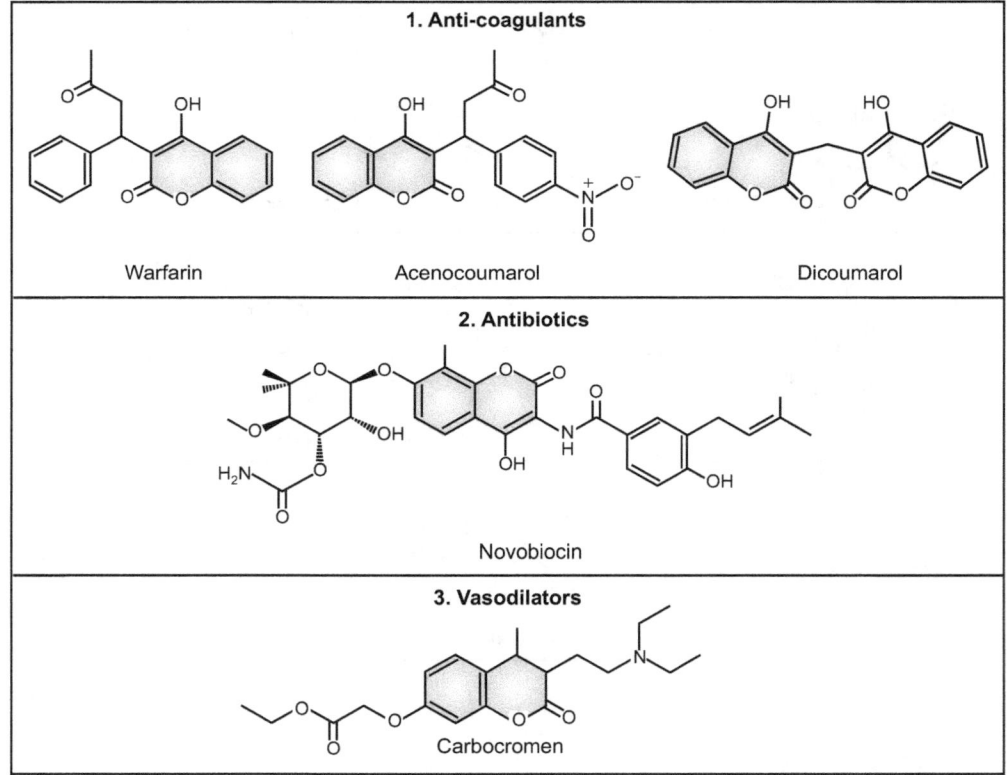

FURAN

1. STRUCTURE

Furan is a five membered ring containing 'Oxygen (O)' as the heteroatom.

Mol. formula: C_4H_4O; **Mol. Wt**: 68.1.

Furan is numbered as shown and exists into two partially reduced forms which are systematically named as 2,3-dihydrofuran & 2, 5-dihydrofuran. The saturated or completely reduced from is named as 2,3,4,5-tetrahydrofuran (THF).

However, Δ (delta) can be used to indicate the position of double bond.

2,3-Dihydrofuran   2,5-Dihydrofuran
(Δ^2-dihydrofuran)   (Δ^2-dihydrofuran)   2,3,4,5- Tetrahydrofuran
                                                        (THF)

Orbital Structure of Furan

Furan has planar pentagonal structure in which four carbon atoms and oxygen atom are in sp^2 hybridized state. The sp^2 hybridized orbitals overlap with each other and with s-orbitals of hydrogen to form carbon-carbon, carbon-oxygen and carbon-hydrogen bonds. Two lone pairs of electrons on oxygen are in different orbitals ; one lone pair of electrons is sp^2 hybridized orbital, while other is in π orbital. Four π-orbitals of four carbon atoms and π-orbitals of oxygen atom are parallel to each other and are perpendicular to the plane of the ring. The lateral overlapping of π-orbitals produces a π-molecular orbital containing six electrons

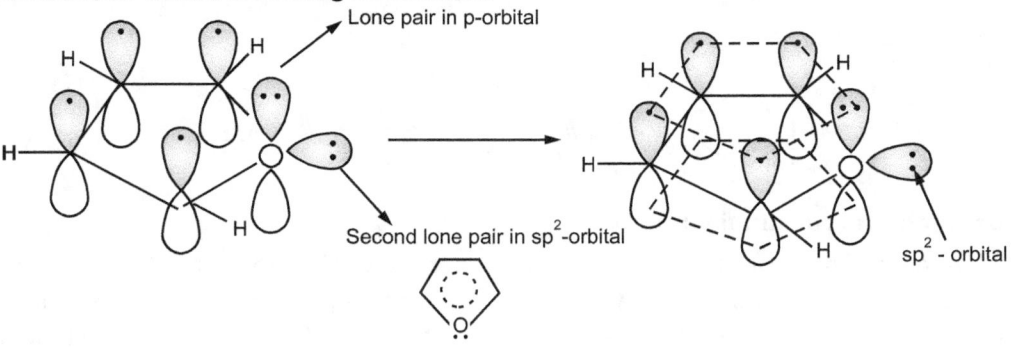

2. PHYSICAL PROPERTIES
- **Colour:** Colorless liquid; **Odour:** Chloroform like; **Boiling point:** 31-32°C
- **Solubility:** Soluble in most organic solvent but slightly miscible with water.
- **Stable** to alkali but polymerizes in presence of acids.
- **Resonance energy and structure:** 15.8 Kcal/Mol;

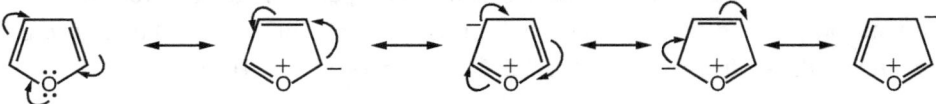

The lone pair on the oxygen atom is donated to the ring carbon atom. The aromatic character of a molecule is dependent on the availability of the lone pair of electrons for resonance and this in turn will depend on the electronegativity of the hetero atom. More electronegative atoms will have a greater hold on the lone pair which will therefore, be localized. *Furan as a result is less aromatic than pyrrole or thiophene.*

3. CHEMICAL REACTIONS:

The aromatic nature of furan makes it resist addition reactions but undergo readily electrophilic substitution. It behaves chemically as a typical diene ether which is resonance stabilized.

(a) Electrophilic Substitution: Reactivity towards Electrophilic Substitution and Orientation Effects:

Furan undergoes electrophilic substitution preferentially at the C-2 and C-5 positions and these positions are comparatively more reactive than that at a benzene position. If these positions are occupied, the substitution takes place at the C-3 and C-4 positions and these positions are more reactive than a position of benzene.

Orientation of Substitution:

Although the α positions of furan are more reactive than the β positions towards electrophilic substitutions, the ratio of α substitution to β substitution depends upon the balancing effect of the ring oxygen and the substituent. The presence of substituent with +I or –I effect at position 2 of furan causes substitution to occur at the position 5, while the substituents exhibiting-I effect deactivate C-5 position due to the mesomeric effect. But this effect is usually overpowered by the powerful orientational effect of the ring oxygen and directs the substitution occur at the C-5 position. However, the –M effect of the substituent is enhanced in the presence of a Lewis acid with the deactivation of C-5 position and the substitution takes place at the C-4 position, although this effect competes with the orientational effect of the ring oxygen.

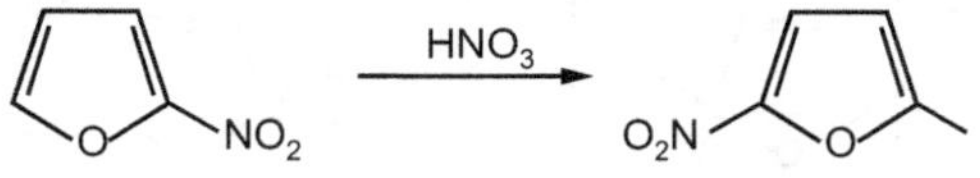

(b) Protonation:

Furan reacts only slowly with hydrogen chloride either as the concentrated aqueous acid or in a non-hydroxylic organic solvent. Hot dilute aqueous mineral acids cause hydrolytic ring-opening.

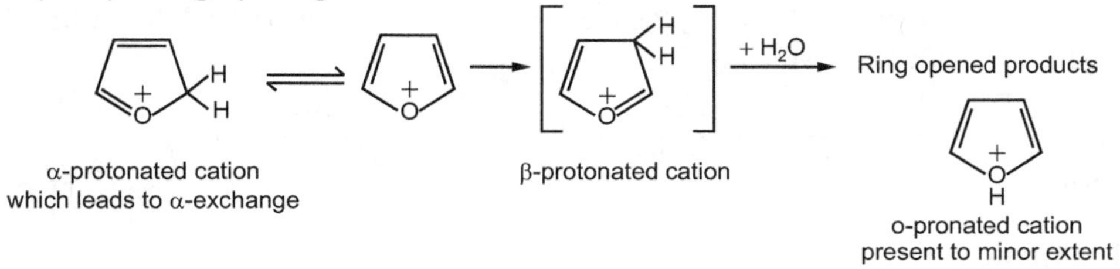

α-protonated cation
which leads to α-exchange

β-protonated cation

o-pronated cation
present to minor extent

(c) Nitration:

Nitration requires mild conditions as usual concentrated acid nitrating mixture will destroy it. Thus, acetyl nitrate is used in presence of pyridine. Reaction of furan with acetyl nitrate produces non-aromatic adducts, in which progress to a substitution product has been interrupted by nucleophilic addition of acetate to the cationic intermediate, usually at C-5. Further nitration of 2-nitrofuran gives 2,5-dinitrofuran as the main product.

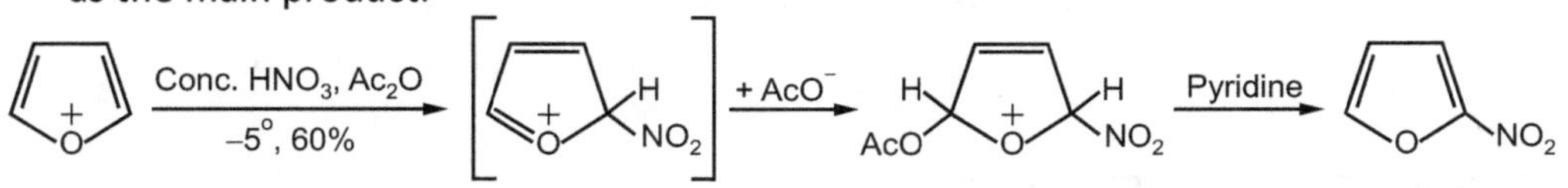

(d) Sulfonation:

Furan and its simple alkyl derivatives are decomposed by the usual strong acid reagents, pyridine sulfur trioxide complex can be used, disubstitution of furan being observed even at room temperature.

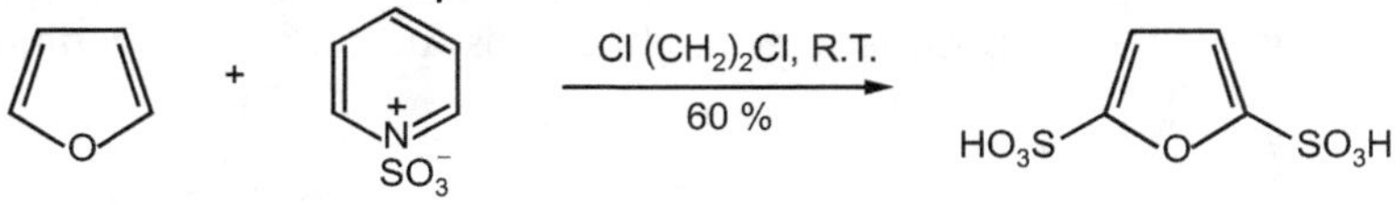

(e) Halogenation:

Furan reacts vigorously with chlorine and bromine at room temperature to give polyhalogenated products, but does not react at all with iodine. More controlled conditions can give 2-bromofuran in a process which probably proceeds via a 1,4-dibromo-l,4-dihydro-adduct. Reaction with bromine in dimethylformamide at room temperature smoothly produces 2-bromo- or 2,5-dibromofurans.

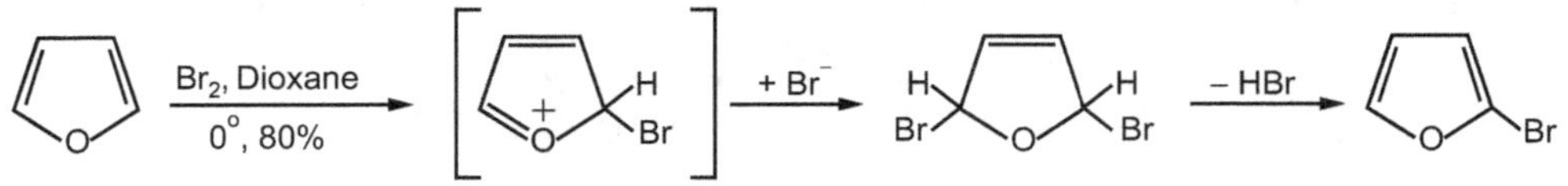

(f) Acylation:

The rate of aluminium chloride catalysed acetylation of furan with acid anhydrides or halides shows the α-position to be more reactive than the β-position. 3-Alkyl furans substitute mainly at C-2; 2,5-dialkylfurans can be acylated at a β-position, but generally with more difficulty.

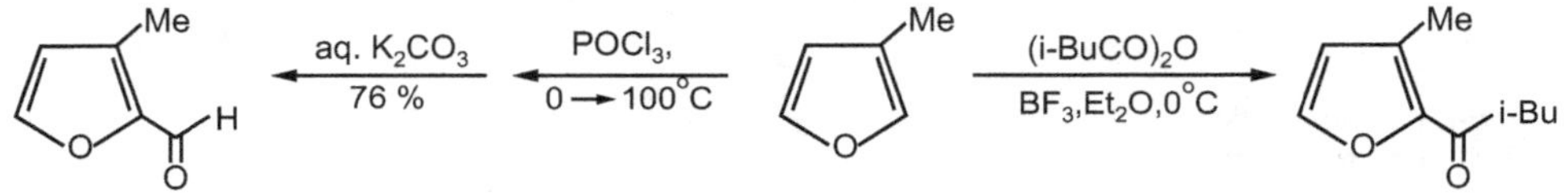

(g) Alkylation:

Traditional Friedel-Crafts alkylation is not generally practicable in the furan series, partly because of catalyst-caused polymerization and partly because of polyalkylation, as well as sensitivity to acid by furan. The alkylation is affected by alkenes at the position 2 in presence of mild catalyst (phosphoric acid or boron trifluoride).

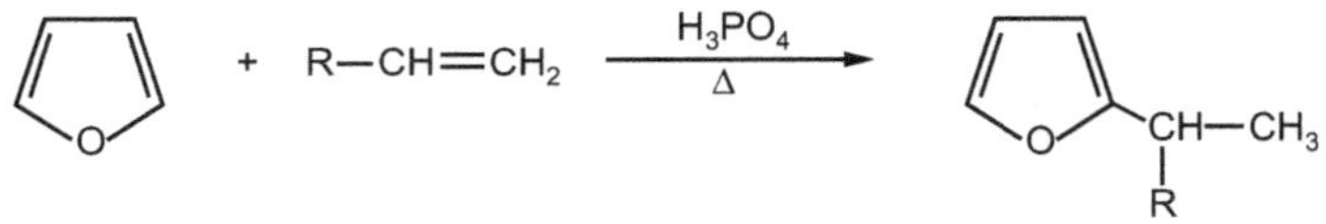

(h) Reactions with diazonium salt:

Furan undergoes phenylation rather than diazo coupling on reaction with benzenediazonium salts. Moreover, the reaction of furan with 2,4-dinitrobenzenediazonium salt in the presence of acetic acid results in formation of pyrrole derivative involving either electrophilic substitution or cycloaddition.

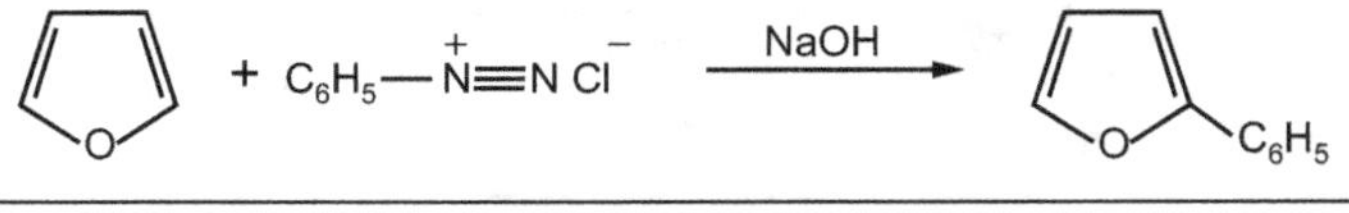

(i) Reactions with Free Radicals:

Furan undergoes free radical substitution as well as free radical addition depending on the generation of the free radicals.

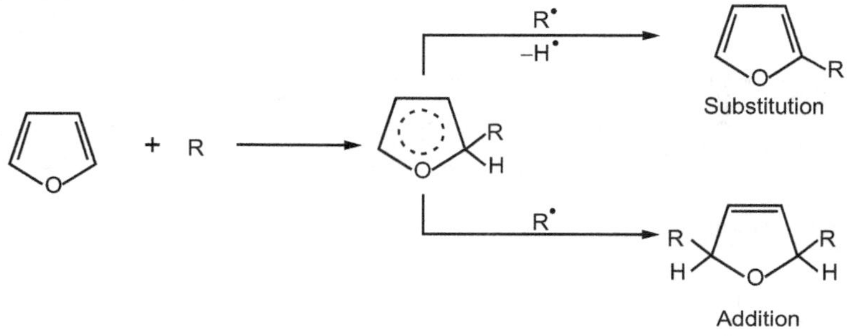

(j) Reactions with reducing agents:

The best way to reduce a furan to a tetrahydrofuran is using Raney nickel catalysis, though ring opening, *via* hydrogenolysis of C-O bonds can be a complication. Most furans are not reduced simply by metal/ammonia combinations, however furoic acids and furoic acid tertiary amides give dihydro-derivatives.

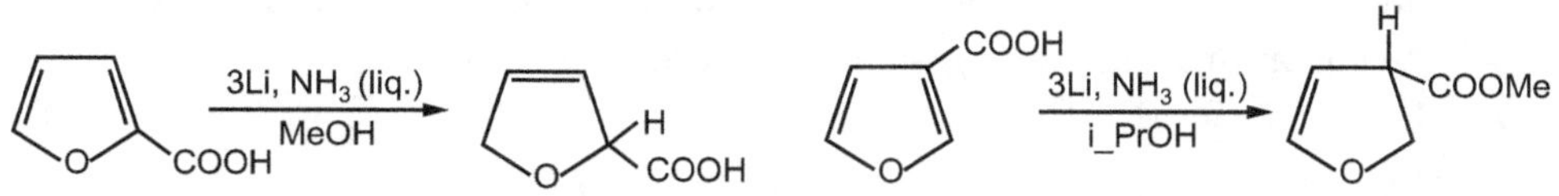

4. SYNTHESIS OF FURAN

(I) **Commercial Methods (From Aldopentoses or Ketopentoses):** Acid catalysed consecutive dehydrations of aldoses or ketoses result in formation of α-ketoaldehydes *via* 1,2-enediol. The resuting α-ketoaldehyde undergoes acid catalyzed cyclization involving carbon-oxygen bond formation to provide furfural which on steam distillation at 400^0C in the presence of oxide catalyst gives the corresponding furan.

(II) From 1,4-dicarbonyl compounds: 1,4-Dicarbonyl compounds can be dehydrated, with acids, to form furans.

(III) The Paal-Knorr synthesis: The most widely used approach to furans is the dehydrative cyclisation of 1,4- dicarbonyl compounds, which provide all of the carbon atoms and the oxygen necessary for the nucleus.

(IV) From γ-hydroxyl α,β-unsaturated carbonyl compounds: γ-Hydroxy α, β-unsaturated carbonyl compounds can be dehydrated, using mineral or Lewis acids, to form furans.

(V) The Feist-Benary Synthesis: This classical synthesis rests on an initial aldol condensation at the carbonyl carbon of a 2-halocarbonyl component; ring closure is achieved *via* intramolecular displacement of halide by enolate oxygen. Intermediates supporting this mechanistic sequence have been isolated in some cases.

(VI) Synthesis of furoic acid and furan from mucic acid: Dry distillation of mucic acid, yields furioc acid. Further it is heated in presence of quinoline and copper powder, for decarboxylation to give furan.

Mucic acid → (Dry distillation, $-CO_2, -3H_2O$) → Furoic acid → (Heat or Quinoline and Cu power) → Furan

(VII) Synthesis of tetrahydrofuran from 1,4-butanediol: Tetrahydrofuran is obtained by removal of water molecule from 1,4-butanediol[1].

1,4-butanediol → (P_2O_5, Heat, $-H_2O$) → Tetrahydrofuran

PYRROLE

1. STRUCTURE

Pyrrole is a heterocyclic aromatic organic compound, a five-membered ring with the formula C_4H_5N. As it is a 5-membered nitrogen containing ring system, it falls in the category of azoles.

Orbital Structure of Pyrrole: It has a planer pentagonal structure with four carbon atom and nitrogen atom sp^2 hybridized. Each ring atom form two sp^2-sp^2 sigma bond to its neighbouring ring atom and one sp^2-s sigma bond to hydrogen atom. The remaining unhybridized p-orbital, one on each ring atom are perpendicular to the plane of sigma bond and overlap to form π molecular system with three bonding orbital. The six π electron form aromatic sextet which is responsible for the aromaticity and renders stability to the pyrrole ring. Pyrrole molecule has C2v symmetry with the following molecular dimensions

Pyrrole reflects cylic delocalization with the involvement of lone pair of electrons on the nitrogen. Pyrrole is considered to be resonance hybrid of the resonating structures below, with electron rich carbon which leads to its classification as a π-excessive aromatic heterocycle.

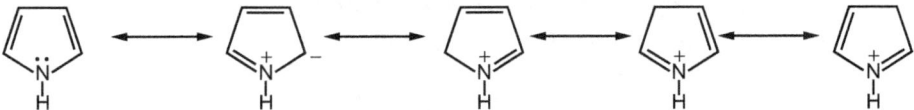

The partially saturated dihydropyrrole are called pyrroline
e.g.:

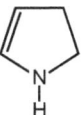   

2,3-Dihydro-2H-pyrroline   4,5-Dihydro-2H-pyrroline   2,5-Dihydro-2H-pyrroline

The fully saturated tetrahydropyrrole is designated as pyrrolidine.

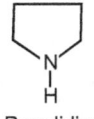

Pyrrolidine

2. PHYSICAL PROPERTIES

Boiling point: -129–131 °C

Basicity: Pyrrole is an extremely weak base because, the lone pair of electrons on nitrogen is involved in the cylic delocalization and is further, less available for protonation. Moreover, pyrrole is weaker base than pyridine and even than aniline in which lone pair on nitrogen atom involved in resonance and not essentially contributes to the aromatic sexlet. The protonation of pyrrole at nitrogen, carbon-2, carbon-3 of the ring reduces its basicity and destroy its aromaticity. However, C- and N- alkyl substituents enhance the basicity of pyrrole but the electron withdrawing substituents on the ring makes pyrrole a weaker base. Thus, pyrrole is a very weak base with a pK_{aH} of about −1 to −2.

3. CHEMICAL REACTIONS

(a) Reactions with Electrophilic Reagents

Whereas pyrrole is resistant to nucleophilic addition and substitution, it is very susceptible to attack by electrophilic reagents and react almost exclusively by substitution. Pyrrole is a π excessive heterocycle in which the π electron density is greater on its carbon atoms. Pyrrole itself undergoes electrophlic substitutaion at the 2-position and if this position is blocked then substitution occurs at other positions.

(b) Protonation

In solution, reversible proton addition occurs at all positions, being by far the fastest at the nitrogen, and about twice as fast at C-2 as at C-3. In the gas phase, mild acids protonate pyrrole *only* on the carbons and with a larger proton affinity at C-2 than at C-3. Thermodynamically the stablest cation, is the *2H-pyrrolium ion*

The *pKa* values of a wide range of pyrroles have been determined: Pyrrole itself is an extremely weak base with a *pKa* value of -3.8; this, as a 0.1 molar solution in normal acid,. However, basicity increases very rapidly with increasing alkyl substitution, so that 2, 3,4,5-tetramethylpyrrole, with a *pKa* of +3.7, is almost completely protonated on carbon as a 0.1 molar solution in normal acid. Thus alkyl groups have a striking stabilising effect on cations - isolable, crystalline salts can be obtained from pyrrole carrying t-butyl groups.

(c) Nitration

Nitrating mixtures suitable for benzenoid compounds cause complete decomposition of pyrrole. But reaction occurs smoothly with acetyl nitrate at low temperature, giving mainly 2-nitropyrrole.

(d) Sulfonation

For sulfonation, a mild reagent of low acidity must be used: the pyridine-sulfur trioxide compound smoothly converts pyrrole into the 2-sulfonate.

(e) Halogenation

Pyrrole undergo halogenation readily. Unless, controlled conditions are used, stable tetrahalopyrroles are the only isolable products.

(f) Acylation

Direct acetylation of pyrrole with acetic anhydride at 200° C leads to 2-acetylpyrrole as main product together with some 3-acetylpyrrole.

(g) Condensation with imines and iminium ions

The imine and iminium functional groupings are, of course, the nitrogen equivalents of carbonyl and O-protonated carbonyl groups, and their reactivity is analogous. Mannich reaction of Pyrrole produces dialkylaminomethyl derivatives, the iminium electrophile being generated *in situ* from formaldehyde, dialkylamine, and acetic acid.

(h) Diazo-coupling

The high reactivity of pyrrole is illustrated by its ready reaction with benzenediazonium salts. Pyrrole itself gives a mono-azo derivative by reacting as a neutral species below pH 8. But in solutions above pH 10 (in more strongly alkaline conditions) 2,5- bisdiazo derivatives are formed.

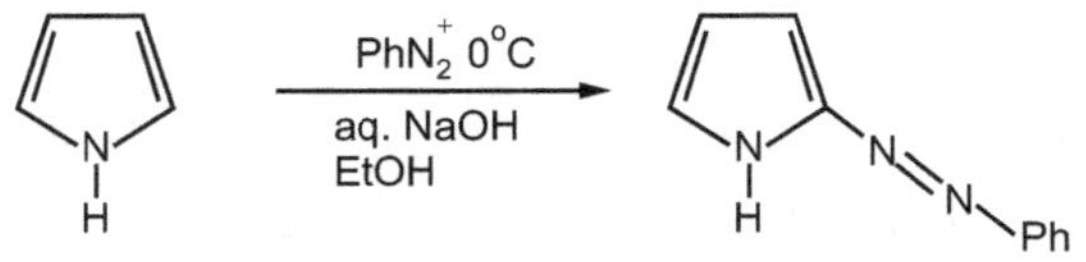

(i) **Nucleophilic Substitution** – The π electron excessive character of pyrrole renders it relatively inert towords nucleophilic substitution or addition reactions.

It also shows some reaction like oxidation, reduction and reactions with free radicals.

4. SYNTHESIS OF PYRROLES

(I) Paal-Knorr Synthesis

Pyrroles are formed by the reaction of ammonia or a primary amine with a 1,4-dicarbonyl compound leading to formation of N - C_2 and N - C_5 bonds. Successive nucleophilic additions of the amine nitrogen to the two carbonyl carbon atoms and the loss of two mole equivalents of water represent the net course of the synthesis. A reasonable sequence for this is shown below using the synthesis of 2,5-dimethylpyrrole as an example.

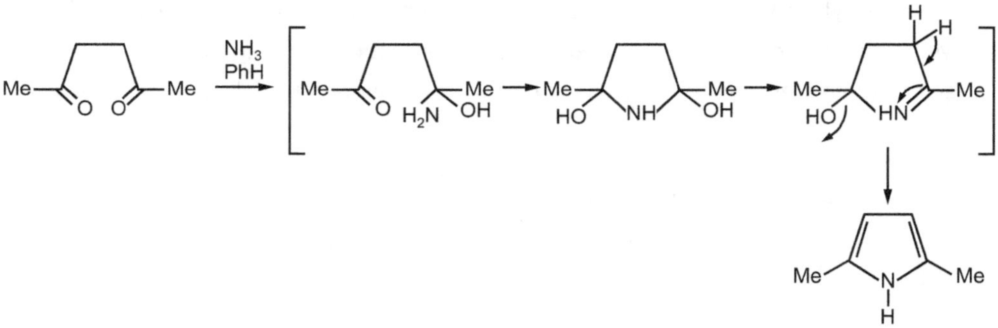

Instead of 1,4 – carbonyl compound, 1,4 – dienes can be used as precursors.

(II) Knorr Pyrrole Synthesis

This is the most widely used method and involves the cyclocondensation of α-aminoketones or α–amino β-ketoesters (three atom fragment –with a nuclophilic nitrogen, a central carbon and an electrophilic carbonyl carbon) with β- diketones or β - keto esters (two atom fragment with electrophilic C_3–C_4 bonds.

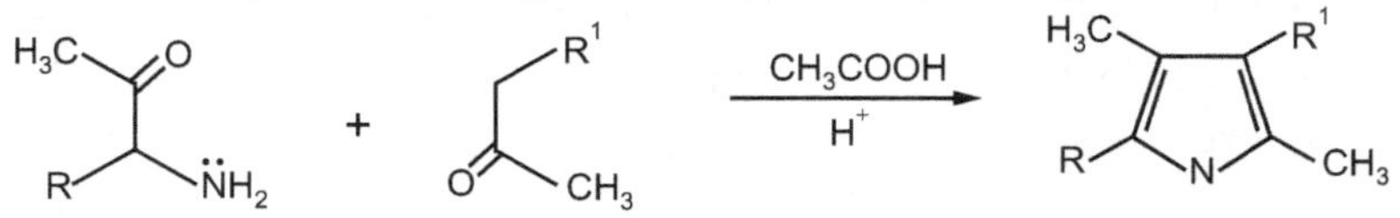

The reaction mechanism is detailed below:

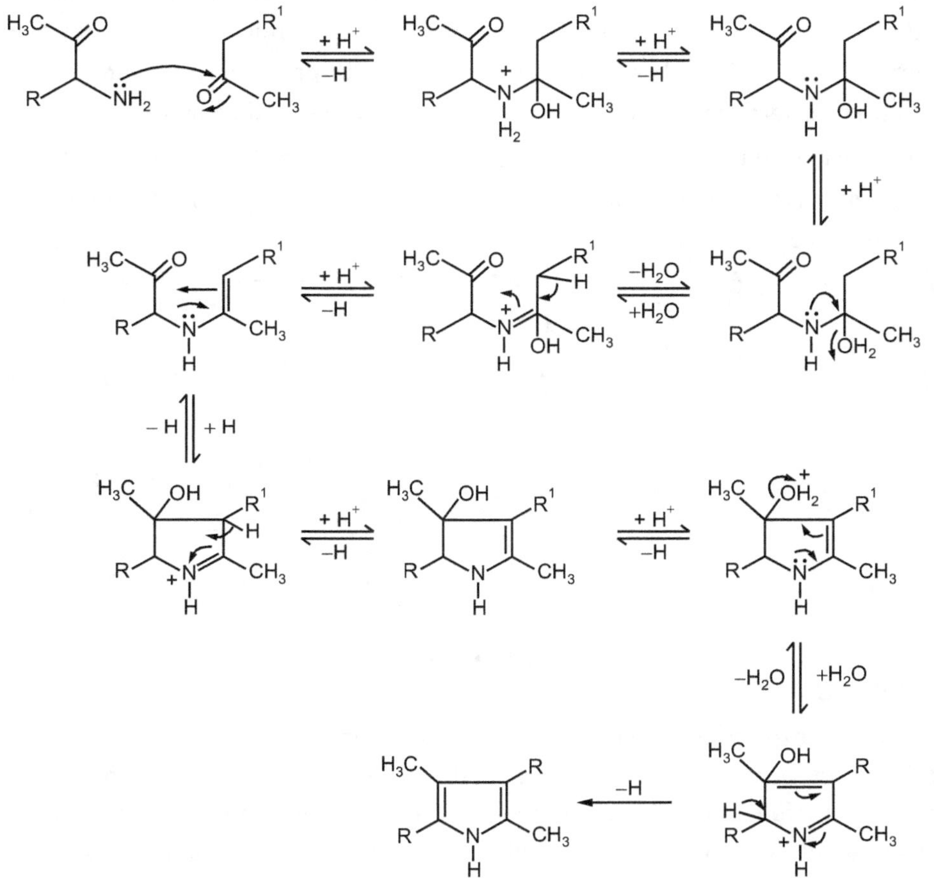

[Reaction mechanism scheme showing stepwise formation of pyrrole from α-aminoketone and β-diketone via enamine intermediate, with protonation/deprotonation and dehydration steps]

The reaction is considerd to proceed with the formation of an enamine intermediate involving attack of nuclophilic amino group of the α-amino ketone or α–amino-β- ketoester on the electrophilic carbonyl carbon of the β-diketone or β-ketoester ($N-C_2$ bond formation). Subsequent cyclization takes place with the nucleophilic attack of the β-carbon of the enamine on the electrophilic carbon of the carbonyl group of the α-aminoketone or α-amino-β-ketoester.

(III) Hantzsch Synthesis

In this modification of the Feist-Benary synthesis of furans, ammonia or a primary amine, is incorporated. The reaction of β-diketone or β-ketoester with α-haloketone or aldehyde in the presence of ammonia or primary amine involving cyclisation with the formation of N – C_2,C_3 – C_4 and N – C_5 bonds affords pyrrole. The reaction proceeds *via* stabilized enamine intermediate which on C alkylation and N alkylation by α - halo ketone leads to the formation of the corresponding pyrrole.

However, in this method the β-ketoester can combine directly with α-haloketone involving a nucleopholic attack on the carbonyl carbon of α-haloketone with the formation of furan as a byproduct

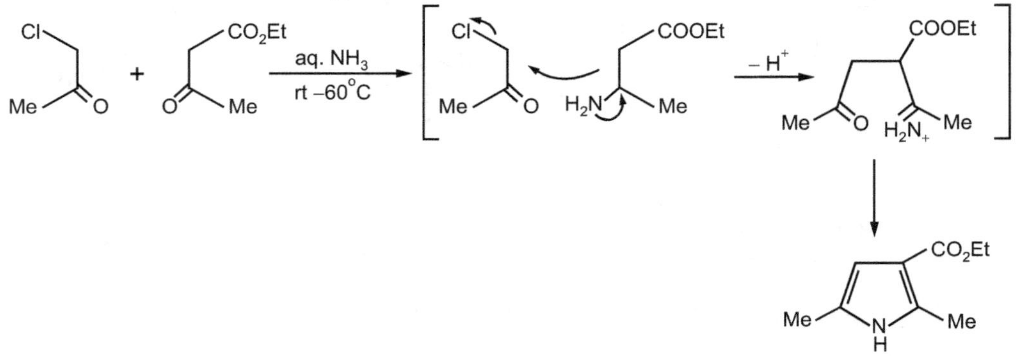

INDOLE

1. STRUCTURE:

Indole (Benzpyrrole) is an heterocyclic organic compound. It has a bicyclic structure, consisting of a six-membered benzene ring fused to a five-membered nitrogen-containing Pyrrole ring. The participation of the nitrogen lone electron pair in the aromatic ring means that indole is not a base, and it does not behave like a simple amine. The indole structure can be found in many organic compounds like the amino acid tryptophan and in tryptophan-containing protein, in alkaloids, and in pigments.

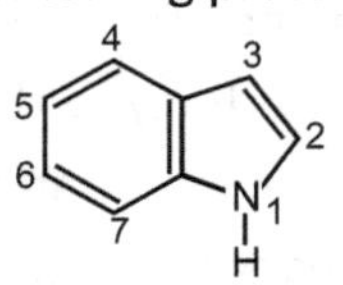

Orbital structure of indole:

Indole is a planer molecule with sp^2-hybridised atom (carbon atom and nitrogen atom) The sp^2 –hybrid orbital of the carbon and nitrogen atom overlap axially with each other and with s orbital of the hydrogen atom forming C-C, C-N, C-H; N-H π-bond. The unhybridized p-orbital on the carbon and nitrogen atom (perpendicular to the plane of π-bond) overlap laterally forming a π-molecular orbital with 10π electrons (2 electron are contributed by nitrogen atom and eight electron by carbon atom.)

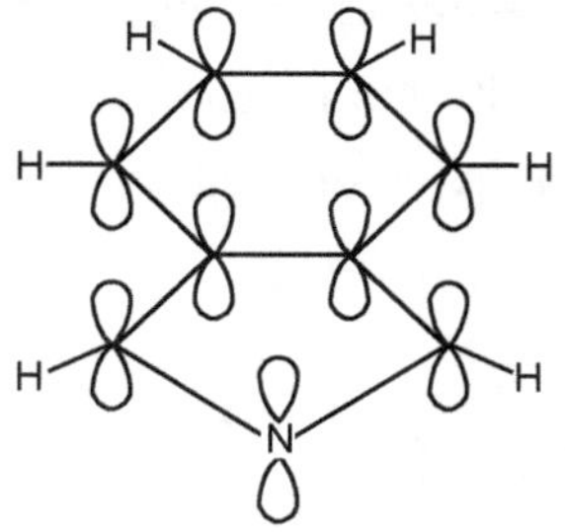

2. PHYSICAL PROPERTIES:

Appearance: White solid; **Density:**-1.22 g/cm³; **Boiling point:** 253 - 254°C; **Solubility in water:** also soluble in hot water; **Acidity (pK_a):**-16.2(21.0 in DMSO); **Basicity (pK_b):**- 17.6; **Molecular shape:**-Planar ;**Dipole moment:**-2.11 D in benzene

Resonance and Aromaticity

Indole is considered to be resonance hybrid of the following resonating structure. Thus, indole is an aromatic heterocyclic as it is cyclic planar with delocalized 10π electrons.

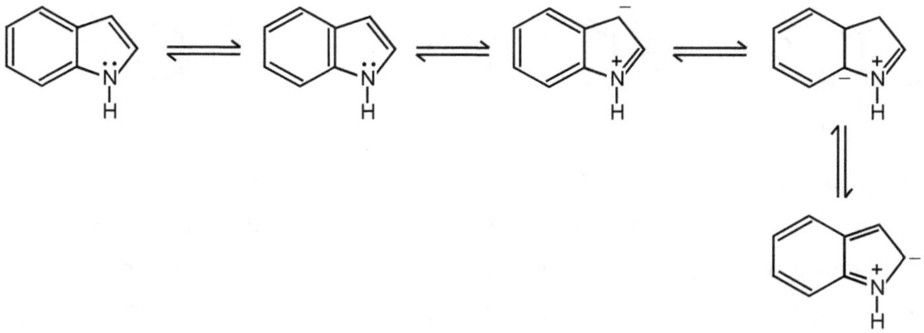

Basicity

Indole is very weak base. The pKa values for indole is -3.6; for 1-methylindole-2.3 and for 2 – methylindole -0.3 and for 3 – methylindole – 4.6. From this it is clear that the methyl group at position 1,2 enhances the basicity 1000 times but methyl group at position 3 decrease the basicity.

3. CHEMICAL REACTIONS OF INDOLE:

(a) Reactions with electrophilic reagents

The π electron excessive character of indole makes it extremely susceptible to undergo electrophilic substitution reaction. The electrophilic substitution at the 3-position (β Substitution) is preferred over the substitution at position 2(α-Substituion).

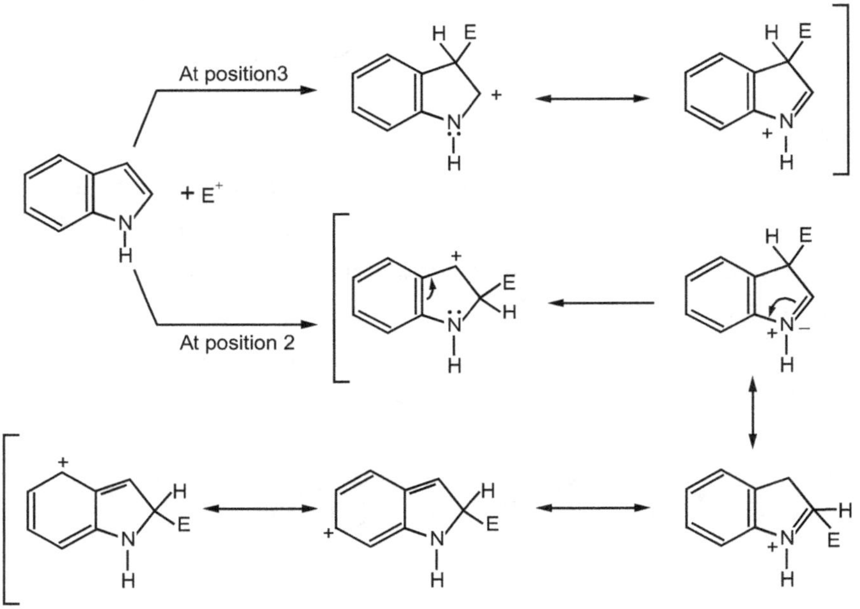

If the position 3 is already substituted the electrophilic substitution in indole occurs at the position 2 initially with the formation of 3,3disubstitued3H-indole which then rearranges to 2, 3 disubstituted indole. The presence of electron withdrawing substituents at the position 1, 2, or 3 of the pyrrole ring deactivates the pyrrol ring of indole towards electrophilic attack and the substitution occurs in the benzene ring in the positional reactivity order:6›4›5›7.

(b) Protonation:
Indoles, like pyrroles, are very weak bases: typical *pKa* values are; indole, -3.5; 3 methylindole, -4.6; 2-methylindole. -0.3. This means, for example, that in 6M sulfuric acid two molecules of indole are protonated for every one unprotonated, whereas 2-methylindole is almost completely protonated under

the same conditions. By NMR and UV examination, only the 3-protonated cation (3H-indolium cation) is dsetectable. it is the thermodynamically stablest cation.

1-H-indolium cation   2-H-indolium cation   3-H-indolium cation

2-methylindole is a stronger base than indole can be understood on the basis of stabilisation of the cation by electron release from the methyl group; 3-methylindole is a somewhat weaker base than indole.

(c) **Nitration:** The nitration using concentrated nitric acid and acetic anhydride at low temperature can be carried out.

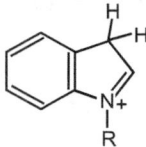

(d) **Sulfonation:** Indole because of its acid sensitivity, is sulphonated with pyridine-sulphur trioxide complex and provides indole-3-sulphonic acid instead of indole 2-sulphonic acid. If the position 3 is already occupied the sulphonation occurs at position 2.

(e) **Halogenation**

   (I) **Chlorination:** Chlorination of indole offers 3-chloroindole but, with excess of sulfuryl chloride the 3-chloroindole so produced react further with sulfuryl chloride and provides 2,3-dichloroindole. 3-Chloroindole is stable at high pH, but under acidic condition it is hydrolyzed to oxindole.

(II) Bromination: Bromination of indole occurs at the position 3 with the formation of 3-bromoindole. If the 3-position of indole is already substitutaed, the bromination takes place at position 2.

(III) Iodination: Iodination of indole occurs at the position 3 with the formation of 3-iodoindole. If the position of indole is already substitutaed, the iodination takes place at position 2 This iodination reaction takes place in chloroform at low temperature.

(f) Acylation

(i) Friedal-Craft Acylation: Indole substituted with electron withdrawing substituents undergo Friedal-Crafts acylation. However ,Indole with acetic anhydride in the presence of acetic acid produces 1-acetyl ,and 1,3-diacetyl,indoles. But with acetic anhydride in presence of sodium acetate the reaction proceeds vva an anion with the formation of 1-acetylindole.

(g) Vilsmeier Hack Formylation:

The Vilsmeier reaction is the most efficient route to 3-formylindoles and to other 3-acylindoles using tertiary amides of other acids in place of dimethylformamide.

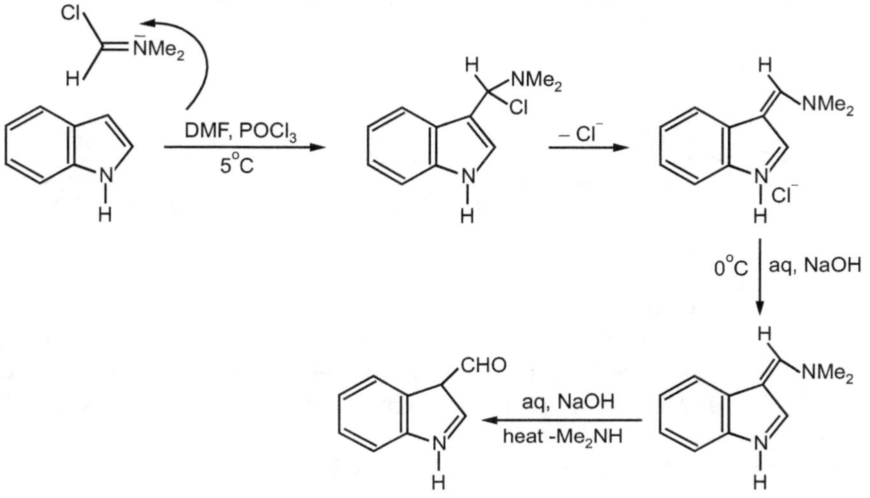

A particularly useful and high-yielding reaction is that between indole and oxalyl chloride, which gives a ketone-acid chloride convertible into a range of compounds. For example tryptamines. The synthesis of serotonin utilises this reaction.

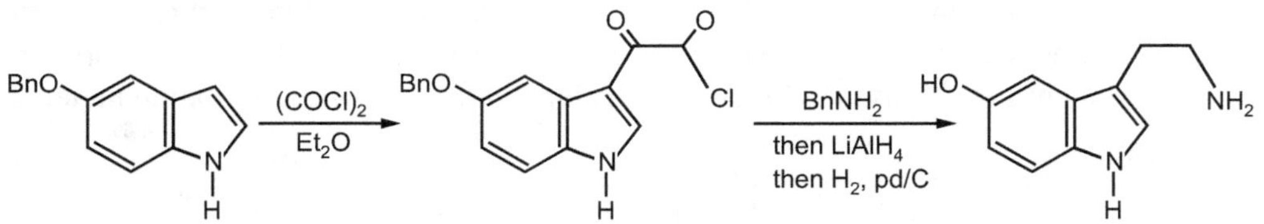

(h) Alkylation:

Indoles do not react with alkyl halides at room temperature. Indole itself begins to react with iodomethane in dimethylformamide at about 80°C, wherein the main product is skatole. As the temperature is raised, further methylation occurs until eventually 1,2,3,3-tetramethyl-3H-indolium iodide is formed.

[Scheme: Indole + MeI, 110°C, DMT, MeOH → 3-methylindole → 3,3-dimethyl-3H-indolium → 2,3-dimethylindole → ... → 1,2,3,3-tetramethyl-3-H-indolium iodide]

The rearrangement of 3,3-dialkyl-3*H*-indolium ions by alkyl migration to give 2,3-dialkylindoles, as shown in the sequence above, is related mechanistically to the Wagner-Meerwein rearrangement, and is known as the Plancher rearrangement.

(i) Reactions with Iminium ions: Mannich reactions

Under neutral conditions and at low temperature indole reacts with a mixture of formaldehyde and dimethylamine by substitution at the indole nitrogen; it seems likely that this reaction involves a low equilibrium concentration of the indolyl anion. In neutral solutions at higher temperature or in acetic acid, conversion into the thermodynamically more stable, 3-substituted product, gramine, takes place. Gramine is formed directly, smoothly and in high yield, by reaction in acetic acid. The Mannich reaction is very useful in synthesis because not only can the electrophilic iminium ion be varied widely, but the product gramines are themselves intermediates for a variety of synthetic manipulations.

[Scheme: Indole + HCHO, Me₂NH, H₂O, 0°C → 1-(dimethylaminomethyl)indole (CH₂NMe₂ on N) → AcOH, R.T. → gramine (3-CH₂NMe₂ indole)

CH₂O, Me₂NH, AcOH → OHCH₂NMe₂ →(+H, −OH₂)→ ⁺CH₂NMe₂]

(j) Reactions with Nucleophiles

The π excessive character of indole makes it relatively inert towards nucleophilic attack. It also exhibits a few oxidation, reduction and free radical reactions.

4. SYNTHESIS OF INDOLE:

(I) Reissert Indole Synthesis (Reaction of o-Nitrotoluene with Diethyl oxalate)

The reaction of o-nitrotolune with diethyl oxalate in presence of the base gives o-nitophenylpyruvate which on reductive cyclisation, followed by dehydration leads to formation of indole 2-carboxylate and on further hydroxylation and decarboxylation gives indole.

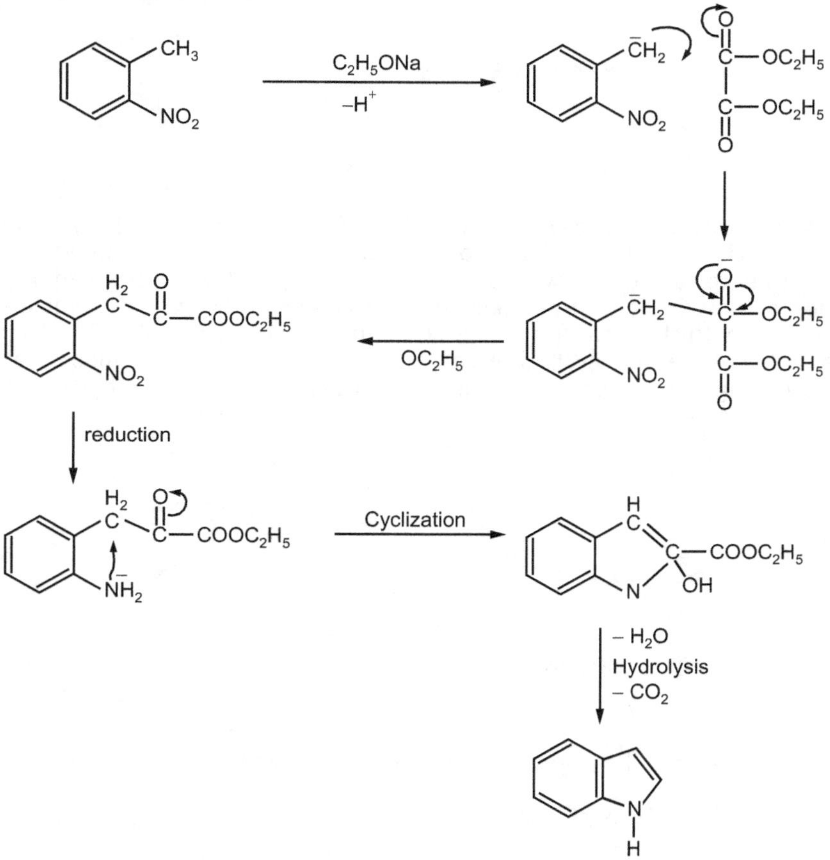

(II) Palladium Catalyse Cyclizations:
The reaction of o-allylaniline with palladium chloride in acetonitrile involves palladium ion catalyzed nucleophlic cyclization and procced with the formation of organopalladium intermediate which on subsequent reaction with trimethylamine provides 2-methylindole.

(III) Gassman Indole Synthesis: The reaction of aniline with *tert*-butyl hypochlorite gives N-chloroaniline which on treatment with β-ketosulfide produces azasulfonium salt, which with a weak base is deprotonated and generates sulfur ylide to undergone intramolecular rearrangement known as Somelet- Hauser Reaction. With the cleavage of N-S bond and the formation of C-C bond providing α-amino ketone the cyclisation of it results into 3-methyl thioindole but the methylthio group can be easily removed by the reaction with Raney-Ni.

(IV) The Fischer synthesis: The Fischer synthesis, involves the acid or Lewis acid catalysed rearrangement of a phenylhydrazone with the elimination of ammonia. The preparation of 2-phenylindole illustrates the process in its simplest form.

In many instances the reaction can be carried out simply by heating together the aldehyde or ketone and phenyl hydrazine in acetic acid; the formation of the phenyl Hydrazone and its subsequent rearrangement takes place without the necessity for isolation of the phenyl hydrazone. Toluene sulfonic acid, cation exchange resins and phosphorus trichloride have each been recommended for efficient cyclisations, sometimes even at or below room temperature. Electron-releasing substituents on the benzene ring increase the rate of Fischer cyclisation whereas, electron withdrawing substituents slow the process down. Electron-withdrawing substituents *meta* to the nitrogen give rise to roughly equal amounts of 4- and 6-substituted indoles; electron releasing groups similarly oriented produce mainly the 6-substituted indole. There is evidence that the loss of the β-nitrogen as ammonia, and in some cases intermediates have been detected. The most important step - the one in which a carbon-carbon bond is made, is electrocyclic in character and analogous to the Claisen rearrangement of phenylallyl ethers

(V) The Bischler synthesis: In the original method, the Bischler synthesis, harsh acidic treatment of α-arylaminoketones (produced from the 2-haloketone and an arylamine) was used to ring about electrophilic cyclisation onto the aromatic ring; these conditions often resulted in mixtures of products *via* rearrangements. It is now known that N-acylated-α-arylaminoketones can be cyclised under much more controlled conditions and in contrast to early work, this approach to indoles can even be used to produce heteroring unsubstituted indoles.

IMIDAZOLE

1. STRUCTURE

Imidazole or *iminazoline* is an azapyrrole. The nitrogen atom being separated by one carbon atom. This compound was earlier also called as glyoxaline as it was first prepared from glyoxal and ammonia. Imidazole is a heterocyclic aromatic organic compound and refers to the parent compound $C_3H_4N_2$

Imidazole is a planar molecule with the following structural parameters. The structure of imidazole is with the combined structural features of both pyrrole and pyridine. Imidazole can act as a base and as a weak acid. The aromatic sextet is contributed by one electron each from three carbon atoms and the pyridine-type nitrogen but two electrons are contributed by the pyrrole - type nitrogen. Imidazole is an aromatic heterocycle with resonance energy of 59 kJ/mol and is considered to be resonance hybrid of the following resonating structures.

The dipolar resonating structures indicate the amphoteric nature of imidazole. The resonating structure (iv) contributes much more to the resonance hybrid as the negative charge is more stabilized on the nitrogen than on the carbon. The resonating structure (v) is also important as the positive charge on C-2 is stabilized by the negative charge on N-3 with the reduction in electron availability at the position-2 due to the electron withdrawing effect of both the nitrogen atoms

2. PHYSICAL PROPERTIES

Appearance	white or pale yellow solid
Density	1.23 g/cm^3, solid
Melting point	89-91°C
Boiling point	256°C
Solubility in water	miscible
Acidity (pKa)	pK$_a$=6.993
Dipole moment	12.8 Cm*10^{30}

Hydrogen bonding: The boiling point of imidazole (b.p. 256°C) is relatively higher as compared to boiling points of other five-membered heterocyclic systems. The higher boiling point of Imidazole is attributed probably to the intermolecular hydrogen bonding of the type N-H...N. But the hydrogen bonding is not possible, if the position-1 of imidazoles is substituted. N-substituted imidazoles, therefore, have much lower boiling points, e.g. 1-methylimidazole; b.p. 198^{0}C.

3. CHEMICAL REACTIONS

Reactivity:

Imidazole is considered to exhibit properties of pyrrole as well as of pyridine because of the presence of pyrrole-type and pyridine-type of nitrogens in the imidazole ring system.

Pyrrole-β and pyridine-α ⟶ N: ⟵ Basic
Pyrrol-α and pyridine-β ⟶ ⟵ Pyrrole-α and pyridine-α

The reactivity of imidazole can be inferred from the structural specificity of the imidazole nucleus relating to the pyrrole-type nitrogen and pyridine-type nitrogen and from the resonating structures contributing maximum to the imidazole nucleus:[2]

(i) electrophillic attack occurs at N-3 (pyridine-type) but not at N-1 (pyrrole-type) because the lone pair on pyrrole-type nitrogen is involved in the aromatic sextet.
(ii) the attack of electrophile also occurs at the annular carbon atoms (C-4 and C-5).
(iii) the attack of nucleophile takes place at C-2 or N-1.
(iv) amphotric nature of Imidazole.

(a) Reactions with Acids

Imidazole is a monoacidic base and forms crystalline salts with acids. It also possesses weakly acidic properties [pseudo acidic]. Imidazole is the most basic [pKa = 7.0] among 1,3-azoles; oxazole [pKa = 0.8] and thiazole [pKa = 2.5], and forms salts with acids. Imidazole is a stronger base even than pyridine [pKa = 5.2]. The abnormally high basicity of imidazole is attributed to the relatively low electronegativity of nitrogen and the symmetrical structure of the imidazolium cation which is resonance stabilized. Thus, with this property imidazole at physiological pH (7.4) exists in both the forms; free base and imidazolium cation, and causes histidine to act as a proton acceptor or a proton donor depending on the environment.

(b) Quaternarisation:

Quatrnarisation of imidazole at the nitrogen atom is normally achieved by the reaction of alkyl halides or dialkyl sulfates under strongly basic conditions in an organic solvent while in water the yields are usually low owing to the strong water solubility of the reaction product. Alkylation of imidazole has been achieved satisfactorily by heating 1-carbo-ethoxyimidazoles obtained by reacting imidazole with ethyl chloroformate.

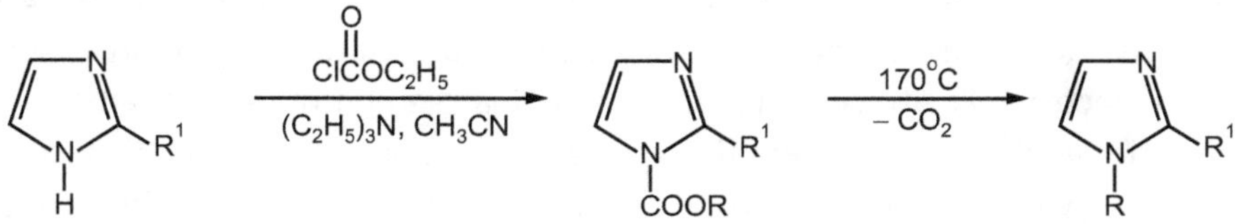

(c) Electrophillic Substitution

(i) **Electrophillic attack at Nitrogen:** Imidazole contains two nitrogen atoms; pyrrole-type nitrogen and pyridine-type nitrogen but the attack of electrophile occurs at pyridine-type nitrogen containing lone pair in the plane of ring (orthogonal to the plane of π-molecular orbital) because the attack of electrophile at pyrrole-type nitrogen disrupts the aromaticity with the use of lone pair oinvolved in aromatic sextet.

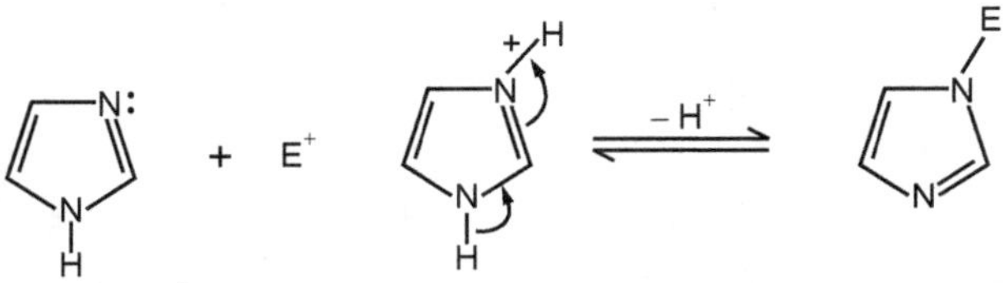

(ii) **N-Alkylation:** Imidazoles substituted at N-1 are alkylated readily at N-3 with the formation of quaternary salts. But the alkylation of imidazole with free N-H group produces protonated N-alkylimidazole.

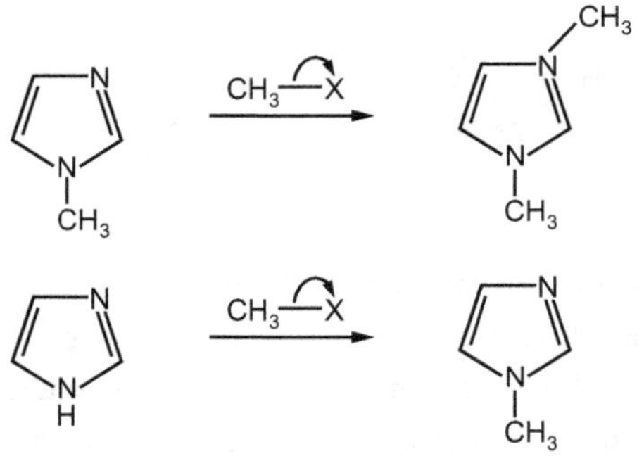

(iii) N-Acylation: Imidazole with free N-H group can N-Acylated by the reaction with acid chloride (2:1 ratio) in an inert solvent at room temperature with the formation of N-acylimidazoles via N-acylimidazolium cation.

(iv) Electrophilic attack at Carbon: Due to the charged structures of imidazole, it possesses increased reactivity toward electrophilic attack. It is more susceptible to electrophilic attack than pyrazole or thiazole and more so than even furan and thiophene. However, the reactivity of imidazole towards electrophiles varies with the reaction conditions. The reactions under acidic conditions involve imidazolium cation which exhibits deactivating effect towards electrophilic attack and therefore the attack of electrophile occurs with difficulty. But the attack of electrophile is facilitated if the reaction involves an imidazole anion or neutral imidazole.

Orientation: In imidazole ring system the attack of electrophile occurs preferentially at C-5 which is the most activated position for the electrophilic attack. However, the tautomerism in imidazole makes C-4 and C-5 positions equivalent. The preferential attack of electrophile at C-5 in imidazole can be explained in terms of the relative stabilities of the σ-complexes (intermediates) resulting from the electrophilic attack at the positions-2, -4 and -5. The electrophilic substitution at the position-2 is unfavourable because the intermediate resulting from the electrophilic attack at the position-2 involves highly unfavoured and less contributing resonating structure (i) with positive charge at N-3.

(e) **Nitration:** Imidazole is nitrated with a mixture of concentrated nitric and sulfuric acids at 160°C with the formation of 4-nitroimidazole. The reaction proceeds to involve the attack of electrophile (nitronium ion) at the position-4 of the imidazolium cation (imidazole conjugated acid).

Nitration of imidazole

(f) **Sulfonation:** When imidazole is treated with 50-60% oleum (H_2SO_4-SO_3) at 160°C, the sulfonation occurs at the position-4 involving the attack of electrophile on the imidazolium cation.

(g) **Halogenation:** Halogenation of imidazole is very complex and varies considerably depending on the substrate, reagents and reaction conditions. Direct chlorination gives undefined products. Imidazole is brominated very readily in aqueous solution or organic solvent with the bromination (Br/CHCl$_3$) at the available vacant nuclear positions providing 2,4,5-tribromoimidazole.

Imidazole   2,4,5-Tribromoimidazole

Imidazole is iodinated only under alkaline conditions and produces 2,4,5-triiodoimidazole involving an imidazolyl anion as the reactive species. The reaction proceeds to involve the attack of molecular iodine at the position-4 of imidazolyl anion.

Imidazole ⇌ (Base, I₂) 2,4,5-Triiodoimidazole

(h) Diazo Coupling: N-Unsubstituted imidazoles substituted with activating substituents (electron releasing) undergo diazo coupling readily in alkaline medium preferentially at the position-2. The reaction proceeds to involve the coupling of diazonium ion with the anion of N-unsubstituted imidazole at the position-2. The presence of electron-releasing substituents on the imidazole ring facilitates diazo coupling, while the electron-withdrawing substituents deactivate the imidazole ring towards electrophilic attack of the diazonium ion to a greater or lesser extent. N-substituted imidazoles fail to undergo diazo coupling as the involvement of an imidazole anion is not possible in the reaction.

R-imidazole + Ar—N≡N⁺ (pH 7-11) → 2-(arylazo)-R-imidazole

Diazo coupling imidazole

(i) Reactions with Aldehydes and Ketones: N-Unsubstituted imidazoles undergo hydroxymethylation at the position-4 (or C-5) when treated with formaldehyde in the presence of DMSO.

Imidazole + HCHO / DMSO → 4-hydroxymethylimidazole

However, with N-substituted imidazole hydroxymethylation occurs at the position-2. The reaction proceeds with the electrophilic attack initially at the position-3 followed by C-2 deprotonation and intramolecular rearrangement (1,2-migration).

N-methylimidazole + HCHO → 1-methyl-2-(hydroxymethyl)imidazole

(j) Oxidation: Imidazole ring is resistant to oxidation, but it is degraded by hydrogen peroxide and perbenzoic acid.

[Reaction scheme: Imidazole (N-H) reacts with H_2O_2 to give CONH$_2$–CONH$_2$; with C_6H_5–C(O)–O–OH to give $NH_3 + NH_2CONH_2$.]

(k) Reactions with Nucleophiles: Imidazoles undergo nucleophilic substitution reactions very readily with the nucleophilic attack at the position-2, if substituted with electron-withdrawing substituents or quaternerized. However, the position of electron-withdrawing substituent can modify the site of nucleophilic attack. Often a nucleophilic attack results in ring fission.

2-Haloimidazoles undergo nucleophilic substitution reactions with the replacement of halogen by nucleophile. The halogen atoms at the -4 and -5 positions of imidazoles are normally unreactive but activated by the α- or γ- electron-withdrawing substituent.

[Reaction: 1-methyl-4,5-diphenyl-2-bromoimidazole + piperidine (HN) → 1-methyl-4,5-diphenyl-2-piperidinoimidazole]

However, in some cases nucleophilic attack results in the cleavage of the ring.

[Reaction: Imidazole (N-H) + C_6H_5COCl / OH^- → 1,3-bis(benzoyl)imidazolium intermediate (N-COC$_6H_5$ at both N) → OH^- → ring-opened product HC(NHCOC$_6H_5$)=CH(NHCOC$_6H_5$)]

(l) Formation of metal complexes: Imidazole forms complex with many metal ions in which the pyridine-like N-atom provides the donor. e.g., dichloroimidazole cobalt (II):[3]

[Structure: two imidazole rings coordinated via N to central Co, with two Cl ligands]

Dichloroimidazole cobalt (II)

4. SYNTHESIS OF IMIDAZOLE

Several approaches are available for the synthesis of imidazoles.

(i) **The Radiszewski Synthesis:** It consists of condensing a dicarbonyl compound such as glyoxal, α-diketones with an aldehyde in the presence of ammonia. Benzil for instance, with benzaldehyde and two molecules of ammonia react to yield 2,4,5-triphenylimidazole. Formamide often proves a convenient substitute for ammonia.

(ii) **Marckwald Synthesis (Reaction of α-Amino Ketones with cyanates, thiocyanates or isothiocyanates):** The reaction of α-amino ketones with cyanates, thiocyanates or isothiocyanates produces 2-mercaptoimidazoles which can be converted readily to the corresponding imidazoles by oxidation or dehydrogenation. If α-amino ketones are treated with cyanamide in place of thiocyanate or isothiocyanate, 2-aminoimidazoles are obtained.

(iii) **Dehydrogenation of Imidazolines:** Imidazole have been prepared by dehydrogenation of imidazolines in the presence of sulphur. However, a milder reagent, barium manganate has been recently reported by Knapp and coworkers. Imidazolines thus obtained from alkyl nitriles and 1,2-ethanediamines on reaction with $BaMnO_4$ yields 2-substituted imidazole.

(iv) **Reaction of Oxamide with Phosphorus Oxychloride (Wallach Synthesis):** The reaction of N,N'-disubstituted oxamide with phosphorus oxychloride produces chlorine containing intermediate which on reduction with hydroiodic acid affords 1-substituted imidazole.

(v) **Reaction of 1,2-Diaminoalkanes with Carboxylic Acids and Aldehydes or Ketones:** When 1,2-diaminoalkanes are treated with carboxylic acids and aldehydes or ketones at high temperature in the presence of dehydrogenating agent (Pt/Al_2O_3), 2-alkylimidazoles are obtained.

(vi) Ring contraction (From Pyrazines): 2-Chloropyrazine undergoes ring contraction to imidazole if treated with potassium amide in liquid ammonia. The reaction proceeds to involve the following mechanism.

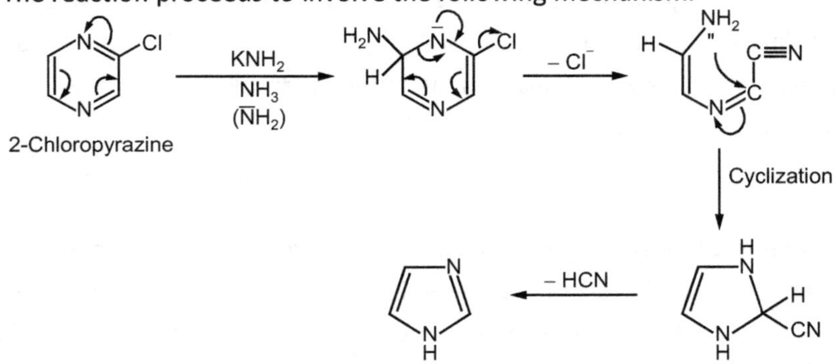

(vii) Ring Transformation (From Oxazoles): Oxazoles undergo ring transformation when treated with ammonia, formamide, hydrazines or amine in the presence of Bronsted acid.(Scheme 8).

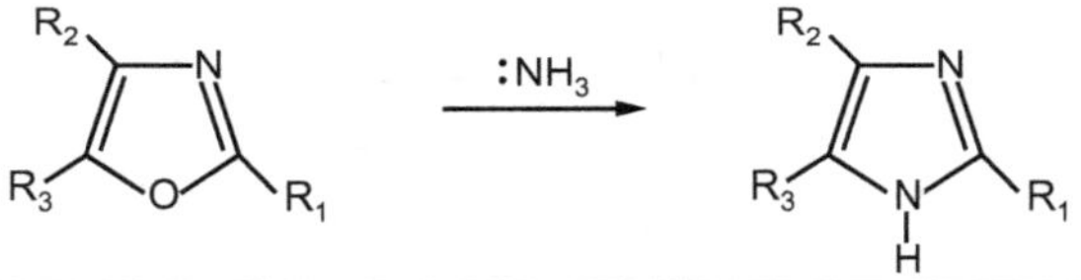

PYRIDINE

1. STRUCTURE, REACTIVITY AND ORIENTATION

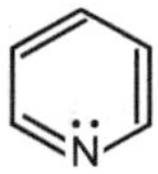

C_6H_5N

(i) Source:

$$\text{Coal tar} \xrightarrow[\text{Fractional distillation}]{80-170°C} \text{Light oil} \xrightarrow[\text{dil. } H_2SO_4]{\text{Extracted with}} \text{acid-extract}$$

↓ NaOH neutralization

$$\text{Pyridine} \xleftarrow[115°C]{\text{Redistilled at}} \text{Distillate at } 115°C \xleftarrow{\text{Fractional distillation}}$$

(ii) Aromatic Character:

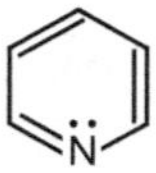

Huckel no. = 4n + 2 = π
4n + 2 = 6
n = 1

In pyridine **6** delocalized π electrons are present in planar hexagonal structure. It obeys Huckel number and hence aromatic in nature.

(iii) Electrophilic attack at position 3 and 5:

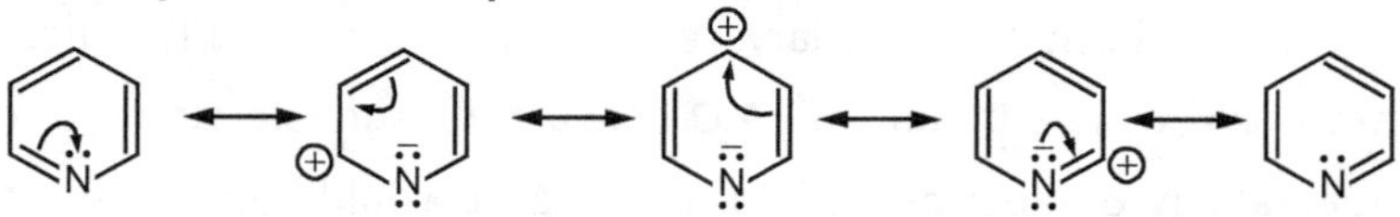

Total **05** resonating structures can be drawn, the partial positive charges on the **2–, 4– and 6–** positions in the resonance hybrid indicates electron dense. Therefore the pyridine ring is deactivated are direction of dipole moment also supports this.

So, pyridine will undergo **electrophilic substitution** reactions **less readily** than benzene.

The resonance hybrid of pyridine further tells us that **3– and 5–** positions of pyridine are **more electron dense** than 2–, 4– and 6– positions. Therefore, incoming electrophile will take 3 (or 5) position preferential. This is also supported by the greater stability of the σ-complex for the **3-attack** than those of σ-complexes for 2 and 4 attack.

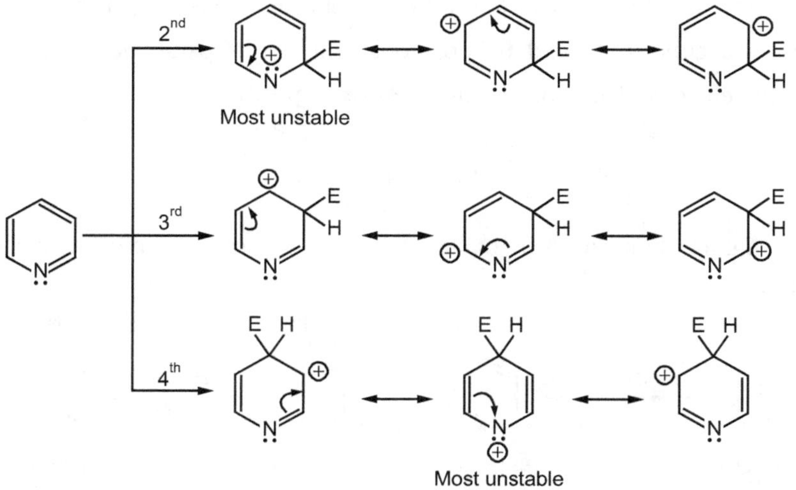

Each of the σ-complexes for the 2-attack and 4-attack contains a very unstable structures in which the more electronegative element nitrogen bears a positive charge; whereas the complex for the 3-attack does not contain such an unstable structures.

(iv) Basic character: Pyridine is appreciably basic; it is more basic than pyrrole since a pair of electrons on the N-atom do not take part in preserving aromatic character of the compound and hence the electrons are available for donation.

Ofcourse, it is much less basic than tertiary amines (pka = 10 – 11); since the donatable electron-pair reside in an sp^2 A.O. having reasonable amount of S character, the donatability of electrons is less than that it would have been if they were in an sp^3 A.O.

2. CHEMICAL PROPERTIES:

(a) Nitration

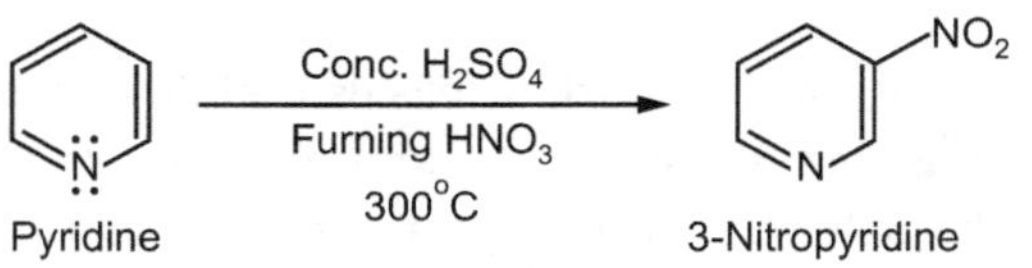

$$\text{Pyridine} \xrightarrow[\text{Furning HNO}_3]{\text{Conc. H}_2\text{SO}_4, 300°C} \text{3-Nitropyridine}$$

The presence of positive inductive group in the ring (– OH, – NH_2 etc.) will accelerate the S_E reactions. When such a group present at 3-position, the electrophilic substitution occurs at 2– and 6– positions; but if the group occupies 2– or 4– position, the electrophilic attack occurs at 3– or 5– position.

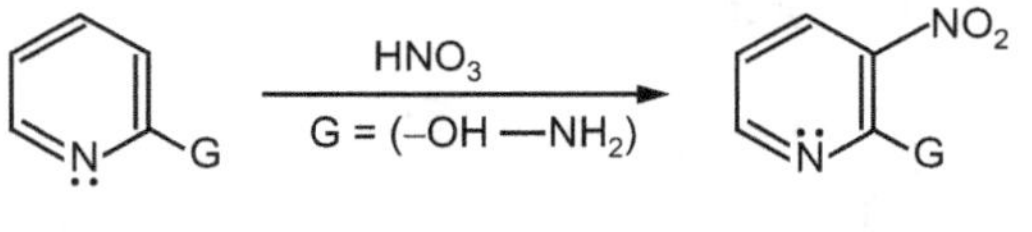

$$\text{Pyridine-G} \xrightarrow[G = (-OH, -NH_2)]{HNO_3} \text{Nitropyridine-G}$$

Pyridine is indirectly nitrated by oxidising 2– and 4– aminopyridine with H_2O_2 and sulphuric acid.

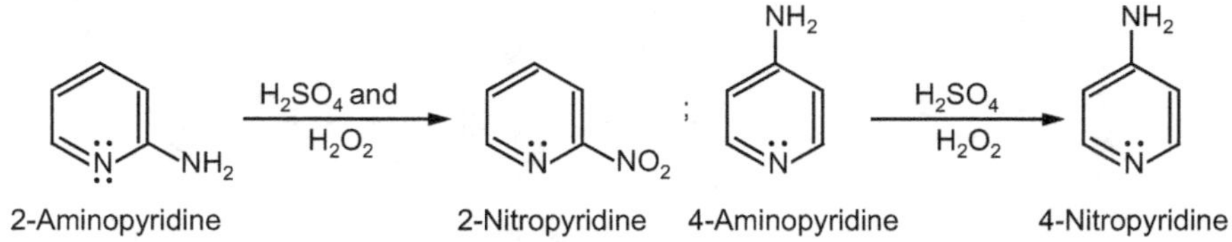

$$\text{2-Aminopyridine} \xrightarrow{H_2SO_4 \text{ and } H_2O_2} \text{2-Nitropyridine} \quad ; \quad \text{4-Aminopyridine} \xrightarrow{H_2SO_4, H_2O_2} \text{4-Nitropyridine}$$

(b) Halogenation

Pyridine + Br₂ / Charcoal at 300°C → 3-Bromopyridine + 3,5-Dibromopyridine

Pyridine + Br₂ / Charcoal at 500°C → 2-Bromopyridine + 2,6-Dibromopyridine

Halogenation at 4-position may also be carried out via pyridine-1-oxide (same as nitration).

(c) Sulphonation

Pyridine + 20% oleium (excess SO_3) (120% H_2SO_4) at 220°C → Pyridine-3-sulphonic acid

(d) Mercuration

Pyridine + Aq. Hg(OAc)₂ → 3-HgOAc pyridine

The Hofmann-Martius rearrangement.

Pyridine-N-methyl iodide —Δ, 300°C→ 2-Methylpyridine + 4-Methylpyridine

(e) Alkylation and acylation

Since pyridine forms salts with Lewis acid, it cannot be alkylated by the Fridel-Crafts method. It can be indirectly alkylated by the Hofmann-Martius rearrangement.

(f) Oxidation

The pyridine ring being deactivated, it is very resistant towards oxidation, on treatment with peracids, however, pyridine forms pyridine-1-oxide.

Pyridine —CF_3COOOH / $-CF_3COOH$→ Pyridine-N-oxide ⇌ (resonance structures) —Pd_3 or $H_2/Pd/HCl$→ Pyridine

(g) Reduction

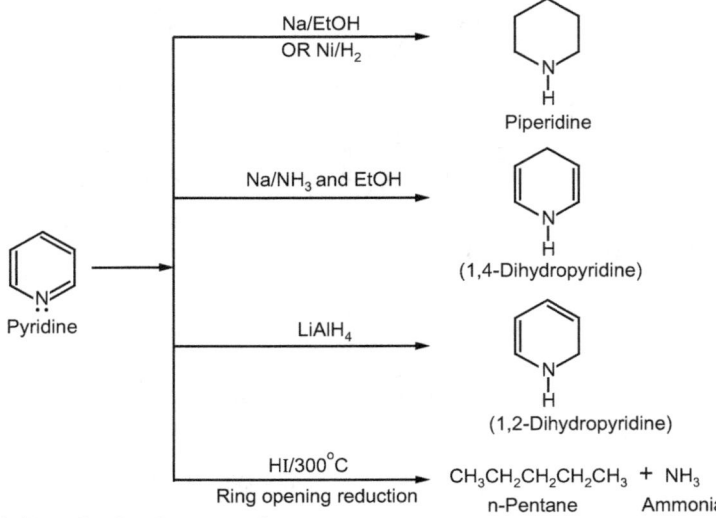

(h) Nucleophilic substitution reactions:

So far as nucleophilic substitution is concerned, the order of reactivity amongst benzene, pyrrole and pyridine is pyridine > benzene > pyrrole. Why is it so?

Let us determine the electronic charge on the constituent atoms of the three given compounds considering their resonance hybrid.

All the C atoms of benzene are equivalent and no extra charge develops on any one of the six C's.

P_z orbital of the N atom contains 2 electrons in pyrrole. It therefore, cannot accommodate further electron. To preserve aromaticity, its electrons move away from it. Thus negative charge appears on each of the carbons in pyrrole with prevents nucleophilic attach.

Because of the greater electronegativity of N atom than that of C atom, the nitrogen draws electron towards itself without disturbing aromaticity in pyridine. The N atom has one C in its P_z orbital. It accommodate another electron electron from neighbouring C atom. Thus the N atom becomes negatively charge and C_2, C_4 and C_6 becomes positively charged. Therefore C atoms are less electron dense than C_3 and C_5 atoms.

Since nucleophilic substitution occurs at less electron dense site, it will occur most readily in pyridine at C_2, C_4 and C_6; in pyrrole it will occur least readily and the position of benzene in this respect in intermediate between pyridine and pyrrole. So the reactivity order (Nucleophilic substitution), Pyridine > Benzene > Pyrrole.

(i) Tischitischibabin Reactions:

It is a reaction by which pyridine and other heterocyclic nitrogen compounds are aminated mainly at α-positions with respect to the nitrogen atom by alkali metal amide ($NaNH_2$) in liquid ammonia at an elevated temperature (100 – 200°C), where H gets displaced by $:\overline{NH}_2$ ion.

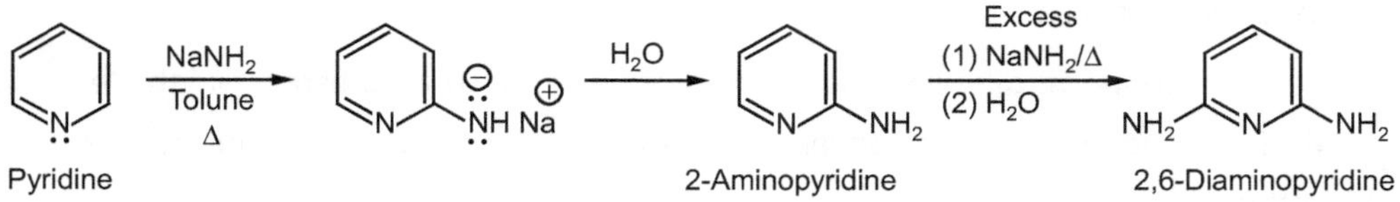

Pyridine → (NaNH₂, Toluene, Δ) → intermediate → (H₂O) → 2-Aminopyridine → (Excess (1) NaNH₂/Δ (2) H₂O) → 2,6-Diaminopyridine

(j) Hydroxylation:

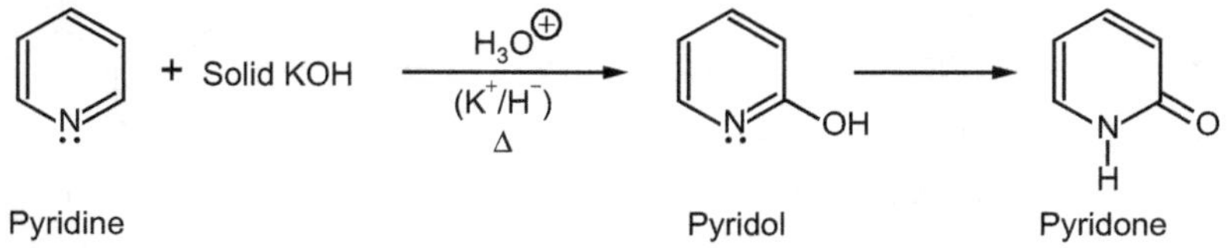

Pyridine + Solid KOH → (H₃O⁺, (K⁺/H⁻), Δ) → Pyridol → Pyridone

3. SYNTHESIS OF PYRIDINE:

(i) From furfural:

Furfural rearranges to pyridine in presence of reducing agent raney-nickel and ammonia at 500°C.

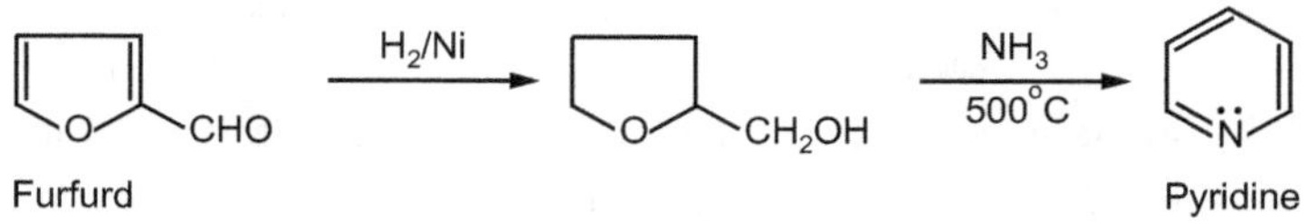

Furfurd → (H₂/Ni) → CH₂OH intermediate → (NH₃, 500°C) → Pyridine

(ii) From pyrrole:

Pyrrole forms salt with sodium ethoxide, which subsequent rearranges to pyridine at 200°C in presence of methylenediiodide.

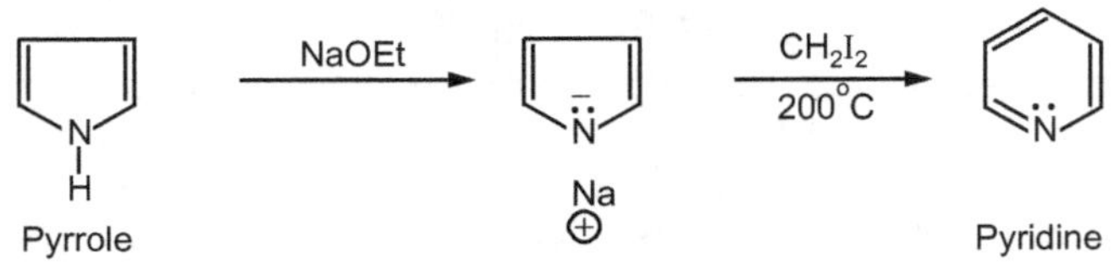

Pyrrole → (NaOEt) → Pyrrole-Na⁺ salt → (CH_2I_2, 200°C) → Pyridine

(iii) From acetylene and hydrogen cyanide.

$$CH{\equiv}CH + CH{\equiv}CH + H-C{\equiv}N \xrightarrow{\text{Passed over red hot tube}} \text{Pyridine}$$

Acetylene + Acetylene + Hydrogen cyanide

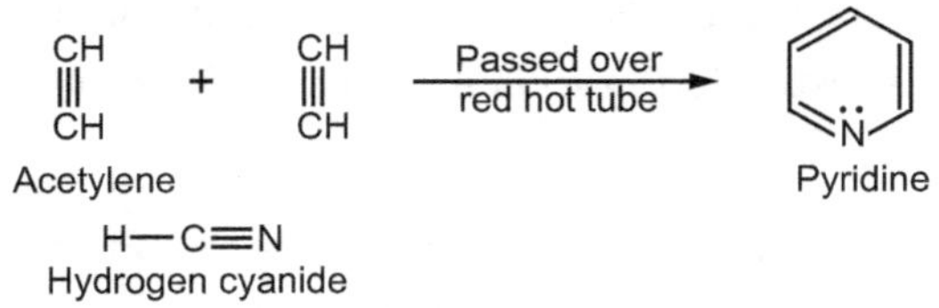

When a mixture of acetylene and hydrogen cyanide is passed over red hot tube, it forms pyridine.

(iv) Hantzsch Synthesis

The formation of dihydropyridine derivative from β-keto-ester, aldehydes and ammonia and subsequent conversion to pyridines is called the "Hantzsch pyridine synthesis".

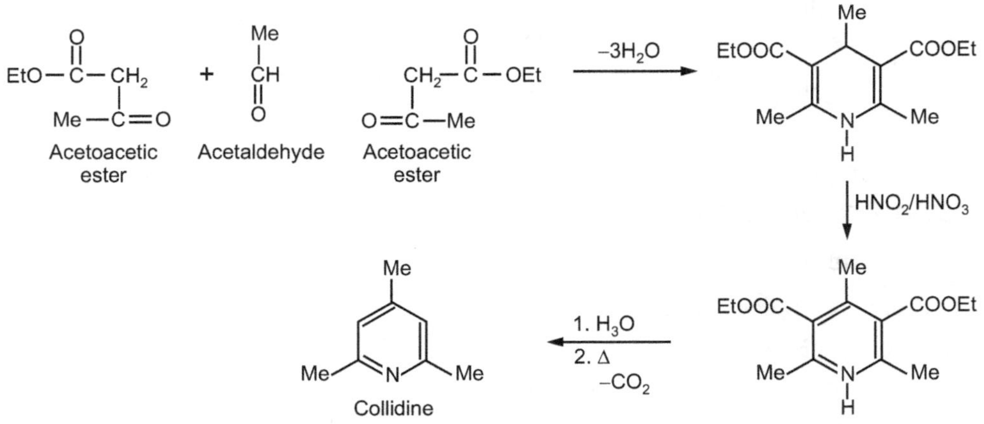

Acetoacetic ester (EtO–CO–CH₂–CO–Me) + Acetaldehyde (Me–CHO) + Acetoacetic ester (Me–CO–CH₂–CO–OEt) $\xrightarrow{-3H_2O}$ 3,5-bis(ethoxycarbonyl)-2,4,6-trimethyl-1,4-dihydropyridine

↓ HNO_2/HNO_3

3,5-bis(ethoxycarbonyl)-2,4,6-trimethylpyridine

$\xrightarrow[\text{2. }\Delta,\ -CO_2]{\text{1. }H_3O}$ Collidine (2,4,6-trimethylpyridine)

HNO_3 or HNO_2 is acts as aromatizing agent. If formaldehyde is used instead of acetaldehyde, the product is 2, 6 dimethyl pyridine.

QUINOLINE

1. STRUCTURE, REACTIVITY AND ORIENTATION:

[Quinoline structure with numbered positions 1-8, N at position 1] C_9H_5N

(i) Source: Coal - tar, bare oil and quinine alkaloids.

Coal tar $\xrightarrow{200 - 250°C}$ Middle oil fraction $\longrightarrow$ distillate $\downarrow$ treated with acid

Quinoline $\xleftarrow[\text{distillation 240°C}]{\text{alkali}}$ acid-extract

(ii) The resonance hybrid of quinoline is written below:

[Resonance structures I through VII shown]

(iii) Electrophile attack at Position 8:

[Resonance structures I through VI shown for electrophilic attack at position 8]

The resonating structures of quinoline show that 2, 4, 5 and 7 positions are electron deficient, but the 3, 6 and 8 positions never acquired as positive charge. Therefore, 3-position is more electron-dense than the 2 and 4 - positions. Hence, electrophilic substitution in quinoline will preferentially at 3-position. However, electrophilic substitution occurs also at 8 and 6. The most preferential position for electrophilic substitution is "8".

From the resonating strs. 2, 4, 5 and 7 are electron deficiency so nucleophilic substitution occurs at 2 and if it is blocked, the reaction occurs at 4-positon.

(iv) Electrophile attack at position 6 (Less stable):

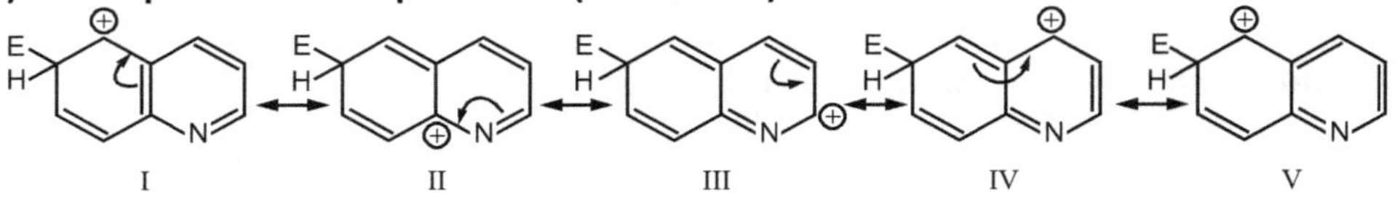

[Resonance structures I, II, III, IV, V shown]

2. CHEMICAL PROPERTIES:

Since quinoline is 2, 3-benzopyridine, it resembles pyridine in many of its reactions. Quinoline is also aromatic compound containing 10 π electrons (Huckle number). Again, since pyridine ring of quinoline is deactivated one, it undergoes electrophilic substitution (S_E) as well as nucleophilic substitution (S_N) reactions.

(a) Basic character:

However, quinoline is a basic compound, because lone pair is intact with nitrogen and does not taking part in preserving aromaticity of quinoline. But it is less basic than pyridine.

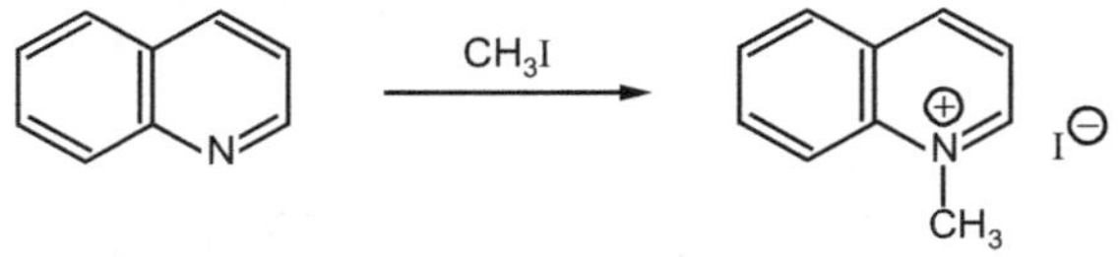

[Reaction: Quinoline + CH₃I → N-methyl quinolinium iodide]

Why electrophilic substitution (S_E) at "8" position is Quinoline?

Like pyridine the electron withdrawing properties of nitrogen atom deactivates the pyridine ring of quinoline towards electrophilic reagents and hence the electrophilic substitution (S_E) occurs preferentially in the benzene ring whereas the nucleophilic substitution occurs preferentially in the pyridine ring, especially if acidic conditions are used.

(b) Oxidation:

Pyridine ring in quinoline being deactivated, it is resistant to oxidation for this reason, the benzene ring opens in this case. The sequential reaction written below shows that quinoline contains a pyridine ring.

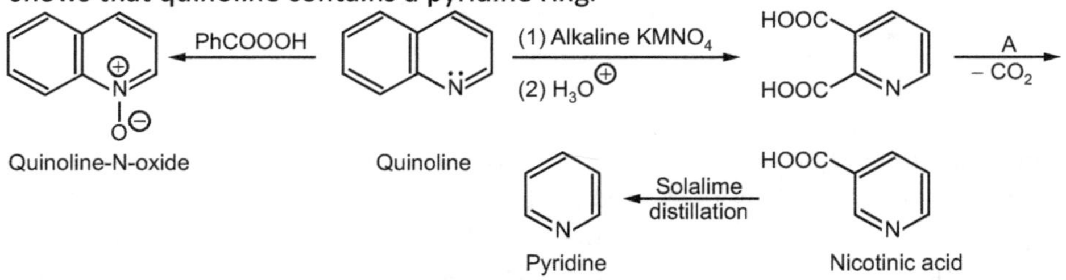

[Reaction sequence: Quinoline-N-oxide ← PhCOOOH ← Quinoline → (1) Alkaline KMNO₄, (2) H₃O⁺ → 2,3-pyridinedicarboxylic acid → Δ, –CO₂ → Nicotinic acid; Pyridine ← Solalime distillation]

Quinoline-N-oxide   Quinoline   Nicotinic acid

Pyridine

(c) Reduction:

Quinoline on reduction gives:
- With Pt/H₂, CH₃COOH → Decahydro quinoline
- With Sn/HCl → 1,2,3,4-Tetrahydro quinoline
- With LiAlH₄ or Na (NH₃Cl) → 1,2-Dihydro quinoline

(d) Electrophilic Substitution Reactions:

Quinoline undergoes electrophilic substitution reactions in the benzene ring preferably at position 8 and 5.

- HNO₃ – Ac₂O → 3-Nitroquinoline
- Fuming HNO₃ and Fuming H₂SO₄ → 8-Nitroquinoline + 5-Nitroquinoline
- Fuming H₂SO₄, 220°C → Quinoline-5-Sulphonic acid + Quinoline-8-Sulphonic acid → (300°C) Quinoline-6-Sulphonic acid
- Vapour-phase Bromination below 500°C → 3-Bromoquinoline
- Above 500°C → 2-Bromoquinoline (By N-oxide mech.)
- Under high acidic medium → 8-Bromoquinoline + 5-Bromoquinoline

(e) Nucleophilic Substitution Reaction:

Quinoline readily gives nucleophilic substitution reactions at 2-position, if this position is blocked the reaction occurs at 4-position.

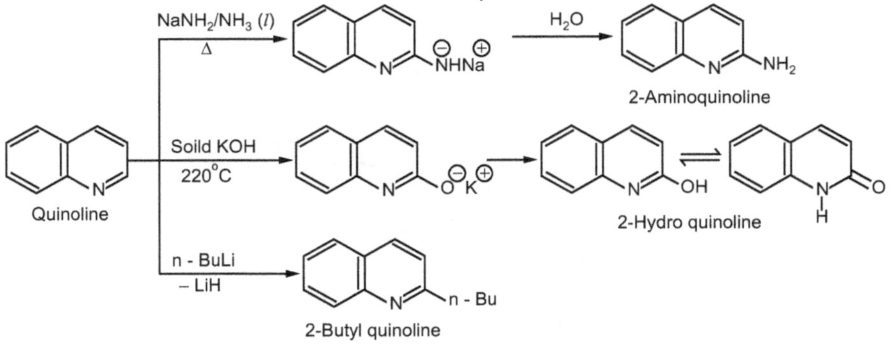

Quinoline reacts via three pathways:
- With $NaNH_2/NH_3$ (l), Δ → 2-(NHNa) intermediate → H_2O → **2-Aminoquinoline** (NH_2 at 2-position)
- With Solid KOH, 220°C → 2-OK intermediate → 2-hydroxyquinoline (**2-Hydro quinoline**) ⇌ quinolin-2(1H)-one
- With n-BuLi, –LiH → **2-Butyl quinoline** (n-Bu at 2-position)

3. SYNTHESIS OF QUINOLINE

(i) Skraup synthesis:

When aniline and substituted anilines are treated with glycerol, conc. H_2SO_4, nitrobenzene (oxidizing agent) and ferrous sulphate (makes reaction less violent), quinoline and quinoline derivatives are formed and the reaction is called "Skraup Quinoline Synthesis". When the aniline derivative is o-aminophenol, the product is 8-hydropxyquinoline.

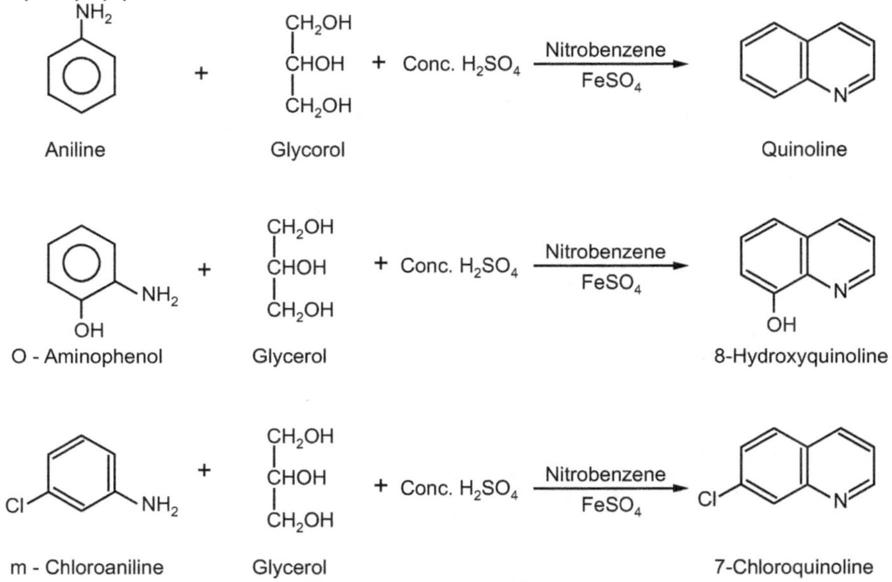

Aniline + Glycerol (CH_2OH–$CHOH$–CH_2OH) + Conc. H_2SO_4 $\xrightarrow{\text{Nitrobenzene}, FeSO_4}$ Quinoline

o-Aminophenol + Glycerol + Conc. H_2SO_4 $\xrightarrow{\text{Nitrobenzene}, FeSO_4}$ 8-Hydroxyquinoline

m-Chloroaniline + Glycerol + Conc. H_2SO_4 $\xrightarrow{\text{Nitrobenzene}, FeSO_4}$ 7-Chloroquinoline

Mechanism:

Step 1: Dehydration of glycerol and formation of acraldehyde.

Here – OH will go as H₂O from secondary carbon, because it forms more stable carbocation than primary.

Step 2: This is a Michael type addition of the primary aromatic amine to the α, β-unsaturated aldehyde, acraldehyde.

Step 3: This step involves the Friedel-Crafts ring closure.

Step 4: Oxidative aromatisation, nitrobenzene is the oxidising agent.

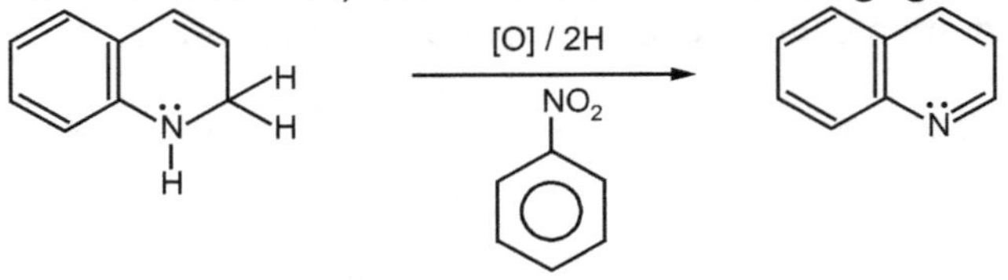

(ii) Friedlander's Synthesis

A condensation reaction between aliphatic carbonyl comp. containing an α-H and an aromatic carbonyl compound with an NH_2 – group at the o-position in presence of a base.

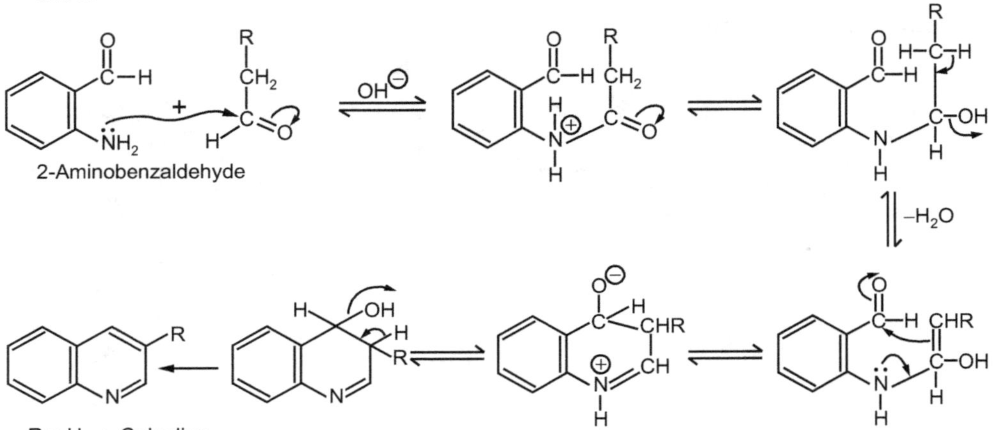

2-Aminobenzaldehyde

R = H → Quinoline

Derivatives of quinoline may be prepared by condensing o-aminoaldehyde or ketone with any aliphatic aldehyde or ketone containing the grouping $-CH_2CO-$.

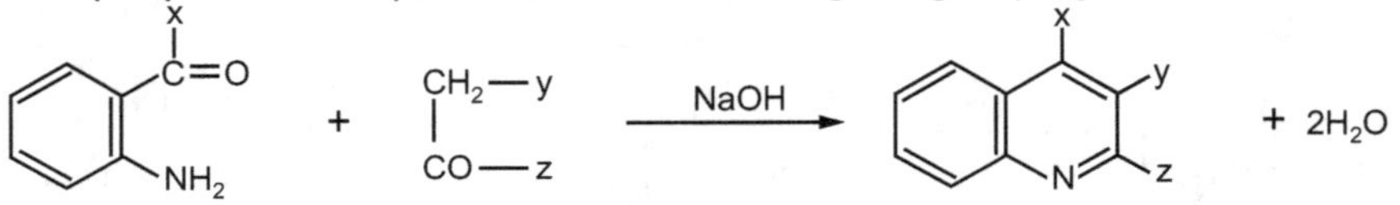

For example: If X = CH_3, y = $COOC_2H_5$, Z = CH_3 (i.e. the comp. y CH_2COZ is ethylacetoacetate), the product is 2, 4-dimethyl quinoline-3-carboxylic ester.

(iii) Knorr Quinoline Synthesis

Condensation between an aromatic amine and a β-keto ester followed by a ring closure reaction is called as Knorr quinoline synthesis.

(iv) Conard-Limpach Synthesis

This involves the condensation between aniline with β-ketoester at elevated temperature results ring closure and formation of quinoline takes place.

(v) From Indole and dichloromethylene in the presence of methyllinium

$$CH_2Cl_2 + CH_3Li \longrightarrow CH_4 + LiCl + :CHCl$$

QUESTION BANK

1. Explain the terms heterocyles and heterocyclic chemistry. Discuss the nomenclature systems of heterocycles and classify heterocycles as per ring size and number of heteroatoms giving suitable examples of each.

PHARMACEUTICAL ORGANIC CHEMISTRY - II   HETEROCYCLIC CHEMISTRY

2. Give the structures with numbering for the following heterocyclic compounds. Also, give the name and structure of atleast one drug from each of the following:
   - furan,
   - thiophene,
   - pyrrole,
   - pyrazole,
   - thiazole,
   - imidazole,
   - oxazole,
   - isoxazole,
   - hydantoin,
   - pyridine,
   - pyridazine,
   - pyrimidine,
   - indole,
   - benzfuran,
   - benzthiazole,
   - benzimidazole,
   - benzoxazole,
   - quinoline,
   - isoquinoline,
   - quinazoline,
   - cinnoline,
   - purine,
   - xanthine,
   - pteridine and
   - coumarin.

3. Explain, why pyridine does not undergo Friedal-Craft reaction?
4. Why furan reacts violently with strong mineral acids?
5. Draw the structures of the following with appropriate numbering
   (i) 1,2,7-Trimethylxanthene.
   (ii) Pteridine
   (iii) 3-Methylquinoline.

(iv) 4-Propylindole
(v) 4H-Imidozo [4,5-d] thiazole
(vi) 7H-Pyrazing [2,3-c] carbazle
(vii) 4H 1.3-Oxathiolo [5,4-b] pyrazole
(viii) Thiazolo [4,5-b] pyridine
(ix) Thieno [2,3-b] furan
(x) 1H-Pyrazolo [4,3-d] oxazole
(xi) 5H-Pyrido [2,3-d] oxazine
(xii) 4-Methyl-2-furancarboxylic acid
(xiii) 5-Ethyl-3-pyrrolecarboxylic acid
(xiv) Isopropyl-4-pyridinecarboxylic acid
(xv) 2-Formyl-3-*tert*-butylpyrrole

6. Discuss the following:
   (a) Fischer-Indole synthesis
   (b) Paal-Knorr synthesis of furan
   (c) Hinsberg thiophene synthesis
   (d) Hantzsch pyridine synthesis
   (e) Skraup Quinoline synthesis

7. Give **two methods of synthesis** of:
   (i) Quinoline
   (ii) Pyridine
   (iii) Imidazole
   (iv) Thiophene
   (v) Indole
   (vi) Furan

8. Write in brief about electrophilic substitution reactions of five membered mono-heterocyclic ring systems and arrange furan, thiophene, as well as, pyrrole in order of stability, as well as, reactivity towards electrophilic substitution reactions.

9. Discuss the nomenclature of five membered heterocycles containing one heteroatom.

10. Write a short note on reactions and synthesis of furan.

11. Write a short note on reactions and synthesis of pyrrole.

12. Write a short note on reactions and synthesis of indole.

13. Write a short note on reactions and synthesis of imidazole.

14. Write a short note on reactions and synthesis of pyridine.
15. Write a short note on reactions and synthesis of quinoline.
16. Write short note on electrophilic substitution in furan.
17. Pyridine undergoes electrophilic substitution reaction at C-2, C-4, C-5. Explain.
18. Explain how pyrrole is both acidic as well as basic.
19. Explain, why electrophilic substitution in quinoline takes place at the 8-position.
20. What is the order of aromaticity amongst furan, thiophene and pyrrole?
21. Indole undergoes electrophilic substitution at 3-position. Explain.
22. Is electrophilic aromatic substitution in furan more facile than benzene? Give reasons.
23. Give the rules for nomenclature of heterocyclic compound with proper examples.
24. Give the molecular orbital structure of:
    (i) furan
    (ii) pyrrole
    (iii) pyridine
    (iv) qunoline
    (v) thiophene
25. Why heterocyclic compounds are more reactive than benzene?
26. Explain why pyrrole is a weak base.
27. Explain why pyridine is less basic than amines and strongly basic than pyrrole?
28. Comment on electrophilic substitution in five membered heterocycles.
29. Discuss the aromaticity of five and six membered heterocycles.
30. Give biological and medicinal significance of pyrrole.
31. Complete the following reactions:

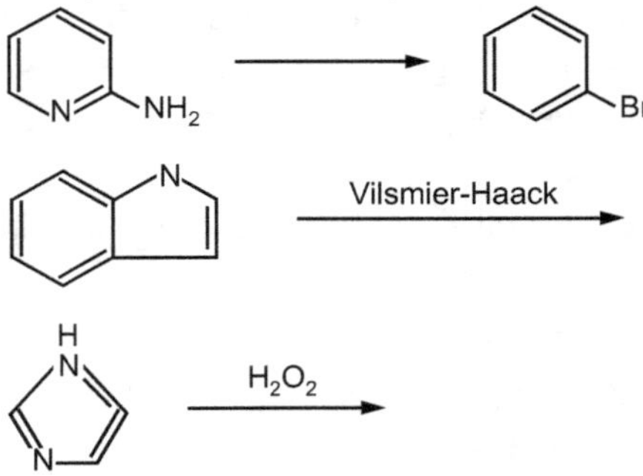

32. Predict the product.

- Indole + DMF / POCl$_3$ →
- Quinoline + Br$_2$ / H$_2$SO$_4$ →
- Furan-2-COOCH$_3$ + HNO$_3$/Ac$_2$O →
- Pyrrole + CH$_3$I + NaOCH$_3$ →
- Pyrrole + CH$_3$I + NaOCH$_3$ →
- Nicotinamide + Br$_2$ / NaOH →
- CH$_3$-O-CH$_2$CH$_2$CH$_2$-CH$_3$ + NH$_3$ → A + B → ethyl 2,4-dimethylcyclopentadiene-1-carboxylate
- Thiophene + HNO$_3$ →
- Pyrrole + DMF/POCl$_3$ →
- Pyridine + HCHO →
- Furan + SO$_3$/pyridine →

33. Pyridine undergoes aromatic electrophilic substitution at position-4. Explain.

34. Complete the following reactions.

(1) 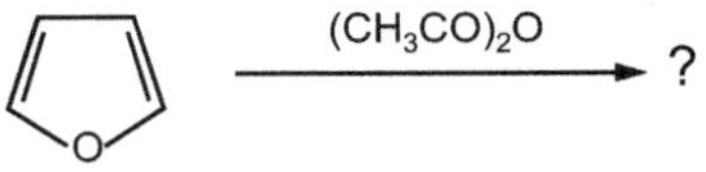 furan + (CH₃CO)₂O → ?

(2) 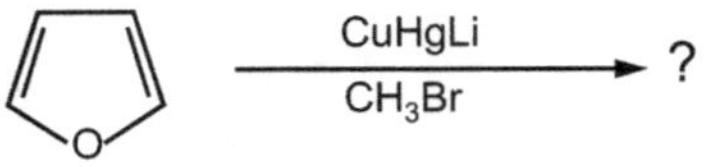 furan + CuHgLi / CH₃Br → ?

(3) 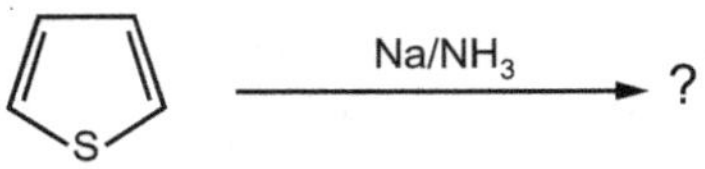 thiophene + Na/NH₃ → ?

(4) 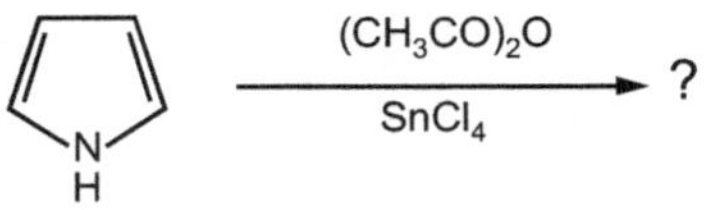 pyrrole (N-H) + (CH₃CO)₂O / SnCl₄ → ?

(6) 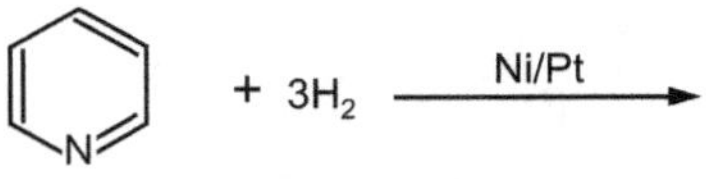 pyridine + 3H₂ → (Ni/Pt)

(7) 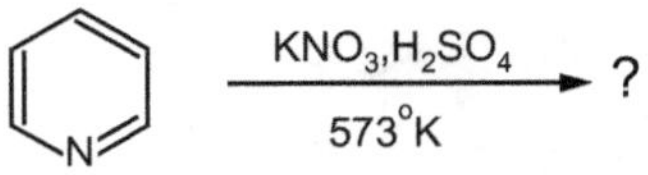 pyridine + KNO₃, H₂SO₄ at 573°K → ?

(8) 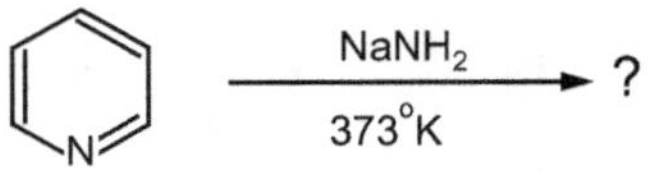 pyridine + NaNH₂ at 373°K → ?

35. Write short notes on:
    (i) Chichibabin reaction.
    (ii) Madelung indole synthesis.
    (iii) Reissert indole synthesis.
    (iv) Friedlander synthesis of quinoline.

Chapter 6 ...

INTRODUCTION TO COMBINATORIAL CHEMISTRY

CONTENTS

- History, Introduction to Linkers and Solid supports.
- Various techniques used in Combinatorial Synthesis (Mix and Split, Parallel Synthesis), Applications.

HISTORY

Combinatorial chemistry was first applied in the 1960's by **Bruce Merrifield**, researcher at Rockfeller University, started investigating the solid-state synthesis of peptides. He introduced most efficient synthesis of peptides on solid support or resin and awarded him **Nobel Price** in 1984.

In **1982**, a Hungarian Chemist, **Arpad Furka** synthesized polypeptides by using combinatorial chemistry. He realised that Merrifield's approach could be extended to allow the synthesis of the possible combinations of given set of amino acids in a limited number of steps.

The first combinatorial chemistry experiments were applied to the study of epitopes - the short sequences of amino acids responsible for antibody recognition and binding to proteins.

The real advance in combinatorial chemistry for drug discovery purpose was the introduction of synthetic methodology to yield true drug-like structures. In **1992, Burin** and **Ellman** synthesized 1,4-benzodinzepine compounds using three components, 2-aminobenzophenone, protected amino acid and an alkyl halide.

In **1994, Zuckerman et. al.** demonstrated synthesis of biologically active peptides by using combinatorial chemistry. He used 24 monomers to generate tripeptides.

In the early 1990's the initial efforts in the combinatorial chemistry arena were driven by improvements made in high throughput screening (HTS) technologies. This led to the demand for access to a large set of compounds for biological screening. The chemists were under constant pressure to produce compounds in vast numbers for screening purposes. The molecules in the first phase were simple peptides and lacked the structural complexity.

In the second phase after 1990s, chemists became aware that it is not just about the members, but something was missing in compounds produced in a combinatorial fashion. Emphasis was thus, shifted towards quality rather than quantity.

In the past decade there has been a lot of research and development in combinatorial chemistry applied to the discovery of new compounds and materials. This work was pioneered by **P.G. Schultz et. al.** in the mid nineties. Since then, the work has been pioneered by several academic groups as well as industries with large R&D programs.

In the decade since the first drug molecules were generated by using combinatorial chemistry, solid-phase syntheses have been discovered for the most common classes of drug structure. An important recent advance in combinatorial chemistry is the use of microwave heating in place of conventional heating methods.

Combinatorial chemistry has emerged as a powerful tool in drug discovery. It is now of prime interest not only in the field of drug discovery but, also in many other domains such as material science and asymmetric catalysis. Combinatorial chemistry is a relatively recent innovation and involves the small-scale synthesis of large numbers of novel structures using automated solid-phase chemistry. There are two main approaches: parallel synthesis and the synthesis of mixtures. The later approach is relatively less used, now-a-days.

A parallel synthesis means that a common synthesis is carried out simultaneously in a series of reaction vessels (vials), using different reactants and reagents for each vial. The method is particularly useful for synthesizing large numbers of analogs for SAR studies and for lead optimization.

INTRODUCTION TO LINKERS AND SOLID SUPPORTS

Solid phase synthesis is carried out on polymeric resins such as beads. Each bead is functionalized with linker molecules, which allow starting materials to be covalently bound to the bead.

The group that joins the substrate to the resin bead is an essential part of solid phase synthesis. The linker is specialised part of solid phase synthesis. The linker is specialised protecting group which will tie up a functional group. The best linker must allow attachment and cleavage in quantitative yield.

Most of the solid state combinatorial chemistry is conducted by using polymer beads of 10-750 μm in diameter. The polymers are inert. In general, the compounds to be synthesized are not attached directly to the polymer molecules. They are usually attached using a **"LINKER"** moiety. In general, about 1 mmol of linker is attached per gram of solid support. To support the attachment of a synthetic target, the polymer is usually modified by equipping it with a linker or anchor group.

Some specialised linkers have been developed to meet particular reaction. The linkers consisting of silyl group ($- Si (CH_3)_2$) is sensitive to acids and can be cleaved to give unsubstituted phenyl or alkyl products. A class of linkers known as "safety-catch" linkers are inert to the synthesis conditions but, have to be chemically transformed to allow final liberation of the product from the resin. Some groups have used linkers that can only be cleaved by enzymes.

The linker used should be stable to the reaction conditions and cleaved selectively, at the end of synthesis. It can be re-usable and facilitate reaction monitoring.

There are around six types of linkers:
1. Acid-cleavable anchors and linkers
2. Base-cleavable linkers
3. Enzyme-cleavable linkers
4. Photochemically cleavable linkers
5. Safety-catch linkers
6. Traceless linkers

A large class of linkers currently available are cleaved by acid treatment. Trifluoroacetic acid (TFA) and hydrofluoric acid (HF) are choice of acid cleavable linkers. Whereas, the ester of 4-hydroxymethylbenzoic acid is a base cleavable linker. A chemical group is transformed from a relatively stable connection to a readily cleavable functionality is termed as safety catch linker. e.g., Disulphone to disulphide.

In a linker whose chemical bond can be broken just by exposure of light and no additional energy is required is called as "photochemically cleavable linker". Example, α-methylphenacyl ester.

Some common linkers used are as follows:

(a) Merrifield resin:	[structure]	for Peptide products
(b) PAM resin:	[structure]	for peptide or carboxylic acid products
(c) Trityl resin:	[structure]	for carboxylic acid products

contd. ...

(d) HMBA resin:	[structure: O—C₆H₄—CH₂—NH—C(=O)—C₆H₄—CH₂—O—]	for peptide products
(e) ADCC resin:	[structure: O—CH₂—NH—C(=O)—cyclohexanone with isopropylidene]	for amine products

In order to prevent polymerisation of amino acids in solid phase peptide synthesis, protecting group are used. Two commonly used protecting groups are **t-BOC** (tertiary butoxy carbonyl) and **f-moc** (9H-fluoren-g-ylmethoxy carbonyl). These protecting group retain usefulness in reducing aggregation of peptides during synthesis. The advantage of f-moc over t-Boc is that it cleaved under very mild basic conditions.

The following types of solid supports used are:
- **(a) Polystyrene resins:** Polystyrene cross-linked with divinylbenzene. These are common resin used in size exclusion chromatography.
- **(b) Tentagel resins:** Polystyrene in which some of the phenyl group have polyethylene glycol (PEG) groups attached in para position. The free OH groups of PEG allows the attachment.
- **(c) Polyacrylamide resins:** These resins swell better in polar solvents and more closely resemble with biological materials.
- **(d) Glass and ceramic beads:** It is not a type of organic resin but sometimes used when high-temp. or high-pressure reactions are needed.

In solid phase support synthesis, the solid support is generally based on polystyrene resin. Light cross-linked gel type polystyrene (GPs) has been most widely used because of its availability and low cost. A prominent characteristic of GPs beads is their ability to absorb large relative volumes of certain organic solvents. GPs have good swelling characteristics in solvents of low to medium polarity ranging from aliphatic hydrocarbons to dichloromethane. Polar, protic solvents such as alcohols and water, do not swell GPs resins and accessibility to all reaction sites may be compromised. Hence, GPs supports are suitable for chemistry performed in solvents of low to medium polarity.

Merrifield resin

Sheppard has designed polyacrylamide polymers for peptides synthesis. These polymers more clearly mimic the properties of the peptide chains.

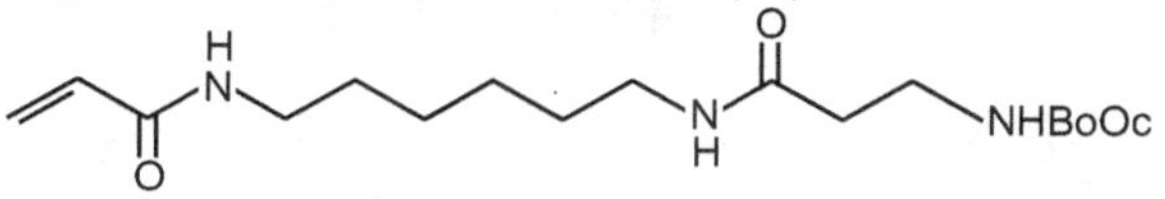

Polyamide resin

Another class of widely used resin supports for organic synthesis which was introduced by Bayer and Rapp is the TentaGel resin. This resin consists of polyethylene glycol attached to cross-linked polystyrene through an ether linkage. The resin was originally prepared by the polymerization of ethylene oxide on cross-linked polystyrene. The tendency of this resin to become sticky makes it difficult to handle it as synthesis progress.

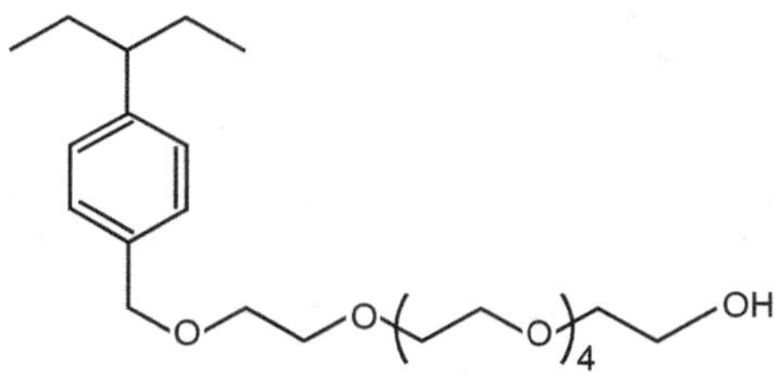

TentaGel resin

Polyethene pins grafted with acrylic acid or 2-hydroxyethylmethacrylate is used as synthetic polymer type of solid support in combinatorial chemistry. Whereas, sephadex, cellulose (cotton fabric/filter paper), chitin, borine serum albumin are used natural polymers for solid support. Silica glass and controlled pore glas are type of inorganic solid supports.

TECHNIQUES USED IN COMBINATORIAL CHEMISTRY

There are two techniques that had greatest initial impact on combinatorial chemistry for the production of large number of peptides or other products:

1. Split and Mix Synthesis (Mix and Split library synthesis)
2. Parallel synthesis

1. Split and Mix Synthesis:

This technique was pioneered by Furka et. al., in 1991. To make 10,000 compounds using orthodox chemistry would normally require 10,000 reaction vessels. This is a necessary pre-requisite for making that number of compounds. But by making the same 10,000 compounds by mix and split synthesis method requires approximately 22 reaction vessels. Hence, the mix and split approach is much more efficient.

The mix and split process relies on the synthesis of the library compounds on small resin beads. A quantity of this support material is divided into a number of equal portions and each of these portions are individually reacted with a different monomeric starting material.

The mix and split synthesis method is illustrated schematically for trimeric product for 3 × 3 × 3 library, giving all 27 possible combinations. A, B and C could be a nucleotide, the final product would be a trinucleotide, where as if A, B and C are amino acids in which case final products would be tripeptides.

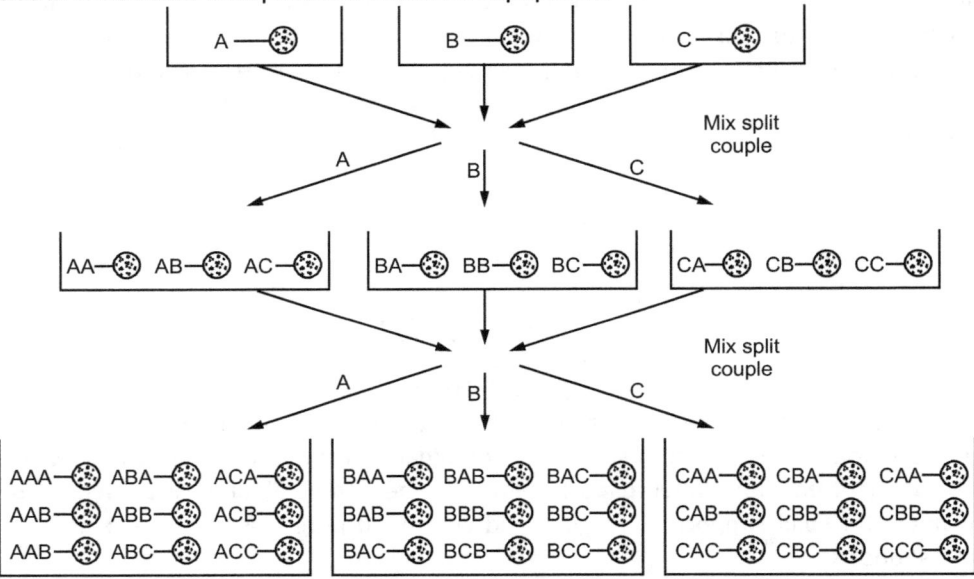

Fig. 1: The mix and split synthetic scheme for the synthesis of a 27 member trimer library

It can be seen that, this mix and split procedure finally gives three mixtures consisting of nine compounds each and there are now several ways of progressing these compounds to biological screening. Identification of the most active compound relies on deconvoluting the most active mixture in the library through future rounds of synthesis and screening. This process has been used successfully by many research groups for making large combinational libraries.

2. **Parallel synthesis:**

This is a simplest method of combinatorial synthesis, where a single reaction product is produced in each reaction vessel.

There are two methods of parallel synthesis:
(a) Houghton's tea bag method
(b) Automated parallel synthesis

The Houghton's tea bag method is a manual approach to parallel synthesis and has been used to synthesize 150 peptides at a time. The polymeric support resin is sealed in polypropylene meshed containers (3 × 4 cm) and each tea bag is labelled. The tea bags are then placed in polyethylene bottles which act as the reaction vessels.

In peptide synthesis, the first amino acid is added to the resin and different amino acid to each bottle used. The tea bags can be redistributed between the bottles for the addition of second amino acid, recombined for deprotection and washing, redistributed for addition of the next amino acid and so on.

The advantage of this approach is that, it is cheap and can be carried out in a laboratory without the need of expensive equipment. The disadvantage of this method is that, it is manual and time consuming.

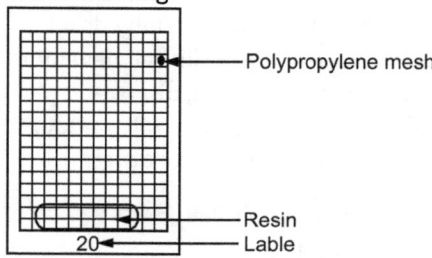

Fig. 2: Houghton's tea bag

Automated synthesizers are available for 42, 96 or 144 compounds to be synthesized at a time. The solid phase support is in the form of sticks or pins, which can be dipped into each reaction tube or well. In case of peptide synthesis, common operations such as washing and deprotection of peptides is done by dipping the rods into large baths, but the coupling is done in the wells such that each well has a unique amino acid. The addition of reagents and the removal of the excess reagents can be carried out automatically. About 80-300 mmol of peptides can be synthesized per rod.

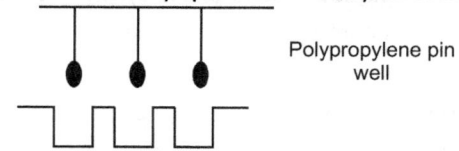

Fig. 3: Automated synthesis

APPLICATIONS

1. The primary benefit that combinatorial chemistry brings to drug synthesis is speed.
2. Combinatorial chemistry is a new beginning in compound library design.
3. Combinatorial chemistry research increasingly involves smaller, focused libraries that serve as the inspiration to get drug like molecules.

4. Most industries and many academic laboratories now regard combinatorial methods as an integral part of their activities towards drug discovery research.
5. Application of combinatorial chemistry are very wide in drug discovery.
   Example: Compound library can be designed, synthesized and screened using HTS.
6. Combinatorial chemistry represents a broad spectrum of techniques that are rapidly becoming a standard part of medicinal chemists tool kit.
7. Solid phase synthesis is highly suited to the synthesis of bipolymers such as DNA, RNA and peptides.
8. Combinatorial is one of the important new methodologies developed by researchers in pharmaceutical industry to reduce the time and costs associated with producing effective and competitive new drugs.
9. This saves significant money in preclinical development costs and ultimately changed fundamental approach to drug discovery.
10. The future of combinatorial chemistry will undoubtedly provide a wealth of pre-clinical lead compounds and potential drugs.

QUESTION BANK

1. What is combinatorial chemistry?
2. Describe history of combinatorial chemistry in brief.
3. Define various terminologies used in combinatorial chemistry.
4. Explain different types of linkers used in combinatorial chemistry.
5. Explain different types of resins used in solid support synthesis.
6. Discuss briefly multiple parallel synthesis.
7. Discuss briefly mix and split synthesis.
8. Describe various techniques of solid phase synthesis.
9. Discuss applications of combinatorial chemistry.
10. Write note on:
    (a) Combinatorial Chemistry
    (b) Types of Linkers
    (c) Types of solid supports
    (d) Multiple parallel synthesis
    (e) Mix and split synthesis
    (f) Methods of solid phase synthesis
    (g) Applications of combinatorial chemistry

Chapter 7 ...

RETRO-SYNTHESIS (DISCONNECTION APPROACH)

CONTENTS

- Introduction to common terms
- General Rules and Guidelines involved in retro-synthesis
- Disconnections involving one and two functional groups
- The retro-synthesis of following drugs to be covered: Ibuprofen, Propranolol, Ciprofloxacin and Sulfamethoxazole

INTRODUCTION

Synthesis is the real test of our ability to use and control organic reactions. In each case the starting material is converted to some desired compound; the target molecule.

Synthetic organic compounds are of wide and varied types. They may be:

- Small or large,
- Simple or complex,
- Straight or branched,
- Cyclic or open chain,
- Carbocyclic or heterocyclic,
- Aromatic or non-aromatic,
- They may bear one or more functional groups.

So, to synthesize these wide variety of compounds, appropriate starting materials are to be chosen. These starting materials are allowed to react and get converted finally to the product molecule called the **Target Molecule**.

Actually, a number of synthetic routes can be written for a given target molecule. But the best will be the simpler, less complex and most reproductive and economical one.

Lets see the following simple example;

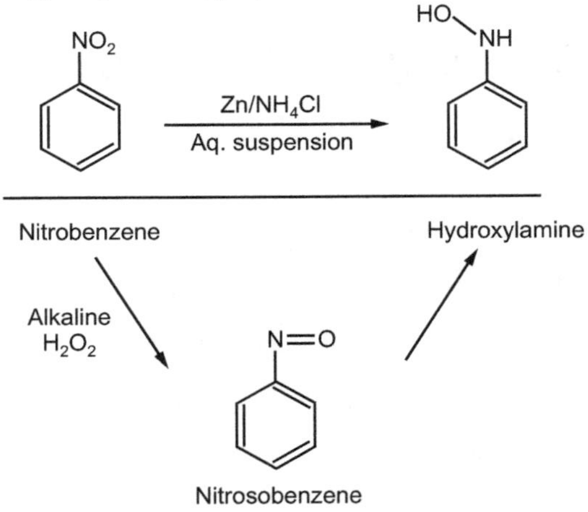

Fig. 1: For the preparation of N-phenylhydroxylamine, a two step or a direct one step route can be used. But in actual synthesis, generally the direct one step route is selected, as it is economical, safe, easy to carry out and it produces the product in maximum yield, in minimum time

Criteria for the selection of a suitable synthetic route include many things as follows,
- Technical feasibility,
- Stability of raw materials used,
- Infrastructural facilities available,
- Availability of raw materials,
- Number of steps involved in the synthesis,
- Conditions of the reactions,
- Isolation, purification, recovery of raw materials, catalyst used,
- By products and yield of the target molecule.
- Overall Final yield of the synthetic scheme adopted.

If any one step has a low yield, then overall yield of the synthetic scheme becomes poor. So, while selecting a good synthetic scheme, following points must be considered.
- Minimum number of steps should be involved.
- High yield reaction should be preferred.
- Competing routes must be absent.
- Prediction of the final product should be easy.

This is where the concept of "Reterosynthesis" comes in picture.

Retrosynthesis (Synthon or Disconnection Approach):

It is exactly the reverse of a normal chemical synthesis. Therefore is called by this name. It helps devising better and easy synthetic routes for complex molecules

Definition: *An analytical approach to Organic Synthesis in which the target molecule is broken into fragments through a series of logical disconnections to get the best possible (plausible) and likely starting materials (Synthons).*

OR

An analytical approach that breaks a bond and converts a molecule into possible starting materials.

INTRODUCTION TO COMMON TERMINOLOGIES

Disconnection: An operation involving breaking of bonds of target molecule to get possible starting materials is called as disconnection and the approach is called as disconnection approach.

Synthon: Synthon is an idealized or imaginary or real fragment obtained after a disconnection. Though, a synthon is usually an ion or radical, sometimes it may also be a neutral molecule. (It may or may not be actually employed in the actual synthesis)

Functional Group Addition (FGA): Addition of a functional group in place of Hydrogen is the FGA.

(CH(CH₃)₂)–H $\xrightarrow{FGA}$ (CH(CH₃)₂)–OH

Synthetic Equivalent: Often, a synthon cannot be straightway obtained from the bottle in the laboratory and hence its synthetic equivalent is used to conduct a reaction. So synthetic equivalent can be defined as a reagent carrying out the function of a synthon (which itself cannot be used because of its instability or non-availability).

$\overset{+}{C}H_2OH \implies HCHO$

$\overset{-}{C}H_3 \implies CH_3MgBr$

Reagent: A compound that reacts to give an intermediate in the planned synthesis or to give a target molecule itself is called as a reagent. The synthetic equivalent of a synthon is often used as a reagent.

e.g., **Synthon** = Me^+, H^+; **Reagent** = Me_2SO_4, $LiAlH_4$

Functional Group Interchange (FGI) or Functional Group Equivalent (FGE): The process of conversion of one group into another, so that disconnection approach becomes easy, is known as functional group interchange or functional group equivalent.

e.g. $-COOH \Rightarrow -CN$; $NH_2 \Rightarrow -NO_2$

OR in simple words it is, writing of one functional group (dummy) for another so that disconnection leads to give a readily available starting material.

e.g.,

HO~~~COOH $\xRightarrow{FGI}$ [γ-butyrolactone]

Examples of some common FGI's

Oxidation	Reduction	Organometallic	Others
$-CH_3 \rightarrow -CHO$	$-COOH \rightarrow -CH_2OH$	$-RLi \rightarrow -RBr$	$-COOH \rightarrow -COCl$
$-CH_3 \rightarrow -COOH$	$-CRO \rightarrow -CRHOH$	$-RMgX \rightarrow -RBr$	$-COOH \rightarrow -CONH_2$
$-CH_2OH \rightarrow -COOH$	$-CHO \rightarrow -CH_2OH$		$-COOH \rightarrow -COCl$
$-CHO \rightarrow -COOH$	$-CHO \rightarrow -CH_2Cl$		$-CONH_2 \rightarrow -CN$
$-CRHOH \rightarrow -CRO$	$-COOR \rightarrow -CH_3$		$-CN \rightarrow -COOH$
$-NH_2 \rightarrow -NO_2$	$-CRO \rightarrow -CRH_2$		$-COX \rightarrow -COOH$
$-NO \rightarrow -NO_2$	$-CHO \rightarrow -CH_3$		$-Ph-NH_2 \rightarrow Ph-H$
	$-CX_3 \rightarrow -CH_3$		
	$-CX_2H \rightarrow -CH_3$		
	$-CXH_2 \rightarrow -CH_3$		
	$-NO_2 \rightarrow -NH_2$		

TgM: It represents target molecule *i.e.*, the molecule whose synthesis is being planned.

SM : It represents starting material.

$\Longrightarrow$ A double lined arrow indicates substitution or reverse of a chemical reaction. (Retrosynthesis arrow).

- This curved arrow is put over a bond indicating which bond is broken. The direction of arrow will indicate which fragment will carry –ve charge.

(∼∼∼ wigly lines indicates breaking of bond)

Analysis/Retrosynthetic Analysis: The process of breaking down of bonds in the (target molecule) to possible starting materials by disconnection and functional group interconversions (FGI).

Reconnection (rec): During retro analysis it means as joining up a bond in the TgM which will be actually broken during the forward synthesis

e.g.,

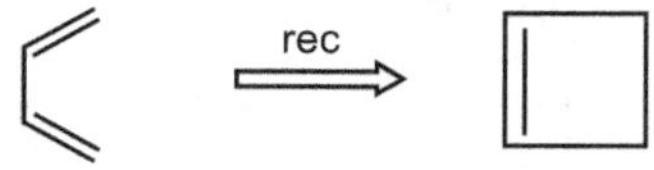

Protecting Group: A group that is required for protecting a labile functionality of the molecule for its survival through reaction conditions. It should be easily removable (de-protection/de-blocking)

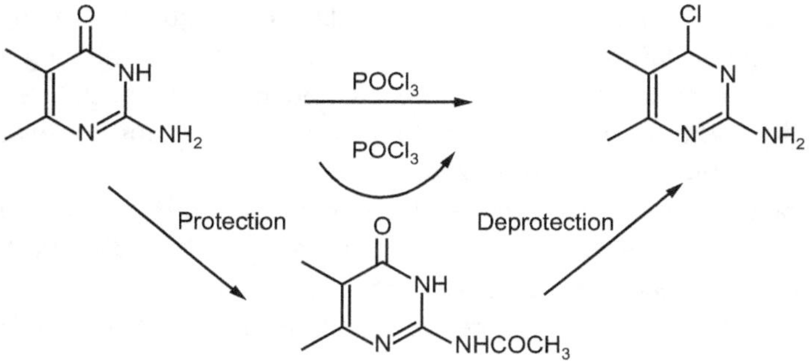

Umpolung Synthesis : Reversal of Polarity:

The transformation of an electrophilic carbon(C=O) into a nucleophilic one(e.g. The deprotonated thiane), i.e., dipole reversal is called as umpolung - the reverse process, that is addition of a electrophile to this dipole reversed (umpolung) nucleophile (e.g., alkylation of an aldehyde on the C=O, carbon using an electrophilic alkylating agent) is said to involve umpolung synthesis.

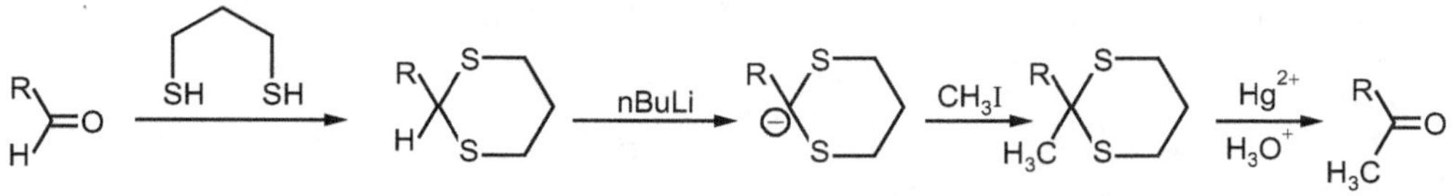

All dipole reversed nucleophiles are illogical nucleophilic synthons. (Illogical means normal polarity reversed). The opposite is also true for the dipole reversed electrophiles.

Illogical Electrophile (ILLE)

The 'ene carbon of enol is nucleophilic' – normal polarity, but by epoxidation of "ene" the polarity is reversed since epoxy carbon is highly eletrophilic.

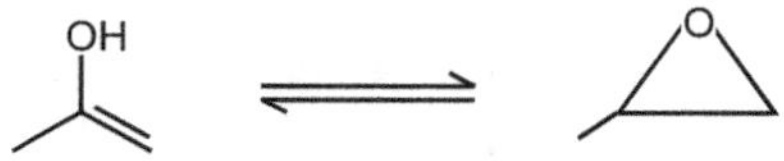

Illogical Nucleophile (ILLNU)

The 'C=O' carbon is electrophilic – normal polarity, but when C=O is converted to cyclicthioketal and then treated with a normal base the C=O carbon is converted to the acyl ion equivalent which is nucleophilic in nature.

METHODOLOGY FOR RETEROSYNTHESIS OR SYNTHON OR DISCONNECTION APPROACH

- First study the structure of the target molecule and go on breaking the molecule successively at different sites or location such that by combining the breakaway fragments in suitable positions, we can build-up the structure of the target molecule, and thus, we can find out starting materials and routes through which target molecule can be synthesized.
- The process of going backwards and finding out starting materials and routes through which target molecule can be synthesized is called as synthetic analysis.
- So, synthetic analysis is a process of stepwise breaking down of target molecule to starting materials by disconnection of bonds and functional group interchange (FGI).
- Every disconnected part is an idealized fragment and is called as synthon and the phenomenon is known as synthon approach.

BASIC RULES AND GUIDELINES IN DISCONNECTION

Rule 1: Disconnection of only One bond should be done at a time and should be such that it should produce stable ion fragments

Usually it generates two fragments, positive and negative.
For example

Route A shall be preferred over **Route B**, as carbocations are stabilised by electron donors and carbinions by electron withdrawing groups.

Rule 2: Generally break the C-Hetero Bond

A bond joining to a heteroatom (like N, O, or S) is always broken with electron pair being transferred to the heteroatom. (Heteroatoms being more electronegative can accommodate an electron pair)

For example,

$$-\overset{|}{\underset{|}{C}} \overset{\xi}{\underset{}{-}} \overset{\cdot\cdot}{N}- \xrightarrow{B} -\overset{|}{\underset{|}{C}}^{+} + -\overset{|}{\underset{\cdot\cdot}{N}}-$$

$$\Updownarrow \qquad \Updownarrow$$

$$-\overset{|}{\underset{|}{C}}-Cl \qquad H-\overset{|}{\underset{\cdot\cdot}{N}}-$$

Rule 3: A Disconnection should generate a minimum number of fragments:

The number of fragments generated from disconnection should be as minimum as possible

For example,

Scheme A

[Retrosynthesis scheme showing disconnection via C-C bond to give acetone enolate and methyl ketone fragments, corresponding to $CH_3COOC_2H_5$ and $CH_3(CH_2)_2COCH_3$; FGI gives $CH_3CO\overset{+}{C}H_2$ + cyclopropanone equivalent ⇌ $HOCH_2CH_2CH_2COCH_3$]

Scheme B (TM₂)

[Retrosynthesis scheme showing C-C disconnection giving $CH_3CO\overset{\ominus}{C}H_2$ + $\overset{\oplus}{C}H_2CH_2COCH_3$, corresponding to acetone and methyl vinyl ketone]

Scheme B is preferred over scheme A

Rule 4: Do FGI if needed

Sometimes a disconnection carried out does not generate sufficiently stable fragments but using FGI or introducing additional electron withdrawing groups and then removing them after synthesis can be useful.

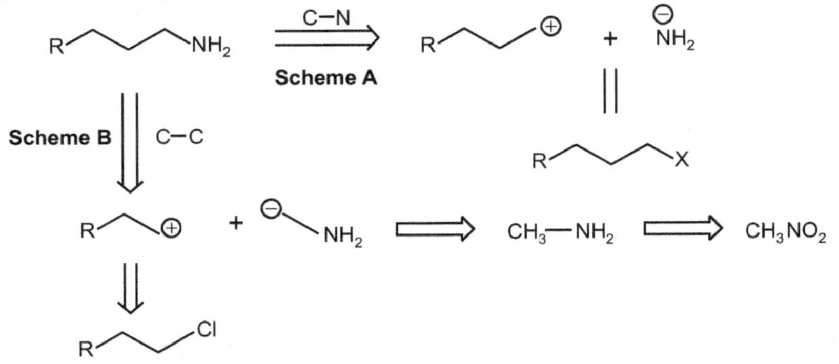

$$R-CH_2CH_2-NH_2 \xrightarrow{C-N} R-CH_2^{\oplus} + {}^{\ominus}NH_2 \quad \text{(Scheme A)}$$

Scheme B ‖ C–C

$$R^{\oplus} + {}^{\ominus}CH_2-NH_2 \Rightarrow CH_3-NH_2 \Rightarrow CH_3NO_2$$

$$\Downarrow$$

$$R-CH_2CH_2-Cl$$

For example,

$$R-CH_2CH_2Cl + CH_3NO_2 \xrightarrow[-HCl]{\text{Base}} RCH_2CH_2NO_2 \xrightarrow{\text{Reduction}} RCH_2CH_2CH_2NH_2$$

Thus, If FGI is needed do it at an appropriate stage. This is required to get the desired effect on orientation. It may alter the directing effect of the group and other substituent should be added either before or after FGI. For example, -CH$_3$ is *o, p*-directing and –COOH is *m*-directing.

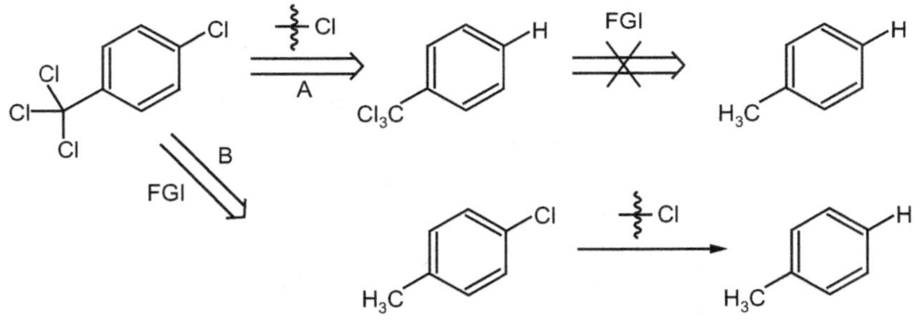

Here CCl$_3$ is *meta* director, but its FGI, CH$_3$ is *p*-director ! Therefore, do FGI prior to C-Cl disconnection.

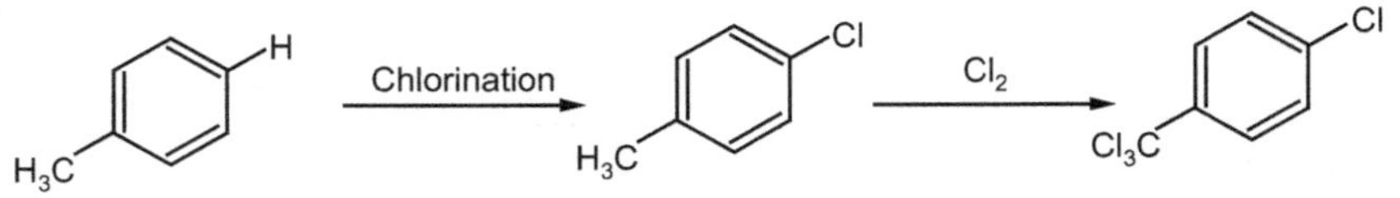

p-methylbenzene $\xrightarrow{\text{Chlorination}}$ *p*-methylchlorobenzene $\xrightarrow{Cl_2}$ *p*-(trichloromethyl)chlorobenzene

Rule 5: Before disconnection examine the relationships between groups

Examine carefully, which group is the proper directing group (disconnect it last) to get the TgM. Thus, the order of disconnection is very important.

For example,

The ketone generated in disconnection (A) is *meta* directing and *iso*-propyl chloride will attach to the *meta* position of acetophenone, while we require *para* substitution.

In disconnection (B) the Isopropyl group on the other hand is *p*- directing and thus, reaction of isopropylbenzene with acetyl chloride gives the target molecule. Hence, synthetic scheme can be written as

Benzene + Isopropyl chloride → Isopropyl benzene → TM

Rule 6: Disconnection of the most electron-withdrawing group is done first.

Disconnection of the most electron-withdrawing group is done first (*to be added last in actual synthesis*) because it deactivates the ring and so it becomes difficult to add or substitute other groups in proper position.

Analysis:

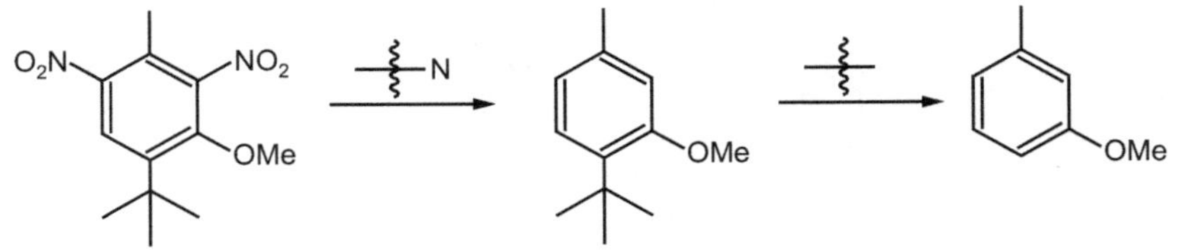

Synthesis:

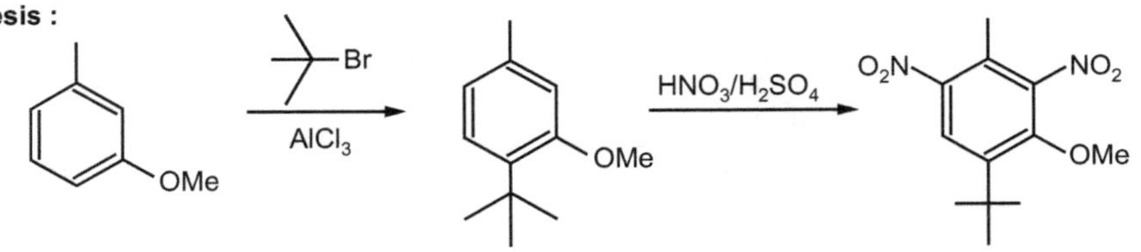

Rule 7: Avoid sequences that may lead to unwanted reaction at other sites of the molecules.

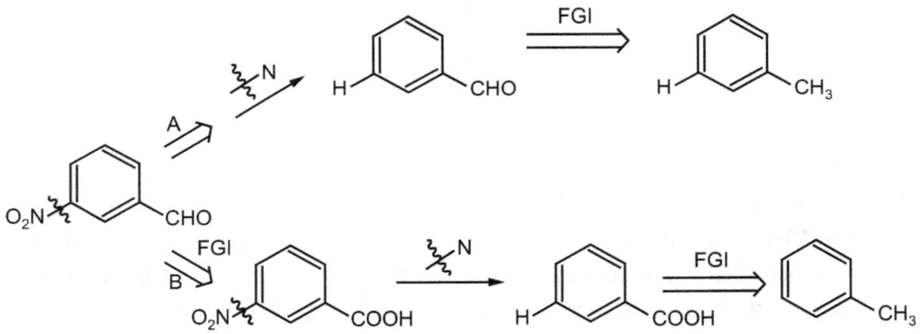

Therefore "B" to be adopted as nitration of benzaldehyde may lead to side reaction. *i.e.*, oxidation. CHO → COOH. Therefore,

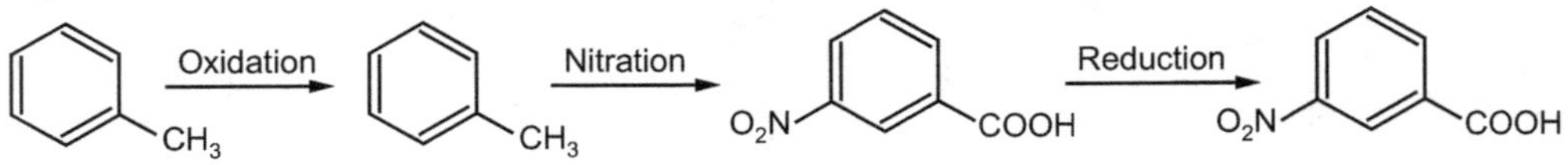

Rule 8: Equivalence:

The –ve and +ve fragments generated by disconnection are replaced by recognizable and meaningful chemical entities.

PHARMACEUTICAL ORGANIC CHEMISTRY - II — RETRO-SYNTHESIS (DISCONNECTION APPROACH)

+ve Fragments	−ve Fragments
$R'CH_2 \equiv R-CH_2-X$ $R-CH_2 \cdot OH$ (alcohol) $R-CH_2-OEt$ (ether) + vely charged alkyl $R-CH=O^+ \equiv R-CO-X$ (acyl halide) $R-COOH$ (acid) $R-CO-OEt$ (ester) + vely charged acyl $\;R-CO-O-CO-R$ (anhydride)	$ROCO-\overset{\ominus}{C}H-R' \equiv ROCO-CH_2-R$ $O_2N-\overset{\ominus}{C}H-R \equiv O_2N-CH_2-R$ $R-\overset{\ominus}{O} \equiv ROH$ $R-\overset{\ominus}{N}H \equiv RNH_2$ $Ph^{\ominus} \equiv Ph$

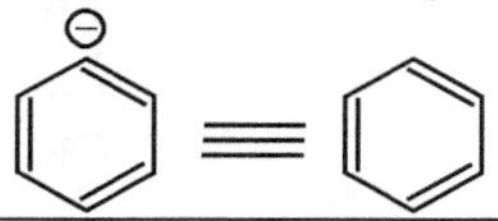

Applying these, lets see an example,

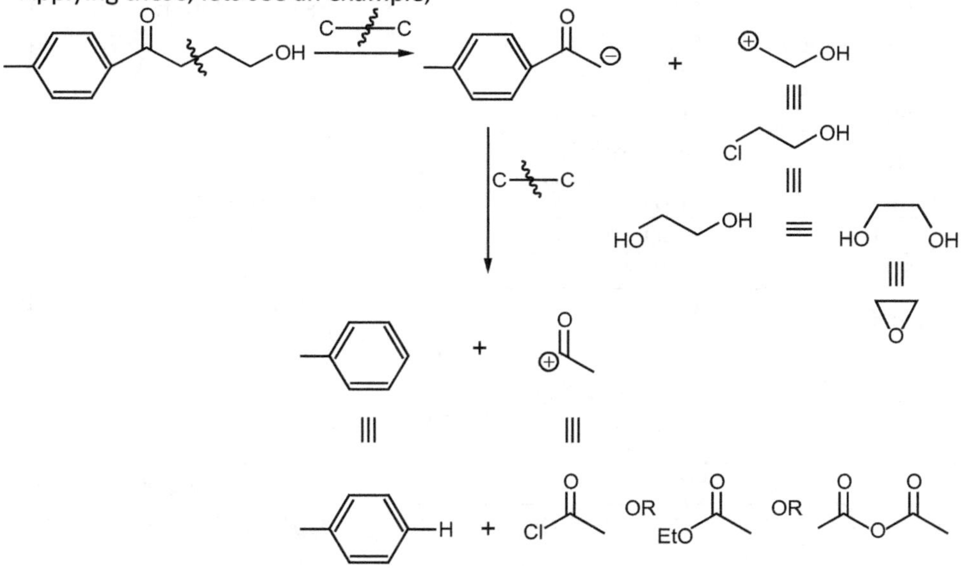

[retrosynthesis scheme showing disconnection of 4-(p-tolyl)-4-oxobutan-1-ol into fragments: p-methylacetophenone enolate + $^+CH_2CH_2OH \equiv ClCH_2CH_2OH \equiv$ ethylene glycol $\equiv$ ethylene oxide]

Further disconnection (C—C) gives:

toluene + $^+COCH_3$ (acylium) $\equiv$ CH_3COCl (a), or CH_3COOEt (b), or $(CH_3CO)_2O$

Thus, we have

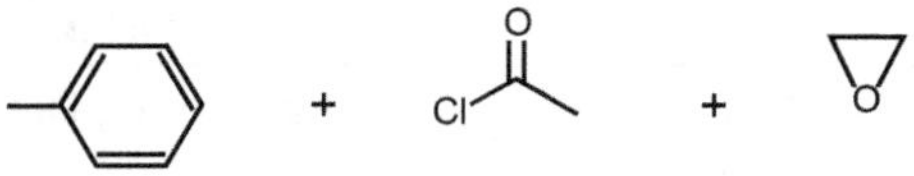

a: toluene + b: CH_3COCl + c: ethylene oxide

Synthesis:

toluene $\xrightarrow[AlCl_3]{\text{F.C. acylation}}$ p-methylacetophenone $\xrightarrow{\text{Base}}$ enolate $\xrightarrow{\text{ethylene oxide}}$ 4-(p-tolyl)-4-oxobutan-1-ol

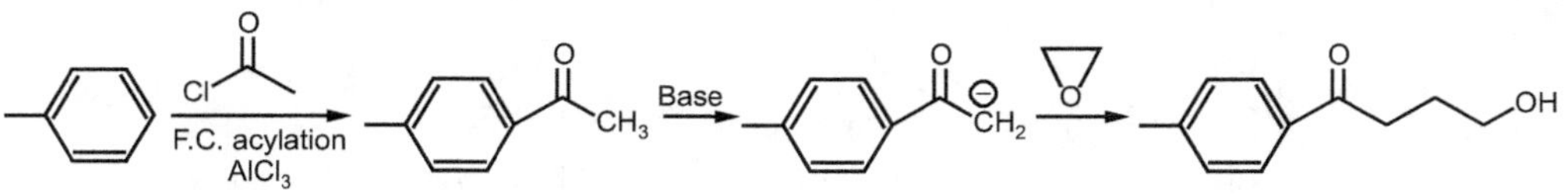

Some important tips on the reagents and conditions to be used for some common synthetic conversions are provided in following tables I-III.

Table 1

X	Reagents	Reaction
CH_2Cl	CH_2O+ $ZnCl_2 + HCl$	Choromethylation
CHO	$CH_2Cl + H_2O$ (OH⁻) OR $(Me_2N=CH-OPCl_2)Cl$ OR $CO + HCl + AlCl_2$	Riemer-Tiemann Vilsmier Haack Formylation Co-Formylation
R^+ (alkyl group)	$RBr + AlCl_3$ $ROH + H^+$ Alkene + H	F.C. Alkylation
RCO^+	$RCOCl + AlCl_3$	F.C. Acylation
NO_2^+	NHO_3/H_2SO_4	Nitration
Cl^+	$Cl_2/FeCl_3$	Chlorination
$^+SO_3H$	H_2SO_4	Sulfonation
SO_2Cl	$ClSO_3H$	Chlorosulfonation
ArN_2^+	ArN_2^+	Diazocoupling

Table 2

	Y	X	Reagent
Reduction	NO_2	NH_2	H_2/Pd-C, Sn/HCl
	COR	CH(OH)R	$NaBH_4$
	COR	CH_2R	Zn/Hg, Conc. HCl or N_2H_4/KOH, glycol
Oxidation	CH_2Cl	CHO	Hexamine, DMSO
	CH_2R, CH_3	COOH	$KMnO_4$
	COR	OCOR	RCO_3H (Peracids)
	CH_3	CCl_3	Cl_2, PCl_5
	CH_3	CF_3	SbF_5
	CN	COOH	$-OH/H_2O$

Table 3

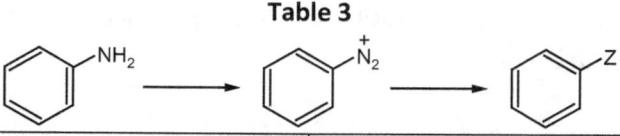

Z	Reagents
OH	H$_2$O
OR	ROH
CN	CuCN
Cl	CuCl
Br	CuBr
I	KI
Ar	Ar-H
H	H$_3$PO$_4$ or EtOH/H$^+$

Rule 9: Use of Dummy Groups:

The difficult task is insertion of two *o, p*-directing groups meta to each other. For this dummy amino group is added to setup the required relationship and then NH$_2$ group is removed by diazotization and reduction

Rule 10: Use of a Protecting group

A protecting group allows us to overcome the problem of chemoselectivity.

Protecting groups should have two important properties:
- It should be easy to introduce and easy to remove.
- It must be resistant to reagents which would attack the unprotected functional groups.

For example, alcohols can be easily obtained by reduction of ketoesters without affecting the keto function.

Rule 11: Procure Specific Starting Materials

For substituents which are difficult to add it is always good not to disconnect these at all, but to use starting materials already containing these substituents (e.g., – OH, -OR).

ONE GROUP DISCONNECTIONS (C-X DISCONNECTIONS)

Disconnection of a target molecule involving one particular functional group i.e., C- X. These are the disconnections involving C-O, C-N, C-S bonds. Under, this we have disconnections involving; Carbonyl Derivatives RCO.X; Ethers ROR'; Sulfides RSR' and Amines RNHR'.

$$R-X \xrightarrow{C \nmid X} R^+ + X^-$$

Where, R = alkyl; X= OR' (ethers), SR' (thiols) or NHR' (amines). R = acyl & X= OR' (esters), NHR' (amides), Halo (acid chlorides), OCOR' (acid anhydrides).

(a) The C-X Disconnections

Carbonyl derivatives: Examples are the esters (RCOOR'), amides (RCONHR') , etc., in which the disconnections will be at the bonds involving the acyl carbon and the group in bold. So we disconnect the bond between the carbonyl carbon and the heteroatom to get synthons leading to acid chlorides and alcohols /amines.

$$R-\underset{\underset{O}{\parallel}}{C}-O-R \xrightarrow{C-O} RCOCl + R'OH$$

$$R-\underset{\underset{O}{\parallel}}{C}-NHR' \xrightarrow{C-N} RCOCl + R'NH_2$$

Ethers, esters and amides, where we have the disconnection to be made between the alkyl/aryl carbon and the oxygen. Which, alkyl/aryl group to be disconnected shall be decided by many factors. Same is the case for sulfides or thioethers, as well as amines.

R'—O—R

PhCH$_2$Cl + HO-CH$_2$CH$_2$CH(CH$_3$)$_2$ PhCH$_2$OH + Cl-CH$_2$CH$_2$CH(CH$_3$)$_2$

(b) The C-C Disconnections

In certain cases, inspite of having a C-X functionality in the TG, still C-C disconnections are to be made mainly due to facile nature of synthesis from the synthons arising from such disconnections or ready availability of the reagents equivalent to the synthons for such syntheses.

These can be done in following events;

1. **One group C-C disconnections in alcohols**

   (i) **1,1-C-C disconnections**: alcohol can be disconnected at a bond next to the OH group.

   [Scheme showing disconnections with MgBr, Acetone, Butyl lithium]

Aldehydes or Ketones via Alcohols

[Scheme: ketone $\xrightarrow{FGI}$ alcohol $\xrightarrow{C-C}$ R-MgBr + ketone; aldehyde $\xrightarrow{FGI}$ alcohol $\xrightarrow{C-C}$ Br-compound]

Carboxylic acids

$$R-Br \xleftarrow{FGI} R-MgBr + CO_2 \xleftarrow{C-C} R-COOH \xrightarrow{FGI} R-CN \xleftarrow{C-C} R-Br + {}^\ominus CN$$

(ii) 1,2-C,C disconnections: alcohol can be disconnected at the second bonds situated next to that adjacent to the C-OH bond (or β to C–OH bond).

2. **One group C-C disconnections in carbonyl compounds**

TWO GROUP DISCONNECTIONS

When the Tg contains two functional groups and if disconnection is done using the two functional group together, i.e., use of one functional group to help disconnect the other.

The position of the groups in the molecules may be 1,3- or 1,4- or 1, 5- to each other, as seen in the following examples.

ROUTINE FOR DESIGNING A SYNTHESIS

Three integral steps in synthon approach are:
1. Analysis
2. Disconnection / FGI
3. Synthesis

Analysis: It involves different steps: before starting disconnection operation, one should examine the target molecule as a whole and recognize the functional groups in the target molecule and also positional relationships between them. Orientation of these groups with respect to each other.

Disconnection: After complete analysis of the TM, one should disconnect the bonds corresponding to the known and reliable reactions or functional group interconversions.

Synthesis:
1. One should write down the plan according to the analysis, adding reagents and conditions.
2. Modify the plan according to the unexpected failures or successes in the laboratory.

Some essential knowledge an organic chemist must have to design synthesis. It may include:
(a) An understanding of the reaction mechanism.
(b) An appreciation that some compounds are readily available.
(c) A working knowledge of reliable mechanism.
(d) An understanding of stereochemistry.

Some examples given below shall illustrate these concepts and their applications

Piperenal
Analysis:

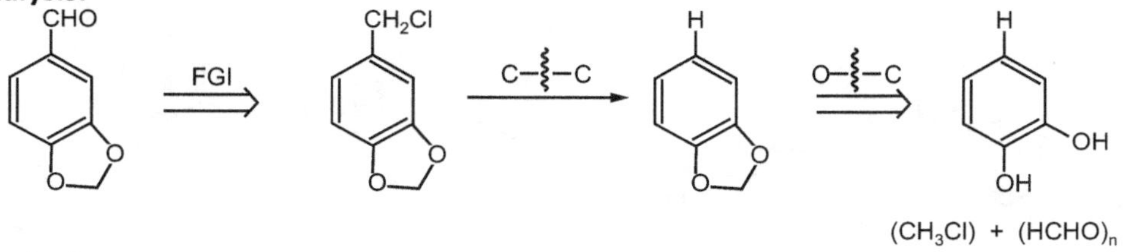

[Retrosynthetic scheme: Piperonal (CHO on methylenedioxybenzene) ⟹ (FGI) CH₂Cl derivative ⟶ (C–C disconnection) methylenedioxybenzene ⟹ (O–C disconnection) catechol (1,2-dihydroxybenzene) + (CH₃Cl) + (HCHO)ₙ]

Synthesis

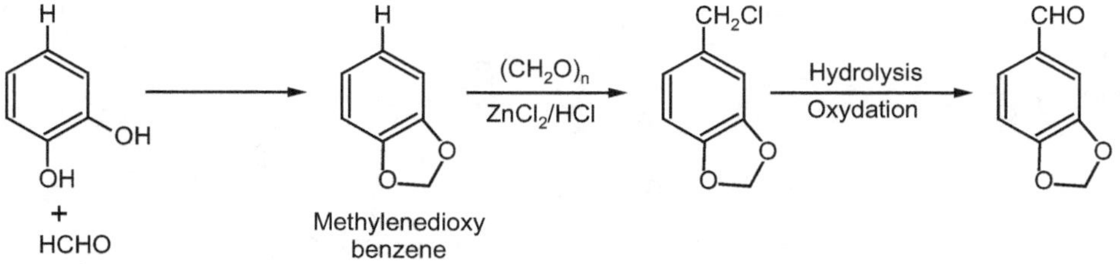

Catechol (with OH, OH) + HCHO ⟶ Methylenedioxy benzene —(CH₂O)ₙ, ZnCl₂/HCl→ CH₂Cl derivative —Hydrolysis, Oxydation→ CHO derivative (Piperonal)

Benzocaine
Analysis:

[Ethyl 4-aminobenzoate ⟹ (C–O disconnection) 4-aminobenzoic acid ⟹ Reduction ⟸ 4-nitrobenzoic acid ⟹ (FGI) ⟸ (C–N disconnection) p-nitrotoluene ⟸ toluene]

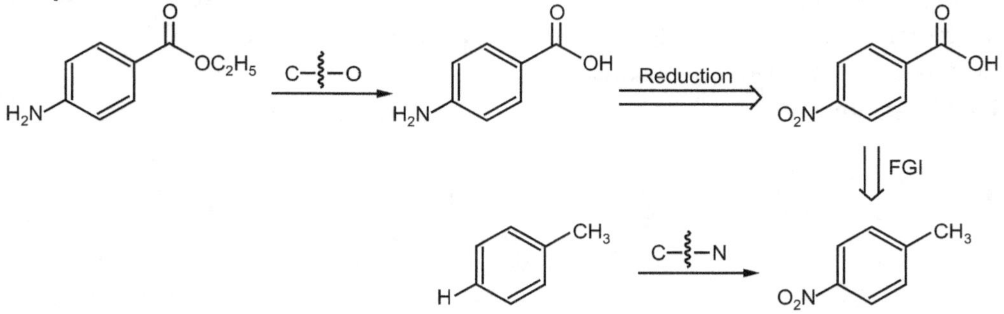

Synthesis:

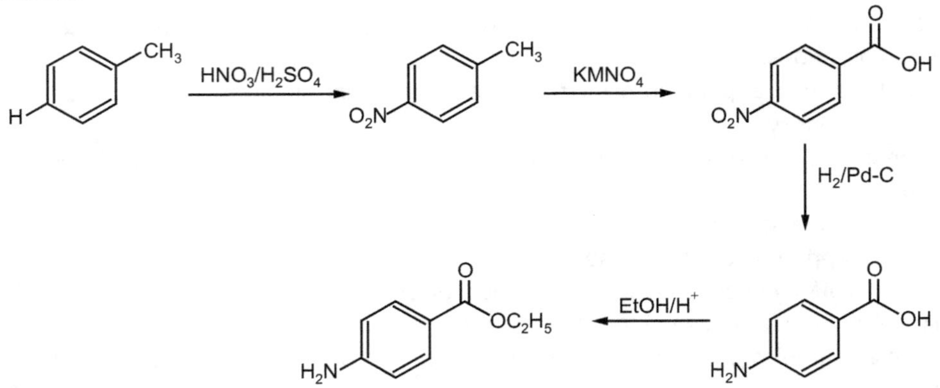

[Reaction scheme: Toluene → (HNO₃/H₂SO₄) → p-nitrotoluene → (KMnO₄) → p-nitrobenzoic acid → (H₂/Pd-C) → p-aminobenzoic acid → (EtOH/H⁺) → ethyl p-aminobenzoate]

p-Methoxyacetophenone
Analysis:

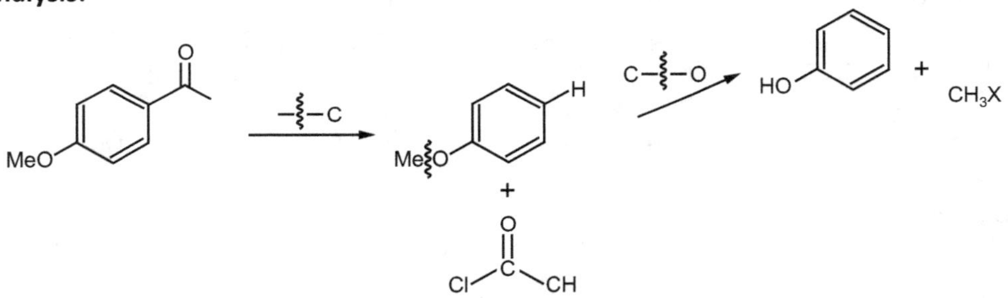

[Retrosynthetic scheme: p-methoxyacetophenone disconnects at C–C bond to give anisole + acetyl chloride; anisole further disconnects at C–O to phenol + CH₃X]

Synthesis:

Anisole + CH₃COCl →(AlCl₃)→ p-methoxyacetophenone

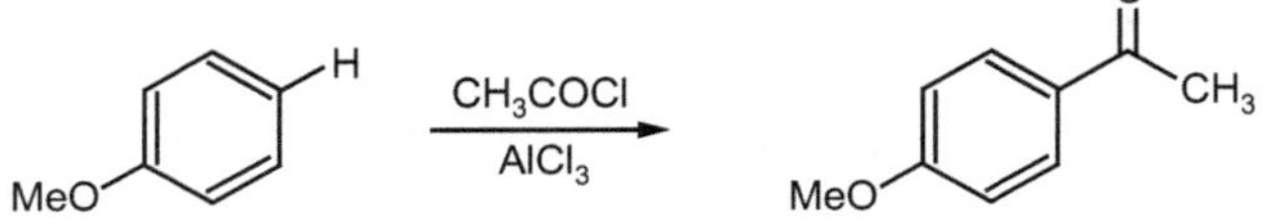

Some heterocyclic ring systems

Reterosynthesis of heterocycles using the criteria of "readily recognizable fragments." e.g., NH_3, NH_2NH_2, NH_2OH, guanidine, urea, thiourea, H_2N-CH_2CH_2-NH_2 are such readily recognizable fragments.

2-Aminopyrimidine

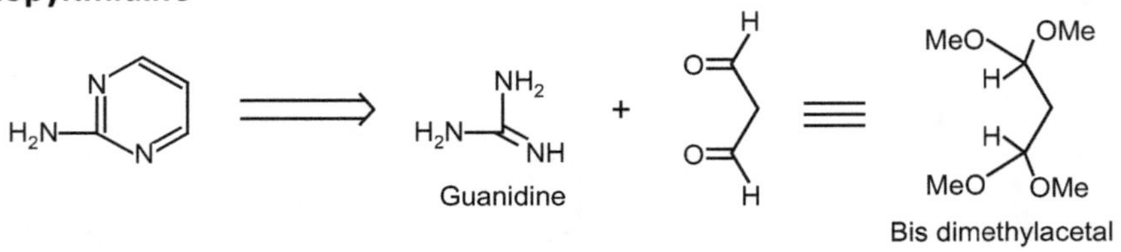

[Retrosynthesis: 2-aminopyrimidine ⇒ Guanidine (H_2N-C(=NH)-NH_2) + malondialdehyde (OHC-CH₂-CHO) ≡ Bis dimethylacetal (MeO)₂CH-CH₂-CH(OMe)₂]

2-Amino-4,6-dimethylpyrimidine

2-Amino-4,6-dimethylpyrimidine ⟹ guanidine (H₂N-C(=NH)-NH₂) + Acetylacetone

Pyridine

Pyridine (R₁, R₂ substituted) ⟹ [2 × C=N, Imine enamine] ⟹ 1,5-diketone (R₁-CO-CH=CH-CO-R₂) ⟹ [FGA] ⟹ 1,-diketone

Pyridine (R₁, R₂ substituted) ⟹ [2 × C=N, Amide enamine] ⟹ R₁-CO-CH=CH-CO-R₂ ⟹ [FGA] ⟹ 1,5-dicarboxylic acid

Pyridine (R₁, R₂) ⟹ [2 × C=N, Imine enamine] ⟹ R₁-CO-CH₂-CH₂-CO-Ph ⟹ [1,5-diCO] ⟹ cyclohexanone enolate + CH₂=CH-CO-Ph

Pyidazine

3,6-dichloropyridazine ⟹ ClCO-CH=CH-COCl + H₂N—NH₂

⟹ HOOC-CH=CH-COOH ↔ (enol form maleic acid)

⟹ [FGI, −H₂O] Pyran (maleic anhydride)

Pyran (maleic anhydride) + NH₂—NH₂ → 3,6-dihydroxypyridazine (HO-pyridazine-OH) → [POCl₃] → 3,6-dichloropyridazine (Cl-pyridazine-Cl)

Isoxazole

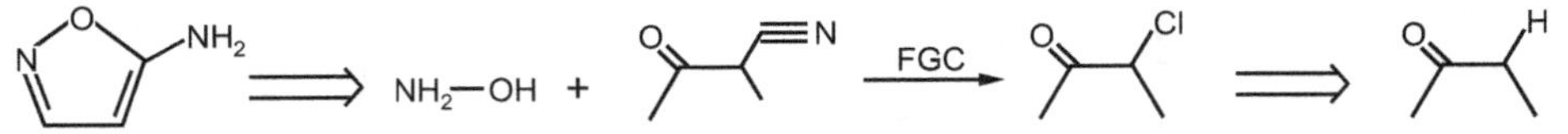

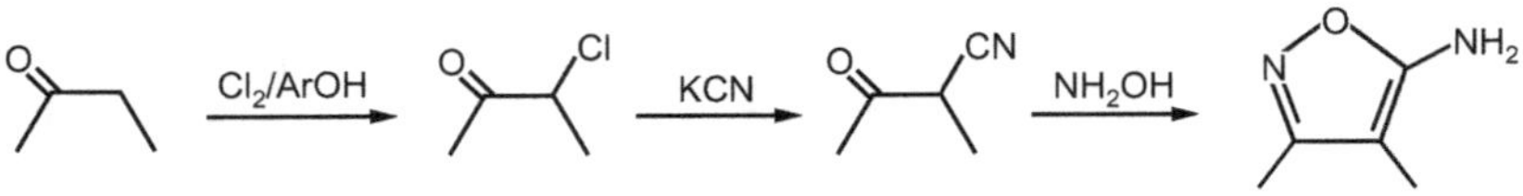

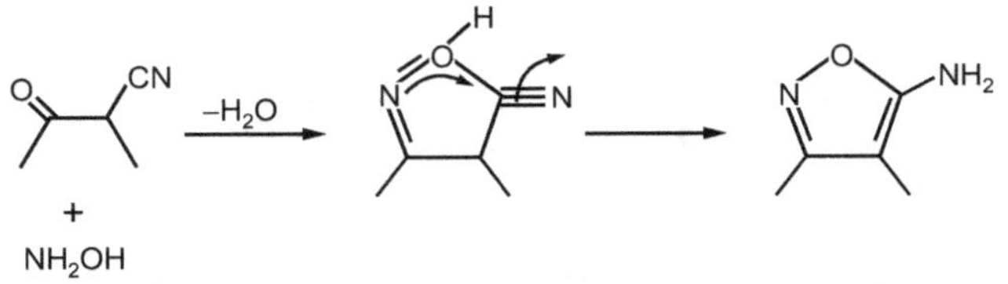

RETEROSYNTHESIS OF DRUG MOLECULES: SOME SELECTED EXAMPLES

1. Ciprofloxacin

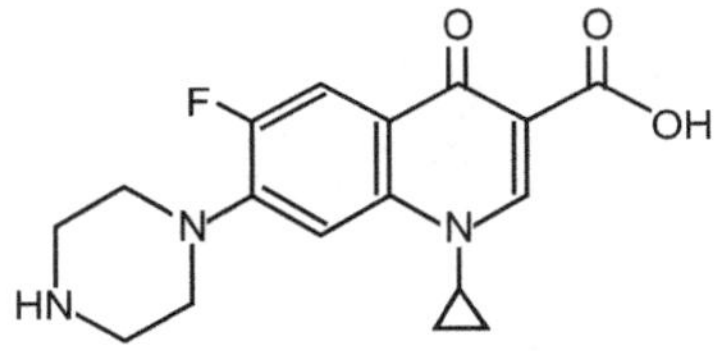

Analysis:

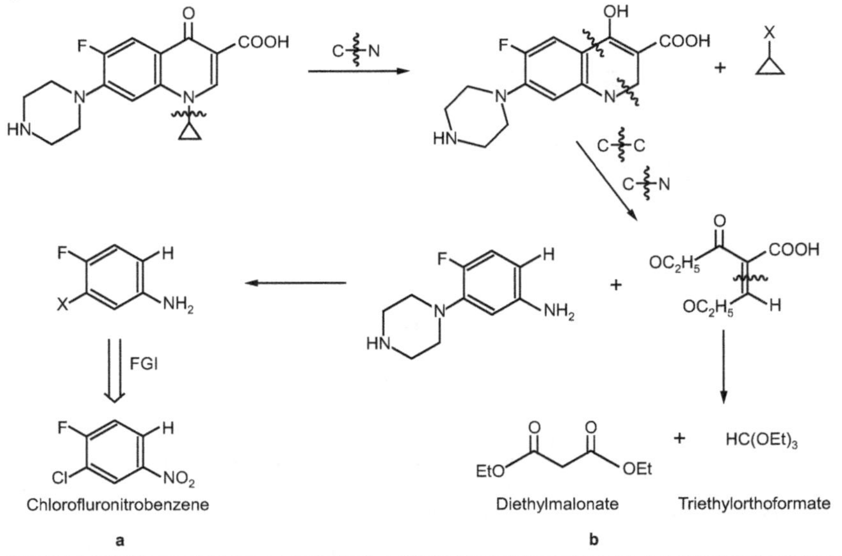

a. Chlorofluronitrobenzene

b. Diethylmalonate + Triethylorthoformate

Synthesis

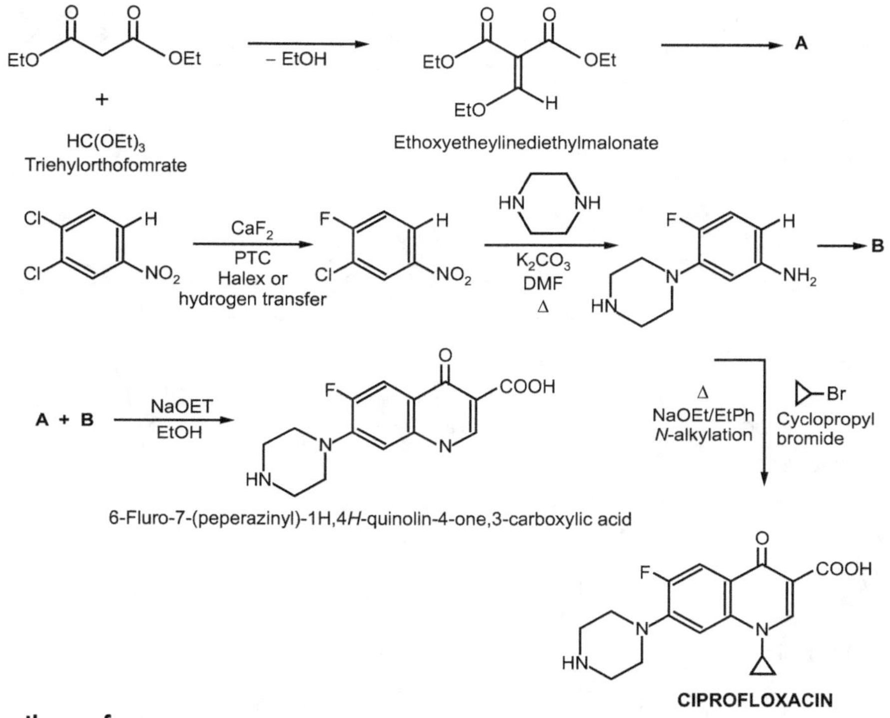

[Scheme: Diethyl malonate + HC(OEt)₃ (Triethylorthoformate) → (−EtOH) → Ethoxyetheylinediethylmalonate → **A**]

[Scheme: 1,2-dichloro-4-nitrobenzene → (CaF₂, PTC, Halex or hydrogen transfer) → 2-chloro-4-fluoro-1-nitrobenzene → (piperazine, K₂CO₃, DMF, Δ) → 4-fluoro-3-piperazinyl-aniline → **B**]

A + B → (NaOEt, EtOH) → 6-Fluro-7-(peperazinyl)-1H,4H-quinolin-4-one,3-carboxylic acid → (Δ, NaOEt/EtPh, N-alkylation; Cyclopropyl bromide) → **CIPROFLOXACIN**

2. Ibuprofen

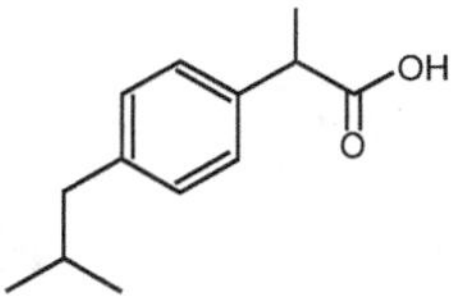

[Structure of Ibuprofen]

Analysis

[Retrosynthetic scheme: Ibuprofen →(FGI)→ nitrile → cyanohydrin ⇒ 4-isobutylacetophenone ⇒ ✗ → benzene + isobutylene (OR isobutyl halide $\diagup\!\diagdown\!X$)]

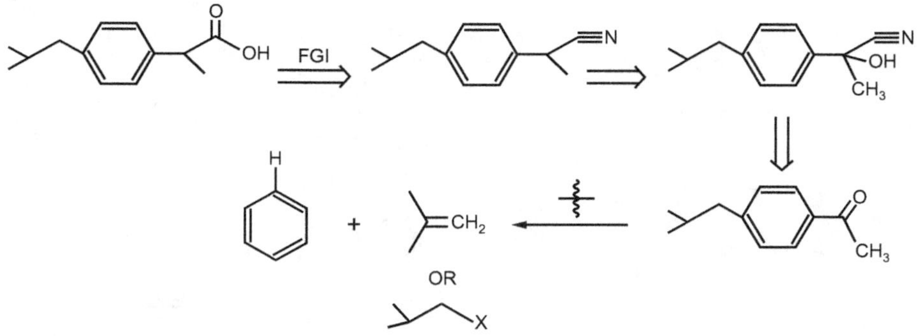

Synthesis

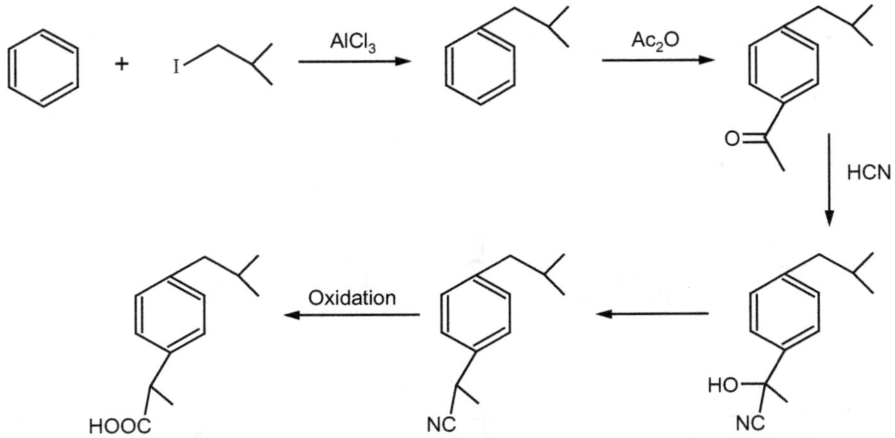

[Reaction scheme: benzene + isobutyl iodide → (AlCl₃) → isobutylbenzene → (Ac₂O) → 4-isobutylacetophenone → (HCN) → cyanohydrin → dehydration to nitrile → (Oxidation) → ibuprofen (HOOC-CH(CH₃)-Ar-iBu)]

3. **Propranolol**

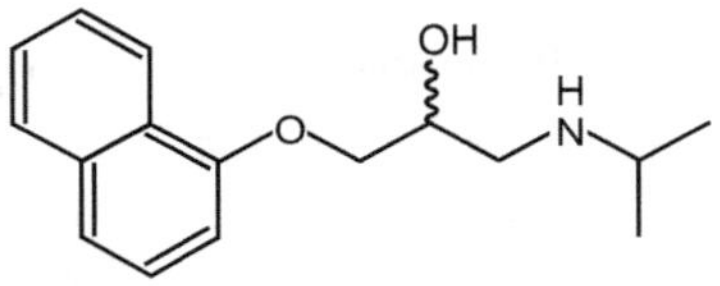

[Structure: 1-naphthyloxy-CH₂-CH(OH)-CH₂-NH-iPr]

Analysis

[Retrosynthetic scheme:
Propranolol → (C–N disconnection) → 1-(naphthyloxy)-2,3-epoxide intermediate + H₂N-iPr
→ FGI → naphthyloxy-epoxide
→ (O–C disconnection) → alpha-Napthol + Epichlorhydrin]

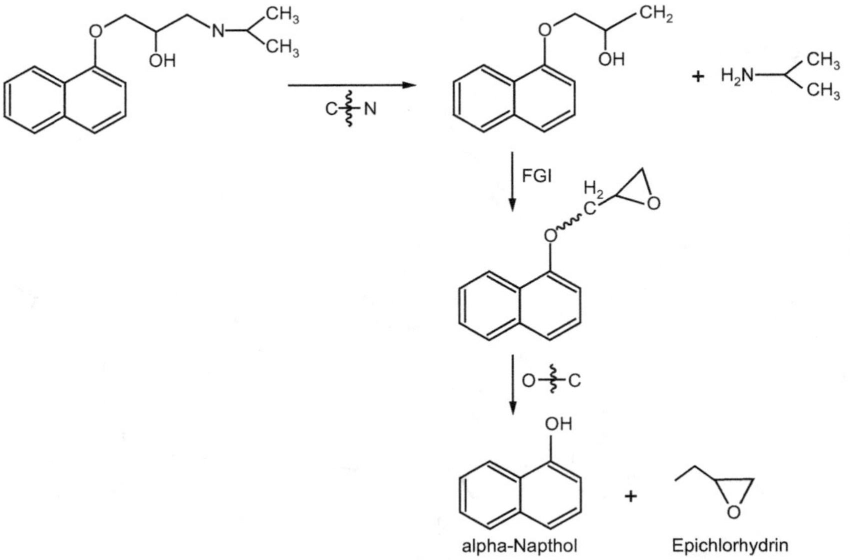

Synthesis

[Reaction scheme: Naphthalen-1-ol + epichlorohydrin (ClCH₂-epoxide) → (base) → 1-naphthyl glycidyl ether → (aq. HCl, Δ) → 1-(naphthalen-1-yloxy)-3-chloropropan-2-ol → (H₂N-CH(CH₃)₂, Δ) → Propranolol]

4. Sulfamethoxazole

[Structure of sulfamethoxazole: 4-amino-N-(5-methylisoxazol-3-yl)benzenesulfonamide]

Analysis

[Retrosynthetic analysis: Sulfamethoxazole ⇒ 4-acetamidobenzenesulfonyl chloride (A) + 3-amino-5-methylisoxazole (B); A ⇒ acetanilide]

Chp 7 | 7.23

Reterosynthesis & Synthesis of B (dimethylisoxazoleamine)

[Retrosynthesis scheme: 3-amino-5-methylisoxazole ⟹ NH₂—OH + acetoacetonitrile-type intermediate —FGC→ α-chloro ketone ⟹ acetone/acetaldehyde precursor]

[Forward synthesis: acetone → Cl₂/ArOH → α-chloroketone → KCN → cyanoketone → NH₂OH → 3-amino-5-methylisoxazole + NH₂OH]

Synthesis

[Scheme: Acetanilide (NHCOCH₃-C₆H₅) → ClSO₃H → 4-acetamidobenzenesulfonyl chloride (SO₂—Cl) → reaction with 3-amino-5-methylisoxazole (H₂N-isoxazole-CH₃), Δ → N-acetyl sulfonamide intermediate (NHCOCH₃ / SO₂—NH-isoxazole) → OH⁻/H₂O → sulfamethoxazole (NH₂ / SO₂—NH-isoxazole)]

CONCLUSION AND FUTURE SCOPE

- The reterosynthesis approach is a very useful analytical tool in medicinal and synthetic organic chemistry. By applying the principles of synthon approach, one can easily determine different routes to synthesize the target molecule, even if the target molecule has never been synthesized earlier.
- Also, it allows us to determine the most economical route for the synthesis. This approach has utmost importance particularly, when we think of synthesis of a new drug molecule obtained from natural resources like plants, animals etc.
- Synthon approach can provide a supply of useful compounds like alkaloids, penicillin's, vitamins, prostaglandins, and insect-attractants not available in adequate quantities from nature.

It is expected that with advancement and development of our knowledge about newer molecules of interest, this approach will continue to help in solving many problems of future for organic / medicinal chemists.

QUESTION BANK

1. Define synthon approach.

2. Give various terminologies used in synthon approach.

3. Enumerate the rules/guidelines for retrosynthesis with suitable examples.

4. How will you make the following molecules?

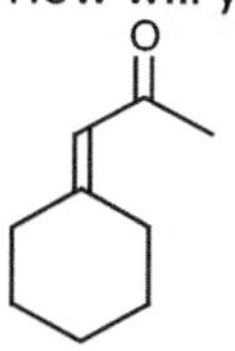

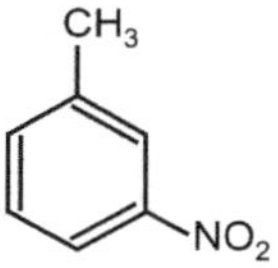

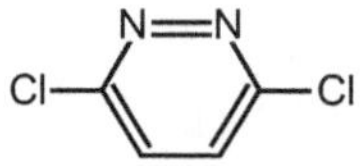

5. Which are the synthesis equivalents for the following:

    (i) $Ph-CH_2-CH_2^{\ominus}$

    (ii) $^{\ominus}CH_2-COOH$

    (iii) $-C+$
    $\quad\quad \|$
    $\quad\quad O$

    (iv) $\overset{\ominus}{N}HR$

6. Write the probable synthons for the following structures.

    (i) 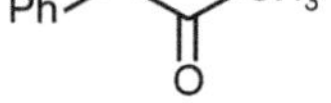 Ph–CH₂–C(=O)–CH₃ (shown as structure)

    (ii) $Ph_3PCH=CH\cdot CH_2COOEt$

7. Where will you disconnect?

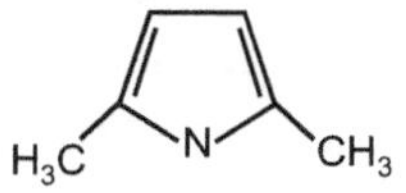

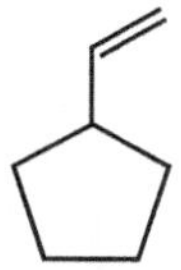

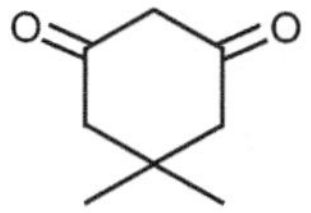

8. Discuss the retrosynthesis of following drugs:
   (i) Ibuprofen
   (ii) Propranolol
   (iii) Sulframethoxazole
   (iv) Ciprofloxacin
9. Give the retrosynthetic analysis and synthesis for the following molecules:
   (i) Piperanal
   (ii) *p*-Methoxyacetopheneone
   (iii) Benzocaine
   (iv) 2, 6-Dimethoxypyrimidine.

Chapter 8 ...

CHEMISTRY OF CARBOHYDRATES

CONTENTS

- Introduction
- Significance and Medicinal Importance of Carbohydrates
- Classification
- Method of Synthesis (Killiani Fischer and Ruff Degradation)
- Reactions of C5 (Arabinose) and C_6 (Glucose and Fructose) sugars
- Mutarotation
- Establishment of structures of Glucose and Fructose

INTRODUCTION

Carbohydrates constitute a very large group of naturally occurring organic compounds. They play a vital role in daily life. Carbohydrates are formed in nature in green plants as a result of photosynthesis - which involves combination of CO_2 and H_2O. When carbohydrates are taken by animals in the form of food, they are ultimately oxidised back to CO_2 and H_2O with liberation of energy. Animals can synthesize carbohydrates from amino acids, but most are derived from plants.

Glucose is the most important carbohydrates present in the nature. It is the major metabolic fuel for mammals and a universal fuel. It is the precursor for synthesis of all other carbohydrates in the body, viz., **glycogen** for storage; **ribose** and **deoxyribose** in nucleic acids, **galactose** in lactose of milk. *Cane sugar is our everyday table sugar.*

The important disaccharides include **maltose**, an intermediate in the digestion of starch; **sucrose** is a dietary constituent containing **fructose** and **lactose** in milk. **Starch glycogen and cellulose** are storage polymers of glucose in plants and animals, respectively. Starch is the major source of energy in the diet.

Complex carbohydrates contain other sugar derivatives such as amino sugars, uronic acids and sialic acids. They include proteoglycans and glycosaminoglycans which are associated with structural elements of the tissues and glycoproteins. They are found in many situations including the cell membrane. The paper we use and the cotton clothes we wear are made of cellulose.

SIGNIFICANCE AND MEDICINAL IMPORTANCE OF CARBOHYDRATES

Carbohydrates are major constituent of animal food and animal tissues. Glucose is the most important carbohydrate in mammalian biochemistry because, nearly all the carbohydrate in food is converted to glucose for metabolism. The physiologically important monosaccharide include glucose, the "blood sugar" and ribose, an important constituent of nucleotides and nucleic acids.

Diseases associated with carbohydrate metabolism include **diabetes mellitus, galactosemia, glycogen storage diseases** and **lactose intolerance**.

Many monosaccharides are physiologically important *viz.*, glucose, galactose, fructose and mannose are most important hexoses. The biochemically important ketoses are D-glyceraldehydes, D-xylose, D-arabinose, D-ribose, D-galactose, D-mannose and D-glucose; aldoses are D-xylulose, D-ribulose, D-fructose.

Table 1: Pentoses of Physiologic Importance

Sugar	Source	Biochemical and Clinical Importance
D-Ribose	Nucleic acids and metabolic intermediates	Structural component of nucleic acids and coenzymes, including ATP, NAD(P) and flavin coenzymes
D-Ribulose	Metabolic intermediate	Intermediate in the pentose phosphate pathway
D-Arabinose	Plant gums	Constituent of glycoproteins
D-Xylose	Plants gums, proteoglycans, glycosaminoglycans	Constituent of glycoproteins
L-Xylose	Metabolic intermediate	Excreted in the urine.

Table 2: Hexoses of Physiologic Importance

Sugar	Source	Biochemical Importance	Clinical Importance
D-Glucose	Fruit juices, hydrolysis of starch, cane or beet sugar, maltose and lactose	The main metabolic fuel for tissues; "blood sugar"	Excreted in the urine (glucosuria) in poorly controlled diabetes mellitus as a result of hyperglycemia

contd. ...

D-Fructose	Fruit juices, honey, hydrolysis of cane or beet sugar and inulin, enzymatic isomerization of glucose syrups for food manufacture	Readily metabolized either *via* glucose or directly	Hereditary fructose intolerance leads to fructose accumulation and hypoglycaemia
D-Galactose	Hyrolysis of lactose	Readily metabolized to glucose; synthesized in the mammary gland for synthesis of lactose in milk. A constituent of glycol lipids and glycol proteins.	Hereditary galactosemia as a result of failure to metabolize galactose leads to cataracts
D-Mannose	Hydrolysis of plant mannan gums	Constituent of glycoproteins	

Sugar forms glycosides and are widely distributed in nature. The glycosides that are important in medicine because of their action on heart (**cardiac glycosides**), e.g. **digitalis** and **stropanthus**. Other glycoside include antibiotics such as **streptomycin**. Several antibiotics *viz.* **amikacin, gentamicin, erythromycin** contain amino sugars, which are important for their antibiotic activity. The physiologically important disaccharides are **maltose, sucrose** and **lactose**.

Table 3: Disaccharides of Physiologic Importance

Sugar	Source	Biochemical Importance	Clinical Importance
Sucrose	O-α D-glucopyranosyl-(1→2)-β-d-fructo-furanoside	Cane and beet sugar, sorghum and some fruits and vegetables	Rare genetic lack of sucrose leads to sucrose intolerance-diarrhea and flatulence
Lactose	O-α D-galactopyranosyl-(1→4)-β-o-glycopyranose	Milk (and many pharmaceutical preparations as a filler)	Lack of lactase (alactasia) leads to lactose intolerance-diarrhea and flatulence; may be excreted in the urine in pregnancy

Physiologically important polysaccharides are **starch** and **glycogen**. Starch is the most important dietary. Carbohydrates are present in cereals, potatoes, legumes and other vegetables. They are the major source of energy in diet. Glycogen is referred as animal starch and is a storage polysaccharide in animals. Approximately 5% of the weight of cell membrane is carbohydrate. **Glycophorin** is a major integral glycoprotein of human erythrocyte.

CLASSIFICATION

Carbohydrates are mainly classified into 4 classes:
1. Monosaccharides
2. Disaccharides
3. Oligosaccharides
4. Polysaccharides

1. Monosaccharides: These are simple sugar units, which cannot be hydrolysed further into smaller molecules. They may be classified as **trioses, tetroses, pentoses, hexoses** (depending upon number of carbon atoms) and as **aldoses** or **ketoses** (depending upon nature of carbonyl group).

Aldehyde group containing monosaccharides are called as **aldoses** where as ketone group containing monosaccharides are called as **ketoses**.

Table 4: Classification of Monosaccharides

No. of carbon atoms	Class	Aldoses	Ketoses
3	Trioses ($C_3H_6O_3$)	Glycerose (Glyceraldehydes)	Dihydroxyacetone
4	Tetroses ($C_4H_8O_4$)	Erythrose	Erythrulose
5	Pentoses ($C_5H_{10}O_5$)	Ribose	Ribulose
6	Hexoses ($C_6H_{12}O_6$)	Glucose	Fructose

Example:

Aldoses

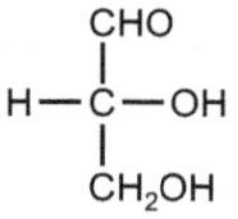

CHO
|
H—C—OH
|
CH₂OH

(I) D-Glyceraldehyde (glycerose)

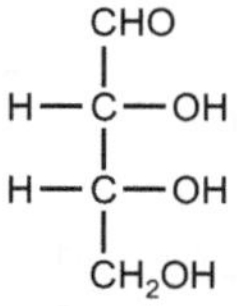

CHO
|
H—C—OH
|
H—C—OH
|
CH₂OH

(II) Erythrose

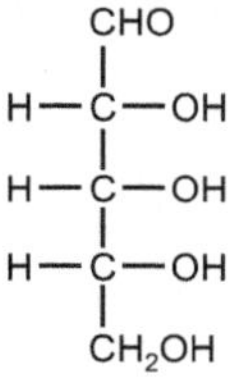

CHO
|
H—C—OH
|
H—C—OH
|
H—C—OH
|
CH₂OH

(III) Ribose

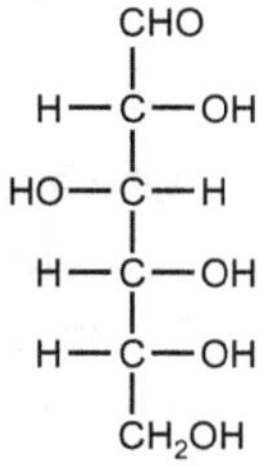

CHO
|
H—C—OH
|
HO—C—H
|
H—C—OH
|
H—C—OH
|
CH₂OH

(IV) Glucose

Ketoses

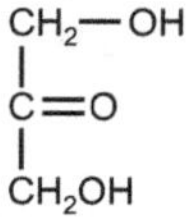

CH₂—OH
|
C=O
|
CH₂OH

(I) Dihydroxyacetone

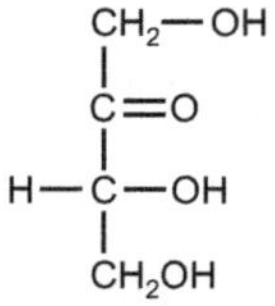

CH₂—OH
|
C=O
|
H—C—OH
|
CH₂OH

(II) Erythrulose

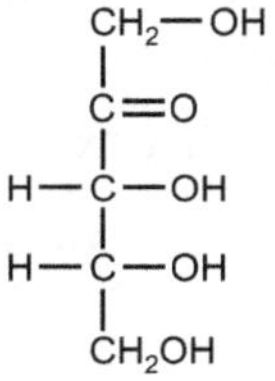

CH₂—OH
|
C=O
|
H—C—OH
|
H—C—OH
|
CH₂OH

(III) Ribulose

CH₂—OH
|
C=O
|
HO—C—H
|
H—C—OH
|
H—C—OH
|
CH₂OH

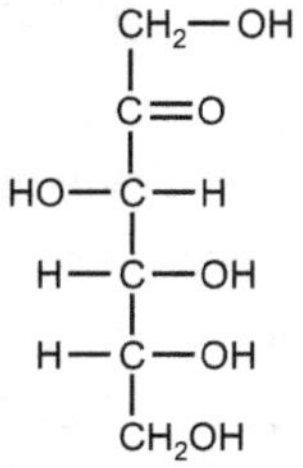

(IV) Fructose

2. **Disaccharides:** These are condensation products of two **monosaccharide units**.

   Example:

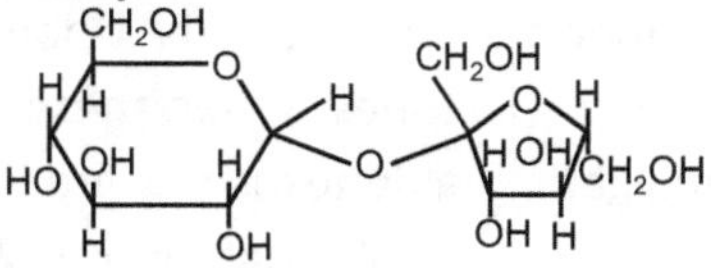

   (I) Sucrose
   (Glucose + Fructose)

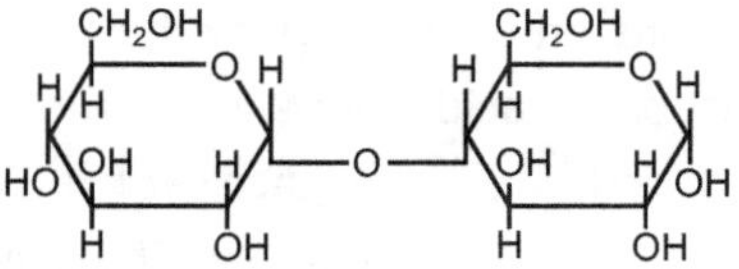

   (II) Maltose
   (Glucose + Glucose)

3. **Oligosaccharides:** These are condensation products of **three to ten monosaccharides units.**

   Example: Raffinose (It is a triasaccharide composed of galactose, glucose and fructose).

   Galactose — Glucose — Fructose

4. **Polysaccharides:** These are condensation products of **more than ten monosaccharide** units.

   Example: Starch, dextrin, cellulose etc.

METHODS OF SYNTHESIS

1. **Killiani Fischer Synthesis:**

   Killiani and Fischer developed an elegant method by which an aldose can be converted into a higher aldose containing one more carbon atom. This method for lengthening the carbon chain of an aldose is called as **Killiani-Fischer synthesis.**

   Here we can illustrate the Killiani-Fischer Synthesis with the synthesis of D-glucose and D-mannose from D-arabinose.

   Addition of hydrogen cyanide to D-arabinose produces two disteromeric cyanohydrins. The cyanolydrin formation gives rise to a new asymmetric centre. These cyanohydrins on heating with dil. HCl gives two isomeric carboxylic acids. Upon heating these carboxylic acids loose water molecules and yield γ-lactones. When these lactones are reduced in presence of sodium amalgam, aldohexoses are formed i.e., D-glucose and D-mannose. These aldohexoses differ in configuration at C-2 carbon and are called as **epimers.** Thus, Killiani-Fischer synthesis leads to the formation of **epimers.**

$$^1\text{CHO}$$
$$\text{HO}—^2\text{C}—\text{H}$$
$$\text{H}—^3\text{C}—\text{OH}$$
$$\text{H}—^4\text{C}—\text{OH}$$
$$\text{CH}_2\text{OH}$$

D - Arabinose (Aldopentose)

↓ HCN

Left pathway:

$$\text{CN}$$
$$\text{H}—\text{C}^*—\text{OH}$$
$$\text{HO}—\text{C}—\text{H}$$
$$\text{H}—\text{C}—\text{OH}$$
$$\text{H}—\text{C}—\text{OH}$$
$$\text{CH}_2\text{OH}$$

↓ Hydrolysis

$$\text{COOH}$$
$$\text{H}—\text{C}—\text{OH}$$
$$\text{HO}—\text{C}—\text{H}$$
$$\text{H}—\text{C}—\text{OH}$$
$$\text{H}—\text{C}—\text{OH}$$
$$\text{CH}_2\text{OH}$$

Δ ↓ Dehydration

$$\text{C}=\text{O}$$
$$\text{H}—\text{C}^\alpha—\text{OH}$$
$$\text{HO}—\text{C}^\beta—\text{H}$$
$$\text{H}—\text{C}^\gamma—$$
$$\text{H}—\text{C}—\text{OH}$$
$$\text{CH}_2\text{OH}$$

Reduction ↓ Na/Hg

$$^1\text{CHO}$$
$$\text{H}—^2\text{C}—\text{OH}$$
$$\text{HO}—^3\text{C}—\text{H}$$
$$\text{H}—^4\text{C}—\text{OH}$$
$$\text{H}—^5\text{C}—\text{OH}$$
$$^6\text{CH}_2\text{OH}$$

D - Glucose

Right pathway:

$$\text{CN}$$
$$\text{HO}—\text{C}^*—\text{H}$$
$$\text{HO}—\text{C}—\text{H}$$
$$\text{H}—\text{C}—\text{OH}$$
$$\text{H}—\text{C}—\text{OH}$$
$$\text{CH}_2\text{OH}$$

↓ Hydrolysis

$$\text{COOH}$$
$$\text{HO}—\text{C}—\text{H}$$
$$\text{HO}—\text{C}—\text{H}$$
$$\text{H}—\text{C}—\text{OH}$$
$$\text{H}—\text{C}—\text{OH}$$
$$\text{CH}_2\text{OH}$$

Δ ↓ Dehydration

$$\text{C}=\text{O}$$
$$\text{HO}—\text{C}^\alpha—\text{H}$$
$$\text{HO}—\text{C}^\beta—\text{H}$$
$$\text{H}—\text{C}^\gamma—$$
$$\text{H}—\text{C}—\text{OH}$$
$$\text{CH}_2\text{OH}$$

Reduction ↓ Na/Hg

$$^1\text{CHO}$$
$$\text{HO}—^2\text{C}—\text{H}$$
$$\text{HO}—^3\text{C}—\text{H}$$
$$\text{H}—^4\text{C}—\text{OH}$$
$$\text{H}—^5\text{C}—\text{OH}$$
$$^6\text{CH}_2\text{OH}$$

D - Mannose

Labels (center): Cynohydrins; Carboxylic acid; −H₂O; γ - Lactones; Aldohexoses

2. Ruff Degradation:

The Ruff degradation involves shortening of the carbon chain by one carbon from the aldehyde end in aldose. Thus, an aldose can be converted to the next lower aldose in two steps:

I. Oxidation of the aldose to aldonic acid using bromine water

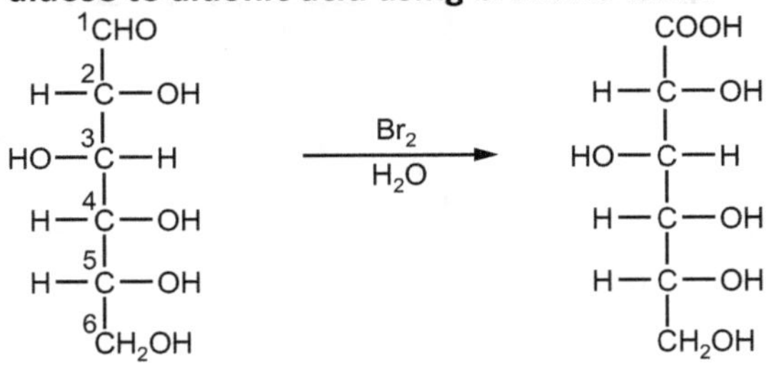

$$\begin{array}{c} {}^1CHO \\ H-{}^2C-OH \\ HO-{}^3C-H \\ H-{}^4C-OH \\ H-{}^5C-OH \\ {}^6CH_2OH \end{array} \xrightarrow{Br_2 / H_2O} \begin{array}{c} COOH \\ H-C-OH \\ HO-C-H \\ H-C-OH \\ H-C-OH \\ CH_2OH \end{array}$$

Aldohexose (D-Glucose) → Aldonic acid

II. Oxidative decarboxylation of aldonic acid by treating with calcium salt, hydrogen peroxide in presence of ferric sulphate.

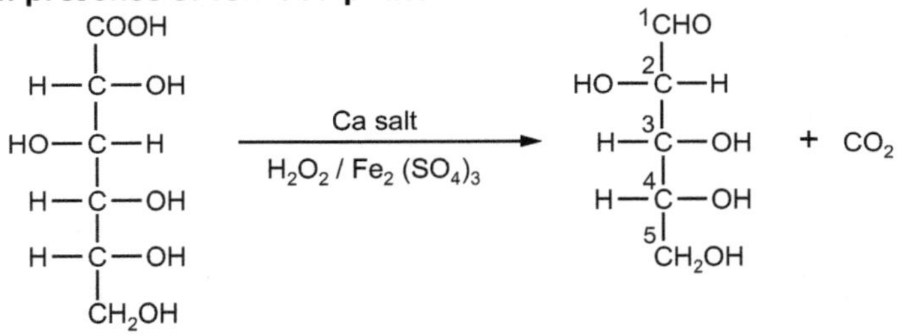

$$\begin{array}{c} COOH \\ H-C-OH \\ HO-C-H \\ H-C-OH \\ H-C-OH \\ CH_2OH \end{array} \xrightarrow{Ca\ salt \\ H_2O_2 / Fe_2(SO_4)_3} \begin{array}{c} {}^1CHO \\ HO-{}^2C-H \\ H-{}^3C-OH \\ H-{}^4C-OH \\ {}^5CH_2OH \end{array} + CO_2$$

Aldonic acid → Aldopentose (D-Arbinose)

REACTIONS OF GLUCOSE

1. Oxidation:

(a) On treatment with a weak oxidising agent, such as bromine water, glucose is oxidised to **gluconic acid**.

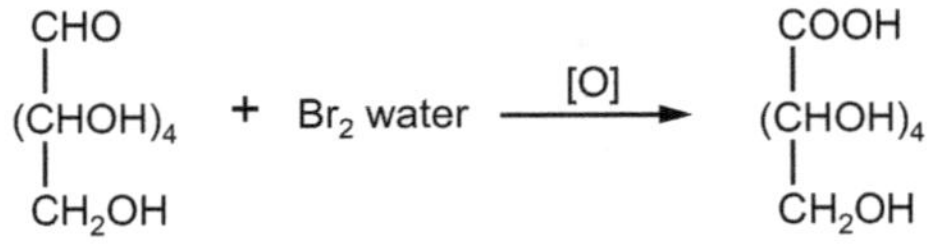

$$\begin{array}{c} CHO \\ (CHOH)_4 \\ CH_2OH \end{array} + Br_2\ water \xrightarrow{[O]} \begin{array}{c} COOH \\ (CHOH)_4 \\ CH_2OH \end{array}$$

D - Glucose → Gluconic acid (Mono carboxylic acid)

(b) Glucose is oxidised to **glucaric acid** in presence of strong oxidising agents such as conc. HNO_3.

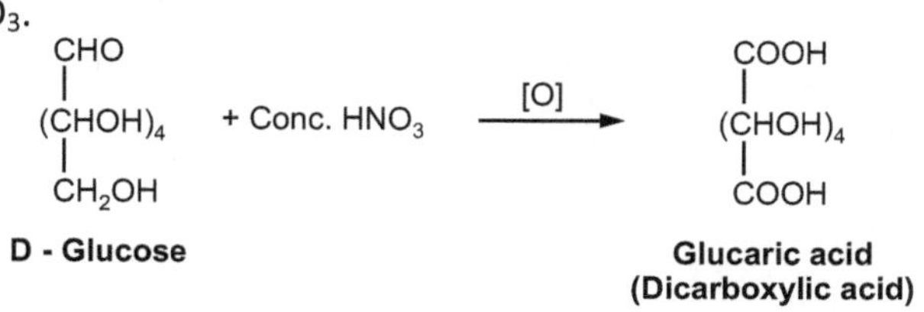

$$\begin{array}{c} CHO \\ | \\ (CHOH)_4 \\ | \\ CH_2OH \end{array} + \text{Conc. } HNO_3 \xrightarrow{[O]} \begin{array}{c} COOH \\ | \\ (CHOH)_4 \\ | \\ COOH \end{array}$$

D - Glucose → Glucaric acid (Dicarboxylic acid)

2. Reduction:

Glucose on reduction with sodium borohydrate ($NaBH_4$) or catalytic reduction (H_2/Pd), yields the corresponding alcohol, **sorbitol**.

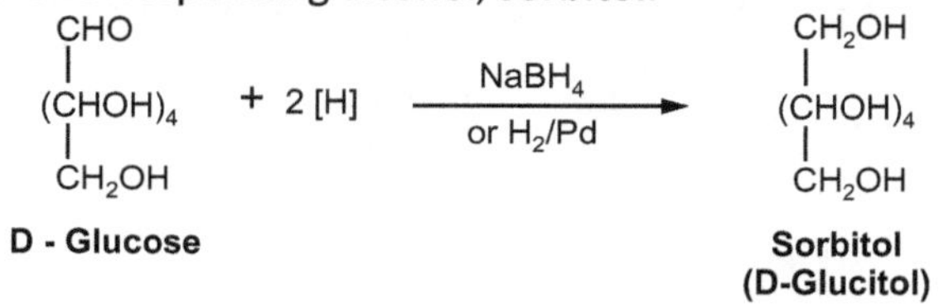

$$\begin{array}{c} CHO \\ | \\ (CHOH)_4 \\ | \\ CH_2OH \end{array} + 2[H] \xrightarrow[\text{or } H_2/Pd]{NaBH_4} \begin{array}{c} CH_2OH \\ | \\ (CHOH)_4 \\ | \\ CH_2OH \end{array}$$

D - Glucose → Sorbitol (D-Glucitol)

3. Reaction with HCN:

Hydrogen cyanide adds to the aldehydic carbonyl group to form glucose cyanohydrin. *This reaction is important while synthesizing a higher aldose from a lower member.*

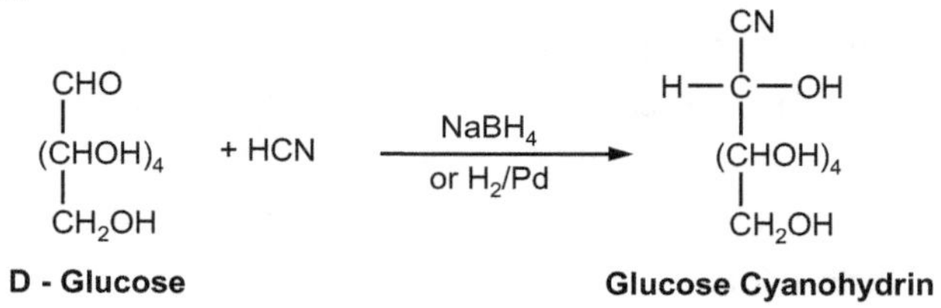

$$\begin{array}{c} CHO \\ | \\ (CHOH)_4 \\ | \\ CH_2OH \end{array} + HCN \xrightarrow[\text{or } H_2/Pd]{NaBH_4} \begin{array}{c} CN \\ | \\ H-C-OH \\ | \\ (CHOH)_4 \\ | \\ CH_2OH \end{array}$$

D - Glucose → Glucose Cyanohydrin

4. Reaction with hydroxylamine:

Glucose condenses with hydroxylamine (NH_2OH), to form glucose oxime.

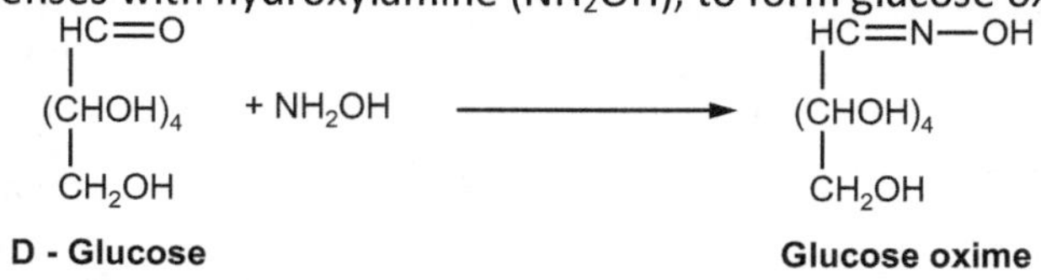

$$\begin{array}{c} HC=O \\ | \\ (CHOH)_4 \\ | \\ CH_2OH \end{array} + NH_2OH \longrightarrow \begin{array}{c} HC=N-OH \\ | \\ (CHOH)_4 \\ | \\ CH_2OH \end{array}$$

D - Glucose → Glucose oxime

5. Reaction with Phenyldrazine:

Glucose when warmed with excess of phenylhydrazine, a product **glucasozone (osazone)** is formed. Osazones are well defined crystalline substances formed by aldoses and ketoses. *This is used for identification of monosaccharides.*

$$\underset{\text{D - Glucose}}{\begin{array}{c}\text{CHO}\\|\\(\text{CHOH})_4\\|\\\text{CH}_2\text{OH}\end{array}} + \underset{\begin{array}{c}\text{Phenyl hydrazine}\\(1^{st}\text{ molecule})\end{array}}{C_6H_5-NH-NH_2} \xrightarrow{\text{Warm}} \underset{\text{Glucose phenylhydrazone}}{\begin{array}{c}\text{CH}=\text{N}-\text{N}-C_6H_5\\|\quad\quad\quad\text{H}\\\text{CHOH}\\|\\(\text{CHOH})_3\\|\\\text{CH}_2\text{OH}\end{array}}$$

$$\downarrow \underset{(2^{nd}\text{ molecule})}{C_6H_5-NH-NH_2}$$

$$\underset{\begin{array}{c}\text{Glucosazone}\\\text{(Osazone)}\end{array}}{\begin{array}{c}\text{CH}=\text{N}-\text{N}-C_6H_5\\|\quad\quad\quad\text{H}\\\text{C}=\text{N}-\text{N}-C_6H_5\\|\quad\quad\quad\text{H}\\(\text{CHOH})_3\\|\\\text{CH}_2\text{OH}\end{array}} \xleftarrow{\underset{(3^{rd}\text{ molecule})}{C_6H_5\,NHNH_2}} \begin{array}{c}\text{CH}=\text{N}-\text{N}-C_6H_5\\|\quad\quad\quad\text{H}\\\text{C}=\text{O}\\|\\(\text{CHOH})_3\\|\\\text{CH}_2\text{OH}\end{array}$$

REACTIONS OF FRUCTOSE

1. **Oxidation:**
   (a) Bromine water oxidises glucose to gluconic acid, but does not react with fructose. **This reaction can be used to distinguish between glucose and fructose.**
   (b) Action of strong oxidising agent such as conc. HNO_3, oxidises fructose to **glycolic acid** and **tartaric acid**.

$$\underset{\text{Fructose}}{\begin{array}{c}\text{CH}_2\text{OH}\\|\\\text{C}=\text{O}\\|\\\text{CHOH}\\|\\(\text{CHOH})_2\\|\\\text{CH}_2\text{OH}\end{array}} \xrightarrow[HNO_3]{[O]} \underset{\text{Glycolic acid}}{\begin{array}{c}\text{CH}_2\text{OH}\\|\\\text{COOH}\end{array}} + \underset{\text{Tartaric acid}}{\begin{array}{c}\text{COOH}\\|\\(\text{CHOH})_2\\|\\\text{COOH}\end{array}}$$

2. **Reduction:**
   Fructose gives two epimeric hexahydric alcohols when reduced in presence of sodium borohydride ($NaBH_4$).

Fructose → Sorbitol + D-mannitol (NaBH₄ reduction)

$$\underset{\text{Fructose}}{\begin{array}{c}CH_2OH\\|\\C=O\\|\\(CHOH)_3\\|\\CH_2OH\end{array}}\xrightarrow{NaBH_4}\underset{\text{Sorbitol}}{\begin{array}{c}CH_2OH\\|\\H-C-OH\\|\\(CHOH)_3\\|\\CH_2OH\end{array}}+\underset{\text{D-mannitol}}{\begin{array}{c}CH_2OH\\|\\HO-C-H\\|\\(CHOH)_3\\|\\CH_2OH\end{array}}$$

3. Reaction with Phenylhydrazine:

Phenylhydrazone is formed, when fructose is warmed with phenylhydrizine. The CH_2OH at C-1 is further oxidised to –CHO by second molecule of phenylhydrizine. Finally, **osazone** is formed when –CHO reacts with third molecule of phenylhydrizine.

$$\underset{\text{Fructose}}{\begin{array}{c}CH_2OH\\|\\C=O\\|\\(CHOH)_3\\|\\CH_2OH\end{array}}+\underset{\substack{\text{Phenylhydrazine}\\\text{(Excess)}}}{C_6H_5NHNH_2}\xrightarrow{\text{Warm}}\underset{\text{Fructose phenylhydrazone}}{\begin{array}{c}CH_2OH\\|\\C=N-NHC_6H_5\\|\\(CHOH)_3\\|\\CH_2OH\end{array}}$$

$$\downarrow C_6H_5NHNH_2$$

$$\underset{\text{Fructosazone (Osazone)}}{\begin{array}{c}C=N-NHC_6H_5\\|\\C=N-NHC_6H_5\\|\\(CHOH)_3\\|\\CH_2OH\end{array}}\xleftarrow{C_6H_5NHNH_2}\begin{array}{c}CHO\\|\\C=N-NHC_6H_5\\|\\(CHOH)_3\\|\\CH_2OH\end{array}$$

CHEMICAL TESTS FOR CARBOHYDRATE

These are polyhydroxy aldehydes and ketones, they do not give all the tests of aldehyde or ketonic group as these groups are not present in free state in the carbohydrates.

Test	Observation	Inference
1. Molisch test: 0.2 g compound +2 ml Molisch's reagent, shake well and add 1 ml concentrated H_2SO_4 from the walls of the test tube.	Violet red colouration at the junction of the two layers.	Carbohydrate is confirmed. Example, glucose.

Reaction:

$$\underset{\substack{\text{CHO} \\ | \\ \text{(CHOH)}_4 \\ | \\ \text{CH}_2\text{OH}}}{} + \underset{\text{Alcoholic solution of α-Naphthol}}{\text{[α-naphthol]}} \xrightarrow{\text{H}_2\text{SO}_4} \text{HO—H}_2\text{C—(CHOH)}_4\text{—C(=O)—[naphthalenone]}$$

Test	Observation	Inference
2. 0.2 g compound + 1 ml concentrated H_2SO_4	Charring of the compound.	Carbohydrate is confirmed.

Reaction:

$$C_n(H_2O)_n + \text{Concentrated } H_2SO_4 \longrightarrow \underset{\text{Charcoal}}{nC} + n(H_2O)\uparrow$$

Test	Observation	Inference
3. **Barfoed's test:** 0.2 g compound + 1 ml freshly prepared Barfoed's reagent. Heat on a boiling water bath for 1-2 minutes and cool under tap water.	Formation of a red ppt of cuprous (Cu_2O) at bottom of test tube.	Monosaccharide is confirmed. This is a test to distinguish between monosaccharides and disaccharides.

Reaction:

$$\underset{\substack{\text{CHO} \\ | \\ \text{(CHOH)}_4 \\ | \\ \text{CH}_2\text{OH}}}{} + Cu^{2\oplus} + 2H_2O \longrightarrow \underset{\substack{\text{COOH} \\ | \\ \text{(CHOH)}_4 \\ | \\ \text{CH}_2\text{OH}}}{} + H^{\oplus} + \underset{\text{Red precipitate}}{Cu_2O}$$

Test	Observation	Inference
4. **Fehling's/Benedict's test:** 0.2 g compound + 2ml Benedict's or Fehling's solution (equal amounts of Fehling's A and B). Heat it.	Formation of a red precipitate of cuprous oxide (Cu_2O).	A reducing sugar is confirmed.

Reaction:

(i)
$$\underset{\substack{\text{CHO} \\ | \\ \text{(CHOH)}_4 \\ | \\ \text{CH}_2\text{OH}}}{} + \underset{\text{Anhydrous}}{(CuSO_4 + 5H_2O + NaCO + Na.Citrate)} \xrightarrow{\Delta} \underset{\text{Cuprous oxide}}{Cu_2O} + \underset{\substack{\text{COOH} \\ | \\ \text{(CHOH)}_4 \\ | \\ \text{CH}_2\text{OH}}}{}$$

(ii)
$$\underset{\substack{\text{CHO} \\ | \\ \text{(CHOH)}_4 \\ | \\ \text{CH}_2\text{OH}}}{} + \text{Fehling's reagent} \left\{ \begin{array}{l} A : CuSO_4, 5H_2O \\ B : KOH + \text{Sodium Tartarate} \end{array} \right\} \longrightarrow \underset{\substack{\text{COOH} \\ | \\ \text{(CHOH)}_4 \\ | \\ \text{CH}_2\text{OH}}}{}$$

Note:
1. It is the general method employed for distinction between reducing and non-reducing saccharides. Copper hydroxide can oxidize some carbohydrate, itself getting reduced to Cu_2O (red precipitate), in the process. Its reactivity is enhanced by the formation of soluble complexes of Cu_2 with either tartarate ions (Fehling solution) or citrate ions (Benedict solution).
2. Non-reducing sugars include some disaccharides (sucrose and trihalose) which on boiling with acts are converted into reducing sugars and hence gives this test positive.

Test	Observation	Inference
5. **Selivanoff's test:** 0.2 g compound + 2 ml water + 0.5 ml concentrated HCl + a crystal of resorcinol is added. Heat it and observe the colour.	Pink colour is formed	Ketoses is confirmed. **Example:** Fructose.

Reaction:

$$\begin{array}{c} CH_2OH \\ | \\ C=O \\ | \\ HO-C-H \\ | \\ HC-C-OH \\ | \\ H-C-OH \\ | \\ CH_2OH \end{array} \longrightarrow \text{Resorcinol (OH, OH)} \xrightarrow{\text{Conc. HCl}} \text{(Phenolic alcohol) Pink colour}$$

Test	Observation	Inference
6. **Osazone formation:** (Monosaccharides, reducing sugars only form osazones). 0.2 g compound + 0.5 g phenyl hydrazine hydrochloride + 0.5 g sodium acetate + 5 ml water in a test tube. Boil them on a water bath with occasional shaking till ppt. appears.	Yellow crystals of osazone formed (Note the time of osazone formation).	0-5 min. — Mannose 2-3 min. — Fructose 4-5 min. — Glucose 8-10 min. — Xylose 10 min. — Arabinose 10 min. — Rhamnose 15-20 min. — Galactose 20-25 min. — Maltose and Lactose (on cooling) 30 min. — Sucrose

Reaction:

$$\begin{array}{c} CHO \\ | \\ CHOH \\ | \\ (CHOH)_3 \\ | \\ CH_2OH \\ \text{Glucose} \end{array} \text{ or } \begin{array}{c} CH_2OH \\ | \\ C=O \\ | \\ (CHOH)_3 \\ | \\ CH_2OH \\ \text{Fructose} \end{array} + 2\, C_6H_5NHNH_2 \longrightarrow \begin{array}{c} CH_2OH \\ | \\ C=N-NHC_6H_5 \\ | \\ (CHOH)_3 \\ | \\ CH_2OH \\ \text{Osazone (yellow crystalline solid)} \end{array}$$

Osazone crystal shapes for Carbohydarts

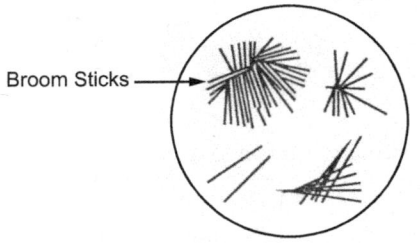

(a) Glucosazone

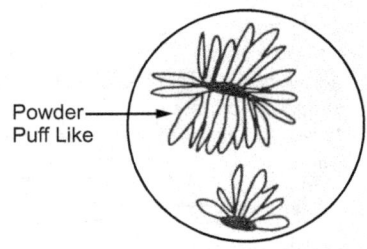

(b) Lactosazone

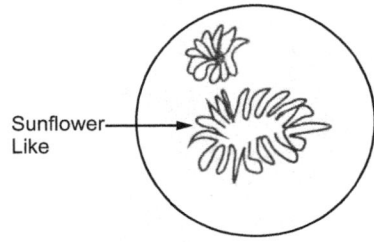

(c) Maltosazone

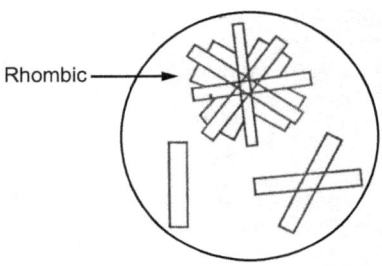

(d) Galactosazone

(e) Arabinosazone

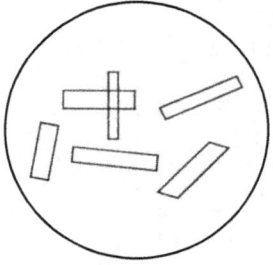

(g) Hydrasazone of mannose
(colourless obtained at room temp.)

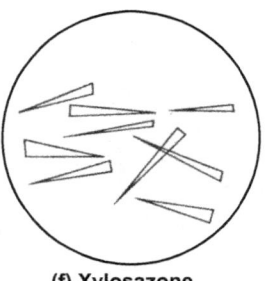

(f) Xylosazone

MUTAROTATION

The crystalline forms of α and β - D (+) - glucose are quite stable, but in aqueous solution each form slowly changes to an equilibrium mixture. This phenomenon of change is specific rotation of an optically active compound with time to an equilibrium value is known as **"Mutarotation"**. Many sugars, other than glucose, also exist in an α and β from and undergo maturation.

Example, α-D-Fructose has specific ration – 31° where as β-D-Fructose has a specific rotation –133° and the constant value is – 92°.

The mutarotation occurs because of the slow interconversion of α-D-glucose and β-D-glucose *via* the open chain form, until equilibrium is established giving a constant specific rotation + 53°.

α - D - Glucose (Specific rotation + 112°) ⇌ D - Glucose (Open chain) ⇌ β - D - Glucose (Specific rotation + 19°)

Mechanism of Mutarotation:

Mutarotation is possible only in presence of an amphiprotic solvent (e.g., water). When mutarotation takes place, the ring opens and then recloses in the inverted position or in the original position. The widely accepted mutarotation mechanism is that, monosaccharides in the solution exist mainly as an equilibrium mixture of the α and β-anomeric pyranoses and a small amount of open chain forms. Lowry in 1925 suggested that it occurred by the simultaneous addition and elimination of a proton, since both acid and base must be present.

α - D (+) - Glucose ⇌ Open chain form of glucose ⇌ β - D (+) - Glucose

A modern chemist can utilise X-ray or NMR spectral techniques to determine the size of the hemiacetal or hemiketal ring structure of monosaccharides.

ESTABLISHMENT OF STRUCTURES OF GLUCOSE AND FRUCTOSE

Glucose:

1. **Molecular formula:** $C_6H_{12}O_6$.
2. **Presence of 6-carbon chain:** n-Hexane is formed upon complete reduction of glucose in presence of hydrogen iodide and red phosphorus. This proves, glucose molecule has a 6-carbon atom chain.
3. **Presence of 5-OH groups:** Glucose penta acetate is formed by reaction between glucose and acetic anhydride. This shows presence of five hydroxyl groups, each attached to a separate carbon.
4. **Presence of aldehyde functional group:** Gluconic acid is formed upon mild oxidation of glucose in presence of bromine water. The gluconic acid when reduced with excess of HI yields n-hexanoic acid. This confirms the presence of an aldehyde group. Also osazone is formed when glucoses is reacted with phenyl hydrazine confirms presence of an aldehyde group.

Glucose:
$$\begin{array}{c} CHO \\ | \\ CHOH \\ | \\ CHOH \\ | \\ CHOH \\ | \\ CHOH \\ | \\ CH_2OH \end{array}$$

HI / Red P, 100°C → $CH_3-CH_2-CH_2-CH_2-CH_2-CH_3$ **n - Hexane**

5 $(CH_3CO)_2O$ / Acetic anhydride →
$$\begin{array}{c} CHO \\ | \\ (CHOCOCH_3)_4 \\ | \\ CH_2OCOCH_3 \end{array}$$
Glucose penta acetate

Br_2 water / Oxidation →
$$\begin{array}{c} COOH \\ | \\ (CHOH)_4 \\ | \\ COOH \end{array}$$
Gluconic acid
HI Reduction → $CH_3-CH_2-CH_2-CH_2-CH_2-COOH$ **n - Hexanoic acid**

$C_6H_5 NHNH_2$ / Phenyl hydrazine →
$$\begin{array}{c} HC=N-NH-C_6H_5 \\ | \\ (CHOH)_4 \\ | \\ COOH \end{array}$$
Glucose phenyl hydrazone (OSAZONE)

5. **Open-chain structure:** Based on these reactions, Bayer in 1890 proposed the following open chain structure for glucose.

$$\overset{1}{CH_2OH}-\overset{2}{CHOH}-\overset{3}{CHOH}-\overset{4}{CHOH}-\overset{5}{CHOH}-\overset{6}{CHO}$$

$$H-\underset{H}{\overset{OH}{\underset{|}{C}}}-\underset{H}{\overset{OH}{\underset{|}{\overset{*}{C}}}}-\underset{H}{\overset{OH}{\underset{|}{\overset{*}{C}}}}-\underset{H}{\overset{OH}{\underset{|}{\overset{*}{C}}}}-\underset{H}{\overset{OH}{\underset{|}{\overset{*}{C}}}}-\overset{H}{\underset{|}{C}}=O$$

6. Configuration of D-Glucose:

The proposed structure of glucose has 4 assymetric carbon atoms (shown by * mark), hence, 16 stereoisomers (n^2, $4 \times 4 = 16$) are possible. All the 16 isomers were identified. (+) - Glucose is one of 16 stereoisomers. The 16 possible configurations consist of 08 pairs of enantiomers. Since, methods of determining absolute configuration were not available, Fischer rejected eight of the 16 possible configurations arbitrarily and retaining only those (I-VIII) configurations in which C-5 carried the –OH on the right hand. Fischer designated the following configuration of D(+)-glucose.

```
      CHO
       |
   H—C—OH
       |
  HO—C—H
       |
   H—C—OH
       |
   H—C—OH
       |
      CH₂OH
```

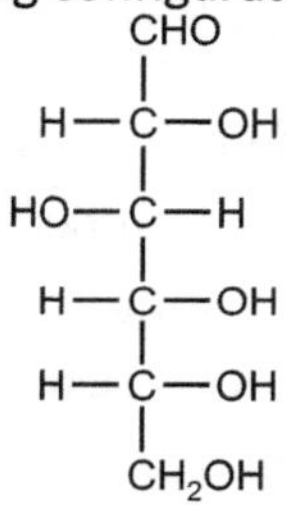

Open chain structures of D-(+)-glucose

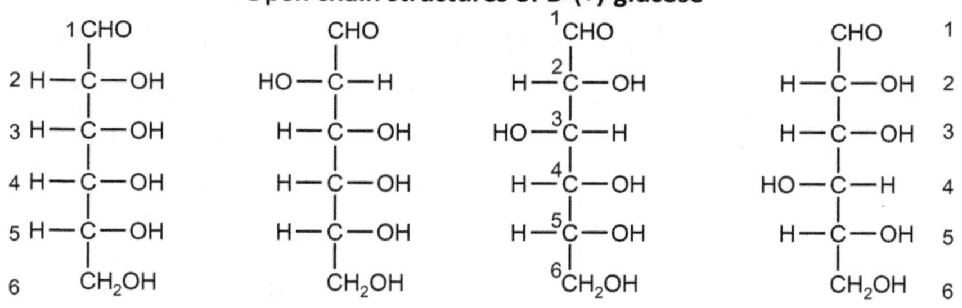

Structures I, II, III (D(+)-glucose), IV, V, VI, VII, VIII — Fischer projections of the eight D-aldohexoses with CHO at C1 and CH₂OH at C6.

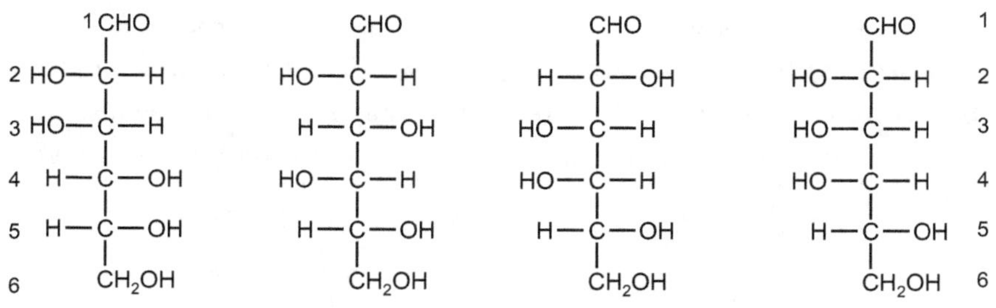

7. **Defects of the open chain structure:** Though, open chain structure of (+)-glucose explains most of its reactions, it fails to explain the following facts:
   (a) Glucose does not form an addition compound with sodium-bilsulphite and does not restore the colour of Schiff's reagent.
   (b) The penta-acetate and pentamethyl-ether derivatives of glucose are not oxidised by Tollen's reagent or Fehling's solution, indicating the absence of CHO group.

8. **Cyclic structures of glucose:** Glycoside formation confirms the cyclic structure of glucose. The glycoside (acetal) is formed when glucose is treated with methanol in presence of dry HCl. The aldehyde group reacts with the hydroxyl group on C_5 of the same molecule to form six membered cyclic hemiacetal structure.

   The cyclic hemiacetal structure of glucose has a new asymmetric centre at C_1. Therefore D(+)-glucose exists in two distereomeric forms, i.e., α and β-form.

   The α-D(+)-glucose has hydroxyl group at C_1 on the right hand side, while β-D(+)-glucose has hydroxyl group at C_1 on the left hand side.

   These two isomers differ in configuration only C_1 are defined as **'Anomers'** and the carbon is known as **'Anomeric Carbon'**.

   α - D (+) - Glucose   β - D (+) - Glucose

9. **Ring size of D(+)-glucose:** According to Haworth, the structures for glucose may be written as more or less regular pentagons and hexagons. Thus, two glucopyranose and two glucofuranose structures may be given as below:

   α - D (+) - Glucopyranose   β - D (+) - Glucopyranose α - D - Glucofuranose   β - D - Glucofuranose

Fructose

1. **Molecular Formula:** $C_6H_{12}O_6$.
2. **Presence of 6-carbon chain:** n-Hexane is formed upon complete reduction of fructose in presence of hydrogen iodide and red phosphorous. This confirms, fructose contains unbranched 6-carbon chain.
3. **Presence of 5-OH groups:** Fructose penta acetate is formed by reaction between fructose and acetic anhydride. It indicates presence of 5-OH group, each attached to a separate carbon.
4. **Presence of ketone functional group:** Fructose forms an oxime with hydroxylamine and hence contains a carbonyl group. Also fructose on oxidation with HNO_3 gives a mixture of carboxylic acids containing the lesser number of carbon atoms than fructose. This indicates the carbonyl group in fructose is "keto group".

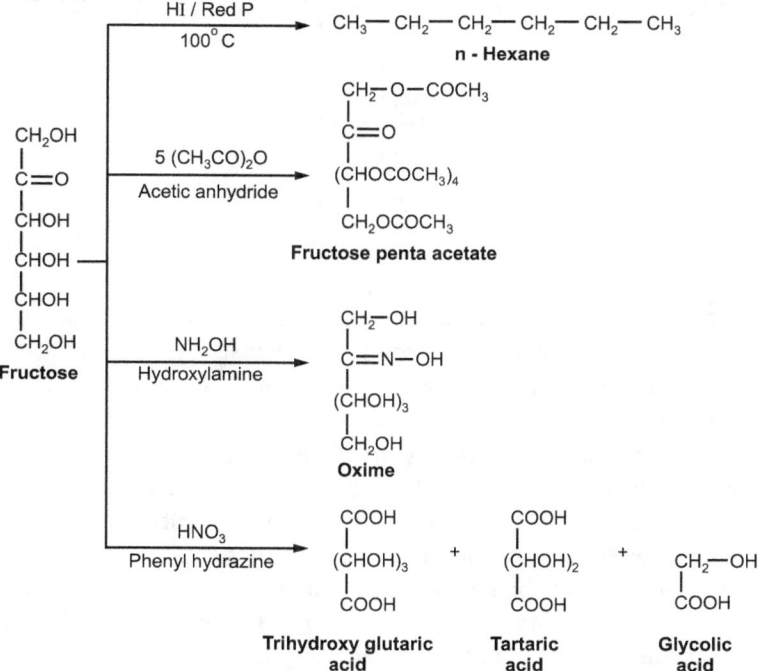

5. **Position of the keto group:** The following reaction proves that the keto functional group present in fructose is adjacent to terminal carbon, i.e., at C-2.

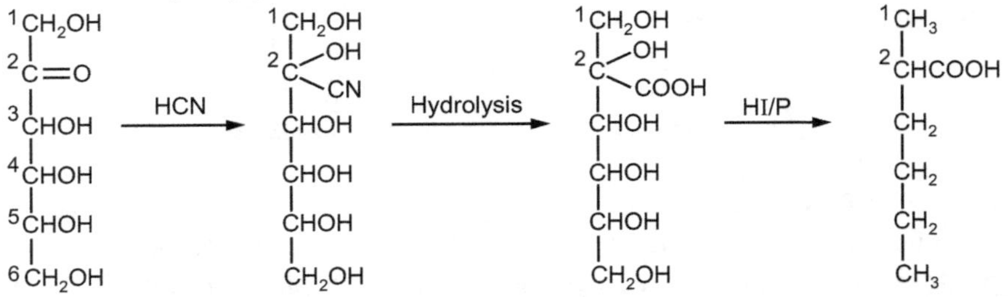

$$\begin{array}{c}^1CH_2OH\\^2C=O\\^3CHOH\\^4CHOH\\^5CHOH\\^6CH_2OH\end{array} \xrightarrow{HCN} \begin{array}{c}^1CH_2OH\\^2C{<}^{OH}_{CN}\\CHOH\\CHOH\\CHOH\\CH_2OH\end{array} \xrightarrow{Hydrolysis} \begin{array}{c}^1CH_2OH\\^2C{<}^{OH}_{COOH}\\CHOH\\CHOH\\CHOH\\CH_2OH\end{array} \xrightarrow{HI/P} \begin{array}{c}^1CH_3\\^2CHCOOH\\CH_2\\CH_2\\CH_2\\CH_3\end{array}$$

Fructose   Cyanohydrin   Polyhydroxy acid   2 - Methylhexanoic acid

6. **Open chain structure:** Considering all the above chemical reactions, the following open chain structure of fructose has been proposed.

$$\overset{1}{C}H_2OH - \overset{2}{C}(=O) - \overset{3}{C}HOH - \overset{4}{C}HOH - \overset{5}{C}HOH - \overset{6}{C}H_2OH$$

7. **Configuration of D-fructose:** The osazone formed by fructose is identical with that obtained from D-glucose. This shows that the configuration of asymmetric carbon atoms C-3, C-4 and C-5 in D-fructose is same as in D-glucose.

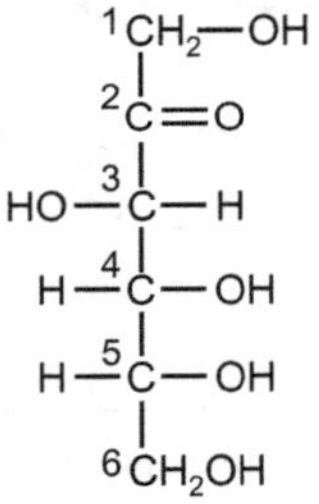

$$\begin{array}{c}^1CH_2-OH\\^2C=O\\HO-^3C-H\\H-^4C-OH\\H-^5C-OH\\^6CH_2OH\end{array}$$

D - Fructose

8. **Defects in the open chain structure:** The open chain structure of fructose is unable to explain many properties of D-(-)-fructose.
   (a) There are two types of naturally occurring D(-) fructoses i.e., α-form and β-form.
   (b) There are two types of methyl fructosides – α and β.
   (c) It exhibits mutarotation, so less possibility of pen chain form.
   (d) It does add HCN but does not add sodium bisulphite.
   (e) It reduces Fehling's solution and Tollen's reagent.
   (f) D-(-)-Fructose probably does not contain a free ketonic carbonyl group and on the other hand it may be a hemiketal since, it reacts with only one molecule of an alcohol to from a full ketal.

(g) **Cyclic structure of fructose:** The carbonyl group of fructose (C_2) must have undergone internal-hemiketal formation with any one of its five hydroxyl groups. Since, D-fructose also exhibits mutarotation, the α and β forms are in equilibrium via open chain form may be represented below:

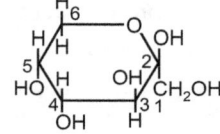

β - (D) - Fructose   Open chain from   α - (D) - Fructose

(h) **Ring size of fructose:** According to Haworth, normally D-fructose is α or β(D)-fructopyranose, but in sucrose it is β-D-fructofuranose.

α - D (–) - Fructopyranose   β - D (–) - Fructopyranose

α - D (–) - Fructofuranose   β - D (–) - Fructofuranose

QUESTION BANK

1. Write down significance and medicinal importance of carbohydrates.
2. Define and classify carbohydrates with examples.
3. What are carbohydrates? Draw the cyclic structures of glucose and fructose.
4. Define monosaccharides, disaccharides and polysaccharides with example.
5. Write various methods of synthesis of carbohydrates with reaction.
6. Write in brief about Killani-Fischer synthesis and Ruff degradation.
7. How will you convert aldopentose to aldohexose?
8. Give the reactions involved in:
    (i) Lengthening of carbon chain in monosccharides
    (ii) Conversion of glucose to fructose
    (iii) Position of carbonyl group in fructose

9. How will you distinguish between glucose and fructose?
10. What will happen when glucose treated with
    (i) Nitric acid,
    (ii) Bromine water
    (iii) Sodium borohydrate
11. What is mutarotation? Explain the phenomenon of mutarotation with examples.
12. Write down reactions of glucose and fructose.
13. Give any four reactions of glucose.
14. How will you confirm the structures of glucose and fructose.
15. Write a short note on:
    (a) Killiani –Fischer synthesis
    (b) Ruff degradation
    (c) Reactions of fructose
    (d) Mutarotation

■■■

Chapter 9 ...

NANOCHEMISTRY AND MICROWAVE ASSISTED SYNTHESIS

CONTENTS
- Basics and Application and Nanochemistry and Microwave assisted synthesis of Pharmaceutical Organic Chemistry.

NANOCHEMSITRY

Nanochemistry is a branch of nanoscience which involves the study of the synthesis and characterisation of nanomaterials. Nanochemistry is a new branch of chemistry concerned with the unique properties associated with assemblies of atoms or molecules on nanoscale. This science uses methodologies from the synthetic chemistry as well as materials science to obtain nanomaterials of specific sizes, shapes, surface properties, specific functions and uses. Nanochemistry is a truly multidisciplinary field, forging a bridge between nanotechnology and biotechnology.

The ultimate frontier of nanochemistry is the chemical manipulation of individual atoms. The use of atoms as building blocks opens new routes to novel materials. This offers the ability to create the smallest features possible in integrated circuits (IC) and explores quantum computing.

Although, nanochemical control was proposed decade ago, recently many tools necessary for studying the nanoworld were developed. These include the **Scanning Tunnelling Microscope (STM)**, **Atomic Force Microscope (AFM)**, X-rays, ion and electron beam probes etc., by which the study of large molecular assemblies in nanochemistry such as, dendrimers, clusters and polymers are carry out. From the studies of assemblies, significant new structures such as - nanotubes, nanowires, three dimensional molecular assemblies have been developed.

Dendrimers are highly branched three dimensional nanoscale molecular objects of the same size and weight as traditional polymers. Dendrimers are ideal building blocks in nanochemistry for the creation of more complex three-dimensional structures. These are already being used in molecular recognition, nanosensing and optoelectro-chemical devices.

Nanocrystals have 1-50 nm dimensions, usually consisting of aggregates of few hundred to tens of thousands of atoms combined into a cluster. Nanocrystals are of great interest because of their promise in high density data storage. They have also found applications as biochemical tags and chemical catalysis.

The **nanotubes** constitute a new form of carbon. Recently hollow carbon tubes of nanometer dimensions have been prepared and studied. Carbon nanotubes may be synthesised with sizes ranging from a few microns to few nanometers. The nanotubes are used in electrical and thermal conductivity.

Nanowires, like nanotubes are very small rods of atoms, solid, dense structures, much like a conventional wire. Nanowires offer the potential for creating very small IC components.

Lab-on-a-chip devices are designed to carry out complex chemical processes at an ultra small scale. They are used to carry out biological, chemical and clinical analyses, performing combinational chemistry and conducting separations. This technology has been aggressively pursued in biotechnology, where better ways to separate and analyse **DNA** and proteins are of great interest.

Carbon is the basic atom or unit of carbon nonotubes whereas, silver is huge array of atoms. Pieces of gold are golden coloured but, gold nanoparticles are deep red or black when mixed with water. Nanoparticles have high surface area to volume ratio, this increases thrice the rate of a chemical reaction and this also enhances their catalytic effect.

APPLICATIONS OF NANOCHEMISTRY

1. Nanochemistry has wide range of applications from electronics to medicine.
2. Nanoparticles of silver are useful to inhibit some viruses and bacteria.
3. Carbon nanotubes are found to be very dense and light weight and are used to make bicycles.
4. Nanochemistry is being popularised in pharmaceutical formulations such as nanosuspensions, nanoemulsions etc.
5. Nanochemistry allows the development of new industrial catalysts.
6. Nanomaterials can be used to make sensors that detect specific molecules. Example, monitoring pollutants in water.

7. Nanotubes can used in aircraft construction and sports equipment.
8. Nanoparticles have a high surface area to volume ratio, this increases their rate of chemical reactions and also enhances their catalytic effect.
9. Nanoparticles are already being used in deodarants, detergents and sunscreen creams.
10. Nanochemistry provides material scientists and chemists with useful atomic and molecular structure with a wide range and ingenious applications.
11. The use of liposome nanoparticles may enable the efficient delivery of chemotherapeutic agents for cancer treatment.
12. In the cosmetic industry, the use of nanosized particles in creams is increasing as the absorption through skin is good due to their small size.
13. The use of inorganic ceramic nanowires is more effective in hip replacement and dental surgery.
14. Nanotubes are stronger than steel, but have only $1/6^{th}$ of its weight, thus, adding strength without adding weight to sports equipment.
15. The effect of nanoparticles on the body is difficult to predict so it must be carefully tested to ensure its safe use.

MICROWAVE ASSISTED ORGANIC SYNTHESIS (MAOS)

Microwave-assisted heating under controlled conditions has been shown to be an invaluable technology for organic and medicinal chemistry and drug discovery applications, since it often dramatically reduces reaction times, typically from days or hours to minutes or even seconds. A massive number of compounds can be rapidly synthesized in either a parallel or sequential (automated) format using this new, enabling technology.

Microwave heating can readily be adapted to a parallel or automatic sequential processing format. In particular, the later technique allows for the rapid testing of new ideas and high-speed organisation of reaction conditions. The fact that a "yes or no answer" for a particular chemical transformation can often be obtained within few a minutes (as opposed to several hours in a conventional protocol), has contributed significantly to the acceptance of microwave chemistry both in industry and academia. The recently reported incorporation of real time, *in situ* monitoring of microwave assisted reactions by Raman spectroscopy allows a further increase in efficiency and speed in microwave chemistry.

Theory of Microwave Assisted Heating

Microwave radiation is an electromagnetic radiation in the frequency range of 0.3 to 300 GHz, corresponding to wavelengths of 1 cm to 1 m. The microwave region of the electromagnetic spectrum (Fig. 1) therefore lies between infrared and radio frequencies. All domestic "kitchen" microwave ovens and all dedicated microwave reactors for chemical synthesis commercially available today operate at a frequency of 2.45 GHz (corresponding to a wavelength of 12.25 cm) in order to avoid interference with telecommunication and cellular phone frequencies.

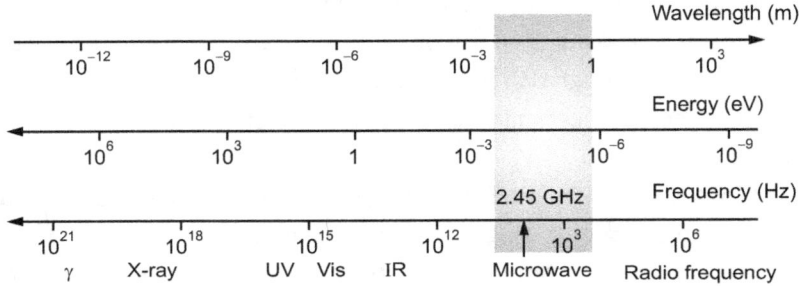

Fig. 1: The electromagnetic spectrum

Mircrowave heating is either by any of the following three mechanisms:

1. Dielectric heating involving dipolar polarization
2. Heating by ionic conductance and
3. Heating by interfacial polarization.

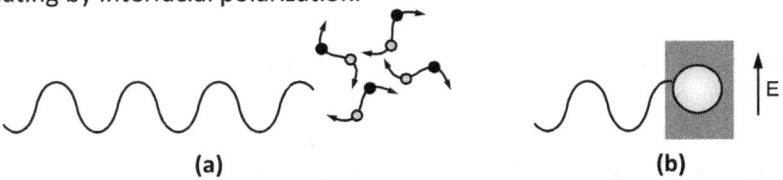

Fig. 2: (a) Dipolar polarization mechanism in which the polar molecules try to align with an oscillating electric field. (b) Ionic conduction mechanism: Ions in solution will move and align with the electric field

Dielectric Properties:

Microwave chemistry generally relies on the ability of the reaction mixture to efficiently absorb microwave energy, taking advantage of "microwave dielectric heating" phenomena or mechanisms. In most cases this means that the solvent used for a particular transformation must be microwave absorbing. The ability of a specific solvent to convert microwave energy into heat at a given frequency and temperature is determined by so called tangent loss (tan δ), expressed as the quotient tan $\delta = \varepsilon''/\varepsilon'$, where ε'' = the dielectric loss indicative of the efficiency with which electromagnetic radiation is converted into heat and ε' is the dielectric constant, describing the ability of molecules to be polarized by the dielectric field. A reaction medium with a high tan δ at the standard operating frequency of a microwave synthesis reaction (2.45 GHz) is required for good absorption and consequently, efficient heating.

The heating characteristics of a particular material (for example, a solvent) under microwave irradiation conditions are dependent on the dielectric properties of the material. The ability of a specific substance to convert electromagnetic energy into heat at a given frequency and temperature is determined by the so-called loss tangent, (tan δ). A reaction medium with a high tan δ is required for efficient energy absorption and consequently for rapid heating. Materials with a high dielectric constant such as water (δ' at 25°C = 80.4) may not necessarily also have a high tan δ value. In fact, ethanol has a significantly lower dielectric constant (δ at 25°C = 24.3), but heats much more rapidly than water in a microwave field due to its higher loss tangent (tan δ : ethanol = 0.941, water = 0.123). In general, solvents can be classified as high (tan δ > 0.5), medium (tan δ 0.1 – 0.5) or low microwave-absorbing (tan δ' < 0.1).

Table 1: Tan δ of various solvents at 2.45 GHz and 20°C

Solvent	tan δ	Solvent	tan δ
Ethylene glycol	1.35	N, N-dimethylformamide	0.161
Ethanol	0.941	1, 2-dichloroethane	0.127
Dimethyl sulfoxide	0.825	Water	0.123
2-Propanol	0.799	Chlorobenzene	0.101
Formic acid	0.722	Chloroform	0.091
Methanol	0.659	Acetonitrile	0.062
Nitrobenzene	0.589	Ethyl acetate	0.059
1-Butanol	0.571	Acetone	0.054
2-Butanol	0.447	Tetrahydrofuran	0.047
1, 2-Dichlorobenzene	0.280	Dichloromethane	0.042
1-Methyl-2-pyrrolidone	0.275	Toluene	0.040
Acetic acid	0.174	Hexane	0.020

Microwave *versus* Conventional Thermal Heating

Microwave irradiation produces efficient internal heating (in core volumetric heating) by direct coupling of microwave energy with the molecules (solvents, reagents, catalysts) that are present in the reaction mixture. Since, the reaction vessels employed are typically made out of (nearly) microwave-transparent materials such as borosilicate glass, quartz or teflon, the radiation passes through the walls of the vessel and an inverted temperature gradient as compared to conventional thermal heating results. (Fig. 3).

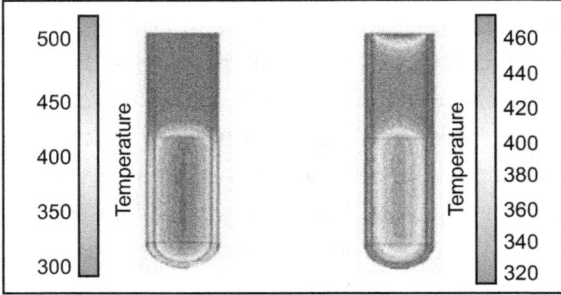

Fig. 3: Microwave irradiation (left) compared to heating in an oil bath (right). Microwave irradiation raises the temperature of the whole volume simultaneously (bulk heating), whereas in the oil heated tube the reaction mixture in contact with the vessel wall is heated first

Examples of Microwave Assisted Organic Reactions:

1. **Catalytic transfer hydrogenation:**

Benzaldehyde + HCOOH $\xrightarrow[\Delta / -CO_2]{RuCl(CO)(PPh_3)_3}$ Benzylalcohol

(Benzaldehyde — CHO; Formic acid — HCOOH; Benzylalcohol — CH$_2$OH)

This reaction is completed in 7 minutes as compared to that in 4 hours under conventional reflux.

2. **Condensation:**

o-Phenylendiamine + Diketone $\xrightarrow[MWI]{C_2H_5OH}$ Quinoxaline

Quinoxalines are effectively synthesized in few minutes by condensation under MWI (Microwave Irradiation).

3. Synthesis of chalcones:

$$Ar'-CO-CH_3 + Ar-CHO \xrightarrow[MWI]{NaOH/C_2H_5OH} Ar'-CO-CH=CH-Ar$$

Ketone + Aldehyde → Chalcone

Various chalcones are synthesised under MWI in sealed vessels in good yields.

APPLICATIONS OF MICROWAVE ASSISTED SYNTHESIS

1. Microwave assisted synthesis involves enhancement of rate of reaction with increase in yield of the product.
2. It also helps in improving purity of the products.
3. Time is saved from hours to minutes and minutes to seconds by MWI.
4. The use of microwave for synthesis of inorganic solids is very efficient and useful technique in material chemistry.
5. Microwaves are put to use in preparing catalysts and reagents. Example, TS-1 zeolite (Titatium silicate), VO_2 (Vanadium dioxide) etc.
6. The advantage of microwave assisted synthesis is in getting proper catalyst system in shorter time with high quality.
7. Microwave heating is reliable methodology for the fabrication of new nanoscale objects by faster and efficient ways.
8. Application of microwave dielectric heating technology has widely being accepted in polymer chemistry for carrying polymer synthesis.
9. Microwave irradiations are effectively used for sample digestion and solvent extraction techniques.
10. Microwave heating technology is also used in drying of materials.
11. Microwave heating is playing an important role in treatment of domestic and hazardous industrial and nuclear waste.
12. Microwave technology can be very easily applied for the control of CFC, methane NOx gases *via* microwave catalysis reactions.
13. The use of microwave assisted heating shown its ability to enhance various physical and chemical reactions. Example, Fischer-indole synthesis, Hoffmann elimination, Perkin reaction, Beckmann rearrangement, Benzillic acid rearrangement etc.

14. In medicinal chemistry, thermal effects of microwave irradiation are used to destroy tumours are now been investigated.

    Example, the cancer patient is administered the drug, which is followed by microwave irradiation at 400-450 MHz on the tumor site. This significantly enhanced the penetration of drug.
15. From the above outcomes, microwave is now moved from kitchen to laboratory.
16. Microwave assisted synthesis allows scale-up from few millilitres to one litre without changing reaction parameters. (Continuous flow type).
17. The reproducibility of synthesis is ensured under microwave heating.
18. Microwave synthesizers are easy to use.
19. As less side product is formed, consequently, also the purification step is faster and easier as well as environment friendly.
20. Microwave assisted synthesis now-a-days is a part of green chemistry.

QUESTION BANK

1. What is nanochemistry? Explain the basic terminologies used into it.
2. Comment on microwave assisted organic synthesis.
3. Write down applications of nanochemistry.
4. Enlist applications of microwave assisted organic synthesis.
5. Write a note on:
   (a) Nanochemistry
   (b) Microwave Assisted Organic Synthesis
6. Discuss the underlying mechanisms for MWI.

■■■

Index

- Stereoisomerism, 1.7
- Geometrical isomerism, 1.8
- E & Z nomenclature, 1.10
- Optical isomerism, 1.11
- Chirality, 1.13
- Fischer representation, 1.24
- R & S nomenclature, 1.26
- Diastereomerism, 1.17
- Racemic modification, 1.20
- Newmann and Sawhorse representation, 1.29
- Conformational isomerism, 1.29
- Conformational isomerism in ethane and n-butane, 1.31
- Conformations of cyclohexane, 1.34
- Monoalkyl and dialkyl cyclohexanes, 1.41
- Conformation in decalin, 1.43
- Bayer-Villiger oxidation, 2.2
- Dakin oxidation, 2.3
- Curtius rearrangement, 2.6
- Lossen rearrangement, 2.7
- Hoffman rearrangement, 2.5
- Schmidt rearrangement, 2.8
- Steven rearrangement, 2.13
- Sommlet rearrangement, 2.14
- Favorski rearrangement, 2.15
- Neber rearrangement, 2.16
- Benzilic acid rearrangement, 2.12
- Fries rearrangement, 2.17
- Claisen rearrangement, 2.19
- Cope rearrangement, 2.20
- Classification and structures of natural amino acids, 3.2
- Iso electric point, 3.5
- General methods of preparation of amino acids, 3.7
- Peptide bonds, 3.17
- Naphthalene, 4.1
- Phenanthrene, 4.16
- Anthracene, 4.9
- Furan, 5.33
- Pyrrole, 5.39
- Indole, 5.46
- Imidazole, 5.56
- Pyridine, 5.74
- Quinoline, 5.66
- History of combinatorial chemistry, 6.1
- Linkers and Solid supports, 6.2
- Mix and Split, Parallel Synthesis, 6.5
- Applications of combinatorial chemistry, 6.7
- General Rules and Guidelines involved in retro-synthesis, 7.6
- Disconnections involving one and two functional groups, 7.14
- Ibuprofen, 7.21
- Propranolol, 7.22
- Ciprofloxacin, 7.20
- Sulfamethoxazole, 7.23
- Significance and Medicinal Importance of Carbohydrates, 8.2
- Classification of carbohydrate, 8.4
- Reactions of C_6 (Glucose and Fructose), 8.8
- Mutarotation, 8.15
- Establishment of structures of Glucose and Fructose, 8.16
- Killiani Fischer Synthesis, 8.6
- Ruff Degradation, 8.8
- Nanochemistry, 9.1
- Microwave assisted synthesis, 9.3
- Applications of Nanochemistry, 9.2
- Applications of Microwave assisted synthesis, 9.7

www.ingramcontent.com/pod-product-compliance
Lightning Source LLC
Chambersburg PA
CBHW080428230426
43662CB00015B/2219